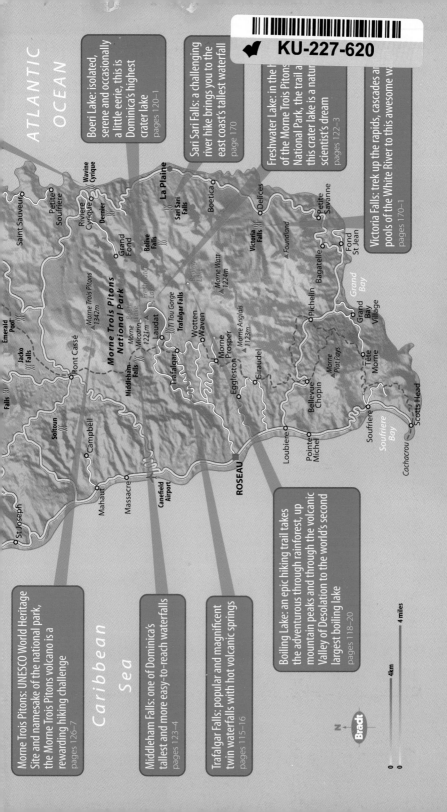

KU-227-620

ATLANTIC OCEAN

Caribbean Sea

Boeri Lake: isolated, serene and occasionally a little eerie, this is Dominica's highest crater lake
pages 120–1

Sari Sari Falls: a challenging river hike brings you to the east coast's tallest waterfall
page 170

Freshwater Lake: in the h[...] of the Morne Trois Pitons National Park, the trail a[...] this crater lake is a natur[...] scientist's dream
pages 122–3

Victoria Falls: trek up the rapids, cascades a[...] pools of the White River to this awesome wa[...]
pages 170–1

Morne Trois Pitons: UNESCO World Heritage Site and namesake of the national park, the Morne Trois Pitons volcano is a rewarding hiking challenge
pages 126–7

Middleham Falls: one of Dominica's tallest and more easy-to-reach waterfalls
pages 123–4

Trafalgar Falls: popular and magnificent twin waterfalls with hot volcanic springs
pages 115–16

Boiling Lake: an epic hiking trail takes the adventurous through rainforest, up mountain peaks and through the volcanic Valley of Desolation to the world's second largest boiling lake
pages 118–20

Saint Sauveur
Wavine Cyrique
Petite Soufriere
Riviere Cyrique
Dernier
La Plaine
Grand Fond
Bolive Falls
Sari Sari Falls
Boetica
Delices
Foundland
Victoria Falls
Petite Savanne
Fond St Jean
Bagatelle
Pichelin
Grand Bay Village
Grand Bay
Tête Morne
Morne Plat Pays
Soufriere
Souriere Bay
Scotts Head
Cachacrou
Pointe Michel
Bellevue Chopin
Loubiere
Giraudel
Morne Anglais 1123m
Eggleston
Morne Prosper
Wotten Waven
Trafalgar Falls
Ti Tou Gorge
Laudat
Trafalgar
Freshwater Lake
Boiling Lake
Morne Watt 1224m
Morne Micotrin 1221m
Morne Trois Pitons 1342m
Morne Trois Pitons National Park
Middleham Falls
Boeri Lake
Pont Cassé
Jacko Falls
Emerald Pool
Falls
Softoun
Campbell
Mahaut
Massacre
Canefield Airport
St Joseph
ROSEAU

N
Bradt

0   4km
0   4 miles

Dominica
Don't
miss...

Rivers and
waterfalls
The magnificent Victoria
Falls on the White River
(PC) pages 170–1

Mountains and rainforest
Dominica's interior is a breathtaking
spectacle of imposing mountains and
vast swathes of rainforest. Pictured
here: Morne Watt in the Morne Trois
Pitons National Park
(CS) pages 107–27

Volcanic landscapes

The Valley of Desolation on the Boiling Lake trail, a mystical domain of steaming fumaroles, hot rivers, bubbling mud and vivid colour
(PC) page 107

Music, dance and cultural festivals

Annual Carnival celebrations include costume parades, the Carnival Queen show and the Calypso Monarch competition
(PC) pages 25–6

Snorkelling and scuba diving

Dominica's pristine marine environment is full of life and reflects the dramatic topography of the island itself
(NC) pages 78–82

Dominica in colour

above   The tranquil and mysterious Freshwater Lake is located in the heart of the Morne Trois Pitons National Park (PC) pages 122–3

left   La Chaudiere river cascade and pool near Bense (PC) page 198

below   Dominica's Boiling Lake is said to be the second largest of its kind in the world (PC) pages 118–20

above   The unusual Red Rocks at Pointe Baptiste (PC) page 197

below left   The 'father' falls, with a drop of around 65m, and the 'mother' falls, with a drop of around 35m, make up the Trafalgar Falls (CS) pages 115–16

below right   Woodford Hill Beach, as pretty as any in the Caribbean (PC) pages 189–90

above — Downtown Roseau is best explored on foot (CS) pages 91–6

left — Wall mural in Roseau, by local artist Hilroy Fingal (CS) page 27

below left — The area around King George V Street is referred to as the French Quarter, and retains the character of a more historic Roseau (CS) pages 93–6

below right — Fresh fruits and vegetables at Roseau's New Market (CS) page 101

AUTHOR

Born in England, **Paul Crask** grew up in Yorkshire and graduated from Leeds University in 1988. He also spent time in former East Germany, studying at what was once the Karl Marx University of Leipzig. After graduating he travelled to Japan where he lived and worked as a teacher for two years before backpacking around the world, from the Far East back to Europe via North America. He worked in London for ten years before dropping out and embarking on a radical lifestyle change with his wife Celia, who was born on Dominica.

Although he has been visiting the island since the mid 1990s, Paul has been living on Dominica permanently since 2005. He is a regular feature writer for travel magazines, writing also for international newspapers, and he publishes his own magazine called *Dominica Traveller*. Paul is also the author of the Bradt Travel Guide to Grenada, Carriacou and Petite Martinique. For more information go to www.dominicatraveller.com.

AUTHOR'S STORY

My wife was born on Dominica and then grew up in England, where I met her in 1991 after living in Japan and backpacking around the world until my money ran out. I spent weekdays commuting by train to London where I worked, and at weekends we would walk the dog, decorate the house, go to movies and a restaurant, stroll to the local pub for a drink; the usual stuff. By 2005 we were ready for a change and we left our jobs, packed up our belongings and moved to the island. My friends told me I was going away to 'live the dream' but I suspect they thought I was heading for the Dominican Republic. No-one had heard of this place. Many still haven't.

Now, over ten years later, I find myself writing the third edition of this book and the Caribbean's 'nature island' feels as familiar to me as England once did. But there is no routine, for life here seems to change from day to day; none is ever the same. Though certainly not without its own set of challenges, life on Dominica offers a freedom and a sense of vitality that reminds me of the carefree tramping around the world of my youth. Perhaps it's the clean air of the rainforest, the freshness of the water, the food I harvest from the fertile soil of my garden, the opportunities to explore – and get lost – and the people I meet along the way. But writing this guide and the other pieces of work that now make up my 'working' life is always a pleasure. Travel to Dominica with an open mind and the spirit for adventure, and I think you will understand what I mean.

PUBLISHER'S FOREWORD   *Hilary Bradt*

I'd had it in mind to publish a guide to Dominica since the 1980s when I recruited Royston Ellis to be a Bradt author. At that time Royston had a house on Dominica and showed me photos of this wonderful lush, mountainous landscape that seemed so different from my preconceived idea of a Caribbean island. Then he moved away and Dominica went on to the back-burner until Paul Crask offered to write the insider's guide we wanted. And what a wonderful job he's done! It's written with such love of his chosen home that you can almost smell the rainforest and ocean, and feel that you have met most of the islanders. Paul wrote in his introduction to the first edition: 'When I set out to write a guidebook to my adopted home it was my aim to be as inclusive and as representative as possible'. He ends up: '… I don't know how well I have succeeded … but … I have given it my best shot'. He's succeeded.

Third edition published October 2016
First published 2007
Bradt Travel Guides Ltd
IDC House, The Vale, Chalfont St Peter, Bucks SL9 9RZ, England
www.bradtguides.com
Print edition published in the USA by The Globe Pequot Press Inc, PO Box 480, Guilford, Connecticut 06437-0480

Text copyright © 2016 Paul Crask
Maps copyright © 2016 Bradt Travel Guides Ltd
Photographs copyright © 2016 Individual photographers (see below)
Project Managers: Anna Moores and Katie Wilding
Cover research: Pepi Bluck, Perfect Picture

ISBN: 978 1 78477 031 0 (print)
e-ISBN: 978 1 78477 186 7 (e-pub)
e-ISBN: 978 1 78477 286 4 (mobi)

British Library Cataloguing in Publication Data
A catalogue record for this book is available from the British Library

Photographers: Alamy.com: nik wheeler (nw/A); Niall Corbet/www.flickr.com/photos/niallcorbet/ (NC); Paul Crask (PC); Pierre Deschamps (PD); Dreamstime.com: 1333809 Ontario Ltd (OL/D), Stubblefieldphoto (S/D); Extreme Dominica (ED); FLPA.co.uk: OceanPhoto (OP/FLPA); Arun Madisetti/Images Dominica (AM); Shutterstock.com: Dennis Sabo (DS/S); Celia Sorhaindo (CS); Superstock.com (SS)

Front cover A view of Soufriere village and bay, southwest Dominica (nw/A)
Title page Kalinago craft in Mahaut River, Kalinago Territory; Hibiscus, in the flower village of Giraudel; Rastafarian Moses James at Zion Valley near Delices (all PC)
Back cover Celebrating Carnival (PC); Sisserou (SS)
Maps David McCutcheon FBCart.S; colour map relief base by Nick Rowland FRGS

Typeset by Ian Spick, Bradt Travel Guides
Production managed by Jellyfish Print Solutions; printed in India
Digital conversion by www.dataworks.co.in

Acknowledgements

CONTRIBUTORS

Stewart Bell is an award-winning Canadian journalist and the author of three non-fiction books, *The Bayou of Pigs*, *The Martyr's Oath*, and *Cold Terror*. For more information go to www.stewartbell.net.

Cozier Frederick (Kalinago name: Chouboutouiba) is a postgraduate student of Kalinago history at the University of the West Indies and a development officer in the Ministry of Kalinago Affairs.

Terri Henry is a writer, health and wellness consultant, ecotherapy facilitator and mother of two beautiful eco-children. For more information go to www.onelovelivity.com.

Dr Lennox Honychurch is Dominica's most prominent historian. He is also a conservationist and responsible for much of the restoration of the Fort Shirley Garrison in the Cabrits National Park. For more information go to www.lennoxhonychurch.com.

Arun Madisetti is a marine biologist and photographer. He has dived Dominica's reefs for many years and you will often find him swimming with sperm whales. For images of his dives, go to www.imagesdominica.com.

Contents

Introduction

Welcome to the third edition of this guide. Quite a few things have happened since I wrote the second edition, but the two that jump right off the page are the disappearance of an entire lake (Lake Matthieu) in 2011, and Tropical Storm Erika in 2015 – the most devastating natural disaster to hit the island since Hurricane David in 1979.

Dominica certainly lives up to its billing as the Caribbean's 'Nature Island', for here you will see nature at its most brutal, its most dramatic, and its most beautiful all at the same time, and all on an island that is only 47km long and 26km wide. And this is why people come to this oft-confused and still relatively unknown Caribbean country; or at least why they try to come – it's quite a journey to get here.

If I were a marketing person I'd tell you the journey is all part of the adventure, but I'm not. The journey can be long, irritating and tiresome. But when I tell you it is worth it, I do mean it. For this is a very special place; the kind that backpackers used to talk of only in whispers when I was a younger man travelling the world; a secret, magical island that only a select few could ever know about. And it does feel like that sometimes.

Dominica has nine active and dormant volcanoes: diverse habitats that include cloudforest, montane forest and swathes of rainforest that cover the majority of the island. Tumbling down from the elevated interior are hundreds of rivers, each one with countless cascades and waterfalls. There are 32 recorded volcanic vents, there are parrots you can find nowhere else, and there is the second-largest boiling lake in the world. The indigenous Kalinago live on the northeast coast in their own territory and are virtually the only survivors of the region's first people.

Dominica's landscape is covered in a vast network of trails mostly historic in origin, now serving as hiking and trekking routes for lovers of the great outdoors, and at around 200km long, the Wai'tukubuli National Trail is unique to the eastern Caribbean. Hikers, scuba divers, nature lovers, seekers of wellness and alternative ways of living, culture vultures, horticulturalists, natural-science researchers, and work-exchange volunteers all love this place. You just have to get here.

A friend came to hike with me while I was updating this guide and remarked that, except for the Bailey bridges and a few broken roads, he would never really have known that the island had suffered the wrath of Tropical Storm Erika. And it is amazing that Dominica has recovered so well. Nature covers up the physical scars, if not the mental ones. Through individual and collective endeavour and creativity, Dominica is recovering well and the best way you can help is to come here and experience this amazing Caribbean island for yourself.

HOW TO USE THIS GUIDE

AUTHOR'S FAVOURITES Finding genuinely characterful accommodation or that unmissable off-the-beaten-track café can be difficult, so the author has chosen a few of his favourite places throughout the country to point you in the right direction. These 'author's favourites' are marked with a ✳.

MAPS
Keys and symbols Maps include alphabetical keys covering the locations of those places to stay, eat or drink that are featured in the book. Note that regional maps may not show all hotels and restaurants in the area: other establishments may be located in towns shown on the map.

FEEDBACK REQUEST AND UPDATES WEBSITE

At Bradt Travel Guides we're aware that guidebooks start to go out of date on the day they're published – and that you, our readers, are out there in the field doing research of your own. You'll find out before us when a fine new family-run hotel opens or a favourite restaurant changes hands and goes downhill. So why not write and tell us about your experiences? Contact us on ☎ 01753 893444 or e info@bradtguides.com. We will forward emails to the author who may post updates on the Bradt website at www.bradtupdates. com/dominica. Alternatively you can add a review of the book to www. bradtguides.com or Amazon.

FOLLOW BRADT

For the latest news, special offers and competitions, subscribe to the Bradt newsletter via the website www.bradtguides.com and follow Bradt on:

🔵 www.facebook.com/BradtTravelGuides
🔵 @BradtGuides
🔵 @bradtguides
🔵 www.pinterest.com/bradtguides

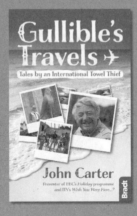

Part One

GENERAL INFORMATION

Location West Indies at 15ºN and 61ºW, between Guadeloupe and Martinique

Size Approximately 47km long, 26km wide and 750km² in area

Capital Roseau

Main airport Douglas Charles (DOM)

Status Parliamentary democracy within the Commonwealth of Nations

Population 71,000

Languages English and French Creole

Economy Agriculture and tourism

Main religion Roman Catholic

Currency East Caribbean dollar (EC$)

Exchange rates US$1 = EC$2.7 fixed; £1 = EC$3.6 variable; €1 = EC$3 variable (July 2016)

Electricity supply 220–240V, 50Hz. Commonly UK-style 3-pronged outlets.

Time GMT –4 hours

International telephone code +1 767

Flag Cross of yellow, black and white stripes on a green background with a red circle at the centre. Within the circle are ten green stars and a sisserou parrot.

National bird Sisserou parrot (*Amazona imperialis*)

National flower Bwa kwaib (*Sabinea carinalis*)

1

Background Information

GEOGRAPHY

Dominica is an independent island nation located in the West Indies at 15°N and 61°W, between the French islands of Guadeloupe and Martinique. It is the most northerly of the Windward Islands and is approximately 47km long and 26km wide. The island is 750km² in area and faces the Atlantic Ocean to the east and the Caribbean Sea to the west. Located on the southwestern coast is the country's capital, Roseau, which is also its main seaport.

The interior of Dominica is one of the youngest and most mountainous landscapes in the eastern Caribbean. At the centre of the Lesser Antilles island chain, Dominica's creation is still very evident in its nine active and dormant volcanoes – one of the largest concentrations in the world – sulphur deposits, hot-water springs and 32 recorded thermal vents that are found both above and below sea level. Running down the centre of the island is a series of volcanic peaks, deep valleys, high ridges, and river gorges, all cloaked in a dense blanket of rainforest, montane thicket and elfin woodland. Dominica's highest mountain is Morne Diablotin, which, at 1,447m, dominates the north of the island.

Rainforest is by far the most widespread vegetation type in the interior, followed by dry scrub woodland growing along the coastal margins. In the higher elevations there are several thousand hectares of montane forest and elfin woodland. Fumarole vegetation can be found in several places including the Morne Trois Pitons National Park (pages 107–27), the Valley of Desolation (page 116), Cold Soufriere (page 195), and the area around the Boiling Lake (pages 118–19).

The coast of Dominica stretches for some 148km and is where most of the population lives. On the Atlantic coastline the inshore waters can be rough and unpredictable, particularly near the mouths of rivers. In stark contrast to this is the west coast, where the Caribbean Sea laps gently along the shore and rough waters are very rarely experienced. Dominica has a combination of black- and white-sand beaches, though most of its coastline is rocky. In many places steep, rugged cliffs plunge dramatically into very deep seas.

CLIMATE

Dominica has a tropical climate with average daytime temperatures typically ranging from around 26°C in January to 32°C in June. Rainfall can be very heavy and sustained, especially on the Atlantic coast and in the mountainous interior of the island. Average annual rainfall is around 700cm in the interior and 100cm on the west coast. Most of the rain arrives with trade winds from the Atlantic, resulting in frequent showers on the east, or *windward* coast, heavy and persistent rainfall inland, and lighter showers on the west, or *leeward* coast. In recent times seasonal weather has been far less predictable but, theoretically, the period between July and December

In August 2015, Dominica was hit by Tropical Storm Erika. There was very little by way of wind, but the volume of rainfall caused widespread devastation. Countless land- and mudslides fell rapidly down steep hillsides and mountain slopes; streams and rivers became raging torrents of water, mud, rocks, boulders and trees. Many roads were damaged by rivers and numerous bridges were swept away, while other routes were blocked by huge landslides. The villages of Delices and Boetica in the southeast were cut off for months after the Boetica River flooded and ripped out earth and road, creating a deep, wide gorge that could only be passed on foot and with rope and pulleys. The villages of Coulibistrie, Dubique and Petite Savanne were severely impacted, the last so much so that it was not only evacuated, it was also officially abandoned. In that village alone, 18 people are believed to have died; at the time of writing, only six bodies have been recovered.

There was an international appeal for help (you may have read some of my articles), and Bailey bridges eventually spanned the gaps where roads used to be; heavy machinery cleared mudslides and people tried to get their lives and businesses back on track. The travel sector upon which Dominica is so heavily reliant was impacted badly but is beginning to recover as travellers are gradually returning. Coming here is the very best way you can help this little island, and certainly more direct and transparent than donating money to its government. As a traveller to Dominica in 2016 and beyond, you will hardly be affected by the aftermath of this particular natural disaster. At the time of writing, all roads except those running through Petite Savanne in the southeast are passable again, and hiking trails and natural attractions are open.

is when Dominica is usually at its wettest, and is also the time when it becomes most vulnerable to tropical storms and hurricanes. The driest and sunniest months usually tend to be from December to June but showers should always be anticipated and some parts of Dominica are wet all year round. The combination of heat and water can also make the island very humid, though breezes from the trade winds often help to make humidity levels a little more bearable, especially on the east coast.

Hurricanes and tropical storms that have the potential to impact Dominica and the other islands of the Lesser Antilles tend to develop from tropical depressions in the Atlantic Ocean to the southwest of the Cape Verde Islands. They are essentially the rains and storms of the African monsoon season that make it all the way across the continent to the west coast and then into the Atlantic as tropical waves or depressions. If sea surface temperatures are warm enough, Sahara dust levels and atmospheric wind shear low, then these disturbances can develop into tropical storms and hurricanes that track westwards to trouble the Caribbean, Central and North America. Historically, the Atlantic hurricane season is usually at its peak, and most threatening to the Lesser Antilles, during the months of August and September. The two worst storms to affect Dominica in recent times were Hurricane David in August 1979 and Tropical Storm Erika in August 2015 (see box, above).

NATURAL HISTORY AND CONSERVATION

HABITATS Found at the highest elevations, along the mountain tops and the tall ridges of Dominica's interior, is **elfin woodland**, or **cloudforest**. Frequently cloaked in a veil of mist and cloud, the moisture and dampness of this environment provide ideal conditions for mosses, lichens and ferns to thrive. A low-growing regionally endemic tree, known locally as the *kaklen* or *kaklin* (*Clusia mangle*), dominates the terrain, growing in a dense, tangled blanket some 2–3m above the ground. *Kaklen* has thick, ovate leaves, dark red, hard-skinned fruit, and small white flowers. The *palmiste moutan*, or mountain palm (*Prestoea montana*), occasionally pushes its way through the *kaklen* and other low-growing trees and ferns to reach heights of up to 7m. Other small- to medium-sized palms include the *Geonoma dussiana* and the *Geonoma pinnatifrons*, known locally as the *yanga*. Also commonly found at these higher elevations is the *kwé kwé wouj* (*Charianthus alpinus*), which is a low-growing tree with small clusters of red flowers with yellow stamens. The flowers and shrubs of the elfin forest typically bear their fruit in these small clusters and include two endemic species of thoroughworts: *Chromolaena impetiolaris* and *Chromolaena macrodon*. Two other endemics are *Inga dominicensis* and *Bealeria peteolaris*; they are more usually found growing in the heights of the Morne Diablotin National Park (page 207).

Located at a slightly lower elevation is a layer of **montane forest**, or montane thicket. This is a habitat of transition that includes mosses and lichens, such as the endemic *Parmelia cryptochlora*, that are also found in elfin woodland. Common trees of the montane forest include the infamous *bwa bandé* (*Richeria grandis*) of the Euphorbiaceae family, and the *resinier montagne* (*Podocarpus coriacius*), a kind of yew. Both of these trees, along with others, can also be found at lower elevations.

Below the montane forest is Dominica's vast and impressive **rainforest**. In this area of more modest rainfall, with deeper, well-drained soil, you will see magnificent trees such as the *gommier* (*Dacryodes excelsa*), also known regionally as the *tabonuco* or *candlewood* because of the flammable gum-like sap that oozes from its bark. These trees tower upwards of 30 or 40m and provide food and shelter for Dominica's endemic parrots (see page 7). The rainforest is also the habitat of several species of *chatanier* (*Sloanea dentate*, *Sloanea caribaea* and *Sloanea berteriana*), both large- and small-leaf varieties, which have huge buttress roots that stretch far out across the forest floor. Other trees known locally as the *mang blanc* (*Symphonia globulifera*), *mang wouj*, *bwa kanno* (*Cecropia peltata*, or the trumpet tree) have prop roots and are also common in this habitat. The *karapit* (*Amanoa caribaea*) produces both buttress and prop roots and is one of the most abundant species of large tree growing in the rainforest. Together with the *balata* (*Manilkara bidentata*), also known as *bulletwood*, these two trees are often used in construction because of their durability and resistance to rain.

Along the unsheltered east coast of Dominica you will see **littoral woodland**. The vegetation here tends to have thick leaves to withstand the wind and salt spray. Shaped by strong Atlantic trade winds, the trees and shrubs along this coast visibly reflect the effects of the weather. Common trees include white cedar, sea grape, almond and coconut.

On the west coast of Dominica, usually sheltered from the severest weather, you will see lots of dry **coastal woodland**. The west coast has less rainfall than the rest of the island and this is reflected in the type of vegetation found here. Many of the trees are semi-deciduous and they shed leaves during excessively dry periods to conserve moisture and nutrients. Common species such as the *kampech* (*Haematoxylum campechianum*, or logwood) also have sharp thorns.

Growing in the volcanically active areas of the island, such as the Valley of Desolation, the Boiling Lake, Wotten Waven, Galion, Cold Soufriere and the

Soufriere Sulphur Springs, are examples of **fumarole vegetation**. The plants found here are able to withstand both steam and sulphur-laden gases. *Kaklen* can also be seen growing in this type of habitat.

PLANTS AND FLOWERS Close to 200 different species of fern have been officially recorded on Dominica, as well as around 20 species of bromeliads, 75 orchids, and a dozen or more other endemic plant species. The tree fern (*Cyathea arborea*), known locally as *fougère* or *fwigè*, is widespread and can be found both within the heart of the rainforest as well as on its more deciduous margins. On forest trails look out for the *pawasol agouti* (*Selaginella*), a low-growing fern that covers the forest floor and provides a hiding place for the elusive agouti (see page 8). The *z'ailes mouches* (*Caludovica insignis*) is a very common rainforest plant with palm-like leaves that split into two lobes. It is one of several plants that were traditionally used by the indigenous Kalinago for thatching shelters and also for waterproofing baskets. Bromeliads include both epiphytes (plants that grow on top of other plants in a non-parasitical manner, deriving nutrients from air and rainfall) as well as terrestrial varieties. *Ananas grand bois* (*Glomeropitcairnia pendulifera*) is the largest bromeliad found on Dominica and is often seen on the branches of trees in rainforest, montane thicket and elfin woodland habitats.

Dominica's **national flower** is the *bwa kwaib* (*Sabinea carinalis*). It is an arboreal blossom found growing in dry coastal areas and, when in bloom, displays bright red flowers. Good examples can be seen in the Botanic Gardens in Roseau (pages 104–5), at the top of Morne Espagnol (page 209) and within the garrison at Fort Shirley in the Cabrits National Park (pages 181–3).

Throughout Dominica, both in the wild and in lovingly tended gardens, it is common to see many varieties of colourful flowers and plants such as allamanda (*Allamanda cathartica*), angel's trumpet (*Brugmansia candida*), anthurium (*Anthurium andraeanum*), bird of paradise flower (*Strelitzia reginae*), bougainvillea (*Bougainvillea*), ginger (*Alpinia purpurata*), hibiscus (*Hibiscus*), heliconia (*Heliconia*) and ixora (*Ixora*). Flowering trees such as the flamboyant (*Delonix regia*) are usually seen growing along the drier west coast and are very bright and colourful when in full bloom.

Dominica also has many interesting and delicious types of vegetables and fruits. Dominicans often tend a family garden of sorts where they grow vegetables and traditional crops such as yams, dasheen, sweet potatoes, or tannias. These *provisions* are staples of the Dominican diet (see page 54). The *calabash* is a large

ROUCOU

Roucou (*Bixa orellana*), also known as *annatto*, is a fruiting tree that grows to around 5m in height and produces prickly, heart-shaped pods, each containing around 50 seeds. These seeds are coated in a reddish pigment that produces a vibrant dye. According to European accounts, Dominica's indigenous Amerindian people, the Kalinago, used this dye as a body paint. For centuries it has also been used as a medicinal plant that is thought to be useful for treating skin prolems, fevers, dysentery, liver disease and even hepatitis. The leaves are used to calm the stomach and also as an antiseptic. Today, roucou is still used worldwide as a food colouring – often as an alternative to saffron – as well as a herbal remedy and an ingredient in skin- and hair-care products.

round gourd that is cultivated on vines and harvested for use both as a vegetable and, when mature, as a functional container, or eating bowl. It is also dried and ornately decorated by local artisans (see page 26) and makes for a unique and pretty souvenir. Coconut palms grow just about everywhere, as do many different varieties of mango. Farmlands of oranges, grapefruits, limes, tangerines, apricots, avocado pears, coffee and cocoa are in abundance throughout the island, as are the commercial smallholdings of banana plants, which are primarily cultivated for export. Other seasonal fruits that can be seen almost everywhere around Dominica include pawpaw (papaya), guava, breadfruit, soursop, passionfruit, cherry, pineapple, watermelon and carambola. For further information, see box on pages 56–7.

Medicinal plants play an important role in Dominican life, despite the increased availability of over-the-counter and prescription drugs. Rastafarians, Kalinago and predominantly the older generation of Dominicans have succeeded in preserving the knowledge of their ancestors, and so a variety of bush teas and other herbal remedies are still in common use, especially in country areas. What may seem like a weed to many could in fact be *verveine* (*Stachytarpheta jamaicensis*) or *tabac zombie* (*Pluchea symphytifolia*), plants that are often used to make tea infusions for colds, fevers and other such ailments. Take a walk in the forest or a cultivated garden with someone who knows about this subject and you will be amazed at the extent and variety of ordinary looking plants that contain extraordinary medicinal properties.

BIRDS Almost 200 species of bird have been recorded on Dominica, including endemics and regional endemics. Most are migratory, of course, and it is thought that only around 60 of the recorded species are actually resident on the island. Dominica's endemic birds include the imperial Amazon parrot (*Amazona imperialis*), commonly known as the **sisserou**. The large and colourful yet extremely elusive sisserou is a highly endangered species and is seen mostly in the elevated mature rainforest of the island's highest mountain, Morne Diablotin (page 207). Dominica's second endemic parrot is the **jaco** (*Amazona arausiaca*), which is smaller than the sisserou, greater in number, and usually found at slightly lower elevations throughout the island's rainforest interior. To date, nine regionally endemic bird species have been recorded: the Lesser Antillean swift (*Chaetura martinica*), the blue-headed hummingbird (*Cyanophaia bicolor*), the Lesser Antillean flycatcher (*Myiarchus oberi*), the Lesser Antillean peewee (*Contopus latirostris*), the forest thrush (*Cichlerminia lherminieri*), the scaly-breasted thrasher (*Margarops fuscus*), the trembler (*Cinclocerthia rufcauda*), the plumbeous warbler (*Dendroica plumbea*), and the Lesser Antillean bullfinch (*Loxigilla noctis*).

Dominica has four recorded species of **hummingbird**: the purple-throated Carib (*Eulampis jugularis*), the green-throated Carib (*Sericotes holosericeus*), the Antillean crested hummingbird (*Orythorhyncus cristatus*) and the regionally endemic blue-headed hummingbird (*Cyanophaia bicolor*).

Along Dominica's inshore waters, especially in the Scotts Head and Soufriere Bay area (pages 133–5), you can see magnificent frigatebirds (*Fregata magnificens*) circling and occasionally fighting other seabirds for their catch. Other coastal birds include brown pelicans (*Pelecanus occidentalis*), brown boobies (*Sula leucogaster*), and occasionally the neotropic cormorant (*Phalacrocorax brasilianus*). The red-billed tropicbird (*Phaethon aethereus*), the white-tailed tropicbird (*Phaethon lepturus*) and several species of petrel and tern may also be observed.

Sandy shorelines, freshwater lakes and rivers provide a habitat for the belted kingfisher (*Ceryle alcyon*), the ringed kingfisher (*Ceryle torquatus*), the cattle egret

1

(*Bubulcus ibis*), the green heron (*Butorides virescens*), and a variety of plovers and sandpipers. Along the swampy and brackish margins of the Indian River (page 196) you are very likely to observe the common moorhen (*Gallinula chloropus*) and the Caribbean coot (*Fulica caribaea*). If you are lucky you may also catch sight of a white ibis (*Eudocimus albus*) and several species of teal and duck.

Dominica's forest habitats are home to a variety of bird species. The mangrove cuckoo (*Coccyzus minor*) and the rufous-throated solitaire (*Myadestes genibarbis*), commonly known as the **mountain whistler**, or *siffleur montagne*, are particularly vocal. The unmistakable call of the mountain whistler sounds rather like a squeaky bicycle wheel and accompanies hikers throughout Dominica's elevated rainforest interior. The ground dove (*Columbina passerina*), the bananaquit (*Coereba flaveola*), the Lesser Antillean saltator (*Saltator albicollis*), over 20 species of warbler and around five species of flycatcher can also be seen and heard in the island's vast tracts of forest and woodland.

Birds of prey observed on Dominica include the northern harrier (*Circus cyaneus*), the broad-winged hawk (*Buteo platypterus*), the merlin (*Falco columbarius*), the American kestrel (*Falco sparverius*), the barn owl (*Tyto alba*) and the peregrine falcon (*Falco peregrinus*).

MAMMALS The **agouti** (*Dasyprocta leporina*) is a wild land mammal that is thought to have been introduced by Amerindians and is still common in the forests of South America. Roughly the size of a rabbit, it is a ground-dwelling rodent that is related to the guinea pig. It has dark fur and pink ears and is built for running at speed. A herbivore, the agouti may be spotted scouring the forest floor looking for fallen fruit and nuts. During the hunting season (usually October to December) it is targeted by bush hunters and eaten for its meat.

The **manicou** (*Didelphys marsupialis insularis*) is a tree-dwelling opossum that is thought to have been introduced at the beginning of the 19th century. Though common, it is nocturnal and therefore rarely encountered. **Wild pigs** (*sus scrofa*) are common but very elusive. They live in the depths of Dominica's interior, particularly in the southern and eastern foothills of Morne Diablotin, where local hunters have reportedly come across some very large and aggressive specimens. Unless you are hiking in the deep bush, it is extremely unlikely your paths will ever meet.

Twelve species of **bat** have been recorded on the island, of which four are endemic to the region: the Lesser Antillean long-tongued bat (*Monohyllus plethodon*), the Lesser Antillean tree bat (*Ardops nichollsi*), the Antillean cave bat (*Brachyphylla cavernarum*), and the mouse-eared bat (*Myotis dominicensis*). It is the Antillean cave bat that makes its home in Tou Santi (Stinking Hole) on the Middleham Falls hiking trail (page 123). Dominica's largest bat is the fisherman bat (*Noctilio leporinus*), which is rufous-coloured and lives in sea caves. Bats are most common in the forest though many can be seen emerging from the corrugated gaps of galvanised-steel rooftops at dusk.

REPTILES AND AMPHIBIANS The **zandoli** (*Anolis oculatus*), or tree lizard, is endemic to the island. Zandoli are small and very well camouflaged lizards. They live in woodlands and gardens throughout the island, though they are more prominent on the west coast. The adult male has an orange and yellow throat fan that he extends to attract females. The **abòlò** (*Ameiva fuscata*), or ground lizard, is also endemic to Dominica. It is very common on the west coast and is much larger than the zandoli. It is often seen and heard in dry coastal woodland and gardens.

The house **gecko** and tree gecko are lizards that usually appear at night, on the prowl for moths. They are both known locally as the *mabouya*, the Kalinago name for an evil spirit. The Lesser Antillean **iguana** (*Iguana delicatissima*) is also quite commonly seen, particularly on the drier west coast (good places to see them are in the gardens of the Sunset Bay Club at Batali, and alongside the boardwalk to Champagne Beach, pages 81 and 140 respectively). A recent arrival to the island is the Puerto Rican crested anole lizard (*Anolis cristatellus*), which appears to be increasing in number in the southwest. It is an invasive and aggressive species which, it is feared, may threaten the native zandoli.

Of the four species of snake recorded on the island, none is venomous. The largest is the **boa constrictor** (*Constrictor nebulosa*), or *tête chien*, which can grow to 3.5m (8ft) and is particularly unusual because it does not lay eggs, but instead gives birth to live young. There are also two types of common grass snake which are regionally endemic and are known locally as the *kouwès nwé* (*Alsophis antillensis*), also known as the Antilles racer, and *kouwès sayga* (*Liophis juliae*). Both snakes are usually seen in drier coastal woodlands – though they can also be found in semi-deciduous woodland and rainforest margins.

The largest frog found on the island is known locally as the **mountain chicken** (*Leptodactyllus fallax*), or *crapaud*, and is endemic to both Dominica and Montserrat. Mountain chicken used to be considered the national dish, though the chytrid fungus disease that has plagued and devastated amphibians around the world also reached Dominica, sparing the *crapaud* from the restaurant menu but nevertheless seriously reducing its number to near extinction. Dominica responded to the threat of this disease by banning amphibian imports, protecting the *crapaud* from hunting, and by establishing a captive breeding facility at the Botanic Gardens under the Darwin Initiative Project, and with assistance from the Zoological Society of London. Though working very closely with their colleagues on the island of Montserrat in an attempt to protect and save the mountain chicken, experts fear the future remains uncertain for this species which is now very rarely encountered.

Far more common than the mountain chicken is the **tree frog**, also known as the *tink frog*. This frog can be found in wet habitats throughout Dominica, from the depths of the rainforest to an upturned plant pot in an urban garden. It actually carries the same disease that has decimated the mountain chicken but is unaffected by it. This makes life even harder for the *crapaud*, given the high population of tree frogs on the island, as it means the disease simply cannot be contained in the wild. The tree frog is one of the members of the extremely lively chorus you hear coming from the forest when the sun has gone down.

BUTTERFLIES AND OTHER INSECTS
Over 50 species of **butterfly** have been recorded on Dominica, two of which are endemic to the island. They are the Dominican Snout (*Libytheana fulvescens*) and the Dominican hairstreak (*Electrostrymon dominicana*). Both are usually found in dry areas, particularly along the west coast of Dominica. To date, seven of the recorded species are considered regionally endemic. They are: the St Lucia mestra (*Mestra cana*), the lesser whirlabout (*Polites dictynna*), the sub-tailed skipper (*Urbanus obscurus*), Godman's leaf (*Memphis dominicana*), Godman's hairstreak (*Allosmaitia piplea*), the bronze hairstreak (*Electrostrymon angerona*), and the broken dash skipper (*Wallengrenia ophites*). Perhaps the most commonly observed butterfly on Dominica, however, is the monarch butterfly (*Danaus plexippus*), which is very widely distributed across the island.

Dominica is home to over 60 endemic beetle species, including one of the largest in the world, the Hercules beetle (*Dynastes hercules*). Other notable insects include moths, fireflies, stick insects, grasshoppers, crickets, centipedes and millipedes. Several insect species are endemic to Dominica, others to the region.

FRESHWATER FISH AND CRUSTACEANS Dominica's many rivers are home to several species of fish, the most common of which is the mountain mullet (*Agonostomus monticola*). You may also come across over ten recorded species of freshwater shrimp, crayfish and other edible shellfish. Within the Morne Trois Pitons National Park, the Freshwater Lake (page 122) is home to a species of tilapia (*Tilapia mossambica*) that was introduced to this natural reservoir.

There are around 20 recorded species of river and land crab on Dominica. The cyrique (*Guinotia dentata*) is usually seen in wet places, around rivers and pools, and is cooked for food. The black crab (*Gegarcinus ruricola*) is usually found in dry forest areas along Dominica's west coast and is the primary ingredient of *crab back*, a delicacy that is eaten during the Creole and Independence season (see page 59).

Titiwi is the Kalinago name that is still used today for a type of goby (*Sicydium punctatum*) that hatches in fresh water, develops in the sea, and then returns to the rivers to spawn. Usually in September, at night-time and accompanied by seasonal storms that are known locally as 'titiwi lightning', coastal villagers catch nets full of these small fish at river mouths and traditionally cook them as an *ackra*, a small fritter that is fried in oil (see page 55). The mouth of the Layou River on the west coast is a good place to see this.

MARINE ENVIRONMENT The powerful deep seas of Dominica's rugged north, east and south coasts are beautiful in their strength. Fierce waves crash wildly against cliffs of volcanic rock, generating tall plumes of white spray. A formidable undertow toys with large boulders and pebbles, causing them to rumble like thunder as they are dragged up and down this weather-beaten shoreline. Sheltered bays and inshore reefs along these coasts offer some respite from the mighty Atlantic. In the northeast, between Marigot and Hampstead, alluring beaches of light sand and shallow water lie undisturbed on the fringes of dense forests of coconut palms.

In the calmer Caribbean Sea along the west coast of Dominica it is possible to see whales and dolphins all year round, and the underwater environment is developing a reputation for some of the very best scuba diving in the region. Beneath the surface there are steep drop-offs descending into the abyss, sea pinnacles rising from the seabed, expansive coral reefs, volcanic fumaroles and an exuberance of aquatic life. Reflecting the dramatic topography above the water, Dominica's pristine marine environment is a miracle of nature, a spectacular fusion of life, colour and depth.

Coral reefs Dominica's reefs have a foundation of granite cliffs and large boulders. Reef topography is varied, though many consist of steep walls and pinnacles. Shallow reefs tend to run quickly away into deeper waters or lie on narrow ledges above precipitous drop-offs. The waters around the reefs are usually clear due to their depth and the fact that silt in water-borne run-off from the island's heavy deluges tends to dissipate very quickly. They are also very nutrient-rich, providing the essential ingredients for life and an extremely healthy marine environment. Hard and soft corals are found on Dominica's reefs. Common gorgonians include sea fans and sea whips. Stony coral varieties include finger coral, star coral, sheet coral and brain coral.

Fish Large numbers of fish live in and around the reefs and occasionally the shadows of migratory pelagics can be seen passing by in the deep blue of the ocean

THE INVASION OF THE LIONFISH

Discarded pets in Florida may well be the reason for the invasion of lionfish in the Caribbean, but we may never know for sure. What we do know is that they do not belong here – their home is in the waters around Asia – and marine biologists are concerned they will disrupt the balance of the marine ecosystems here.

Laying thousands of eggs a day and eating unsuspecting reef fish in both the shallows and at depth, there seems to be no stopping them.

Some of Dominica's scuba-diving professionals now spend time as lionfish hunters and an interesting spin-off to this rather unnatural situation is the appearance of lionfish on restaurant menus (inexplicably expensive given there is an abundance of them).

Some marine operators are now beginning to observe interesting developments beneath the waves, however. On the expansive coral reef off Salisbury Beach, for example, very little spear fishing for lionfish takes place, yet their numbers are very small. The reason? The sudden appearance of large grouper, a natural predator. Perhaps the best way of dealing with the invasion of these very pretty, yet far-from-home, visitors is simply to let nature take its course.

beyond. The abundance of fish life, and in particular the huge numbers of juveniles, is testament to the purity of the environment. The reefs are nursing grounds to many species including damselfish, butterflyfish, angelfish and surgeonfish. Large shoals of yellow- and blue-striped grunts hover along the margins of reef edges, groups of soldierfish may be found suspended beneath overhangs or in the shadows of arches or small caverns, and goby, blenny, jawfish and flounder find their home in patches of sand. Parrotfish, cowfish, trunkfish, trumpetfish and spotted drum are just some of the many common varieties decorating an already colourful reef system, where in every nook and cranny a moray or sharptail eel may also be making its home.

Sharks are rarely seen along the west coast. The most common is the nurse shark, which can sometimes be found resting on the sand beneath plate coral. Whale sharks have been recorded, as have hammerheads and reef sharks. Rays are more regular sightings, including the stingray and the spotted eagle ray. Barracuda are also present, as are large schools of predatory jacks and mackerel.

It is perhaps the more unusual species of fish that are of greatest appeal to recreational divers, conservationists and marine photographers. The longlure frogfish (*Antennarius multiocellatus*) is one such example. Through the use of camouflage, the frogfish is able to make itself look like part of the sponge or coral it is inhabiting. The first spine of its dorsal fin is highly modified and acts as a lure to fish that swim by. The frogfish then makes a movement thought to be one of the fastest of all animals alive: in around one-sixth of a second it extends its mouth and sucks in prey which can be even larger than itself. The frogfish has a voracious appetite and is also cannibalistic. If fishing is bad in one area, it simply takes its rod and lure and moves to the next. In addition to the frogfish, Dominica's reefs are home to a variety of other interesting fish such as the sea horse, the scorpionfish, pipefish, batfish and flying gurnard.

Other marine creatures Along the east coast of Dominica endangered **giant leatherbacks** (*Dermochelys coriacea*), the largest of all living sea turtles, return to lay their clusters of eggs in the sand. The giant leatherback is one of four species of turtle observed in the waters around Dominica. The hawksbill turtle (*Eretmochelys imbriocota*) is by far the most common. The green turtle (*Chelonia mydas*) and the loggerhead turtle (*Caretta caretta*) may also be seen, though more rarely.

Dominica's waters are home to a number of echinoderms including the very aptly named donkey dung sea cucumber, long-spined urchins and a variety of colourful crinoids. Octopus and squid are also evident and there are several varieties of crab, lobster and shrimp. Fanworms, fireworms, feather duster worms and Christmas tree worms are widespread. There are lots of sponges inhabiting Dominica's reefs, including tube, vase, volcano and rope varieties. Perhaps the most impressive, however, is the giant barrel sponge, which can be found in large numbers all along the dramatic coral formations of the west coast.

Whales and dolphins Several species of whale routinely visit the deep coastal waters of Dominica. The most prevalent is the sperm whale (*Physeter macrocephallus*), which actually breeds here and is observed, often with calves, all year round. Other species of whale that may be sighted here include short-finned pilot whales (*Globicephala melaena*), humpback whales (*Megaptera novaeangliae*) and false killer whales (*Pseudorca crassidens*).

Pods of dolphin are often spotted along the west coast, even from the shore. The most common visitors are spinner dolphins (*Stenella longirostris*) though other frequently observed species include bottlenose dolphins (*Tursiops truncatus*), Atlantic spotted dolphins (*Stenella frontalis*) and Fraser's dolphins (*Lagenodelphis hosei*).

CONSERVATION Reflecting the need to protect and preserve its rich natural environment, both above and below sea level, Dominica has a number of national parks, and forest and marine reserves.

National Parks The most well-known national park is the 7,000ha **Morne Trois Pitons National Park**, which is a UNESCO World Heritage Site. The south of Dominica is dominated by a concentrated cluster of forest-covered volcanoes and many lie within the boundaries of this park. The highest is the three-peaked summit of Morne Trois Pitons itself, at 1,342m.

Morne Micotrin, occasionally also called Morne Macaque, is 1,221m tall and is located a short distance to the south of Morne Trois Pitons. Nestled within a circular crater between these two mountains is the 2ha **Boeri Lake**. At an elevation of 853m, it is the highest mountain lake on the island. A short distance to the east of Morne Micotrin is the 4ha **Freshwater Lake**, at an elevation of 762m.

A high ridge runs southwards from Morne Micotrin until it reaches the pointed and weather-beaten summit of Morne Watt at 1,224m. To the east of this imposing mountain is the **Valley of Desolation**, an active volcanic landscape of steaming gas vents, heated rivers and cascades, bubbling mud and a crust of colourful, sulphur-stained rock. Located at the northern end of the valley is the famous **Boiling Lake**, a flooded fumarole some 66m in diameter. It is one of the largest of its kind in the world, second only, it is said, to Frying Pan Lake and the interconnected Inferno Crater Lake in Waimangu Volcanic Rift Valley, New Zealand. The lake's nebulous, boiling hot waters spill over a cleft on its eastern margins and create the White River, which runs from this turbulent source down a deep valley beneath the Grand Soufriere Hills, passing over several waterfalls, including the Victoria Falls near Delices (pages 170–1), until it joins the Pointe Mulâtre River and, finally, the Atlantic Ocean. At the park's southern tip is Morne Anglais, which rises to 1,123m above Dominica's western shore.

In January 2000 the 3,335ha **Morne Diablotin National Park** was established. The park contains rainforest, montane forest and elfin woodland habitats and has some of the most dense and least explored terrain in all of Dominica. At the heart of the park is Dominica's highest peak, Morne Diablotin, which rises to 1,447m, and dominates the landscape in the north. This park was created primarily to protect the habitat of Dominica's two endemic and endangered Amazon parrots, the sisserou and the jaco (see page 7), but is also home to many other bird species, as well as mammals such as the agouti and wild pigs (see page 8).

The 525ha **Cabrits National Park** was established in 1986. It is located to the north of Portsmouth, on a peninsula formed by two volcanic peaks, East Cabrit at 140m and West Cabrit at 171m. Within the park, and its most prominent feature, are the semi-restored ruins of the 18th-century Fort Shirley Garrison (pages 181–3). The park contains dry coastal woodland and is connected to the mainland by the island's largest swamp and wetland area. Around the coastline is 421ha of marine environment that has been designated the Cabrits Marine Reserve.

Forest Reserves When it was formed in 1977, the **Northern Forest Reserve** covered 8,900ha, but it ceded land to the formation of the Morne Diablotin National Park in January 2000. Located in the north of Dominica, it is a vast tract of montane and rainforest habitats and contains some of the island's largest tree species.

Extending down from the Northern Forest Reserve to the valleys of the Layou and Pagua rivers are further high ridges and areas of dense forest. The Layou is Dominica's longest river, and the area to the north and east of the Layou River valley is the 410ha **Central Forest Reserve**, Dominica's oldest forest reserve, which was established in 1952.

Soufriere Scotts Head Marine Reserve (SSMR) The SSMR is located in the southwest of Dominica and contains some of the island's most visited and well-known dive sites. The aim of the reserve is to protect the marine environment at the same time as providing structure and balance to the demands of both tourism and the traditional fishing heritage of the villages in this region. The reserve runs from the isthmus of Cachacrou to the Champagne Reef system south of the coastal community of Pointe Michel, and is comprised of priority zones for fishing, scuba diving and marine nurseries. Within the reserve, dive sites such as L'Abym, La Sorciere, Danglebens Pinnacles and Scotts Head Drop-off provide visiting scuba divers with a spectacular combination of life, colour and dramatic reef formations. The waters here are extremely deep, and the reefs largely bereft of sand, so turbidity is rarely a problem and thus visibility is usually excellent all year round. Scuba diving and snorkelling in the SSMR draws a US$2 fee per snorkeller or scuba diver, which goes towards its management, much in the same way that the site pass system is designed to work for designated 'eco' attractions on land.

Organisations A selection of government ministries and organisations that are involved in the management and preservation of Dominica's natural environment and cultural heritage:

Forestry, Wildlife & Parks Division Roseau; 767 266 3429. Government department responsible for the management & conservation of Dominica's forests, wildlife & national parks.

Dominica Organic Agriculture Movement (DOAM) www.doamdominica.org. Non-governmental organisation (NGO) providing advice, news, classes, workshops & seminars on organic methods for Dominica's farmers.

Society for Heritage Architecture Preservation & Enhancement (SHAPE)
☎767 275 5031 or 767 440 3430; www.shape. dm. A non-profit group promoting awareness & appreciation of Dominica's buildings of architectural & historic interest.

Wai'tukubuli Ecological Foundation
☎767 440 1764; e bernardwiltshire@cwdom. dm. Environmental NGO promoting & lobbying for increased environmental awareness, preservation & development of Dominica.

A BRIEF HISTORY OF THE ISLAND

EARLY SETTLERS Dominica's first arrivals are believed to have been Orinoco River tribes who made their way up the island chain from South America some 5,000 years ago. Archaeologists and historians describe these people as basic hunter-gatherers, living off wild plants and shellfish. Around 400BC these tribes are thought to have been displaced by an Arawak tribe called the **Igneri** who also migrated from the Amazon River Delta and occupied the Windward Islands, from Grenada to Guadeloupe, for many years. Like the Taino tribes who settled in the Greater Antilles, the Igneri are believed to have probably worshipped nature spirits, often represented by three-cornered *zemi* stones or conch shells. They also carved curious designs in rock faces, often close to water sources, which we now refer to as Amerindian petroglyphs, several examples of which have been discovered in the southeastern Caribbean. So far on Dominica only one very small and quite inaccessible petroglyph has been uncovered in the very north of the island. This leads some to wonder if there could be more.

Archaeologists, historians and anthropologists have suggested the Igneri probably engaged in inter-tribal trade; they also farmed, built thatched houses, made pottery, wove cotton and crafted ocean-going canoes. They are believed to have lived on the island for around 1,000 years before the arrival of another Arawakan people called the **Kalinago**.

Considered by archaeologists and anthropologists to have been a more warrior-like Amerindian tribe, the Kalinago probably displaced the Igneri by around the end of the 14th century, just a hundred years before the arrival of Columbus and the first Europeans to the region. Like their predecessors, the Kalinago are thought to have worshipped ancestors and nature spirits in the form of iconic *zemis*, and they also excelled at boat-building and fishing. These are traditions that live on. Carved out of the trunks of *gommier* trees (see page 5), their larger boats, called *canoua*, were said to be up to 15m long and capable of travelling long distances across open seas. Smaller craft included the *couliana*, also carved out of whole tree trunks, and *pwi pwi*, a very simple raft that was probably used more for inshore fishing. These vessels would carry Kalinago men on hunting trips for fish, lobster and other shellfish and conch, as well as on trading and perhaps raiding parties to neighbouring islands. Kalinago women would, in all likelihood, have had a more domestic role, taking care of the children, cooking, running the farms, weaving hammocks and making baskets from the dried outer bark of the *larouma* reed (see page 155).

NEW ARRIVALS On 3 November 1493 Columbus's fleet sighted the island the Kalinago had called **Wai'tukubuli**, meaning 'tall is her body'. He named it Dominica.

Through enslavement and disease, it is said to have taken just 30 years of Spanish occupation to eradicate the Taino people of the Greater Antilles and, as slave labour became a scarce commodity, the Spanish turned their attention to capturing the Amerindian people of the Lesser Antilles. Amazingly, the Kalinago steadfastly resisted these raids for two whole centuries and Dominica remained largely untouched by Europeans.

In 1635 France claimed Dominica as her own and in 1642 French missionaries arrived on the island for the first time. The Kalinago continued to hold the French and the British in check, however, and in 1686 both countries signed a treaty stating that Dominica would be a neutral island belonging to this indigenous tribe.

For around a hundred years or more it is assumed the Kalinago lived in peace on Dominica, as did escaped West African slaves from the neighbouring French islands of Martinique and Guadeloupe. What took place on Dominica during this period and whether there was interaction between Africans and Kalinago is as unknown as it is intriguing.

In spite of their agreement with the British, French incursions from Martinique and Guadeloupe increased and small lumber, cotton and tobacco settlements were eventually established. Needing more land to grow sugarcane crops, the French shipped in African slaves to work their new and expanding estates but it was not until the 1760s, after Dominica was ceded to the British following the Seven Years War, and then again 18 years later following the Battle of the Saints, that these estates boomed and the population of African slaves became comparable to those of other Caribbean islands. African slaves were seen as a cheaper and more durable alternative to traditional white indentured labour. Unused to the tropical Caribbean climate, these indentured servants from England, Ireland and Scotland were soon replaced by large numbers of slaves from West Africa. In the meantime the Kalinago population was declining rapidly. Years of intense fighting, resistance, and disease had severely diminished their numbers, and in 1730 there were thought to be fewer than 500 Kalinago on the island.

In 1795 the French attempted to recapture Dominica from the north but failed. Then again in 1805 they launched a fierce siege of Roseau. The British defences were outnumbered by ten to one and soon Roseau was ablaze. Retreating all the way to the Cabrits garrison near Portsmouth, the British regrouped and prepared for a final battle. However, it did not materialise. Instead, the French commander demanded a ransom for the return of members of the British legislature, looted the now completely destroyed town of Roseau of everything of value, including slaves, and then sailed back to the French colonies.

The British were brutal masters and the flogging and execution of slaves was common. Many slaves managed to escape captivity by running away into the dense forest and forming small settlements in remote mountain locations. Plantation owners in the Caribbean region referred to these bands of runaway slaves as **Maroons**. Towards the end of the 18th century Dominica's Maroon population had grown significantly in number. They were fairly well-armed and launched many successful and violent raids on estates, plundering food, setting fire to buildings, and, on occasion, killing plantation workers.

In 1813 Major General George Robert Ainslie arrived and became Governor of Dominica. A violent, oppressive, perhaps even psychopathic man, his brutality against runaway slaves and those who helped them is captured in the public and military trial transcripts of Polly Pattullo's *Your Time is Done Now. Slavery, Resistance and Defeat: the Maroon Trials of Dominica: (1813–1814)* (Papillote Press, 2015). With scant regard for British slave laws (though many would question the premise of slavery as a lawful activity in the first place) he set about 'eradicating the evil' of Dominica's Maroons.

A legion of 500 men was formed to deal with the Maroons, and those captured were often tortured and executed in public at the Sunday Market in Roseau (see pages 93–4). Their heads were cut off and put on stakes on the estates from which they had escaped or on roads into the town to serve as a very visual warning to others.

On 12 July 1814, Chief Jacko, one of the island's most famous Maroon leaders, was shot and killed by John LeVilloux in a bloody battle with the Loyal Dominica Rangers – a militia of 'trusty' slaves who were offered the reward of freedom in exchange for killing a Maroon chief. According to witness testimony, Jacko had killed two Rangers, wounded a third and was preparing to fire on another when LeVilloux's musket delivered a fatal blow to the head. According to Ainslie, Jacko had been a Maroon for 'upwards of 40 years'. His death marked the end of what are commonly referred to as the second Maroon wars.

Dominica became an island of isolated village communities and small plantation estates that grew sugar, coffee, limes and coconuts. Despite the fact that it was under British rule, Dominica's main influences came from the neighbouring French colonies of Martinique and Guadeloupe. When British landowners were forced either to abandon or sell off failing estates, it was often the increasing number of 'free people of colour' or *mulattos* (now considered a derogatory term) arriving from Martinique and Guadeloupe who took over and made them viable again. The

RESEARCHING *BAYOU OF PIGS*   Stewart Bell

The mercenaries who decided to invade Dominica in 1981 were an unlikely alliance of misfits – Vietnam vets, Ku Klux Klansmen, militant Rastafarians, disgruntled Dominican soldiers, the ex-prime minister and a gun-loving mobster from Toronto. Dominica was having a tough time back then. Hurricanes had battered the island, the economy was struggling and the government had all but collapsed. The American and Canadian mercenaries who decided to take advantage of Dominica's troubles had a simple plan: invade Roseau by sea, overthrow Prime Minister Eugenia Charles and get rich. Financed by US investors, they were going to strip the island of its resources and open casinos, drug labs and arms depots. What could go wrong?

When I began investigating this little-known piece of Caribbean history for my book, *Bayou of Pigs*, I soon realised this was the strangest story I had ever come across in two decades of journalism. Nobody could make up a tale this bizarre. To find out what had happened, I tracked down the members of the conspiracy one by one. I soon found that some were dead. One had been murdered in Canada, another was executed by hanging, and a financier had killed himself with a shotgun. The leader of the coup, Mike Perdue of Houston, had died of AIDS in prison. Even those still alive weren't easy to find. One had changed his name and was living in a Colorado trailer park. Another was in a Canadian prison, serving time for gun trafficking. When I told him I wanted to put his mugshot in the book, he told me not to. He said he had better photos. A week later an envelope arrived in the mail. Inside were a half-dozen pictures showing him posing with machine guns and ammunition belts. One of the group had undergone a sex change. She suggested we meet in person so that, following the interview, we could 'have a little shag on the couch'. Let's stick to phone interviews, I said. A few people would not talk to me but most did. In fact, some of them still had papers from the plot – photographs taken during reconnaissance missions to Dominica, even plane tickets and hotel and car rental receipts. I was also able to get copies of the invasion plans, which diagrammed how the mercenaries would land at Rockaway Beach and storm the police headquarters in Roseau.

When I began to read the US government's file on the coup, I was confused at first. The memos contained a lot of references to GOD, which isn't usually something you find in FBI correspondence. It puzzled me until I figured out that

African slaves who had been brought by French settlers began to absorb French language and culture, and so it was not long before **Creole**, a combination of French vocabulary and strong African dialect and syntax, was spoken as a first language. A new Creole culture was born which, in addition to language, was also reflected in dance, games, music, instruments and modes of dress.

INDEPENDENT PEOPLE In 1838, following the abolition of slavery, Dominica became the first and only British Caribbean colony to have a legislature that was not controlled by the white planter class. However, it was not to last. The planters began lobbying for greater British rule and in 1871 Dominica became part of the Leeward Island Federation. In 1896 Crown Colony government was re-established.

Dominica's first Crown Colony administrator was a man called Hesketh Bell. In a six-year period from 1899 to 1905 he constructed Dominica's first highway, the Imperial Road, which ran from Roseau to Bells; he connected Portsmouth to Roseau by telephone; he initiated the first electricity service; he designed the Public

GOD was Washington shorthand for the Government of Dominica. So I guess you could say that Dominica is GOD's paradise. When I began visiting the island, hiking to waterfalls and walking the beaches, I quickly realised that was true, even if it almost became a crooks' paradise. In the weeks before the coup, the conspirators met in Toronto, Louisiana and Antigua. They plotted. They recruited. They raised money and bought guns. And they carefully mapped out how they would remove Prime Minister Charles from office and install Patrick John in her place. 'Imagine what you could do if you owned your own country,' said Wolfgang Droege, the Canadian KKK boss who was deputy-leader of the plot. The problem was, the conspirators were not only ambitious, they were also imbeciles. The ship they hired to transport them and their guns to Dominica was immediately infiltrated by US agents. The ship's captain, Mike Howell, had tipped off the Bureau of Alcohol, Tobacco and Firearms. Special Agents John Osburg and Wiley Lloyd Grafton posed as crewmen on the ship as they secretly tape-recorded the conspirators. The ATF called its investigation Bayou of Pigs – a Louisiana take on the infamous Bay of Pigs invasion of Cuba. Canadian police also found out. The mercenaries wanted to bring a news reporter along with them to document their invasion for posterity, so they 'embedded' a Toronto radio reporter named Gord Sivell. Once he found out that lives would be lost, Sivell went to the police. Police on Dominica got wind of the plot as well, through their own inquiries. The FBI knew, the US State Department knew. The Royal Canadian Mounted Police knew. The Dominica coup may have been one of the worst kept secrets in the history of mercenaries. On 27 April 1981, as the soldiers of fortune were about to set sail from New Orleans, police moved in and made the arrests. They seized guns, ammunition, inflatable rafts, Tennessee whiskey and Nazi flags. More than two dozen people were arrested and ultimately convicted in the US, Canada and Dominica. 'It was an exercise in stupidity,' Bob Prichard, an Army veteran who was convicted for his role in the plot, told me. 'The worst part was, I was stupid enough to go along with it.'

Stewart Bell is an award-winning Canadian journalist and the author of three non-fiction books, The Bayou of Pigs, The Martyr's Oath *and* Cold Terror. *For more information go to www.stewartbell.net.*

1

Library for which he had secured funding from the famous philanthropist, Andrew Carnegie; he opened a new jetty at Roseau; and he made proposals to set aside some 1,530ha for the island's indigenous Amerindians, the Kalinago. Over the next 60 years Dominica's population increased and its infrastructure and social institutions slowly developed to support it. In 1967 Dominica achieved Associated Statehood, giving the island total self-governance, and on 3 November 1978, exactly 485 years to the day after Columbus had first sighted the island, Dominica was granted full independence from Britain.

The birth of the new **Commonwealth of Dominica** was testing. On 29 August 1979 Hurricane David hit the island, causing widespread devastation, and in 1981 a very odd incident took place. A group of North American mercenaries and former Dominica Defence Force officers attempted an overthrow of the government of Eugenia Charles. The mercenaries were made up of Canadian and US right-wing extremists, gangsters, former soldiers, and even Ku Klux Klan Grand Wizard Don Black. This bizarre operation, code-named Red Dog, was meant to restore former Dominica premier Patrick John to power in a kind of puppet regime which would allow this group to exploit the island and turn it into a form of criminal paradise that would launder money and manufacture and export illicit drugs. For countless bizarre reasons, the coup attempt was a disaster and failed before it left the shores of the United States. In Dominica Patrick John faced trial and was found to have been a supporter of the attempted coup – a charge he has consistently rejected. Eugenia Charles, the Caribbean's first female prime minister, went on to lead Dominica for 15 years.

For a very interesting account of the Red Dog incident, pick up a copy of *Bayou of Pigs* by Canadian journalist Stewart Bell (see box, pages 16–17).

The powerful influences of nature, together with a turbulent history, are still evident in contemporary Dominica. Direct descendants of the Kalinago live in a semi-autonomous territory on the east coast. They weave *larouma* reed baskets for visitors and for export, and they hand-carve *gommier* canoes for both local and regional fishermen. Ruins of estate houses, fortifications and mills can be found across the island, many people have reconnected and have strong affiliations with their African roots, and the culture of French Creole is very much alive in language, food, dance and traditional costume. Village communities retain strong identities, and very many Dominicans continue to eke out a living from land, river and sea.

GOVERNMENT AND POLITICS

Dominica is a parliamentary democracy within the Commonwealth of Nations. The head of state is the president who is appointed by parliament for a five-year term. The president and prime minister make up Dominica's executive branch. Dominica's legislative branch, or parliament, is the House of Assembly, of which 21 are ministers elected by popular vote in single-seat constituencies, five senators are appointed by the president on the advice of the prime minister and four on the advice of the leader of the opposition.

Dominica has ten administrative divisions, or parishes. They are St Andrew, St David, St George, St John, St Joseph, St Luke, St Mark, St Patrick, St Paul and St Peter. The Ministry of Kalinago Affairs represents the interests of the Kalinago population and the affairs of the Kalinago Territory, together with the Kalinago Council. Dominica's village councils are elected by popular vote and are responsible for local amenities, services and sanitation.

There are two main political parties in Dominica. The Dominica Labour Party (DLP) and the United Workers Party (UWP). A third party, the Dominica Freedom

Party, was the party of Eugenia Charles but in recent times it has lost much of its popular support and become marginalised.

LAW Dominica's judiciary is independent of both executive and legislative branches and its legal system is based on English common law. Dominica's law upholds freedom of speech and freedom of religion, and it prohibits discrimination based on race, gender, place of origin, colour and creed. The island's only security force is the Dominica Police Force, which is overseen by the prime minister's office. Dominica's law prohibits arbitrary arrest and it does not detain political prisoners.

ECONOMY

Dominica's economy is for the most part dependent on a combination of tourism and agriculture. Its foreign relations are driven by the need for economic and social development and Dominica usually seeks financial assistance in the form of low interest loans and grants when it comes to major infrastructure projects. Key donors and economic partners are the European Union, China, Venezuela, Japan, Morocco, and the US via the Caribbean Development Bank (CDB), the IMF/World Bank, and the US Agency for International Development (USAID).

Dominica is a member of the Organisation of Eastern Caribbean States (OECS) and is committed to an agreement to allow the free movement of goods and labour across OECS-participating countries. The OECS is in turn committed to the CARICOM (Caribbean Community) ambition to develop the Caribbean Single Market Economy (CSME). Dominica is also a member of ALBA (Alianza Bolivariana para los Pueblos de Nuestra América – the Bolivarian Alliance for the Peoples of our America). The aim of ALBA is to attempt economic integration of member nations of South America and the Caribbean based on a premise of social welfare, bartering and mutual financial assistance.

Dominica's economic welfare is also underpinned by remittances from its diaspora – Dominicans living and working overseas. These remittances are significant and a major source of external funding and benefits in kind for individuals and families living here. In recent times the government has embarked on a programme of economic citizenship: a much maligned and controversial 'passports for cash' initiative that aims to attract overseas investment in capital projects – notably hotels – in exchange, one assumes, for a means to secure relief from taxation.

AGRICULTURE Historically, agriculture has been and still is the traditional mainstay of the Dominican economy. Growing produce for domestic consumption and overseas trade is a practice that has sustained the people of the island ever since they first arrived here. In recent times, in the face of world trade and overwhelming competition from large-scale food producers, Dominica's agriculture industry has waned. The farming of bananas for export to Britain and other EU countries was struck a severe blow by successive changes to trade rules, removing subsidy support for small island growers and pitting them against the economies of scale that are enjoyed by mass producers. Many Dominican farmers have not been able to survive these events and have left the industry altogether, sometimes preferring to sell their land to real-estate developers and speculators. Those who remain in this troubled sector have had to change the way they manage and operate their businesses, producing and selling to specialist markets both at home and abroad. The damage inflicted by globalisation has also extended to the image and attraction of farming for the young people of Dominica, with many no longer considering it a viable or worthwhile occupation. Indeed it is all too often seen as a last-resort occupation.

Organic and sustainable farming is becoming popular with some, though it is far from the norm as there are few incentives for farmers to switch to more nature-friendly agricultural practices. Weedkillers, pesticides and chemical fertilisers still appeal to those who grow produce in bulk to supply supermarkets. The government does little to support and promote organic agriculture and so it is usually practised by those who grow food for their own consumption or for specialist markets.

Agrotourism is linking a fragile organic farming movement with the developing ecotourism sector (see below). Some rural groups have enthusiastically embraced organic farming and have established educational farm tours for visitors as a means to supplement income as well as promote their products.

Dominica's Wai'tukubuli National Trail (pages 223–51) passes through or nearby several farmlands and the hope is that more farmers will embrace the presence of hikers and use the opportunity to develop agrotourism businesses of their own. This is a painfully slow process, however.

FISHERIES Fishing is a traditional occupation on Dominica and every coastal village has its community of fishermen. Colourful boats can be seen pulled up on the beach or moored close to the shore, and there is usually a regular spot where daily catches are sold. Many fishermen sell directly to hotels, restaurants and supermarkets, some sell at established fish markets in Roseau, Marigot and Portsmouth, and others simply meander around village communities either in a pick-up truck or pushing a barrow, blowing a conch shell to let people know there is fish for sale. You will also see fishermen selling by the roadside on makeshift benches or cable drums. (Be careful when you do – cars and buses tend to pull over and stop without any kind of warning.)

Migratory pelagics such as marlin, tuna and dorado are usually caught from small boats using long hand lines and homemade artificial lures. This takes place several miles offshore using fish-attracting devices (FADs) that are usually floats made from an assortment of tree branches or palm fronds. Small fish are drawn to these floating structures, creating a concentrated food source for larger predators.

Inshore fishermen use basketware or chicken-wire traps and seine nets to catch mackerel, ballyhoo, jacks and small tuna. Almost all lobsters that are caught are sold directly to hotels and restaurants, and you will rarely see them for sale elsewhere. Unlike most of the Eastern Caribbean, conch is fairly uncommon as the sea around Dominica's coastline gets very deep very quickly.

Lionfish hunting has become common in recent times (see box, page 11). It is an attempt by some scuba divers and fishermen to rid Dominica's reefs of this invasive predator while at the same time earning income by selling their catch to restaurants.

TOURISM Because of its dramatic and largely unspoiled natural environment, Dominica is rightly promoted as an ecotourism destination. In addition to hikers, scuba divers, researchers, botanists, birdwatchers and other nature enthusiasts, Dominica receives around 300,000 cruise ship passengers each year. These day-visitors are an important source of income for local people, in particular tour operators, bus drivers, and souvenir vendors, though income per visitor is in actual fact very low compared with stay-over travellers. Despite this anomaly and the negative impact large cruise ships can have on the natural environment, cruise lines and their passengers offer direct marketing and revenue opportunities, and continue to be courted.

The government-sponsored agency responsible for tourism marketing is the **Discover Dominica Authority** (*1st Floor Financial Centre, Roseau;* \ *767 448 2045;* e *tourism@dominica.dm; www.dominica.dm*). Also promoting the island as well as representing its members is the **Dominica Hotel & Tourism Association** (*17 Castle St, Roseau;* \ *767 616 1055;* e *dhta@cwdom.dm; www.dhta.org*).

Community tourism was a strategy aimed at assisting local communities to develop and implement tourism-related initiatives. Since the decline of the agriculture sector in the majority of Dominica's rural areas, the government sought to arrest the slump by trying to get people involved in the tourism industry. 'Tourism is everybody's business' is a phrase you may well come across during your visit to the island. Although community tourism initiatives sprang up all around the island, the enthusiasm and support for many has since waned.

COTTAGE INDUSTRIES Handmade soaps, wood and tree fern carvings, rum punches, Kalinago basketwork, essential oils, honey, decorated calabash bowls, and exotic fruits are just some of the products developed or grown by small cottage industries scattered throughout the island. From roadside vendors selling *braf* or *souse* on a Saturday morning (see page 55) to seasoning peppers, bay oil, tonics, herbal teas, coconut water, coffee, mineral water and beer, Dominica's home-grown businesses are important for the development of the country's economy and, in particular, the local communities where these cottage industries are based. For a list of some local products see page 102.

PEOPLE

For outsiders the Dominican psyche can be difficult to understand and first impressions are often somewhat misleading. However, serious, sometimes stern outward countenances usually give way to broad smiles and friendly conversation (though you may have to work hard for it sometimes), and what may look like a heated exchange is often just a lively discussion or debate that ends in jokes and laughter. Of course there are exceptions, but visitors should have no reservations about engaging with a friendly and interesting people. Once the ice is broken, Dominicans are very keen to talk about their lives and their country and will indulge themselves by offering you, the visitor, plenty of information, help and advice. Politics and social commentary are always hot topics, though Dominicans will willingly offer you an opinion on absolutely any subject at all, from world affairs to how best to park your car.

POPULATION Dominica's population is estimated at around 71,000, with some 20% or so living in or around the capital, Roseau. The population has remained fairly unchanged in recent years due to the migration of many young people abroad, particularly to the United States (often via the US Virgin Islands), the UK and Canada, where they go in search of opportunity and prosperity. Though the estimated size of the Dominica diaspora varies considerably, commonly quoted statistics are that around half of Dominica's households have at least one close family member currently living abroad and that 30% of households have experienced close family migration abroad over the last ten years.

ETHNICITY The majority of Dominicans are descendants of slaves brought to the island by the French and British from West Africa. Dominica is the only island in the eastern Caribbean that is still home to a people who were here before the

The weapon of choice for sailors and pirates in the 17th and 18th centuries was the cutlass. It is a short sabre with a broad curved blade and was useful for close combat on ship and shore, as well as for cutting through rope and wood. On land it was also used as an agricultural tool, particularly effective for cutting through rainforest and harvesting sugarcane.

Also used both as a weapon and an agricultural tool was the machete. Very similar in shape and length to a cutlass, the machete has a broad blade with a very thin, sharp cutting edge. It is, however, much less elegant in design than the naval cutlass, and is sometimes called the 'poor man's sword'. Variations of the machete exist in many countries across the world. The *parang*, *golok* and *bolo* are similar long knives used in Malaysia, Indonesia and the Philippines. In Nepal it is the *kukri* and in China the *dao*.

In Dominica today the machete continues to be used as an agricultural tool for cutting overgrown bushes, trees and weeds, and for harvesting crops, and the household that does not possess at least one is very much in the minority. Commonly referred to as a cutlass, the tool is in fact a simple machete, rather than its upmarket relative. Visitors to Dominica may see both men and women walking along the roadside carrying one. This should not cause alarm, although it almost certainly will at first.

arrival of Columbus in 1493. The Kalinago are of Amerindian descent and number approximately 3,000, the majority of whom live on the east coast in or around the 1,530ha Kalinago Territory (pages 153–8).

LANGUAGE

The official language of Dominica is English, which is spoken throughout the island. The unofficial language of Dominica, and very commonly used, is **French Creole**, also called *Kwéyòl*, *Patwa* or *Patois*.

The European settlers on Dominica and throughout the Caribbean brought with them many slaves from West Africa to work on their estates. These slaves developed an indigenous language that combined the syntax and vocabulary from their native African languages with those of their European oppressors. On Dominica, together with Martinique, Guadeloupe and St Lucia, a French Antillean Creole was born.

Often considered rudimentary, sometimes not even a real language, many Creoles have been in a state of decline and loss. When Dominica became a British Crown Colony, English was firmly established as the language of the ruling classes and for many years Creole was viewed as a dialect spoken only by servants, farmers and peasants. The influence of the French has remained strong, however, and in recent times Creole language and culture has undergone significant recognition and revival, ultimately resurfacing as a key part of the island's national heritage. These days Creole is very commonly used and you will often hear Dominicans using it to converse with each other.

In the northeast of the island, around the villages of Marigot and Wesley, it may still be possible to hear a dialect that combines African with English rather than French. This is because the British estate owners in this area brought African slave workers from English-speaking islands such as Antigua. This English Creole is known locally as **Kockoy**.

The English spoken by Dominicans reflects both the past and the present. Sentence structure frequently resonates with the syntax of African languages and the continued

Some examples of French Creole, or *patwa*, from Marcel D'jamala Fontaine's *Dominica's Diksyonnè* (2003):

Good day	*Bon jou*
Good afternoon	*Bon apwé midi*
Good evening	*Bon swé*
How are you?	*Sa ka fete?*
My name is Paul	*Non mwen sé Paul*
I love Dominica	*Mwen enmé Domnik*
It is a beautiful day	*Jòdi sé yon bèl jou*
It is raining	*Lapli ka tonbé*
I am thirsty	*Mon swèf*
I am hungry	*Mon fen*
I would like a drink	*Mon vlé on bwè*
How much is it?	*Konmen ou sa?*

influence of Creole. A high English remains and reminds us that a Dominican class society, particularly in and around the capital Roseau, is still mirrored in the language spoken by its people. Inevitably, through the prevalence of cable TV and contact with an increasing number of tourists, a North American English is now also spoken on the island and you may well experience people '*Yanking it*' with you. Please ask them to be proud of their own heritage, rather than yours.

RELIGION

From the moment Columbus arrived in 1493, the *zemi* stones and ancestral spirit worship of the Amerindian tribes across the region were brutally replaced by the crucifix and the Roman Catholic Church. Vieille Case (or Itassi as it was known to the Kalinago) was the site of the island's first Roman Catholic Mass in 1646, and in the early 18th century French Jesuits erected the first Roman Catholic church in Roseau. Many more churches were built across the island as well as schools, health services and the Credit Union movement were established. Today, with around 80% of the population as followers, Roman Catholicism is by far the dominant religion. Faith is very strong and the Church's influences and principles find themselves deeply woven into the fabric of modern Dominican society.

A number of other Christian denominations are present on the island, including Methodists, Pentecostals, Seventh Day Adventists, Baptists and Jehovah's Witnesses. Other minority religions include Islam, Baha'i and Rastafarianism. Dominica's constitution provides for religious freedom of all faiths.

Although religion is strong and most Dominicans have very conservative beliefs, Dominica has many social issues such as the abuse of women and children, teenage pregnancies, alcoholism, and having children outside of marriage.

EDUCATION

Primary school education is mandatory on Dominica. It lasts for seven years and ends with the common entrance exam. Secondary education was made universal in 2005 and lasts for five years. It is completed by pupils sitting examinations for the Caribbean Examinations Council Secondary Education Certificate, or GCE O-levels. There are also a number of non-governmental primary and secondary schools operating on the island.

Dominica's State College opened its doors in September 2002. Its formation amalgamated a number of disparate tertiary education establishments under one roof with the aim of better organising standards, policies and opportunities. The college offers further education in traditional as well as vocational subjects such as hospitality and tourism, nursing, agriculture and teacher training.

The University of the West Indies (UWI) Open Campus offers Dominicans the opportunity to enrol in some degree programmes that may take place entirely within Dominica, or may be split between the Dominica school and the main UWI campus.

Dominica's tertiary education system receives small but welcome boosts through scholarships that are awarded by individuals, organisations or governments. It is through such scholarships that talented Dominicans of all backgrounds are able to pursue further education in institutions abroad that, under normal circumstances, would be well beyond the reach of most pockets.

CULTURE

Following the decline and subsequent retreat of the Kalinago population to the northeast of the island, it was left to the European colonists and their West African slaves to stamp a new cultural identity upon the rugged face of Dominica. Of the Europeans it was the French who made the greatest impression, due largely to the proximity of Guadeloupe and Martinique, and the movement of traders and 'free people of colour'. African tribal traditions including dance, dress and belief systems merged with the culture of France, from the dances and festivals of its royal courts to the language, music and fashions of its Caribbean settlers. Whilst Kalinago place names fared better than those concocted by the British, it was without doubt the emergent **French Creole** that dominated the cultural landscape of Dominica from the 19th century onwards. Despite Dominica becoming a British Crown Colony, Creole culture not only survived, it also continued to prevail in the villages and among the island's freed slaves.

Today Creole is one of the essential ingredients of Dominica's cultural landscape and, together with a fresh movement in 'Kalinago consciousness' history and tradition, and the continued revival of African roots and heritage, a bewitching brew of the past merges with the present to leave us with a multi-cultural bouillon of sound, colour, words, and a little bit of magic.

TRADITIONAL COSTUME Commonly worn by women from the 1800s to the 1960s, the *wob dwiyet* is now only seen at national festivals such as the Creole and Independence celebrations that take place during October and November each year. Starting life as a dress worn on Sundays or feast days when enslaved women were permitted to discard their drab uniforms and dress up in the kind of colours to which they were more accustomed, the traditional Creole *wob dwiyet* dress was born. Over the years the style has been modified and accessories have been added to develop this attire, but the combination of bright skirt over white chemise, with lace adornments, coloured headscarf and kerchief is in essence the same as the national dress that is worn today.

The wearer of the *wob dwiyet* is known as the *matador* and for formal occasions she may choose to wear a headpiece, or *tête en l'air*, made of a square piece of **madras**. This square of Indian cotton, made by the Kalabari in the vicinity of

Chennai (formerly Madras), was known as the *mouchoir madras* and became very popular with Creole women towards the end of the 18th century. French, English and Portuguese merchants were involved in the trade of madras, or *injiri*, as it is known in India, around 400 years ago. It is thought these merchants brought the material to West Africa where it was worn by the Igbo in southern Nigeria. Traditionally madras was made with vegetable dyes which ran, or 'bled', each time the material was washed, becoming blurred over time. Today most madras is still made in India but with chemical dyes.

MUSIC AND DANCE Traditional music and dance finds its roots in the island's history. From the slaves of West Africa and the influences of their British and French oppressors, songs, music and dance emerged that can still be enjoyed today. The drum, or *la peau cabwit*, provides a traditional beat that has echoes of Africa, whereas lyrics are often sung by women in an enchanting French Creole.

The **bélé** is a Creole dance of African origin. The *tambou twavail* or *tambou bélé* drum is the centrepiece and the dance moves, particularly in the *bélé rickety* variant, reflect a courtship between the man and the woman as they move in turn towards the drum and its resonating rhythm. By the time the dance reaches its conclusion, the drum is booming loudly and the man and woman are dancing together with quick steps and vigorous body movements, symbolising their union.

The **quadrille** is a more formal square dance that originates in the French courts of the 19th century. Four couples traditionally dance together. The ladies, known as the *dam*, dance in *wob dwiyet* costume, with the men, known as the *kavalyé*, leading. Often referred to as 'heel and toe', the quadrille's style is aristocratic, graceful and elegant, and today it is a key part of Dominica's Independence celebrations. Its traditional accompaniment is a **jing ping** band. This is usually a four-instrument ensemble that comprises a tambourine (*tambal*), a long boom pipe (*boumboum*), a rattle or scraper (*shak-shak*, or *gwage*), and an accordion, which replaced the original bamboo flute.

Dominica's popular music scene really began in the 1960s with **calypso** and **steelpan** music. These genres are still very popular and the Swinging Stars calypso band that was formed in Roseau in 1959 still performs to packed houses today, though the line-up has changed somewhat. In the 1970s a new Dominican music style called **cadence-lypso** became fashionable across the Caribbean. This music combined calypso with *kompa*, a Creole music genre from Haiti. Popular Dominican exponents of cadence-lypso include Ophelia Marie and Gordon Henderson with his band Exile One. **Zouk** music from Martinique and **soca** from Trinidad arrived on Dominica in the 1980s and eclipsed the cadence-lypso scene. Zouk takes its influences from reggae and salsa, and soca is a fusion of calypso and Trinidad's Indian music, sometimes called *chutney* music. One of Dominica's most popular soca bands, Windward Caribbean Kulture (WCK), combined cadence-lypso with jing ping to produce **bouyon** music, which has also become a very popular genre on Dominica, Martinique and Guadeloupe.

CARNIVAL The festival of Carnival, or *Mas Domnik*, that takes place on the Monday and Tuesday before Ash Wednesday each year, is a time when Dominicans party hard, 'jump up', 'free up' and really let their hair down. Although today the music is a modern combination of calypso, steelpan and bouyon, usually transported in electronic format with huge amplifiers and speakers crammed on to flat-bed trucks, the colourful costumes and the spirit of dancing are still tantalising reflections of the past. French settlers may have brought the festival of *masquerade* to Dominica, but it was the African slaves who added a raw rhythm, vibrancy and just a hint of rebellion. It is that colour, spirit and edge that is still in evidence in today's Carnival.

The calypsos that are sung in competition prior to Carnival hark back to the *chante-mas*, a tradition of song and satire that evolved as part of the preparations for Carnival. The female *chanteulles* would sing short, cutting ballads that ridiculed administrators or perpetrators of bad deeds. Today calypso songs are much longer, though the lyrics still contain a large dose of irony or political and social commentary.

Carnival costumes were originally little different from those worn in African tribal festivals. Most notable is the **sensay** costume, its fierce mask and horned headpiece with ruffles of cloth strips completely covering the wearer and cascading in layers from the head down to the ground. Although one or two of these original themes survive, today costumes are of modern materials and design, and in more recent years have become far more mainstream – lots of bikinis and feathers – a trend that is bemoaned by traditionalists.

ARCHITECTURE Many of the small wooden houses that can be seen in villages across Dominica are based on a simple design that goes back to the days of the earliest settlers. These small houses, called *ti kai* or *kai kwéyòl*, typically have a half-hip shingle roof designed for hurricanes, quick water run-off, and to enable air circulation. They have a small veranda, jalousie-style windows with strong hurricane shutters and are sometimes raised on piles or pillars. Today the roofs are often made of modern galvanised steel, which sound like thunder when it rains. Elements of the French Creole style are evident in some of the older buildings across Dominica, but especially in the French Quarter in Roseau. King George V Street provides an excellent example of beautiful verandas, jalousie windows, wooden shutters, ornate and intricately designed fretwork beneath the eaves of the upper floors.

Unfortunately, due to fire, sackings and hurricanes, many of Dominica's original buildings are gone. Those that remain and are being preserved, however, offer a glimpse into the island's colonial past. There are some interesting military fortifications and ruins such as those at Cachacrou, Fort Young, Fort Shirley and Capuchin. Also there are a number of estate houses and ruins of estate buildings dotted across the island. Bois Cotlette, Clarke Hall and Morne Rouge estates are great examples. The Kalinago Barana Auté, or Kalinago model village by the sea, is an interesting representation of traditional Kalinago building design and construction.

ARTISTS One of Dominica's most famous historic painters is actually Italian. Born in Rome in 1730, **Agostino Brunias** was hired by Sir William Young, governor of Dominica in 1771, as his personal artist. Brunias fell in love with the island and stayed there until his death in 1796. During his life he painted many scenes of Dominica: detailed images of people working the fields, washing, cooking and dancing that offer an interesting insight into the Dominica of the day. Brunias's works were reproduced in prints, many of which left the country. You can see examples of his work in the Dominica Museum opposite the Roseau cruise ship berth.

Today Dominica has a number of very talented artisans, including painters, illustrators and sculptors. Here is a selection.

Painters A young Dominican artist, **Shadrach Burton**'s scenic landscapes are inspired by the drama and beauty of his island. For more information visit his website: www.shadrachburton.com.

Earl Etienne is perhaps the country's most established contemporary artist. Though his style changes, he is best known for his technique of *bouzzaille*, which incorporates smoke and soot patterns from which images of Dominican folk life emerge. His paintings of traditional *bélé* are also excellent. Earl Etienne has a gallery in Roseau (page 102); for more information: www.earletienne.com.

Hilroy Fingal is an artist who is inspired by Dominica's natural environment and its African heritage. His colourful paintings and intricately decorated calabash bowls and glassware are well worth seeking out.

Marie Frederick (*www.mariefrederickgallery.com*) was born in France and now lives and works on Dominica. Her inspiration is the daily life of the island and she paints in acrylic, ink, watercolour and oil. Her unique Indigo studio and gallery is located in the northern village of Bornes.

Pauline Marcelle (*www.paulinemarcelle.com*) is a modern artist who has received international acclaim at exhibitions in New York and Vienna, where she now lives. Her artworks combine painting, objects, film and text.

Petros Meaza (*www.petrosart.com*) was born in Ethiopa and now lives and works on Dominica. His colourful paintings are inspired by his new home and the spirit of his native Africa.

Ellingworth Moses is a Dominican artist who paints scenery and very colourful abstracts that incorporate the use of thread. He has a gallery in Roseau (page 102), and a website: www.emosesart.com.

Lowell Royer works in acrylics to create colourful, eye-catching and beautiful depictions of people and life on the island. For more information http://lowell-royer.fineartamerica.com.

Other talented painters you could look out for on your travels include: Gharan Burton, Aaron Hamilton, Hilary St Hill, Marvin Fabien, Marcus Cuffy, Ray Francis, Kelvin James, David G Wilson, Arnold Toulon, Tiffany Burnette-Biscombe, Kelo Royer, Arthurly Richards, Carla Armour.

Sculptors Born in England and now living on Dominica, **Roger Burnett** is a figurative sculptor, watercolour painter and illustrator. His studio is located in Antrim Valley, between Roseau and Pont Cassé. For more information: www.sculpturestudiodominica.com.

Louis Desire was a Haitian-born sculptor who lived and worked on Dominica. Sadly he died in 2015. His wood carvings are quite exquisite and much sought-after.

Other artisans Dominica is home to some very imaginative and talented craftspeople who create ornaments, batiks, calabash bowls and bags, jewellery, masks and so on. Absolutely the best resource for discovering many of them is the website of the **Dominica Arts and Crafts Producers Association** (*www.dominicacraft.com*). It has a very useful artisan directory with contact information as well as a fun and interesting documentary about the association and some of its members. Try, if you can, to shop for genuine Dominica crafts and mementos rather than all the mass-produced imported tat that swamps many of the market stalls and souvenir shops.

WRITERS, POETS AND STORYTELLERS
Dominica's two most famous literary icons, Jean Rhys and Phyllis Shand Allfrey, lived around the same time and were daughters of British settlers. In more recent times a number of home-grown writers have achieved success and today, thanks to the annual Nature Island Literary Festival and Book Fair (see page 61), and a grass-roots movement of poets and storytellers, there continues to be a healthy interest in the written and spoken word.

Jean Rhys was born in Cork Street, Roseau in 1890. Her father was a Welsh doctor and her mother a member of the Lockhart family who owned the Geneva

Estate at Grand Bay. Rhys left Dominica at the age of 16 for schooling in England, during which time the Geneva Estate house was razed to the ground by arsonists. In 1936 she made a last trip to Dominica, which included a visit to the remains of Geneva, and it was the attacks on this family estate that were reflected in the burning of 'Coulibri' in her acclaimed 1966 novel, *Wide Sargasso Sea*. Jean Rhys died in 1979.

Phyllis Shand Allfrey was born in 1908, a year after Jean Rhys left Dominica for England. In 1954 her only novel, *The Orchid House*, was published. It is a largely biographical story of the three daughters of a once wealthy but now impoverished white family, told through the eyes of Lally, a black nurse. The book received praise and was even made into a film for British television. A grass-roots activist and Fabian socialist, Allfrey returned to Dominica in 1954 and founded the Dominica Labour Party, the country's first political party. Phyllis Shand Allfrey died in 1986.

Elma Napier was born in Scotland in 1892 but settled on Dominica in 1932 where she spent the remainder of her life. She lived with her husband at Pointe Baptiste (page 190) and became the first woman to be elected to a Caribbean legislature. She loved exploring the island and wrote an autobiography of her life on Dominica called *Black and White Sands*. Napier died in 1973 and was buried next to her husband 'in a quiet place under trees' on the Pointe Baptiste Estate.

Lennox Honychurch is the author of a number of non-fiction works including *The Dominica Story – A History of the Island*, first published in 1975, and still Dominica's definitive historical reference, and *Negre Mawon: The Fighting Maroons of Dominica*, published in 2014. A Doctor of Philosophy and an anthropologist, Dominica-born Honychurch is also an artist, poet and conservationist. In recent times he has been actively involved in the preservation of the Fort Shirley Garrison in the Cabrits National Park (pages 181–3).

Irving André is a novelist. His work *A Passage to Anywhere* is the poignant story of a young man's journey into adulthood and the decision to stay on Dominica or seek his fortune abroad. Other works by André include *Distant Voices* and *The Island Within*.

Gabriel Christian is a novelist whose work includes *Rain on a Tin Roof*, which is a collection of short stories portraying life on Dominica.

Giftus John is a storyteller and poet. His book *Mesyé Kwik! Kwak!* is a collection of short stories set against the backdrop of the west coast village of St Joseph where he grew up. He has also written a collection of poems called *The Island Man Sings His Song*.

Alick Lazare is a writer and poet. His popular novel *Pharcel* tells the story of a runaway slave in colonial Dominica, and his most recent work *Kalinago Blood* was published in 2013.

For more about Dominica's writers and publishers, and for further reading please see *Appendix 3* on pages 256–8.

Kont is a form of traditional storytelling that draws upon history, superstition and legend. **Lawrence Brumant** of the northern village of Paix Bouche (page 192) is one of Dominica's best-known tellers of *kont*, with stories such as *How Dominica Got its Name*, *The Wise Lawyer* and *Désirée*.

FOLKLORE Dominican culture is embellished with a number of colourful myths and legends that have their origins in the spirit tales, practices and beliefs of West African tribes as well as in later Creole folkloric influences. For some Dominicans this lore extends beyond simple superstition and is still to be found lurking in the shadows of the island's more contemporary practices and belief systems.

Obeah, a kind of magic or witchcraft, is still practised by traditional shamans or herbalists. Based on a belief in supernatural forces that can forge or quell evil spirits, Obeah men or Obeah women may be engaged to cast spells or create potions.

There are two night spirits the unassuming visitor may wish to look out for. The *soucouyan* of West African origin sheds her skin and flies through the forest in a ball of flames on the lookout for the blood of people and animals. If her skin happens to be found it can be rubbed with salt to make it difficult and painful for her to put back on, or alternatively a calabash of peas can be placed next to it which she must count before she is able to transform herself back into a human. Successful escape from a *soucouyan* may just place you in the hands of **La Diablesse,** however, which is altogether bad news. This beautiful woman walking through the forest by the light of the moon lures men deeper and deeper into the woods, where she transforms herself into a wild old crone who causes her victims to either go mad or die. Avoiding the *soucouyan* and La Diablesse does not mean you are out of those deep woods just yet, however. Go for a swim in a river and you may come across **Mama Glo,** a female spirit of lakes and rivers who also takes on the appearance of a beautiful woman or even a mermaid. She may command you to undertake a series of menial tasks with a promise of reward, but if you choose to disobey she may turn very nasty indeed. Take a nap on the forest floor and you may be visited by a *jombie,* or evil spirit. If it finds you sleeping, the *jombie* could destroy your health or bring you a lifetime of bad luck. Fortunately there is a remedy for its curse. Unfortunately it requires the help of Obeah…

SEND US YOUR SNAPS!

We'd love to follow your adventures using our *Dominica* guide – why not send us your photos and stories via Twitter (@BradtGuides) and Instagram (@bradtguides) using the hashtag #dominica. Alternatively, you can upload your photos directly to the gallery on the Dominica destination page via our website (*www.bradtguides.com*).

2

Practical Information

WHEN TO VISIT

Dominica is never overrun with tourists ('If only it were!', scream some) but the 'busiest' time of year is the **annual cruise ship season** which starts fitfully in October and peaks in December through March before limping to a halt by the end of April. During this period around 200 cruise ships will call at Roseau and occasionally Portsmouth. On some days there may be no ships at all, on others there can be two or three, even four offloading at the Bay Front, the ferry terminal or the port. Convoys of buses and taxis taking these day-visitors on island tours mean that some roads become congested – especially up the Roseau Valley – and some of the more accessible sites, such as Emerald Pool, Trafalgar Falls and Ti Tou Gorge, get rather crowded with people who may not be entirely sure where they are. It is also more difficult to catch a public bus as many drivers drop their loyal passengers and village routes in favour of the more lucrative cruise ship tour business, meaning you'll often see school children enduring long treks home or people laden with shopping bags or low-pressure gas bottles trying to hitch a ride by the roadside. Roseau becomes a little more crowded with meandering, often disorientated tourists looking for something interesting to photograph, or searching for the Botanic Gardens with out-of-date photocopied island maps they picked up on the ship, occasionally pausing to take selfies while trying to avoid being run over by traffic that seems to come from every direction and never end. It is a lively time of year on the island and, whatever its pros and cons, very many Dominicans depend on cruise ship tourism for a living.

Creole Week and **Independence celebrations** take place in the latter half of October and the beginning of November. At this time you can usually see traditional costume parades and cultural shows, and enjoy regional and local music events such as steel pan, Creole in the Park and the World Creole Music Festival. Creole Week (usually the last week in October) is especially busy and droves of visitors from the neighbouring French islands of Guadeloupe and Martinique arrive by ferry for the festivities. If you plan on coming to Dominica at this time of year then consider booking early as flights, ferries and accommodation book up quickly.

Carnival preparations and events start in early January and reach their peak on the Monday and Tuesday before Ash Wednesday. On an island of seemingly endless parties and fetes, Dominicans and visitors can enjoy uninterrupted days of around-the-clock festivities during the Carnival period. Many Dominicans love and look forward to absolutely any reason to 'fete' and this is the biggest excuse of all. There is much to enjoy and experience during Carnival, even if you are not a rum drinker: street parades, Carnival Queen and Calypso Monarch competitions, live music, dancing, and plenty of street food. Though it is certainly not on a par with Rio or Trinidad, Dominica's version of Carnival is a colourful and lively time to be on the island.

The **weather** from January to June grows hotter and the rains eventually peter out during the dry season. April, May and June are great months for hiking the interior and climbing the high peaks as cloud cover is usually minimal and views across the island are often unrestricted. Trails, though in places wet all year round, become a little less so at this time of the year and rivers and waterfalls are far more predictable. As the cruise ship season has usually wound down by the end of April, the more popular and accessible sites are also less crowded.

The Atlantic hurricane season starts in July and ends in November, though it usually peaks in the Caribbean region in the months of August and September. Hurricanes begin life on the west coast of Africa or mid-Atlantic and make their way westwards towards the Caribbean and the Gulf of Mexico. Whether tropical depressions become tropical storms and then develop into hurricanes is down to sea temperatures, high and low pressure areas, Sahara dust and wind shear. Due to the island's vulnerability during this period, August and September tend to be very quiet months and many hotels and tour operators choose to close and take a holiday themselves. The last 'direct hit' was in 1979 with Hurricane David, though near misses in more recent years have brought landslides, minor damage and flooding. In 2015, Dominica was struck by the outer bands of Tropical Storm Erika (see box, page 4), now considered to be one of the most destructive storms in living memory.

From October to December the weather is usually changeable, and often rainy. Days of clear skies and sunshine can be followed by an equal number of days of downpour and squall. But whatever time of the year you decide to visit, you should always prepare to get wet. Consider it part of the experience! Tour operators like to call it 'liquid sunshine' but make no mistake, it is rain, and it can be heavy. Dominica's mountainous, rainforest-covered interior is lush and green for a reason.

HIGHLIGHTS

Travellers come to Dominica for its dramatic, unspoilt and diverse natural habitats. Its cluster of nine active and dormant volcanoes and swathes of undisturbed rainforest make it unique to this region. This means it is an island for travellers who enjoy nature and the great outdoors. Its vast network of hiking trails are the main draw. The 200km Wai'tukubuli National Trail is a trek without equal in the eastern Caribbean and the island's signature hike, the Boiling Lake Trail, is on most hikers' bucket lists.

Dominica is also a popular destination for scuba divers and natural science enthusiasts. The island has endemic reptile, amphibian and bird species, sperm whales can be seen all year round, and the coral reefs and marine life are pristine and diverse.

Dominica is also home to the Kalinago, descendants of the region's first people. Most of them live in the Kalinago Territory, a semi-autonomous region in the east of the island where they still retain a tenuous, though increasingly firm, grasp of their history and heritage.

Wellness, alternative and natural living are also reasons travellers enjoy this island. Dominica has numerous hot volcanic spas and its unspoilt natural environment offers a pure and fresh alternative to hectic lifestyles, traffic jams and offices. It's the perfect place to recharge batteries.

SUGGESTED ITINERARIES

SURF AND TURF Getting to Dominica is no easy feat and it's not always possible to do it in a single day. You may have to overnight in Antigua, Barbados, St Martin, Guadeloupe or Martinique – it all depends where you are coming from. Often when people consider coming to Dominica they think about their connecting flight first, then their long-haul flight, and then somewhere to stay. Believe me, you really have to want to come here; but it is worth it!

Although Dominica does have beaches, that's not the reason you come here. You come to get wet, muddy and sweaty; to free up and feel alive. So if you're looking for all of this with a side of powder-white sand beaches, fine dining and cocktails at sunset, I would recommend making your stay on Dominica part of an eastern-Caribbean multi-destination holiday. Spend a few nights on Antigua, Barbados or St Martin either side of your visit to the island, sandwiching the adventure of Dominica between beachside relaxation: surf and turf.

GREAT DAYS OUT If you are here for more than a week, I think it's a good idea to split up your accommodation rather than stay in one place for the entire duration. It cuts down on the driving around and you can see more of the island at a relaxed pace. If you have arrived here by plane then start in the south and work your way back up north to the airport. If you are renting a car, pick a company that will let you drop it off at the airport when you leave.

National Trail aside, many of the main **hikes** are in the southern half of the island and can be accessed from the southwest, the southeast or the 'Heart of Dominica' (pages 207–9). Some of the easier trails, the Kalinago Territory, the Cabrits National Park, and a selection of very nice beaches and bays can be enjoyed in the upper half of the island.

If you are **scuba diving**, again start in the south and head up the west coast; the underwater topography is diverse. In the south you'll experience a lot of wall and pinnacle diving, and on the mid-west coast you'll dive to more expansive coral reef formations.

Assuming you are adventurous and plan on doing a little exploring, here are some ideas for great days out. You will find more suggestions throughout the book.

The interior

- The Boiling Lake hike followed by a swim up Ti Tou Gorge and then a hot sulphur bath at Wotten Waven to work on those tired and aching muscles. Dinner in the Roseau Valley; try Papillote Wilderness Retreat or River Rock Café.
- Climb Morne Trois Pitons and follow it with a cool down at Mero Beach, where there are several nice places for drinks and eats; Romance Café is a great option.
- Hike to Middleham Falls from the Laudat end, or walk the circular trail around the Freshwater Lake. If you are feeling energetic, tag on the Boeri Lake Trail too. Dine in the Roseau Valley or in town. Le Petit Paris Bakery serves wood-oven baked pizza on Friday evenings.

The north

- Cabrits National Park trails, Fort Shirley garrison, a swim at Purple Turtle Beach or Douglas Bay, and then a late afternoon trip up the Indian River. Purple Turtle is handy for lunch and there are several decent restaurants in the Picard area for dinner. Try Iguana Café at Glanvillea for something a little different, or some great seafood at Sisters Beach Bar in Picard.
- La Chaudiere, Red Rocks, Pointe Baptiste Estate Chocolate, Woodford Hill Beach or Batibou Beach. For lunch or dinner head to Calibishie for the Rainbow Restaurant, Coral Reef or Calibishie Lodges' Bamboo Restaurant. If you go to Batibou Beach on a Sunday, there's a beach restaurant serving lunch (check out the desserts).

Back for this edition by popular request (!) here's my list of top-ten things to see and do.

1. The Boiling Lake Trail
2. The Victoria Falls Trail
3. A Roseau Valley hot volcanic spa
4. Scuba diving (if you are not certified, do a 'try-dive')
5. Canyoning
6. The Jacko Steps Trail
7. The red rock coastline
8. A garden and/or farm tour
9. Freshwater Lake Trail
10. Cabrits National Park

I think the most important thing you can do, however, is get out of your car and take a walk – especially through a rural or Kalinago village; it is the best way to get to know Dominica and meet its people.

The east

- Victoria Falls and/or Sari Sari Falls (but only when it isn't raining). Riverside Café at Citrus Creek Plantation is a great place for a late lunch and a bathe in the Taberi River.
- Kalinago Territory including the KBA, back into the Heart of Dominica for short walks to the Emerald Pool and Soltoun Falls. Riverstone Bar & Grill on the Layou River near Bells is a good dining option and there is sometimes live music on Sundays.

The west

- Snorkelling at Champagne then down to Scotts Head for a climb up to the top of Cachacrou and then a swim and some more snorkelling to cool off. Late lunch and a cold beer in Scotts Head or Soufriere; Cocoyea by the church in Soufriere is a good choice and if you fancy lobster, give Anna a call at Chez Wen.

TOUR OPERATORS

Despite the best efforts of its tourism marketing people, Dominica is still very much off the beaten path and often confused with the Dominican Republic. International tour operators offering accommodation and activity packages here are definitely increasing in number, though there are still not that many of them to choose from. Most tend to offer accommodation in the larger and better-known hotels only so if you want to break things up a bit or stay in cheaper or alternative lodgings (for example, some of the many eco cottages) then the most flexible way to do things is to work out a rough itinerary first (using this excellent guidebook, naturally!) and then book flights, accommodation and transport independently online or over the phone. Most hotels, eco cottages, car rental agencies and inter-island flight operators have working websites, so it's quite straightforward to do this. Some hoteliers don't respond to emails especially quickly, so phone them before giving up, and others prefer to use booking agencies such as Airbnb and Booking.com.

The majority of hoteliers will help you organise activities when you get here, some will also help you do so in advance. Check with them when you book. For listings of specialist activities operators, see pages 69–85.

INTERNATIONAL OPERATORS

These international operators offer flights, accommodation & activity packages to Dominica.

Airbnb www.airbnb.com
Caradonna Dive Adventures US: 1 800 328 2288; Canada: 1 800 803 1383; www.caradonna.com
Caribtours UK: 020 77510660; www.caribtours.co.uk
Explore! UK: 01252 883946; www.explore.co.uk
HomeAway UK: www.homeaway.co.uk
Inn Travel UK: 01635 617000; e holidays@inntravel.co.uk; www.inntravel.co.uk. See ad, 2nd colour section
Kenwood Travel UK: 020 77499245; www.kenwoodtravel.co.uk
Motmot Travel UK: 01327 359622; www.motmottravel.com
Newmont Travel UK: 020 8920 1155; www.newmont.co.uk
Responsible Travel UK: 01273 600030; www.responsibletravel.com
Spafari US: 1 800 488 8747; www.globalfitnessadventures.com

LOCAL AGENTS

The following local agents offer tailor-made destination management services, pre-booked accommodation, transportation & activity packages.

Decide on Dominica 767 255 1104 or 767 448 2181; e decideondominica@whitchurch.com;

www.decideondominica.com. This destination management company offers bespoke travel arrangements to & from Dominica including flights, connections, accommodation, tours & excursions, even cruises. They work with international agents & offer assistance & tours in English, French, Spanish & German for a holiday tailored to fit your needs. Team-building vacations for corporations & linguistic tours for non-native English speakers wishing to learn the language are just some of the specialities offered. Outbound travel & tour arrangements, including worldwide cruises, also offered.
Dominica Tours 767 448 2638 or 767 617 7650; e info@experience-dominica.com; www.experience-dominica.com. This family-run destination management company will organise your land- & sea-based activities as well as accommodation at Anchorage Hotel, Picard Beach Cottages, Portsmouth Beach Hotel, Aywasi Kalinago Retreat & Harmony Villa.
Going Places Travel 767 448 2550 or 767 448 2552; e dominica@going-places.tv; www.going-places.tv. Organises flights, cruises & accommodation – usually to the larger, high-profile hotels.
Ken's Hinterland Adventure Tours (KHATTS) 767 448 1660 or 866 880 0508 (toll-free); e info@khatts.com; www.khattstours.com. Respected operator specialising in organising land- & sea-based adventure activities as well as airport transfers, bus & taxi tours.
Whitchurch Travel Agency 767 448 2181; e travel@whitchurch.com; www.whitchurch.com. Long-established agent specialising in cruises, ferries, inter-island flights & island tours.

TOURIST OFFICES

For up-to-date details of Dominica's tourism representatives in Europe and North America, check the contact page of the Discover Dominica Authority's website. Their office on the island is located at First Floor Financial Centre, Roseau (767 448 2045; e tourism@dominica.dm; www.dominica.dm).

RED TAPE

ENTRY REQUIREMENTS All visitors to Dominica require a valid passport. You may also be asked to show either a return or an onward ticket, though this rarely happens. Arriving passengers must complete an immigration form which, if you have not been given one prior to landing on Dominica, you can pick up in the arrivals area. You must be able to provide details of your hotel or the address of family, friends etc, so be sure to have this written down somewhere. Complete your form before standing in line or you may be sent to the back. There is no hurry; relax, you are on island time now.

CUSTOMS It is common practice for customs officers to ask you to open your luggage at ports of entry on Dominica, so do not think you are being singled out in any way. Arriving passengers must complete a customs declaration form and hand it to a customs officer prior to inspection. Usually the customs officer will ask you where you are staying, whether you are here on business or vacation, whether you are bringing any food items and so on. Just answer honestly, be polite and smile – even though you may be very hot, tired, delayed and ready for a rum punch and a shower by now. Among other things, you must be sure to declare fruits, plants, cut flowers, vegetables, meat, pharmaceuticals, toy guns, commercial merchandise and currency above US$10,000 or equivalent.

DEPARTURE TAXES When you leave Dominica you have to pay departure tax of EC$59 (US$22) after check-in. Children under 12 are exempt.

COMMERCIAL FILMMAKERS If you are bringing film-making equipment here you may well be asked to show a permit. Contact the Discover Dominica Authority (*www.dominica.dm*) regarding permits, fees and waivers in advance of your journey.

MARRIAGE REQUIREMENTS If you are planning on getting hitched on Dominica there is a bit of red tape, but authorities have streamlined the process in an attempt to market the island as a wedding destination. Assuming your wedding is being organised by your hotel, they will help you with it all as part of their service. Bring with you: a certified copy of your birth certificates (copies have to be certified by a solicitor or notary); if previously married, a decree of divorce or the death certificate of your former spouse; a passport-sized photograph. Your application form must be accompanied by a EC$7.50 stamp and the following fees: EC$300 if on Dominica for up to two days (eg: cruise ship visitors); EC$500 if on Dominica for longer than two days; and an extra EC$204 for a weekend wedding. Any questions, queries or requests for up-to-date information should be made to either your hotel's appointed wedding organiser or the Discover Dominica Authority (*www.dominica.dm*).

CONSULATES AND EMBASSIES

Visitors from the United States and Canada should note that there is no representative consulate on Dominica. Instead you will be referred to your consulates in Barbados. For the other consulates listed, do not be surprised if you are put through to a Dominican business, an individual's home, or a law firm as that is where the consular representative may be located.

Belgium ☎767 448 2168	**France** ☎767 445 4508
Brazil ☎767 440 8007	**Germany** ☎767 449 7395
Canada (Barbados) ☎246 429 3550	**Netherlands** ☎767 448 3841
Cuba ☎767 449 0727	**Norway** ☎767 449 1733
Finland ☎767 878 5425	**People's Republic of China** ☎767 449 0080

Spain ✆767 445 5355	UK ✆767 275 7800
Sweden ✆767 448 2181	US (Barbados) ✆ 246 436 4950
Switzerland ✆767 445 4501	Venezuela ✆767 448 3348

GETTING THERE AND AWAY

BY AIR Dominica has two airports, both too small for commercial passenger jets. This means that for long-haul journeys you have to fly to another Caribbean island and then transfer to an inter-island air service. The most popular hubs are Puerto Rico, Antigua, Barbados and St Martin. You can also get here via the French islands of Guadeloupe and Martinique.

Dominica's main airport is **Douglas Charles Airport (DOM)** (formerly known as Melville Hall Airport) in the northeast. Seaborne Airlines, Winair and Liat have scheduled flights to and from this airport. Liat and Winair also fly to and from **Canefield Airport**, in the southwest, just a few kilometres north of the capital Roseau.

FROM THE US AND CANADA
Most of the major North American airlines have flights to Antigua (ANU), Barbados (BGI), Puerto Rico (SJU) or St Martin (SXM) where there are regular connecting Liat, Seaborne & Winair services to Dominica (see below). Please check their websites for latest prices & offers. Caribbean island governments heavily tax air travel (around 50% of ticket prices is tax), making them pricey. High demand at peak times (carnival, public holidays etc) also makes inter-island flying an expensive business.

Liat www.liat.com. Liat has a service between Dominica & San Juan, Puerto Rico (SJU), sometimes stopping at Antigua *en route*. Liat also flies to Martinique, where you can connect to Boston & New York with low-cost airline, Norwegian (*www.norwegian.com*).
Seaborne Airlines www.seaborneairlines.com. Seaborne flies between Dominica & San Juan, Puerto Rico (SJU). It has a codeshare agreement with JetBlue, which is handy for connecting flights to mainland USA.
Winair www.fly-winair.sx. Winair flies between Dominica & St Martin where you can get connecting flights to mainland USA.

FROM THE UK
Flights from the UK to Dominica are usually via Antigua or Barbados. Prices are usually very similar. Same-day connections may not always be possible. Please check tour operator or airline websites for latest prices, schedules, & whether you have to overnight *en route*.

British Airways www.britishairways.com. Flights are daily from London Gatwick (LGW) to Antigua (ANU) & Barbados (BGI) where you can connect to Dominica.
Virgin Atlantic www.virgin-atlantic.com. Flights are daily from London Gatwick (LGW) to Antigua (ANU) & Barbados (BGI) where you can connect to Dominica.

FROM FRANCE
Air France www.airfrance.com. Flights are daily from Paris Orly (ORY) to Guadeloupe (PTP) & Martinique (FDF) where inter-island flights or high-speed ferry services connect to Dominica.

INTER-ISLAND FLIGHT SERVICES AND CONNECTIONS
Liat www.liat.com. Liat serves the islands of the Eastern Caribbean & has its main hubs in Antigua & Barbados. Liat flights to & from Dominica arrive & depart from both Douglas Charles & Canefield airports.
Winair www.fly-winair.sx. Winair operates inter-island flights between Dominica, Puerto Rico & St Martin.

Connect via the French islands It is definitely worth considering getting to Dominica via Martinique or Guadeloupe. At the time of writing, low-cost airline Norwegian is flying from Boston, Baltimore and New York to Martinique. You can also get to Martinique from Miami. From Europe, you can get to both of the French islands via Paris. From Martinique or Guadeloupe you simply catch the high speed inter-island ferry to Roseau or fly with Air Antilles (*www.airantilles.com*). For up-to-date options contact a Dominica-based agent such as Decide On Dominica (page 35).

Douglas Charles Airport Although there is constant talk of an international airport one day, a project the country could never seriously afford, Dominica's Douglas Charles Airport is currently the island's primary air terminus and will probably continue to be so for some time to come. It is located on the Atlantic Ocean shoreline of Londonderry Bay in the northeast of Dominica, between the villages of Marigot and Wesley. It has a very simple layout of departure and arrivals halls with a small bar and restaurant in between. The main airline check-in desks (Liat, Seaborne and Winair) are clearly marked. The airport has a travel information office and an ATM located near the arrivals/customs hall.

Once you have cleared immigration and customs you will exit the arrivals hall and be greeted by official Airport Taxi Association drivers asking if you need a ride. All prices and drivers are regulated and there is information posted on the wall outside the arrivals door. If you are unsure about anything, check at the travel information booth. Confirm the price of the trip (and currency) with the driver before leaving. If you are collecting a hire car, make your way past the restaurant and departure hall to the wooden buildings up the steps. Car hire firms have their desks here. Be sure to bring your domestic licence with you.

Canefield Airport Located just a few miles from Roseau, Canefield is a very handy airport if you are staying in the south or west. The airport is very small, with a short runway, and is predominantly used by smaller inter-island hoppers, charter aircraft and courier services. Flights are usually to and from Antigua or the French islands but schedules do tend to change quite often. It is always worth checking, though, as prices may be a little higher than flights to and from Douglas Charles Airport. You can get taxis and buses at Canefield without too much difficulty, but you will have to let any car rental companies know in advance that you plan to arrive at and depart from this airport.

Baggage Please check airline websites for up-to-date information on baggage allowances and restrictions. Inter-island airlines are often very strict with baggage allowances.

Make sure your checked bags are properly tagged with your name and address. Should your bags not turn up at the airport with you (sadly, this does happen), make your way to the check-in desk in the departure hall and complete the requisite forms. Usually baggage delays are short and you can expect it to arrive the following day. Your hotel may well collect it for you.

BY FERRY L'Express des Iles (*www.express-des-iles.com*) operates a high-speed ferry service between the islands of Guadeloupe (including Les Saintes), Dominica, Martinique and St Lucia. The ferry arrives at and departs from the terminal on Roseau's Bay Front regularly throughout the week, although the schedule does change at certain times of the year. For timetables, pricing and bookings see the website. Tickets and updated schedule information may also be obtained on Dominica from H H V Whitchurch Travel Agency (*Old St, Roseau;* ☏ *767 448 2181;* e *travel@whitchurch.com; www.whitchurch.com*).

BY PRIVATE YACHT Visitors to Dominica arriving by private or charter vessel should contact the Dominica Port Authority on VHF channel 16. Customs clearance is mandatory before anchoring. Two copies of the crew and passenger list are required and you must pay an environmental levy. Ports of entry are in Portsmouth on the northwest coast, Roseau on the west coast, and Anse Du Mai on the east coast. While there is no properly established marina on Dominica, popular anchorages are Prince Rupert Bay on the northwest coast, Mero and Batali Bay on the mid-west coast, and Castle Comfort and Loubiere in the southwest. The Soufriere Scotts Head Marine Reserve on the southern tip of Dominica is out of bounds as an anchorage.

Dominica's marina and provisioning services are fledgling but they are also very personal.

ALDive Loubiere; ☎767 440 3483 or 767 275 3483; e aldive@aldive.com; www.aldive.com

Cobra Tours & Yacht Services Ltd Portsmouth; ☎767 245 6332 or 767 613 6332; e info@cobratours.dm; www.cobratours.dm

Dominica Marine Center Newtown, Roseau; ☎767 448 2705 or 767 275 2851; e info@dominicamarinecenter.com; www.dominicamarinecenter.com & www.dominicayachtservices.com

Pancho Services Castle Comfort; ☎767 448 1698 or 767 235 3698; e panchoservices@yahoo.com

HEALTH   *Dr Felicity Nicholson*

BEFORE YOU GO There are no immunisation requirements for visitors to Dominica except proof of vaccination against **yellow fever** for those over one year of age if coming from a yellow fever endemic area (eg: certain countries in sub-Saharan Africa and South America) or anyone transiting for more than 12 hours in a yellow fever endemic area. If the vaccine has been deemed unsuitable for you, travellers should obtain an exemption certificate from a registered yellow fever centre (eg: some GPs and most travel clinics). If you are unsure whether this applies to you, then check with a doctor ideally before you leave home and at least ten days before entering Dominica. There is no endemic malaria but there are other mosquito-borne diseases to avoid, including dengue fever and zika virus. Dominica's water is safe to drink though travellers who have particularly sensitive stomachs may wish to consider bottled water as an alternative. Even if the water is clean the different mineral content can lead to an upset stomach. It is recommended that standard vaccinations such as tetanus are up to date. These days **tetanus** is combined with **diphtheria** and **polio** in an all-in-one vaccine (Revaxis), which lasts for ten years. Travellers should also consider protecting themselves from **hepatitis A.**

Visitors requiring health care on Dominica are required to pay up front for treatment. Medical insurance is strongly recommended, particularly if participating in activities such as hiking or scuba diving. Ensure that your policy covers you for the activities you wish to enjoy. Vaccination against **hepatitis B** is recommended for long stays, for those working with children, or in a medical setting. Carriage of the virus in the local population is estimated at 2–10%. The course comprises three doses of vaccine given over a minimum of 21 days if time is short for those aged 16 or over. For those under 16 the minimum time to complete three doses is two months. Both these schedules require a booster dose in one year to give longer-lasting protection. Wherever possible the longer course of 0, 1, and 6 months is preferred for more sustained protection.

TRAVEL CLINICS AND HEALTH INFORMATION A full list of current travel clinic websites worldwide is available on www.istm.org. For other journey preparation

2

information, consult http://travelhealthpro.org.uk (UK) or http://wwwnc.cdc.gov/travel/ (US). Information about various medications may be found on www.netdoctor.co.uk/travel. All advice found online should be used in conjunction with expert advice received prior to or during travel.

INSECT BITES
Mosquitoes and sand flies Although there is no risk of malaria on Dominica, mosquito bites can still spoil your trip. You should bring insect repellent and ensure you apply it both day and night when you are out and about. Scratching bites can result in open wounds and infections so try to resist. Most hotels on Dominica will either have mosquito screens or bed nets though you could consider bringing your own to ensure that they are freshly impregnated with permethrin and do not have holes. Failing this, electric standing or ceiling fans usually work well as a night-time deterrent.

LONG-HAUL FLIGHTS, CLOTS AND DVT   *Dr Felicity Nicholson*

Any prolonged immobility, including travel by land or air, can result in deep-vein thrombosis (DVT) with the risk of embolus to the lungs. Certain factors can increase the risk and these include:

- Having a previous clot or a close relative with a history
- People over 40, with increased risk in over 80s
- Recent major operation or varicose-veins surgery
- Cancer
- Stroke
- Heart disease
- Obesity
- Pregnancy
- Hormone therapy
- Heavy smokers
- Severe varicose veins
- People who are tall (over 6ft/1.8m) or short (under 5ft/1.5m)

A deep-vein thrombosis causes painful swelling and redness of the calf or sometimes the thigh. It is only dangerous if a clot travels to the lungs (pulmonary embolus). Symptoms of a pulmonary embolus (PE) – which commonly start three to ten days after a long flight – include chest pain, shortness of breath, and sometimes coughing up small amounts of blood. Anyone who thinks that they might have a DVT needs to see a doctor immediately.

PREVENTION OF DVT
- Keep mobile before and during the flight; move around every couple of hours
- Drink plenty of fluids during the flight
- Avoid taking sleeping pills and excessive tea, coffee and alcohol
- Consider wearing flight socks or support stockings
  (see *www.legshealth.com*)

If you think you are at increased risk of a clot, ask your doctor if it is safe to travel.

Dengue fever occurs throughout the Caribbean. This virus is transmitted by a day-biting mosquito (*Aedes aegypti*), which is why it is important to use DEET-based insect repellents during the day. Use your sun screen first and the insect repellent second. If you are in forested areas then you would be advised also to wear long-sleeved cotton clothing and trousers for added protection. There are four types of dengue fever for which there is currently no cure. Dengue is rarely fatal if you have not had it before. However, even a primary infection can be unpleasant and causes a fever, with a headache, joint and muscle pains and sometimes a rash. It can be likened to a prolonged attack of influenza. Repeated infections with different strains can lead to a more serious haemorrhagic form of the disease, which can result in death. It is important, therefore, to avoid mosquito bites whenever possible by applying a good insect repellent (see above) during the day as well as in the evening to avoid other biting insects.

Chikungunya is also a virus that is transmitted by the daytime biting Aedes mosquito. Its symptoms are similar to those of dengue; headache, muscle pain, joint swelling or a rash, and there is no vaccine or medicine to prevent chikungunya infection. To protect against chikungunya, follow the advice above.

In March 2016, the first case of **zika virus infection** was reported on Dominica. Symptoms of zika virus occur in about 25% of patients. These include itchy red eyes, an itchy rash, and sometimes fever and muscle aches; symptoms are mostly short-lived. However, there are implications for women who are pregnant and travelling in risk areas, and for those who are planning pregnancy. Up-to-date guidance can be found at http://travelhealthpro.org.uk/zika-virus-update-and-advice-for-travellers-including-pregnant-women/. Like dengue and chikungunya, the zika virus is spread by day-biting Aedes mosquitoes so the same precautions taken to prevent those infections apply.

Sand flies are members of the subfamily *phlebotominac* and are tiny blood-sucking insects. They are attracted to warm-blooded animals, such as you, and can sometimes be a nuisance on beaches and in areas of mangrove. As with the mosquito, the small bites of the female can irritate and become inflamed if you rub or scratch them. Insect repellent will help.

Chiggers (*Trombicula alfreddugesi*)
Chiggers are known locally as *bête wouj*, and are the parasitic larvae of the harvest mite that move to the tips of leaves and grasses. When you brush against them, they migrate to your body and then spend a time rummaging around, trying to find a nice protected warm spot (often beneath the waistband of underwear or in other places you would really rather they not venture) where they pierce your skin and suck up the tissue. An extremely irritating rash appears which is caused by an allergic reaction to the salivary secretions of the larvae which drop off the skin once they have had their fill of you. They leave you with the rash as a memento of their visit, however, which can develop into severe welts if you scratch them a lot or if you are particularly sensitive to having insects partying in your nether regions. Insect repellents containing DEET help to prevent them hopping aboard your body in the first place, as do Vaseline and coconut oil.

Biting ants
These little – and sometimes rather large – critters can catch the unaware by unpleasant surprise. Bites are usually the result of either standing and pausing on a nest or brushing against or holding on to branches or foliage where ants are going about their business. They are all over you in seconds and their bites are like needles. Take care where you put your feet and hands and, if you have rested clothes or shoes anywhere, give them a good shake before putting them on again.

The larger carpenter worker ants (known locally as *tac-tacs*) bite hard, sometimes breaking the skin and spraying formic acid. This can result in a painful swelling that may last a couple of days.

TRAVELLERS' DIARRHOEA Around 50% of travellers will get a bout of diarrhoea which can spoil a good holiday so it is always wise to take basic precautions. Try to be sure water is safe to drink. Even though the tap water may be fine on Dominica it is always wise to drink bottled water instead. You should clean your teeth in bottled water too. Avoid food that has been left around or looks like it has been reheated – buffet meals are often the worst culprits. Food should be thoroughly cooked and served piping hot. Remember to wash your hands before eating. If you do get diarrhoea, in most cases it will settle down after 24 hours with rest, drinking plenty of fluids and taking rehydration salts (eg: Electrolade). Many people these days prefer to stop the diarrhoea at the first sign. Using a single dose of the antibiotic ciprofloxacin (500mg) taken together with two Imodium or other stopping agent will do the trick in most cases. A second dose of ciprofloxacin should be taken 10–12 hours later. The ciprofloxacin should always be taken with plenty of fluids and alcohol must be avoided. If the diarrhoea comes with a fever and/or blood and/or slime then you should seek medical help immediately as it is important to get the correct diagnosis and if necessary the appropriate antibiotics. That said, by taking sensible precautions you can minimise your chances of getting diarrhoea while still being able to eat and enjoy local foods.

PRICKLY HEAT A very itchy red skin rash known as *miliaria*, or prickly heat, is caused by sweating a lot in humid weather conditions. This can be a common problem for visitors who are not used to tropical climates. Dead skin cells and bacteria block sweat glands and the skin becomes inflamed. Air conditioning, cold showers, calamine lotion or, in severe cases, steroid creams can bring relief. Aloe vera may also help. If you find you are suffering from heat rash, try to avoid exerting yourself for a couple of days to reduce sweating and give your skin a chance to recover. Cool shaded rivers and easily accessible waterfall pools are alternative outings, as is a nice shady bar with a fresh juice or a cold beer, of course.

DEHYDRATION, HEAT EXHAUSTION AND HEATSTROKE High temperatures, humidity, exertion and a lack of adequate fluids will inevitably result in dehydration, heat exhaustion and possibly heatstroke. It is incredibly easy to become dehydrated in a tropical climate. Most people do not even realise that their irritability, weariness and dizziness is actually due to a lack of water, and travellers frequently underestimate the volume of water they should consume to remain healthy. Exertion in the tropics can require up to three litres a day, which is quite a rehydration challenge. When out walking take as much water as you can carry – at least one to two litres per person. Drink plenty of water before hiking and drink at regular intervals during your outing. Do not wait until you are thirsty. Carbonated soft drinks or beer are no substitute for water.

Dominica's rivers are usually very clean – as long as they are upstream from urban areas and farms. Rainforest hiking usually means a ready supply of water is on hand and many people drink it with no ill effect. If you are concerned about it, or have a sensitive stomach, then there are many good portable water filters on the market these days and it is really worth having one in your backpack.

Heat exhaustion occurs when the body's cooling system hits overdrive. Profuse sweating, pale clammy skin, fast shallow breathing, nausea, headaches, rapid weak pulse and stomach cramps are all signs of heat exhaustion. It is important to counter this quickly by trying to cool the body down. Sit in the shade, take a dip in a river or pool, drink plenty of water and relax.

Heatstroke can be fatal. This occurs when the body's cooling system has collapsed completely. Skin becomes hot and red, breathing slows and confusion and dizziness lead to unconsciousness. Cooling the body down is paramount and immediate medical assistance is essential.

SUN DAMAGE In a very short period of time the hot Caribbean sun will redden and burn your skin. Try to stay in the shade as much as you can, wear a hat, consider protecting sensitive skin with a sunscreen (at least SPF 25), and wear good-quality sunglasses to protect your eyes. Sun reflecting on the water can be especially damaging if you are exposed to it for too long without adequate protection. If your skin is not used to the sun, limit direct exposure as much as possible. Wearing a T-shirt to protect your back when snorkelling is also a good idea. If you absolutely must sunbathe, try to limit direct exposure to no more than 20 minutes and stay out of the sun during the hottest part of the day. That will easily be enough to send you home with a tan. Sunburn is not only harmful to your skin, it is very painful and can ruin your holiday. Wearing light-coloured, loose shirts, skirts and trousers made from cotton is the best solution.

SCUBA DIVING INJURIES Certified scuba divers should always dive conservatively and within recreational dive limits. If you do not know what they are, or have forgotten, check with your certifying organisation or dive centre professionals. Do not dive beyond your training and avoid alcohol and strenuous activities before and immediately after dives. Diving on Dominica is mostly easy, though wall diving means you are exposed to very deep waters. Maintain good buoyancy and always check your depth and no decompression limits. Dive with a buddy but do not share a dive computer.

Decompression sickness can be avoided by diving conservative profiles, ascending slowly and making safety stops at 5m. Signs and symptoms of decompression sickness include tingling or numbness in extremities, aching joints, rashes, headaches, dizziness and nausea. If affected, request 100% pure oxygen and seek medical assistance. Decompression sickness can be fatal and whilst the most severe symptoms become apparent within the first two hours of surfacing, problems can emerge up to 24 hours after diving. Allow dive crew to help and advise you. They are trained in managing dive emergencies.

Dominica has a recompression chamber located at the Princess Margaret Hospital, Roseau. It is always a sensible precaution to take out dive insurance to cover the cost of any evacuation and emergency recompression treatments that may be required.

AQUATIC LIFE INJURIES Whether scuba diving, snorkelling or just having fun in the sea, it is always possible to pick up an injury from aquatic life. Dominica's seas are very safe, there are no dangerous sharks patrolling the shore, and aquatic life injuries tend to come from contact with sea urchins or small jellyfish. Sea urchins are bottom dwellers, usually found around rocks. They have sharp spines that can pierce the skin of your feet if you stand on them. Typically the tips of the spines break off and embed themselves under the skin. This can be very painful and if not treated may cause an infection. It is prudent to seek medical assistance. A local remedy for the removal of sea urchin spines is to heat up some soft wax (a special soft wax that can be bought at a pharmacy), place the hot wax over the affected area and cover with a bandage. Leave it on overnight and the spines disappear. Incredibly, it works.

Contact with small jellyfish can result in a small but painful sting. Rubbing makes it worse. If possible remove any visible traces of tentacles with tweezers (not with your fingers, as the tentacles still retain their sting) and douse the affected area with white vinegar. Most dive boats and operators will carry a bottle of white vinegar in their first aid kit especially for this type of injury.

You should also avoid contact with fire worms. They look a little like hairy caterpillars and you may see them crawling over rocks or reef formations in both deep and shallow water. Touching them causes the bristles to embed into your skin, resulting in irritation and a rash.

The most environmentally friendly way of scuba diving and snorkelling is not to touch anything.

SEXUALLY TRANSMITTED DISEASES Unprotected sex is risky in any part of the world and Dominica is no exception. The official incidence of HIV infection is relatively low, however discrimination and the stigma attached to the disease may mean that reported cases do not reflect the true picture. Common sense and caution is the best advice. If you must indulge, use condoms or femidoms, which help reduce the risk of transmission – these are best brought from home to ensure their quality. If you notice any genital ulcers or discharge, get treatment promptly since these increase the risk of acquiring HIV. If you do have unprotected sex, visit a clinic as soon as possible; this should be within 24 hours, or no later than 72 hours, for post-exposure prophylaxis.

USEFUL CONTACTS
Emergencies ☏999
Princess Margaret Hospital Federation Dr, Roseau; ☏767 448 2231

Grand Bay Hospital ☏767 446 3706
Marigot Hospital ☏767 445 7091
Portsmouth Hospital ☏767 445 5237

SAFETY

Dominica is a relatively safe country for visitors but you should not take anything for granted. Precautions here are no different from those you would take anywhere else in the world. It is usually safe to walk around, both by day and by night but there have been occasional incidents of late-night muggings by youths in Roseau. Avoid walking alone at night-time in the capital if you can. Generally speaking, Dominicans are sensitive to issues concerning tourists and recognise that unpleasant experiences will inevitably affect everyone in the long run. But that doesn't prevent it from happening, of course. There are relatively few incidents of visitors experiencing crime, particularly violent crime, but it does happen and it is not always reported in the news; fear of bad publicity for the island occasionally trumps the truth, sadly. Travellers should take common-sense precautions such as dressing conservatively, avoiding conflict and not flaunting wealth openly. If approached by people asking for money (and this is very likely to happen in the capital), either give them a few dollars, or politely decline and walk on. Do not lose your temper or decide to give someone a lecture. It is simply not worth it and it will ruin your day. It is not uncommon for Dominicans themselves to admonish people they see asking visitors for money. If you do find yourself in a threatening situation, your focus should be on getting through it as peacefully as possible and not fighting back or getting into an argument. Smile lots.

The destitute, the homeless and the addicts have increased in number in Roseau and very little is done to help them. Sadly they are viewed as a nuisance rather than as human beings in need of help, and people are often very intolerant towards them. I used to think that giving them money would simply encourage them to hound visitors even more or just prolong their addictions, but now I give them a few dollars whenever I can. The bottom line is that they need help.

There is no social safety net on Dominica and if you have no caring family members either to take you in or help you out, then your situation can quickly become desperate. The situation never really seems to improve – in fact the number of beggars on Roseau's streets seems to grow. I can think of few capital 'cities' in the world where people know most of the beggars by name; that is a mark of how long they have been living on the streets here.

There have been occasional incidents of violent robbery and attack on some of the **northern beaches**. Despite this sort of incident being rare, I would suggest you go to Batibou Beach, Woodford Hill Beach and Hodges Bay (page 194) in groups or on weekends when there are plenty of locals also out enjoying themselves. Avoid evenings. And finally, **L'Escalier Tete Chien** (page 158) has a poor reputation for the hassle visitors receive from the drinkers who hang out at the bar above the trail.

Without doubt the riskiest part of any visit to Dominica is when driving. Some of the roads are challenging, often narrow with pot-holes, deep drainage gutters and sharp corners but it is Dominican driving practices that present the greatest potential hazard. There appears to be no happy medium when it comes to the way local people drive and you should simply expect the unexpected. See page 51 for more information about both car hire and the challenges of driving on Dominica.

WOMEN TRAVELLERS

Inevitably, as a visitor, you will attract attention – whatever your gender or age. This attention should not, however, be misinterpreted as a threat. Dominica is a safe place and most people are either just curious, perhaps looking for a conversation or friendship, or interested in trying to make a few dollars. Try to relax and always be polite, even if you are not really in the mood for it.

Women travellers are likely to be more vulnerable to unwanted attention than men, but you should not let this spoil your experience nor prevent you from exploring and enjoying the island. The best advice, as always, is to use common sense. If you can, try to avoid going to remote places alone, both by day and by night, try to dress as conservatively as your taste in fashion will allow, and do not bathe topless. Consider carrying a flashlight at night and trying to blend in as much as you can. Wearing similar clothing to local people is one way of doing this, as is not wearing nor flaunting ostentatious jewellery. If you do attract unwanted attention from amorous men, be as polite and good humoured as possible in the way you express your wish to be left alone – assuming you do. Try to extract yourself as quickly from the situation as you can – the longer you converse, the harder it is to leave. Avoid conflict, resist becoming angry and do not try to humiliate or belittle those you feel are harassing you. Some recommend wearing dark sunglasses as this helps you avoid eye contact and may also enhance your confidence.

TRAVELLERS WITH A DISABILITY

Dominica is not very disabled-traveller friendly at all. There are few provisions at hotels though some have ground-floor rooms and a couple (Garraway and Fort Young, page 97) also have elevators. Cottage-style accommodation is also an option worth considering as many are fairly obstacle free.

Roseau, however, is a nightmare if you use a wheelchair. Most footpaths are narrow and very uneven, often with drops, steps, gratings, potholes, vendors or parked cars to negotiate your way around. The road is your only option and then you have vehicular traffic to deal with. Most banks and ATMs are accessible.

Private minibus or taxi tours may be the most comfortable way for you to experience Dominica. Your hotel may also be able to arrange something specific to your needs. Accessible sights include: the Botanic Gardens (pages 104–5), some areas of the Kalinago Barana Auté (pages 154–6), Touna Auté (pages 157–8), beaches such as Purple Turtle (page 194), Mero (page 213 – the beach is disability friendly and Romance Café has a wheelchair ramp), Woodford Hill (see page 189), Douglas Bay (page 184) and, if you are interested in a hot sulphur bath, Tia's (page 112) has a very accessible and private pool, close to the entrance. A good time to visit may be during Creole and Independence festivities in October when you can enjoy traditional dancing, steel pan, music and food at reasonably accessible village, town and park venues.

For help, information and advice contact the Dominica Hotel and Tourism Association (*PO Box 384, 17 Castle St, Roseau;* \ *767 440 3430;* e *dhta@cwdom.dm*).

TRAVELLING WITH CHILDREN

Dominica is a great place to explore with children – they can enjoy a sense of freedom and adventure in a natural environment that may simply not be possible at home. There are lots of good hotels, cottages and self-catering options to choose from. All of the west coast beaches are safe for bathing (Purple Turtle and Douglas Bay are perhaps the best, see pages 194 and 184) as are many in the northeast, such as Hodges Bay (page 194), which is particularly good. There are plenty of outdoor activities that are fun for families: some of the shorter, less demanding hikes such as Syndicate Nature Trail (pages 216–18), Cabrits trails (pages 180–1) and WNT segment 10 (pages 245–6); rivers and waterfalls such as Trafalgar Falls (pages 115–16), Emerald Pool, Spanny Falls (pages 220–1), and La Chaudiere (page 198); and other activities such as river tubing (page 78), snorkelling, Indian River boat ride (page 196), Kalinago Barana Auté (pages 154–6), Kalinago Touna Auté (pages 157–8), and whale watching (pages 83–5). If you decide to take on any of the more challenging hikes, please take a good guide with you (see pages 476–7). It will enhance your experience as well as your safety.

If you are travelling with very young children you will find baby products in most of the better-known supermarkets as well as in the numerous pharmacies in Roseau (page 103). As they are imported, they can be quite expensive, however, so you will need to balance cost with convenience when planning your trip and deciding what to bring with you from home.

GAY TRAVELLERS

Roman Catholicism is by far the predominant religion on the island and majority views on homosexuality are in accord with traditional (rather than some of the more modern) church doctrine. It is a taboo subject and Dominica's homosexuals are essentially a silent community, forced to maintain a low profile and unable to express their sexuality openly without prejudice.

However you choose to deal with this is your choice, of course. But you should be aware that overt displays of your sexuality will certainly draw attention, and it will always be unpredictable and possibly confrontational in nature.

WHAT TO TAKE

Dominica has a hot and humid climate. It can also get very wet. You will need to bring shorts, light skirts and tops, and at least one swimming costume. Bring a hat to protect your head and sunglasses to shield your eyes from the sun. For hiking, a pair of training shoes is fine, but if you prefer proper hiking footwear then try to find something that has a good grip in the wet. Hard plastic soles are not very good for this. Many hikes require river crossings or scrambles over rocks, so your choice of footwear is quite important. Bring a light and breathable rain jacket. If you are staying in the interior, on the east coast or at a high elevation, bring a sweater too, as it can become cool in the evenings. Lightweight trousers are also good for the evenings when mosquitoes are on the prowl.

You will need a small backpack for day trips – a waterproof one is best. Take a small first-aid kit, sunscreen, after-sun and mosquito repellent.

If you are a photographer, it is always worth bringing sufficient digital storage media with you as well as a supply of extra batteries. A waterproof bag, to protect your gear in the rainforest, at waterfalls, when you are crossing rivers and on dive or whale-watching boats, is also a prudent addition.

Roseau's supermarkets and pharmacies (see page 103) have a good selection of toiletries and medicines, but if you are taking prescription drugs please ensure that you bring them with you.

You should not have too many difficulties with electrical appliances. The supply is 220V, 50Hz with UK-style three-pin plugs and sockets, but many hotels and self-catering accommodations have duel voltage systems, and so 110V with two-pin sockets is quite common these days. It is certainly worth checking in advance whether your choice of accommodation offers the supply you need. With regards to electrical appliances themselves, please remember that you are travelling to a tropical climate where heat, exposure to direct sunlight, Sahara dust, and high levels of humidity may have a detrimental effect on sensitive equipment if it is not adequately protected. Moisture absorbing sachets are quite inexpensive and can be placed in camera bags, backpacks and so on during your trip. They are worth the investment.

MONEY AND BUDGETING

CURRENCY Dominica's currency is the Eastern Caribbean dollar (commonly written EC$ though officially XCD) and it has been fixed to the US dollar at a rate of US$1 = EC$2.7 since 1979. Notes come in denominations of EC$100, EC$50, EC$20, EC$10 and EC$5. Coins come in denominations of EC$1, and then 50, 25, 10 and 5 cents. The Eastern Caribbean dollar is also the official currency of Anguilla, Antigua and Barbuda, Grenada, St Kitts and Nevis, St Lucia, Montserrat and St Vincent. It is issued by the Eastern Caribbean Central Bank which is based in St Kitts and Nevis.

US dollars are widely accepted across the island and you will usually be quoted prices in both EC and US dollars. You will also find that euros are accepted though not as commonly as the US dollar. Please be aware that the euro to EC dollar rate is not fixed.

Travellers' cheques can be exchanged at the main banks and in some of the larger hotels. ATMs can be found at the main banks in Roseau, at both airports, at some of the large supermarkets, and at the National Bank of Dominica in Portsmouth near the Indian River. Most stores and hotels accept all major **credit cards** though many do not accept American Express.

BANKS Banking hours are usually Monday–Thursday 08.00–14.00 and Friday 08.00–16.00, but some banks and branches have a slight variation on this.

First Caribbean International Bank
Roseau branch Old St, Roseau; ✆767 255 7900; ⊕ 08.00–14.00 Mon–Thu, 08.00–17.00 Fri

National Bank of Dominica
Head office Hillsborough St, Roseau; ✆767 255 2300; ⊕ 08.00–14.00 Mon–Thu, 08.00–16.00 Fri
Roseau branch Independence St, Roseau; ⊕ 08.00–14.00 Mon–Thu, 08.00–16.00 Fri
Canefield branch Imperial Rd, Canefield; ⊕ 09.00–16.00 Mon–Thu, 09.00–17.00 Fri

Portsmouth branch Bay St, Portsmouth; ⊕ 08.00–14.00 Mon–Thu, 08.00–16.00 Fri

Royal Bank of Canada
Bay Front, Dame Eugenia Charles Bd, Roseau; ✆767 448 2771; ⊕ 08.00–14.00 Mon–Thu, 08.00–16.00 Fri

Scotiabank International
Hillsborough St, Roseau; ✆767 448 5800; ⊕ 08.00–14.00 Mon–Thu, 08.00–16.00 Fri

MONEY TRANSFERS There are **Western Union** and **Moneygram** agents in Roseau, Portsmouth and several village locations around the island. You will also find one at the Roseau Ferry Terminal on the Bay Front.

BUDGETING Although you can find very reasonably priced hotel and self-catering accommodation, Dominica is not a cheap destination. In fact some restaurant prices are not too far off those you would expect to see in New York or London. Unfortunately, the standard is not always comparable. The same goes for the price of goods in supermarkets, with imported products especially high. This can really take you by surprise if you are not prepared for it. Nevertheless, with a bit of planning, you should be able to find a combination of accommodation, dining and daytime activities that suit both your taste and your wallet. Here are some basic tips on how you can do it. This is a very broad guide for two people.

Low budget You can find guesthouse and self-catering apartment accommodation for as little as US$50–75 per night (see listings, pages 252–3) and, if you arrive in the low season, you can probably find or negotiate good rates at some of the smaller hotels and lodges. You can also camp for up to US$20 per night. If you confine your dining to local eateries you can enjoy a traditional lunch (see page 54) for around US$5–7. *Rotis* (see pages 56–7) are good value at around US$4–5. Roadside barbeques are also fairly cheap options. Ask at your hotel for suggestions. Buy a weekly site pass for US$12 per person (see pages 67–8), which works out at less than US$4 per day in total for the two of you. Walk, hitch rides, or take public buses everywhere. The highest one-way bus fare is only around US$4 per person (see page 50). Another great way of travelling on Dominica on a low budget is via a work exchange (see page 85).

Medium budget The choice of mid-priced accommodation is wide and varied with rates falling somewhere between US$75 and US$175 per night. It is a nice idea to stay in at least two different places if you can. This cuts down travelling time to sites and gives you a little more variety and local colour. Car rental rates work out at about US$60 per day for a standard 4x4 jeep. It costs in the region of US$40 to fill up with fuel. Consider renting a car for half your stay and using public buses or hitchhiking to more accessible places on other days. Buy a weekly site pass and try to eat locally (*see above*). Give yourself an occasional dining treat at one of the fancier restaurants where a main course costs around US$20–30. Ask at your hotel for suggestions and recommendations.

High budget You can stay at a high-end hotel or villa for upwards of US$175 per night (it can get much, much higher) and either rent a car for the whole week or go on organised, guided excursions with a tour operator. Whatever your preference, a weekly site pass is still a good option (some tour operators will include this in the price). Treat yourself to some wellness therapies, a relaxing massage or yoga classes, for example, and dine out at a combination of local eateries, hotels and international restaurants.

GETTING AROUND

The best way to get around Dominica is by car, but you may well find the roads and local driving practices more than a little challenging. Some visitors find driving around Dominica quite a stressful experience, especially if they are used to wide, straight motorways. Having said that, a bus ride can also be a seat-of-your-pants affair that may leave you with a renewed lust for life, not to mention a case of motion sickness, by the time you get off. Organised tours and private taxis usually go at a more sedate pace, though they can be a more expensive option.

BUSES Roseau is the main hub for bus transport, but there is no central terminus. Local people have become accustomed to knowing where all the different bus stops are in the capital, but as a visitor you may find it very confusing. Buses to different parts of the island depart from bus stops located on different streets and at no fixed times. They tend to leave when the driver is happy he has enough passengers, or when he has finished eating his lunch, chatting with his friends, done his shopping and so on. During rush-hour times in the early mornings and late afternoons, and also when children leave school, buses are at their busiest and run more frequently. They are usually crammed full and their drivers apply a very heavy foot to the accelerator in order to return and collect more fares as soon as possible. From time to time you may also come across a somewhat bizarre situation where there is a bus in a village waiting to depart for Roseau, and there are people standing there also wishing to travel to the capital, but they would rather try to hitch free rides with passing vehicles than pay a bus fare. This can be frustrating as the driver will rarely leave with a near empty bus. Nevertheless, despite its peculiarities, hair-raising speeds, questionable overtaking practices, no timetable, no organised central terminus and no bus or route numbers, if you do ever manage to get to grips with it in your short stay on Dominica, the bus network can actually be quite a fun and very inexpensive way to get around. You will meet local people and you will get a glimpse of the real life that goes on beyond the tourist attractions. So give it a try.

Dominica's buses are small minivans and can be identified by the letters 'H', 'HA' or 'HB' on the licence plate. Many bus drivers also decorate the windscreen of their vehicles with a name or a slogan so that they become recognisable along the routes they drive. In addition to designated bus stops, simply flagging down a bus along the roadside is the most common method of reaching your destination. If travelling

BUS STOPS AND FARES

Here are the locations of bus stops in Roseau and Portsmouth, together with routes and a selection of fares.

ROSEAU BUS STOPS

Kennedy Avenue (*near the Arawak House of Culture*) Buses to Rosalie, Riviere Cyrique, La Plaine, Morne Jaune and Boetica.

King George V Street (*opposite Jolly's Pharmacy*) Buses to Newtown, Castle Comfort, Loubiere and Pointe Michel.

Old Street (*near the Old Market*) Buses to Soufriere and Scotts Head.

Old Street (*next to Whitchurch supermarket*) Buses to Eggleston and Giraudel.

Corner of Castle Street and Cross Street Buses to Stowe, Bagatelle, Fond St Jean and Petite Savanne.

River Bank, along from the New Market (*outbound traffic bridge*) Buses to Portsmouth and villages along the west coast highway, Castle Bruce, Kalinago Territory, Marigot, Wesley, Calibishie (via Portsmouth) and Vieille Case (via Portsmouth).

River Bank, between Independence Street and Great George Street (*inbound traffic bridge*) Buses to Goodwill, Canefield, St Aroment, Massacre, Mahaut and St Joseph.

Cross Street Buses to Morne Bruce and Kings Hill.

Hanover Street (*Old Market end*) Buses to Bellevue Chopin, Pichelin, Grand Bay and Tete Morne.

Hanover Street (*New Market end*) Buses that go all the way to Delices and Boetica.

King George V Street (*near Astaphans*) **and Valley Road** (*just over the junction with King George V St – look for 'Keep Clear' markings on the road*) Buses to Trafalgar, Wotten Waven, Shawford, Morne Prosper and Laudat.

PORTSMOUTH BUS STOPS

By the mini roundabout on the southern end of Bay Street Buses to Roseau and villages along the west coast.

Along the south side of Benjamin's Park (*right at the mini roundabout above*) Buses to Calibishie, Vieille Case, Wesley and Marigot.

Bay Street (*near the market*) Buses to Pennville, Toucari, Cottage, Clifton and Capuchin.

BUS FARES Just to give you an idea of how much things cost, here is a sample of typical one-way bus fares from Roseau.

Calibishie (via Portsmouth) EC$11	Portsmouth EC$9
Canefield EC$2.50	Rosalie EC$7
Castle Comfort EC$1.75	Scotts Head EC$4
Grand Bay EC$5	Soufriere EC$4
Kalinago Territory EC$11	Trafalgar EC$3.50
Laudat EC$4	Wotten Waven EC$3

Ask the driver to let you know when you get to your destination and pay either when you get on or off. Try to have some change or small notes. To stop the bus, call out 'Stopping!'. Public bus fares are regulated by parliament and you are not expected to tip. Some bus drivers may try to offer you private taxi tours.

to remote areas or across the island, expect to use a number of different buses to get from one place to another (changing bus in Portsmouth to go to the top end or Calibishie, for example); and be prepared to wait. Some bus drivers may simply not go beyond a certain point (it's always worth offering them a bit extra just in case) and walking the final stretch may be your only option. Note that most buses stop running in the evening and there are reduced numbers on Sundays.

TAXIS Dominica's taxi drivers are licensed by the government and should display official credentials. There are no standard rates for private taxi hire so it is down to the individual driver and a little negotiation on your part. Most taxi drivers offer island tours but they must have additional credentials as tour guides to show you around sites or take you hiking. Some taxi drivers have this dual licensing, and others work in partnership with tour guides. See the listings on pages 69–70 for operators offering island tours.

CAR HIRE New car rental companies seem to spring up every week – there are so many to choose from. The difference is usually price, quality of vehicle and selection, with the smaller companies being a little cheaper but with a limited choice of vehicle models. Privateers may not always keep their rental vehicles in the best shape, or have a large enough fleet to bring you a change of vehicle should yours break down. Check this first. The most common rental cars are small 4x4 vehicles. Prices vary but you should expect to pay about US$60 per day depending on the vehicle, with discounted rates usually offered for longer rental periods. Collision damage waiver is usually an additional cost; check in advance. Some rental companies offer free drop-off and pick-up at airports and hotels.

The government requires the purchase of a visitor's temporary driving licence. This costs US$12 for a one-month licence (this is the minimum) and is usually obtained from the car hire company itself. Visitor licences can also be purchased at either Canefield or Douglas Charles airports (ask customs officers), or in Roseau from the Inland Revenue building which is located on the street to the side of the House of Assembly. In order to rent a car and purchase a visitor licence, you must be able to present either your domestic or international driving licence, so make sure you bring it. If you are renting a car it is a good idea also to carry a mobile phone with you in case you break down, have an accident, lose your keys or lock them in the vehicle.

It is definitely worth contacting car hire companies for quotes and bookings prior to arrival, especially at busy periods such as Carnival and Creole. Also check to see if it is possible to collect the car and drop it off at the airport. Here is a selection of car hire companies.

🚗 **Bonus Car Rentals** ☏767 448 2650 or 767 445 8042 (Douglas Charles Airport); e cphillip@cwdom.dm

🚗 **Calabash Motors** ☏767 445 7816; e calabashmotors@gmail.com

🚗 **Courtesy Car Rental** ☏767 448 7763 or 767 445 7677 (Douglas Charles Airport); e courtesyrental@cwdom.dm

🚗 **Edge Car Rental** ☏767 445 8999 (Douglas Charles Airport); e kdtbazil@gmail.com

🚗 **Garraway Rent A Car** ☏767 448 2891; e garrawaye@cwdom.dm

🚗 **Gem Car Rental** ☏767 449 0654; e gemcar@hotmail.com

🚗 **Happy Car Rentals** ☏767 276 4659; (Douglas Charles Airport) e happycarrentals@gmail.com

🚗 **Island Car Rentals** ☏767 255 6844 or 767 445 8789 (Douglas Charles Airport); e reservations@islandcar.dm

🚗 **Lindo Park Car Rental** ☏767 448 2599; e lindopark@cwdom.dm

🚗 **Road Runner Rental** ☏767 440 2952; e roadrunnercarrental@gmail.com

🚗 **Valley Rent A Car** 📞767 448 3233;
📧 valley@cwdom.dm; www.valleyrentacar.com

Check the car over very carefully prior to signing any documentation. Look for scratches and bumps, test lights and brakes, and examine tyre tread. Make sure any bodywork defects are properly recorded on the rental agreement. If the vehicle has poor tyre tread, request a replacement. If the car handles poorly when you first take it out, return it and request a replacement straight away. Do not settle. Dominica has some unforgiving, tricky and remote roads.

It will cost between EC$100–120 to fill up your car. There are filling stations all around the island, but it is always prudent to ensure that you have a full tank before setting off. One thing you should note is that not many filling stations accept debit or credit card payment, so don't depend on it. Carry cash and ask about card payment before you fill up.

DRIVING ON DOMINICA Driving on Dominica can be quite stressful for visitors. It is, however, the most convenient way of getting around, especially if your stay is a short one and you want to see and do as much as possible.

Driving on Dominica is on the left, though it may not seem like it sometimes. Roads are slowly being improved after Tropical Storm Erika, but this is a long, ongoing process and you may come across roadworks and diversions during your stay. Many roads are narrow with many sharp, blind corners and very steep precipices or deep drainage gutters on one side or another, so you need to exercise caution and always keep your speed low. Whenever you approach a blind corner, hit your horn several times to let anyone coming the other way know you are there. Do not be shy about this. Beeping horns is like a language on Dominica and it may prevent a very nasty surprise. Look out for pot-holes. Dominica's heavy rains erode surfaces and wash away makeshift repairs very quickly. Though they are definitely improving, some roads are very bad and pot-holes can be deep and wide. Drive around them when the roads are clear but be really careful on bends.

Unfortunately, driving practices on Dominica also present a risk to you. Many people drive far too fast for the roads, they overtake on corners, they overtake even if there is oncoming traffic, they pull out without either looking or giving any warning, they may suddenly stop in the middle of the road for a conversation with a friend, or they may even decide to reverse. Driving safety and road etiquette is a problem and sadly it seems to be getting worse rather than better.

Inevitably there will be a vehicle right up against your rear bumper and the driver will probably hit his horn to indicate he wishes to pass. Let him pass every time, even if it means slowing down and pulling over. Do not race, or be stubborn; it is not worth getting angry about; it will happen often. Though you may find it hard to relax, do try to remember that you are on holiday and smile about it! Wherever you are, always watch for vehicles pulling out from the side of the road without any warning, and look out for very deep drainage ditches, especially on bends and when parking. When passing parked cars that you suspect may be about to pull out or are indicating, blow your horn to tell them you are coming. Try to encourage etiquette if someone stops for you or lets you pass by thanking them or giving them a couple of quick bursts of the horn. Keep your speed slow at all times and do try to enjoy the ride!

HITCHING Hitching or *riding* is very common on Dominica. It is often possible to wave down a pick-up truck and jump on the back for a free ride. Conversely, when driving, expect to see people asking for a ride along the main highways or on the outskirts of villages. Hitching a ride is quite an effective way to get around, though it may involve long waits, sometimes in heavy downpours. It is also a nice way to meet Dominicans and experience a side to the island that is not possible in other circumstances.

SCOOTER HIRE Whatever you do, be careful. A scooter is a handy way to get around Roseau and environs but it is not without its fair share of hazards. Look out for vehicles pulling out or stopping in front of you without warning and take care in the rain.

C & S Scooter Rentals Newtown, Roseau;
📞 767 277 7460, 767 315 3675

ACCOMMODATION

The pick of Dominica's accommodation reflects a congruity of design with the natural environment and cultural heritage in mind. Sometimes this design is simple and traditional, other times it is luxurious and modern. Whether money is no object or you are travelling on a tighter budget, whether you want to get back to basics or you prefer to keep the jungle at arm's length, there should be something for you here.

Accommodation is spread all around the island, and staying in more than one place is a good idea as it gives you the opportunity to explore different regions without having to travel too far each day. Take time to plan what you would like to do and then look for your preferred type and price of accommodation in those places. Some hotels have free airport shuttle buses which is useful for getting back to Douglas Charles Airport. You may also want to think about staying in the northeast, not too far from the airport, towards the end of your stay, so you do not have too far to go when it is time to leave.

CHARGES AND RATINGS Hotel accommodation charges are subject to a 10% government tax (VAT). Some hotels will also add an additional 10% service charge. Be sure to check prior to booking whether the rates quoted include or exclude these charges, especially the latter.

There is no official hotel grading or ratings system on place in Dominica though the Discover Dominica Authority together with the Dominica Hotel and Tourism Association attempt to implement their own idea of standard requirements. If you

ACCOMMODATION PRICE CODES

Codes are used to accompany accommodation listings in this guide. They are meant to give a basic indication of price based on a double room per night in the high season. Please check websites or call ahead of booking to confirm exact rates and whether government taxes and a service charge are included. Most hotels on Dominica quote their prices in US$ rather than EC$.

$$$$$	US$225+
$$$$	US$175–225
$$$	US$125–175
$$	US$75–125
$	<US$75

have any questions about accommodation standards, please get in touch with the Dominica Hotel and Tourism Association (📞 767 440 3430; e **dhta@cwdom.dm**).

Note The accommodation listed in this guide is deliberately selective and by no means comprehensive. You will find more options online, especially via services such as www.airbnb.com, where many hotels and villas may offer discounted rates. Price codes quoted are current at the time of writing and are based on double occupancy per room per night during the peak season, or roughly the equivalent for self-catering accommodation with weekly rates, unless stated otherwise. Please be aware that price codes are meant as guides only and are subject to change.

CAMPING Opportunities to camp are still quite limited on Dominica though more and more are beginning to appear. It is illegal to camp on beaches or in any other public places, but it is fine to camp on private land so long as you have the owner's permission. Camping on the Wai'tukubuli National Trail is a grey area but there is no way to through-hike unless you do and the authorities are aware of this fact.

EATING AND DRINKING

When the Amerindians arrived on Dominica it was a combination of seafood and cassava that formed the basis of their diet. As agricultural practices developed on the island, root crops such as yams, sweet potatoes and tannias were cultivated for food. Among other things, the European settlers introduced bananas, breadfruit, mangoes, plantain, cocoa, coffee and sugar. West African slaves working the coffee and sugar plantations tended to have a staple diet of root crops, or *provisions*, which they spiced up with seasonings such as peppers, bay leaves, parsley, celery and thyme, adopting the influences of the French. Following the abolition of slavery, these Caribbean Creole culinary practices continued to develop, particularly with the arrival of freed slaves from the French islands, and are the foundation for the local traditional dishes served in many of Dominica's snackettes and Creole restaurants today.

LUNCH Sometimes it seems that Dominicans would not be able to survive the day without having their lunch. Despite busy lifestyles and the influence of fast foods, almost everything comes to a standstill for what many Dominicans continue to regard as the main meal of the day. In local eateries a menu board may simply say 'fish lunch' or 'chicken lunch' and typically it will consist of a main ingredient, such as fish or chicken, with a fairly standard selection of rice, red beans and boiled *ground provisions*.

PROVISIONS

When eating out or shopping for food, you will come across *provisions*, also known as *ground provisions*. This term refers to any one or a collection of root crops such as varieties of yam, eddoe, dasheen, sweet potato or tannia. The term is occasionally stretched to include breadfruit, plantain, and green bananas (rather confusingly known as *figs*) though purists will contest this inclusion. *Provisions* are usually boiled and served with a main meat dish. They also appear prominently in traditional soups or one-pot *brafs* (broths). *Provisions* are very filling and are high in carbohydrates. Grown and eaten by slaves working plantations and estates, they remain a staple food across the Caribbean, especially for those whose work involves a lot of physical activity.

LOCAL DISHES There are many traditional dishes for you to try. Perhaps one of the oldest and most basic is the one-pot dish, or *braf*. One-pot cooking simply means placing all the ingredients you have, whatever they may be, in one large pot, cooking them up in water and seasoning to create a nutritious broth. This dish tends to be eaten in homes rather than in restaurants, though some local eateries do serve it, especially on Friday nights (fish *braf*) and Saturday mornings (pig's and cow's foot *braf*).

Most local dishes are rich in vegetables and seasonings. You may find meat and seafood dishes in some local eateries a little overcooked for your liking. This is a legacy of the past, and a lack of proper refrigeration. The Dominican palate has become accustomed to eating meat dishes in this way. Larger restaurants are more likely to cook meat and seafood in a more international manner, though you should always check when ordering. **Hot pepper sauce**, made from scotch bonnet peppers, is used to spice up dishes. Be very careful with it: just a few drops can completely transform a dish, and maybe not in the way you want!

Calalou **soup** is a very traditional dish made from young *dasheen* leaves (a *ground provision*), and occasionally spinach. It is a thick green soup that is often served with crab and dumplings. It is delicious and usually a speciality on restaurant menus during the Creole season (see page 59). Other popular soup dishes are pumpkin soup, **goat water**, which is a goat meat stew, and *chatou* **water**, a soup made with octopus. *Sancoche* is a traditional dish made from coconut milk, *provisions* and usually codfish. *Ackra* is a kind of seasoned and fried fritter, often made from codfish, breadfruit, tannia and, from September to November, in the days after the moon's last quarter, *titiwi*, which is a juvenile goby caught in fine nets at the mouths of rivers. In September each year the west coast village of Layou usually hosts the Titiwi Fest where, along with music, river and beach activities, you can sample a wide variety of *titiwi* dishes. **Crab backs** are a delicious savoury dish and are also available during the Creole season. The land crab's flesh is mixed with a secret combination of spices and seasonings and then stuffed back into the shell, sprinkled with breadcrumbs and baked in a hot oven. **Curried goat** is a popular spicy meat dish (and yes, it is goat), usually served with rice, and, when in season, **stewed agouti** is another local delicacy. A common staple is a heavily seasoned rice dish called *pelau*, usually a lunch dish served as chicken *pelau*.

RESTAURANT PRICE CODES

The following codes are used in this guide to indicate the average price for a main course in a restaurant or local eatery. Typically, the most expensive thing you can eat in a restaurant is usually lobster which may run to EC$80 or so. One of the cheapest dishes is probably *roti* which costs around EC$10. Excluded are prices for roadside snacks such as barbecue chicken, plantain and so on, which cost less than EC$10.

$$$ EC$50+
$$ EC$20–50
$ <EC$20

Please remember that some menu prices, especially in hotel restaurants, may exclude local tax (VAT = 15%) and service charge (usually 10%). This can make quite a difference to your bill, so please check.

Seamoss is the name given to a red algal genus called *Gracilaria* which is cultivated in many parts of the world for its *agar*, a gelatinous polymer that is used as a preservative jelly, a culture medium, a laxative, a clarifying agent in brewing, a thickening agent in baking and cooking, and in the Caribbean as the basis for a thickened milk drink or dessert. On Dominica, Seamoss comes in several flavours including ginseng, peanut, linseed and *bois bandé* (see page 58). The drink is said to be vitamin-rich and a useful tonic for a variety of medical conditions.

Vegetarians should have few problems finding good food on Dominica. With a preponderance of fresh fruit and vegetables, the choice is varied. *Tannia ackra*, rice and peas, fried plantain, breadfruit puffs, *provisions*, vegetable *sancoche* and macaroni cheese are all staple foods and very common dishes.

If you happen to hear the distinctive sound of a **conch shell** being blown then it means a fisherman is selling his catch. The fish caught locally and used in Dominican cooking will typically include tuna, marlin, flying fish, jacks, snapper and dorado (*mahi mahi*), also known locally as *dowad* or *dolphin*.

Popular roadside snacks include **bakes**, a fried flour-and-water dough that is usually stuffed with seasoned saltfish, tuna or cheese. You will also see people selling fried or barbecue chicken, corn and plantain. A filling snack is **roti**, a flatbread most

FRUITS AND VEGETABLES

Some of the less familiar fresh fruits and vegetables you may come across on Dominica are:

Ackee Related to the lychee, toxic when immature or overripe, commonly grown and eaten in Jamaica, usually fried with salt fish.

Barbadine Large fruit grown on a vine, eaten as a fruit or cooked and served as a vegetable when unripe. Sometimes combined with lemon and sugar as a juice.

Breadfruit Large round fruit with white flesh that is sometimes fried in butter or served in a salad.

Canep Small round fruit with thin green skin and soft, tart flesh. Often sold in bunches by the roadside.

Carambola Also called star fruit, eaten as a fruit or blended as a juice.

Christophene A pear-like green-skinned squash, usually eaten boiled or fried as a vegetable.

Custard apple Heart-shaped fruit with sweet, custard-like flesh. Usually eaten as a dessert.

Dasheen A small, starchy tuber, usually eaten like a potato.

Green banana Confusingly referred to as *figs*, actually unripe bananas, usually boiled and eaten as a *provision*.

Guava Original Arawakan name for this scented fruit which is eaten raw, turned into jam or blended as a juice.

Mangosteen A reddish purple fruit when ripe with sweet and creamy white flesh.

Noni Fruit with a pungent odour when ripe (hence the name *vomit fruit* in some countries). Considered medicinal, it is either eaten as a fruit or blended as a drink.

commonly stuffed with either curried vegetables or chicken. It is a very inexpensive dish that is very filling and great if you are on a tight budget.

You may also come across the term *ital*. This is a term commonly used by Rastafarians to mean wholesome, natural food. It is always vegetarian.

LOCAL DRINKS

Non-alcoholic Freshly made juices are always available, the selection being determined by season and what is ripening. Lime squash and freshly made ginger beer are particularly refreshing drinks on hot days. Passionfruit, pineapple, orange and grapefruit juices are also commonly served. Less familiar drinks may include cherry juice, barbadine punch, soursop and carambola. All of them are worth trying if available. *Sorrel*, known in some parts of the Caribbean as hibiscus tea, is a delicious drink, usually available around the festive season. It is made from the sepals of the sorrel flower (*Hibiscus sabdariffa*) and is fruity and fragrant. It is also served as a warm, spiced tea or as a wine, and tastes rather like a European Christmas mulled wine. **Coconut water** extracted from unripe *jelly* coconuts is an acquired taste, though it is very refreshing, especially direct from a coconut. Always drink coconut water and/or fresh fruit juice in moderation. Too much may have the effect of a laxative.

When thirsty, drink water. Tap water is usually clean and safe to drink, though after heavy rains it may become dirty for a short period and so should be avoided. Usually the water supply is temporarily suspended if it has been contaminated with

Okra Long, crisp green pods, often used as a flavouring for stews and soups. Also eaten parboiled and fried.

Passionfruit Round yellow fruit with soft, sweet pulp. Usually blended for juice.

Pawpaw Also called papaya, with an elongated shape, yellow when ripe and eaten as a fruit. Green, unripe pawpaw is often used in salads or pickles.

Plantain A type of banana that is either fried or boiled and eaten as a *provision*. Also seen as fried plantain chips, a popular snack.

Pommerac Large fruit with bright red skin, often used to make jam.

Sapodilla Round fruit with reddish brown skin. Fleshy pulp is often used to make custard or ice cream.

Sorrel Member of the hibiscus family, a plant with edible flowers, fruits and leaves. Usually brewed as a tea or blended for juice. Also used as a natural medication and traditionally consumed at Christmas.

Soursop Large green ovoid fruit with soft spines. Tart white flesh is sweetened to make a delicious juice or ice cream. A sweet version is also found (called sweetsop) and can be eaten as a fruit.

Sugar apple Similar to a custard apple but with sweet white flesh. Usually eaten as a dessert.

Sweet potato Not a yam, and not a potato. Actually belonging to the bindweed family, this elongated vegetable has a sweet flavour. It is often boiled, roasted or mashed.

Tamarind Segmented pod with a reddish-brown shell. The inner pulp is mixed with sugar to make tamarind balls, a popular confectionery.

Tannia A small, starchy tuber, usually eaten like a potato.

Taro Also called eddoe, a small potato-like tuber. Usually eaten like a potato.

Yam Large tuber that is boiled, fried or roasted as a staple *provision*.

dirt. Following reconnection, always run the tap until the water runs clear again. If in doubt, boil it first. Local bottled water is also available from most food stores, restaurants, bars and petrol stations.

Arabica coffee is cultivated in the heights of Dominica's interior, and ground and sold as **Café Dominique** by local firm Parry W Bellot & Co Ltd, or as **Café Locale** by growers in Giraudel. Some villagers will also cultivate their own. You can buy Dominican coffee in supermarkets and also in souvenir shops. There are also several blends of **cocoa tea** available which are made from locally grown cocoa and mixed with a variety of spices to make a delicious hot beverage. You should also try local **bush tea**. These teas are made from an assortment of plants and are believed to have medicinal properties for many conditions from colds, headaches and fevers to stomach aches and even insomnia. They can be drunk as hot teas or cooling teas and whether they work or not, they are certainly very refreshing. Ma Pampo, who is claimed by many Dominicans to have been the world's oldest person, put her longevity down to 'dumplings and bush tea'. She died in 2003 and is said to have been 128 years old. Ask for bush tea at local snackettes, bars and eateries or take a farm or garden tour with an expert such as Moses James at Zion Valley (page 72) or Roy Ormond at Harmony Gardens (page 135).

Alcoholic drinks Dominica has two main rum distilleries. The Belfast Estate produces blends called Soca rum, Red Cap rum and Bois Bandé rum, and the Shillingford Estate produces dark and light Macoucheri rum which is distilled from sugarcane grown on its own grounds. Dominicans will decant rums from these distilleries into bottles as a basis for their own individual blends of **rum punch** and **bush rum**, the latter being white cask rum with an infusion of herbs, spices or tree bark. Some simply make their own from molasses in backyard sheds. One of the island's most famous blends of bush rum is *bois bandé* which is said to have a tumescent effect upon male drinkers. Locals will often refer to it as a 'natural Viagra'. Stripping pieces of the bois bandé tree's much sought-after bark is common practice, though illegal in the national parks where it is mostly found. Other popular bush rum blends are *spice*, which has cinnamon added, *pueve* with pepper, *nannie* with rosemary, and *l'absent* with aniseed. Bush rums are usually sold in local rum shops and bars, though you may also find them in regular bars and restaurants. Try Rudy's Islet View Restaurant near Castle Bruce for just about the widest selection of bush rums on the island (see page 152).

Rum punch is usually a little smoother than bush rum blends. Popular varieties are those made from lime and from passionfruit. Take care when drinking rum punches as their mild flavour masks what is often a very high alcohol content.

Dominica's national beer is **Kubuli** which is brewed using natural spring water by the Dominica Brewery at Snug Corner near the southern village of Loubiere. In 2002 this lager beer won a gold prize at the Brussels Monde Selection Awards.

PUBLIC HOLIDAYS AND EVENTS

JANUARY Public holidays for New Year's Day and New Year's Holiday (Merchants' Day) are on 1 and 2 January. Calypso 'tents' or heats take place at various venues during January in the build up to the Calypso Monarch Final that is held at Carnival time in February/March.

FEBRUARY/MARCH Dominica's Carnival, or *Mas Domnik*, takes place on the Monday and Tuesday before Ash Wednesday. These two days are also public holidays.

The Carnival season runs throughout the month and includes: the Carnival Queen Show, the Calypso Monarch competition, Pan By The Bay (steel pan drumming on Roseau's Bay Front), costume parades, T-shirt band parades, street jams and 'jump-ups', and traditional *la peau cabwit* drumming. Tewé Vaval is the symbolic burial, or sacrificial burning, of the spirit of Carnival that takes place on Ash Wednesday. Formerly a fairly sombre ceremony at which people dressed in funeral attire carried a coffin with an effigy of Carnival to a funeral pyre, this traditional event, like several others on Dominica, seems to have transitioned into a fete or 'jump up' and an excuse to extend the partying by an extra day. Visitors can experience Tewé Vaval at Bataca in the Kalinago Territory and in the west coast village of Dublanc. For more information about the heritage of Carnival, see pages 25–6.

APRIL Good Friday and Easter Monday are public holidays.

MAY Labour Day on 1 May is a public holiday. The **Dominica Festival of Arts (DOMFESTA)** takes place throughout the month of May. DOMFESTA is designed to promote and celebrate the arts on Dominica. Look out for a schedule of events and entertainment. May is the month for Dominica's **Hike Fest** at which a series of hikes are organised by the Dominica Hotel and Tourism Association. The Giraudel and Eggleston village **flower show** also usually takes place in May.

JUNE Whit Monday is a public holiday.

JULY Dominica's annual **Dive Fest** takes place over one week in July. This event is organised by the Dominica Watersports Association and includes introductory pool and ocean scuba diving experiences, children's events, Kalinago canoe racing, evening cruises and parties. The aim of Dive Fest is to promote diving and watersports on Dominica, particularly to local people. It is also yet another excuse to party.

AUGUST Dominica celebrates Emancipation Day in August, which is also a public holiday. It is often accompanied by the annual Emancipation Hike. The annual **Nature Island Literary Festival & Book Fair** is usually held over one weekend in August (but there has been talk of moving it). Writers, poets and performance artists from Dominica and the wider Caribbean converge to celebrate the literary word and encourage everyone to discover the artistic side in themselves. The village of Cochrane usually hosts its annual **Rabbit Festival** during the month of August; a rather odd festival that combines rabbit racing and stew.

SEPTEMBER Look out for Kalinago cultural celebrations taking place during September and don't miss the annual **Titiwi Fest** at Layou village. Enjoy a wide variety of fish dishes, music, river and beach activities at this very popular family day out.

OCTOBER October is the month for Creole and Independence celebrations. Look out for published events such as traditional dancing, music and singing. It is also a great time to eat; be sure to try a crab back at the very least (see page 55).

Creole Week takes place during the last week of October and includes **Creole in the Park** (held at Roseau's Botanic Gardens), **Creole Bod La Mer** (on Roseau's Bay Front), and the three-night **World Creole Music Festival** which is held at the Windsor Park Sports Stadium. Often there will be a number of other Creole events taking place, such as **Creole in the North** and **Creole in the East**. This is a great time to visit Dominica. The island is full of colour, music, dance and good food.

NOVEMBER 3 November is **Independence Day**, and the following day is **National Day of Community Service**, both of which are public holidays.

DECEMBER Christmas Day and Boxing Day, 25 and 26 December, are public holidays.

SHOPPING

Shopping for food, drink and toiletry items is rarely a problem on Dominica, though you will usually have to visit a number of different places to get everything you need. In Roseau the larger supermarkets, Astaphans, Whitchurch and Save A Lot, are usually well stocked, as are the very handy Miniya's 7–11 outlets, and throughout the island there are numerous small general stores and minimarts that hold basic essential items. The major shops also carry a good stock of baby foods, nappies, and cleaning and sanitary products. If you are visiting from the US, you will recognise many brands. There are also plenty of pharmacies selling medicines, toiletries and prescription drugs. Generally speaking you will find prices on a par with those back home and in the case of some imported goods, a little more expensive. Do not expect to find shopping cheap on Dominica – it isn't.

Markets and roadside vendors sell fresh locally grown fruit and vegetables. The best time to go to the Roseau New Market is late on Friday evening or early Saturday morning. Expect the market to have wound down by Saturday afternoon. Most villages will have some form of Saturday market, though they are much smaller affairs. There is also a good Saturday morning market in Portsmouth. If you pass through interior farming villages such as Bells, for example, look out for people selling fresh produce along the roadside. If you see people selling jelly coconuts, do stop and treat yourself to a refreshing drink.

You can buy fresh fish from the fish markets at Roseau, Marigot and Portsmouth, from fishing villages such as Fond St Jean, Saint Sauveur, and Scotts Head, to name just a few, and also from wherever you hear the distinctive sound of a conch shell being blown.

Most shops open from around 08.30 and close between 16.00 and 17.30. Some stay open longer. The majority close from around 14.00 on Saturdays and are closed all day on Sundays.

Imported goods, particularly luxury items, are quite expensive, though there are a few duty free shops in Roseau where you can buy jewellery, watches, clothing, leather goods, souvenirs and so on. Bring your passport and onward ticket. In addition to the somewhat unimaginative, mass-produced souvenirs, there are some excellent original crafts sold in small stores, galleries and on some stalls. Try to buy local if you can (see page 102).

ARTS AND ENTERTAINMENT

CONTEMPORARY MUSIC Dominica's premier international music event is the **World Creole Music Festival** that takes place during the last week of October each year. This three-night event falls within Creole Week, which is part of Dominica's Independence celebrations. **Creole in the Park** is a four-day live music and Creole cultural event that is held in the Botanic Gardens, Roseau. It is a family event that runs from lunchtime to early evening. There are stalls selling traditional Creole food and crafts, activities for children, and a mix of music. National and regional musicians arrive on the island to perform during the Creole festival period. Although the week is a celebration of Creole culture and tradition, the music festival does not appear to limit itself to a particular genre.

Concerts are staged throughout the year, some in aid of good causes. Many live music concerts take place on village *savannahs*, which are local playing fields, while others may be completely impromptu street jams. Look in the local press, listen to the radio (see page 62), check social media, and ask your hotel for information about anything that may be happening during your stay. There is sure to be something going on.

Popular today is the *bouyon* style of music, though reggae, soca, cadence and jazz are also performed. Musicians that have achieved success internationally include Nelly Stharre (tragically deceased), Michele Henderson, Nasio Fontaine, and Ophelia Marie. Dominica's two main *bouyon* bands, WCK and Triple Kay, have achieved regional success, particularly among young people.

PERFORMING ARTS The **Dominica Festival of Arts (DOMFESTA)** takes place each May. The festival is designed to promote and celebrate the arts on Dominica and is a good time to catch a play, a choral performance or some traditional dancing. Your hotel should be able to help you find out about scheduled events. You could also check social media.

Theatre performances occasionally take place at the Arawak House of Culture in Roseau, and the Old Mill Cultural Centre in Canefield. Sadly there is no regular schedule of events and performances are very ad hoc and often poorly publicised. The **Alliance Française** (\ 767 448 4557) hosts music, dance and films fairly regularly and it is always worth passing by or calling to see what may be on during your stay. It is located outside the eastern boundary of the Botanic Gardens, just next to the Bath Estate bridge on the Roseau Valley road (see map, page 88).

Choral performances and traditional dancing take place from time to time at the Arawak House of Culture and the Old Mill Cultural Centre. Ask at your hotel, listen to the radio, call in at the Old Mill Cultural Centre, or look out for billboards advertising forthcoming events.

The **Nature Island Literary Festival & Book Fair** is usually held every August (there has been talk of moving it) in the grounds of the University of West Indies campus, next to the Alliance Française, with related events also taking place in other parts of the island. The event attracts writers, poets and performance artists from around the region and is also meant to support and promote home-grown talents. There are readings, workshops, open mic sessions, book stalls, and more. Previous guests have included Kwame Dawes, Colin Channer, Earl Lovelace and Derek Walcott. Both Dominica and the wider Caribbean have a number of talented performers and there is a growing subculture of young poets who are worth seeing and hearing if you get the chance. For more information: ☐ NatureIslandLiteraryFestival.

Many of the villages of Dominica have their own cultural groups. Some specialise in traditional *bélé* and quadrille dancing (see page 25), others have very talented steel pan, drum or jing ping players (see page 25). These groups are invited to perform at cultural events throughout the year, but you are most likely to see them during the month of October when it is Creole and Independence time. Dominica's Kalinago also have a couple of excellent cultural groups. One of Dominica's most celebrated choral companies is the **Sisserou Singers**. If they are performing, go and see them.

MEDIA Dominica has two independent national newspapers, *The Chronicle* and *The Sun*, each published once a week in English. Both have political bias. There are two cable television companies, **Marpin 2K4** and **Digicel Play**, each broadcasting a range of US television stations as well as local news and government information programmes. The main radio stations broadcasting on Dominica are **DBS Radio** (88.1FM), **Q95FM** (95FM), **Vibes Radio** (99.5FM) and **Kairi FM** (107.9FM, 93.1FM and 88.7FM). For news and local affairs you could also check www. dominicanewsonline.com.

POSTAL SERVICE The main branch of Dominica's post office (⊕ *08.00–16.00 Mon–Fri*) is located on Bay Front/Dame Eugenia Charles Boulevard opposite the Roseau ferry terminal. Postal delivery times between Dominica and the US and Europe fluctuate. Allow *at least* two weeks, or even months; it's that bad.

If you actually do receive packages from abroad you must collect them from the parcels office on the ground floor of the main post office and open them in the presence of a customs official, who will determine the level of duty that you must pay. Proof of identification is required when collecting packages. The parcels office closes for lunch between 13.00–14.00.

TELEPHONE
International calls
The international dialling code for Dominica is +1 767 followed by a number consisting of seven digits. International dialling codes from Dominica are as follows:

Belgium ✆011 +32 + number	**Netherlands** ✆011 +31 + number
Canada ✆1 + area code + number	**Norway** ✆011 +47 + number
Caribbean ✆1 + area code + number	**Spain** ✆011 +34 + number
China ✆011 +86 + number	**Sweden** ✆011 +46 + number
Cuba ✆011 +53 + number	**UK** ✆011 +44 + number
France ✆011 +33 + number	**US** ✆1 + area code + number
Germany ✆011 +49 + number	**Venezuela** ✆011 +58 + number
Guyana ✆011 +592 + number	

Mobile phones Mobile-phone operators with outlets on Dominica include FLOW and Digicel. If you do not have your own mobile phone or other handheld device with roaming services, it is possible to purchase a prepaid phone from one of these suppliers for as little as EC$60. All you need is identification. Some hotels lease prepaid mobile phones to their guests. If you are planning on hiking on Dominica, doing some exploring, or renting a car, you should think about having some kind of device with you, just in case. Save your hotel and car rental company as a contact and call them if you find yourself in difficulties.

INTERNET Dominica has good high-speed internet services and most hotels and restaurants offer Wi-Fi connections to their guests and patrons. You will also find free Wi-Fi in the Botanic Gardens in Roseau and at Douglas Charles Airport.

COURIERS Private international courier services offer a quick, reliable alternative to the postal system.

DHL Agents: HHV Whitchurch Travel Agency Ltd, located on the corner of Hanover St & Kennedy Av, Roseau; ☎767 448 5887; e dhldominica@ whitchurch.com

Fedex Agents: Express Courier, located on the corner of Cork St & Old St, Roseau; ☎767 448 0992; e expresscourier@cwdom.dm

BUSINESS

Business hours vary, although most will start at 08.00–08.30. In the morning expect traffic to be heavy entering the capital from 07.45 onwards. Many workers will take their lunch at home or in the Botanic Gardens, which usually means a traffic exodus from Roseau at 13.00 with work starting again at 14.00. Most businesses will end their working day between 16.00 and 17.30 so it is also busy at that time. A five-day week is standard though more and more businesses also open on Saturday mornings.

Working practices in some organisations, particularly those associated with government departments, can appear somewhat dated by modern standards. Completing one task may require several trips back and forth between different people with different roles and in different buildings. If you are lucky, the people you must deal with will all be available and located in the same place, but don't count on it. If you are in a hurry or if you tend to be an impatient person, you may well become frustrated by what are often very time-consuming processes, especially in the unforgiving heat of downtown Roseau. On the flip side, some things are surprisingly quick. If you have all the right documentation with you, it is entirely possible to open a bank account, get a cheque book and an ATM card all on the same day.

Service standards are not especially good on Dominica, in fact they are often far from it. Of course there are always exceptions and you may well find that your holiday is replete with pleasant, happy, smiling faces and attentive people. But the chances of this happening, unfortunately, are quite slim. People who serve you may not smile, they may not say anything, they may not look at you, and they may well deal with you while having a conversation with someone else. If you are used to standing in line and waiting your turn, you may also be in for a few surprises. People may simply push in front of you, shout over your head, or even demand service from the person who is actually in the process of serving you – as if you were not there at all. If you are used to a very fast, high standard service culture, you will find all of this quite a challenge.

How to deal with it? Meet it head-on with a flourish of smiles, a hearty 'good morning' or 'good afternoon', a broad grin, a 'please' and a 'thank you' at absolutely every opportunity, and a warm and meaningful 'have a nice day' when you leave. It is the only way to get through it. Frustration, anger and shouting may be a release, but they get you absolutely nowhere and in the end it just spoils your day. Being a little overboard with courtesy will make you smile inside (really, it will) and you never know, some of it just may rub off if everyone makes a point of doing it.

CULTURAL ETIQUETTE

DRESS When walking around Roseau, or any other town or village for that matter, please wear a top. You should also dress appropriately when entering churches and people's homes; bikinis, swimming costumes or no shirt will certainly offend and embarrass, though it is unlikely that anyone will actually challenge you about it.

Sunbathing topless is not a good idea and you will almost certainly draw unwanted attention or cause offence.

DRUGS AND ALCOHOL Please confine your consumption to bars and do not walk around the streets drinking alcohol – unless it is Carnival, of course! Although you may well encounter someone smoking marijuana, and may even be offered some, please remember that it is currently illegal.

DEALING WITH BEGGARS At some point in time you are likely to be asked by a beggar for money, especially in Roseau. Though some may hassle you a little, most are generally polite and do not present a threat.

TAKING PHOTOGRAPHS OF PEOPLE In recent times Dominicans have become very sensitive about photography. The reasons are not clear but it may well have something to do with hordes of cruise ship visitors pointing cameras everywhere when they come ashore. Some visitors can be very rude, sticking cameras and tablets in people's faces (especially when it comes to particularly photogenic subjects such as the elderly, the young, Rastas, Kalinago and so on). It therefore seems fairly understandable that Dominicans have become a little fed up with it.

Please do not assume it is all right to take photographs of people. If you do wish to take a photograph of someone, try the following:

- Ask for permission first.
- Offer to share by email the photograph you wish to take, and then actually email that photograph to the person as soon as possible (if you do not email it, eventually people will simply consider this type of offer a ruse).
- Offer a 'contribution'. Some people will accept a few dollars in return for allowing you to take their photograph.
- If your request is declined, please respect that decision and, however tempting, do not try to take the photograph candidly.

If you are genuinely taking photographs of scenery that just happens to have people in it, there is not much you can do; take the photograph. If anyone ever challenges you (some people can be a little too sensitive, or are perhaps even seeking conflict or an argument), simply tell them you are photographing Dominica's beautiful scenery (it is always a good idea to emphasise how beautiful you think Dominica is), and perhaps offer to show them the photographs you have taken. Try to avoid confrontation.

THE LAST WORD No matter how ridiculous or irritating the situation, do not get into arguments and always resist conflict. One thing is certain: it will spoil your mood, your day, perhaps even your entire holiday. Some Dominicans seem to love an argument or a debate. Sometimes everything seems so serious that you are certain things must end badly, but then someone makes a joke or laughs and you realise it was either not serious in the first place or the situation has been deliberately defused before it got out of hand. People will often see how hard they can push each other.

With this in mind, swallow your pride and back down with a laugh, a smile or a joke; the louder and more exaggerated the better. Keep laughing and smiling, massage your opponent's ego (do not belittle them) and let him or her enjoy the satisfaction of having the last word. If you succeed in defusing the situation, that makes you the real winner, right?

TRAVELLING POSITIVELY

Throughout this guide you will be encouraged to look out for and support local businesses, farmers, artists and so on. Dominica also has many practical problems that a number of NGOs and local groups of volunteers try to resolve or improve upon. Dominicans living abroad are continually a great source of assistance to these organisations by sending materials and helping with fundraising. Visitors to Dominica can also make a big difference. Think about contacting one of these organisations before or during your visit and asking how you might be able to help.

Abilities Unlimited Federation Drive, Roseau; ☎767 448 2203. Craft workshop for the blind & disabled.

Alpha Centre Goodwill, Roseau; ☎767 448 6509. A voluntary school for people with mental deficiencies, sensory, physical & communication disorders. The centre provides education, parental skills training & support for children.

Dominica Infirmary Home for the Aged Independence St, Roseau; ☎767 448 2636. Provides institutional care for the destitute, aged & infirm. Also provides a day care centre for the elderly.

House of Hope Delices; ☎767 446 2208. A home providing 24hr care for severely disabled & neglected children & young persons.

Operation Youth Quake Roseau; ☎767 448 4174. Provides a rehabilitation service for deprived, abused, delinquent, disadvantaged & neglected children.

REACH Roseau; www.reachdominica.org. Dedicated to relieving the plight of the elderly in Dominica, especially those abandoned by their families. REACH also supports many of the other charitable organisations on Dominica & is a good portal for your donations.

Dominica Charity Foundation wwwndominicacharity.org. Set up by Mary Sylvester, a Dominican musician who now lives in Germany. Its aim is to help those who have suffered from natural disasters such as Tropical Storm Erika.

3

Activities and Special Interests

There are many ways to enjoy Dominica, with a wide variety of activities suitable for all budgets, interests, ages and abilities. A healthy interest in the great outdoors, natural history and cultural heritage, plus a positive attitude towards a bit of exercise, adventure and excitement, will all stand you in good stead and help you to get the most out of your stay on this very beautiful and naturally dramatic Caribbean island.

If you are arriving here by cruise ship and are on the island for just a day, then I would urge you either to book a shore excursion or to hire a tour guide when you step ashore. To appreciate this island properly you must be prepared to venture beyond the crowded streets of its diminutive capital.

TOUR OPERATORS AND PRIVATE GUIDES

Dominica has a good selection of tour operators and professional guides. Licensed tour guides are trained and certified by the Discover Dominica Authority and should be able to present an official photo identification card upon request. Unfortunately, the training is generally focused on cruise ship tourism and bus tours, with little instruction offered in other activities. The best hiking guides are those who have learned the trails first-hand, specialise in trails around where they live, and have genuine enthusiasm for the environment. Scuba guides ('divemasters') are usually PADI, SSI or NAUI certified. All certified guides have been trained in emergency first aid.

You are very likely to be approached by people offering you tours during your stay on Dominica, particularly in Roseau when cruise ships are in, or at popular hiking trailheads. The best advice is to do as much forward planning as you can so you are not forced to make spur-of-the-moment decisions that you may feel uncomfortable with or even regret later on. Depending on what you are doing, first of all decide whether you require a guide or not, and then try to engage one in advance. You will find a selection of guide and operator listings with activities and hikes in this book. Hoteliers will also be able to help in this regard as they will usually have established working relationships with reliable guides. Be sure to agree the cost of the activity before you begin – including the currency. Do not engage a guide who seems to avoid giving you a price or who asks you to say how much you think you should pay. The more established tour operators usually publish their tours and prices, which makes it much easier for you. Prices for the same activity can vary greatly, so shop around.

SITE FEES AND PASSES

The **Ecotourist Site User Fee Programme** was established in 1997 to generate revenues from non-residents for the maintenance and upkeep of some of the island's most popular natural attractions. Frankly, I feel the programme is in need of an update.

At the time of writing, the user fee programme covers only 12 designated ecotourism sites: Emerald Pool, Boiling Lake, Freshwater Lake, Boeri Lake, Middleham Falls, Cabrits National Park, Syndicate Nature Trail, Indian River, Trafalgar Falls, Morne Trois Pitons, Morne Diablotin, and Soufriere Sulphur Springs. Rather bizarrely, the Botanic Gardens is also a designated ecotourism site but the fee is not collected. Why the programme doesn't cover more than this (perhaps Morne Anglais, Sari Sari Falls, Victoria Falls, Jacko Steps, Dernier Falls, Chemin L'Etang and many others) is anyone's guess.

Permits can be purchased directly at the Emerald Pool, the Cabrits National Park, the Indian River, Trafalgar Falls, the Syndicate Nature Trail (don't count on this reception centre being open outside the cruise ship season, so consider buying a pass elsewhere) and Soufriere Sulphur Springs. Permits can also be purchased from independent vendors – look for signs – and from tour operators and some hotels.

At present, two types of permit are available. A **site pass** costs US$5 and is valid for one site for one day only. A **week pass** costs US$12 and is valid for all sites for one week.

Just to confuse you even further, there is a separate fee programme for the **Wai'tukubuli National Trail** (pages 223–51). It costs US$12 per day on the trail or US$40 for 15 days of WNT hiking. You can buy tickets from some of the same vendors as the Ecotourist site passes or from the WNT interpretation facility on the Imperial Road near Pont Cassé (where segments 4 and 5 join).

This very confusing system means that it costs US$12 to hike the very short and easy WNT Segment 10, yet only US$5 to hike the far longer and more arduous Boiling Lake Trail. It doesn't make a lot of sense and a more straightforward 'hike anywhere' pass would surely be a better option. But don't hold your breath.

Scuba divers and snorkellers wishing to enjoy the sights of the Soufriere Scotts Head Marine Reserve (page 13) must pay a **marine reserve fee** of US$2 per person. This fee is usually collected by dive and snorkelling operators as part of their charge. If you choose to go snorkelling independently at Champagne Reef (see pages 140–1) then Champagne Reef Dive & Snorkel (page 80), located at the entrance, will usually collect this fee from you.

BIRDWATCHING

Most organised birdwatching tours will incorporate the Syndicate Nature Trail in the Morne Diablotin National Park (pages 216–17) or part of WNT segment 10 (pages 245–6). This region is the primary habitat of the endangered **sisserou** parrot (see page 7). The gently undulating Syndicate Nature Trail passes through a lush rainforest habitat and the reception centre (if open) has washroom and refreshment facilities. The lookout points across the Dublanc River valley offer good opportunities to see parrots in flight. The best time to go birdwatching here is early in the morning or late in the afternoon. Also in this region is the short trail to the Syndicate (Milton) Falls (pages 219–20). The trail is also a good place to see and hear parrots.

The hiking trails throughout the Morne Trois Pitons National Park also provide lots of opportunities to get close to Dominica's birdlife. From the viewpoint at the summit of Morne Nicholls *en route* to the Boiling Lake, it is often possible to see jaco parrots in flight against a background of dense forest canopy. The Middleham Falls trail is also a good place to hear them, though they are much harder to see. The Layou River and the Indian River are especially good for observing water birds, including the ringed kingfisher (*Ceryle torquata*), the green heron (*Butorides striatus*) and the snowy egret (*Egretta thula*). Near the mouth of the Layou River there are often brown pelicans (*Pelicanus occidentalis*), cattle egrets (*Bubulcus ibis*) and royal terns (*Sterna sandvicensis*).

Further information on the birds of Dominica may be obtained from the Forestry, Parks and Wildlife Division just off Valley Road near the Botanic Gardens (see map, page 88). They also sell a book.

Bertrand Jno Baptiste \767 446 6358; m 767 245 4768; e drbirdy2@cwdom.dm. Nicknamed 'Birdy', Bertrand Jno Baptiste is without doubt Dominica's best known birdwatching expert & guide. He offers tours for birders of all levels of interest & will also help you to find the specific birds you are interested in observing & photographing. Birdy is not only very knowledgeable, he is also great company & highly recommended.

BOAT TOURS AND WATER TAXIS

Some of the main dive and whale-watching operators also offer boat trips along the west coast, including sunset or party tours, plus charter trips to the French islands, so they are worth contacting. You can also charter local river boat operators in the Portsmouth area, notably from Purple Turtle Beach and the Indian River visitor centre (see page 196) while some fishermen in the Calibishie area offer a water taxi service across to the French island of Marie-Galante.

Island Style Fishing Fortune, Roseau; \767 265 0518 or 767 613 9935; e islandstylefishing@gmail.com; www.islandstylefishing.com. Experienced Captain Jerry Daway offers chartered boat tours along Dominica's west coast.
Wai'tukubuli Eco Tours (WET) \767 275 7001, 767 275 3150; e info@wetdominica.com; www.wetdominica.com. Aimed primarily at cruise tourists, WET offers exciting coastal rides in custom rigid inflatable boats. Excursions include coastal tours, snorkelling & whale watching, & also day trips to the French islands of Marie-Galante & the Saints. Bring swimwear, sunscreen & towels.

BUS AND JEEP TOURS

If the thought of self-driving Dominica's roads fills you with dread, then bus and jeep tours are very good alternatives. In addition to the operators listed below, you should check with your hotel to see if they run their own tours or whether they recommend anyone. During the peak season (November to May) many of the bus operators may be occupied with cruise ship tours. Check with them before coming to Dominica and then confirm any booking you have made shortly before you arrive.

Here is a small selection of Dominica's many island tour operators.

Alwin's Taxi Service \767 446 4699; m 767 225 2112; e alwinhilltaxi@hotmail.com; www.alwinhilltaxi.com. Offering airport runs & sightseeing tours all around the island.
Dominica Untouchable Tours \767 316 7702 or 767 245 3089; e untouchabletours@yahoo.com. Based in Calibishie, Wendy Marcellin offers island-wide full- & half-day tours incorporating waterfalls & cultural sights.
Eddison Tours & Yacht Services \767 225 3626; e info@eddisontours.dm; www. eddisontours.dm. Portsmouth-based tour operator offering a selection of island-wide sightseeing trips & Indian River boat tours.
Fredo's Taxi & Tours \767 448 5874 or 767 615 5200; e fredos40@hotmail.com; www.fredostours.com. Offering scenic tours to & around the island's main attractions.
Jenner Robinson \767 276 4659; e jenna23dm@yahoo.com. In-demand tour guide with island-wide experience. Jenna offers a range of tours including bus tours & hiking.

Jon Vee Tours 767 315 7772 or 767 235 2375; e jonvee_11@live.com. Offering custom tours throughout the island for individuals, families & groups.

Just Go Dominica 767 245 4328 or 767 277 8360; e justgodominica@gmail.com; www.justgodominica.com. Experienced tour & hiking guide Nahjie & taxi driver Addi combine to offer a very wide selection of island tours.

First Nation 767 614 0418; e firstnation365@gmail.com. Ali Auguiste is a very experienced Kalinago guide specialising in the sights & cultural heritage of the Kalinago Territory as well as island-wide tours & trail hiking.

Green Lizard Eco Tours 767 295 0031; e jeffreyasiedu1@gmail.com. Certified guide fluent in English & German offering a range of island-wide guided tours.

KHATTS (Ken's Hinterland Adventure Tours) 767 448 1660; e info@khatts.com; www.khattstours.com. Established & experienced tour company offering a wide range of island-wide

travel experiences including bus tours to all the island's major attractions.

Petra Tours (Feel Dominica) 767 285 5550; www.petra-tours-dominica.com; f. Experienced German-speaking tour guide offers island-wide tours, short hikes, bird- & turtle-watching excursions to both cruise ship & stayover visitors.

Tana's World 767 265 3760 or 767 315 7979; email: tanaquilpfund@gmail.com; www.enjoy-dominica.com; f. French- & English-speaking Tana offers off-the-beaten-path hiking & 4x4 island-wide tours. She specialises in the east coast but has island-wide knowledge & experience. She also has a lodge (see Vanil Vaness Lodge, page 150).

The Island Fun Tours 767 315 0896; e theislandfuntours@gmail.com; www.theislandfuntours.com. A collective of bus & tour operators offering a range of tours & activities island-wide.

CANYONING

If you are adventurous and want to see and experience something very different on Dominica then you should certainly take a canyoning trip. No experience is necessary as training, along with equipment, is provided before you set off. Most canyoning takes place within the river canyon below Ti Tou Gorge, though there are a number of other exciting and challenging routes for the more experienced. The trip involves rappelling down waterfalls, jumping into pools, and hiking the river – usually for up to 4 hours – until you reach your exit point. The waterfalls, pools and rock formations in the canyons are quite breathtaking and Cathedral Canyon, one of the last you come to, is one of the most naturally beautiful places on the island. Highly recommended.

Extreme Dominica Canyoning & Adventure Tours 767 295 7272; e extremedominica@gmail.com; www.extremedominica.com; f. Extreme Dominica offers a wide range of canyoning trips depending on your experience; from Ti Tou Gorge to the Breakfast River & Trafalgar Falls. All equipment, training & transportation to & from the canyon is included & advanced training courses are available. GoPro helmet cameras are available to rent; bring your own memory card or purchase one.

Ti Nath Kanion 767 616 7118; e email@dominica-canyoning.com; www.canyonspeleo.com & www.canyoning-dominica.com; f; ⏱ Oct–May. With over 20 years' professional canyoning & caving experience in France & Dominica, Nathalie Dalboussières offers great value-for-money French- & English-speaking canyoning trips for both complete beginners & those with experience. Canyoning venues include Ti Tou Gorge (in the canyons above & below), River Blanc, Boetica River & Ravine Dejeuner. Shorty wetsuit, helmet, harnesses & waterproof bag all supplied – just bring swimwear, trainers or wetshoes, & a spirit of adventure.

EDUCATION AND RESEARCH

Whether you are interested in academic study or natural science and archaeology research, Dominica has some good options.

Archbold Tropical Research & Education Centre Springfield; ☎767 449 3026; e nosler@ clemson.edu; www.clemson.edu/public/rec/ archbold. The Archbold Research Centre & Springfield Guest House are an extension of Clemson University, USA. Located in 80ha grounds and with welcoming scientists, research & environmental groups, the facility comprises fully equipped laboratory, classroom, reference library, Wi-Fi & sgl, dbl & dorm-style accommodation in a historic plantation house. A full meal service is available.
Ross University School of Medicine Picard; www.rossu.edu. Located on a large campus in Picard, south of Portsmouth, Ross accepts student 3 times a year on their journey to become physicians. Students complete a rigorous basic science curriculum in which they develop clinical skills before advancing their education via clinical rotations in the US, Canada & UK. The campus is completely wireless & has state-of-the-art teaching & learning as well as recreational facilities. Dedicated student accommodation in Picard is plentiful as are shopping & dining options.
University of the West Indies Open Campus Roseau; ☎767 448 3182; e dominica@ open.uwi.edu; www.uwi.edu/dominica. The Dominica Open Campus of the University of the West Indies is located in Roseau behind the Botanic Gardens (see map, page 88) & offers a range of undergraduate & postgraduate study options. The campus features a library, computer centre, classrooms, teleconferencing room & auditorium.

If you are a scientist bringing students on a field trip or cultural visit, some other places you could consider using as research/field stations include:

Anchorage Whale Watch & Dive Centre (page 80); Aywasi Kalinago Retreat (page 150); D-Smart Farm (page 205); Rodney's Wellness Retreat (page 131); and Roots Jungle Retreat (page 205).

FISHING

While the seas have provided the people of Dominica with food and nutrition since the earliest settlers arrived, the recreational aspect of fishing is so far rather underdeveloped. Doubtless as Dominica's tourism industry grows, more sport fishing operators will emerge to offer visitors a chance to catch some of the marlin, bonito, skipjack, dorado (*mahi-mahi*), tarpon and mackerel that can be found in the island's offshore waters.

Shore fishing is definitely possible and, if lucky, you may be able to catch snapper, jacks or kingfish. You do not need a permit for this. River fishing is restricted to residents, and only at certain times of the year. It is always worth checking with your hotel to see if they know any local fishermen who could take you out with them on an inshore trip, perhaps followed by a barbecue on the shore – if you catch anything, that is.

Island Style Fishing Fortune, Roseau; ☎767 265 0518 or 767 613 9935; e islandstylefishing@gmail. com; www.islandstylefishing.com. Experienced Captain Jerry Daway offers half- & full-day deep- sea sport fishing charters aboard his fully equipped boat, *Bonita Rose*. You can also contact Jerry for personal whale-watching trips & scenic boat tours.

GARDENS, FARMS AND FOOD

If you are interested in horticulture and organic farming then you have a number of options. Perhaps one of the best is simply to visit ordinary gardens where people grow flowers, herbs, fruit and produce for their own consumption and for sharing with their family and neighbours. Of course this is not always practical or possible for visitors, but if you do come across an opportunity, take it. The care and attention people pay to their small pieces of land is extraordinary and the variety of plants and vegetables they grow, equally so. An alternative is to contact community tourism groups such as those in Giraudel, Eggleston and Bellevue Chopin. These community groups have been established in an effort to extend the tourism sector to rural and coastal villages and they could really do with your support. This is positive tourism in action, and a great way to meet ordinary Dominicans, as well as have fun and maybe learn something new. The third option is to visit some of the island's wonderful historic public and private gardens.

Taking Dominica's deliciously fresh produce to its natural conclusion is a Creole cooking lesson. If you are a dab hand in the kitchen and would like to be able to show off some Creole culinary skills back home, then this is definitely for you.

Bellevue Chopin Organic Farmers Group Bellevue Chopin; 767 316 2710 or 767 315 1175; e bellevue@communitytourism. dm, bcofmi@hotmail.com; www. bellevueorganicfarmers.communitytourism.dm. This community tourism group offers tours of a diverse & interesting selection of working organic farms against a gorgeous backdrop of mountains & forests (see also the box, page 135).
Botanic Gardens Roseau. Dominica's historical public gardens are located on the outskirts of Roseau & are home to a number of domestic & exotic species; see also pages 104–5.
Giraudel Eggleston Flower Growers Group Giraudel & Eggleston; e giraudeleggleston@communitytourism.dm; . The communities of Giraudel & Eggleston are nestled on the slopes of Morne Anglais, overlooking Roseau & the Caribbean Sea & are famous for flower growing. This community of growers organises tours of local gardens, flower arranging & even Creole culinary lessons. (For more on the Giraudel & Eggleston area see box, page 133.)

Cooking Caribbean (Rum & Nature) Giraudel; 767 440 5827; e jtasxperience@gmail.com; www.experiencescaribbean.com. An integral part of the Giraudel Community Group, Daria & Michael welcome you to their home where you are invited to learn about local foods, try a bit of cooking for yourself, & enjoy the lovely gardens & views.
Papillote Tropical Gardens Trafalgar; 767 448 2287; e papillote@cwdom.dm; www.papillote. dm. Perhaps Dominica's most celebrated private garden, Papillote has been the destination for horticulturalists for many years. Take a self-guided or an accompanied walk through the 2ha of beautiful tropical gardens where you can also enjoy natural hot volcanic springs & waterfalls. (Also see page 114.)
Zion Valley Fond Toufai, Delices; 767 612 7587; e lngmari@roug.se; . Moses James & his family will be happy to take you around his very natural gardens, teach you about herbal medicines & invite you to dine in his unique 'Rastarant' (page 153) where healthy ital food, fresh fruit juices & bush teas are served. The focus is to teach visitors about the medicinal use of plants & the Rasta way of life.

HIKING

The origin of Dominica's vast network of trails was one of necessity: escaping enslavement, hunting for food, travelling between communities, going to see a doctor, visiting family, getting to school, and so on. Before there were roads, everyone had to travel from one place to another on foot, on horseback, or by boat. Despite an increasing number of cars and motorcycles on the roads these days, Dominicans who live in rural communities still tend to walk a great deal; along tracks to isolated farms in the bush, to hunt agouti, wild pig, crabs and crayfish, and to travel between villages when buses or other forms of transport are scarce or unavailable. Perhaps because walking has traditionally been a necessity rather than a choice, it seems few Dominicans tend to walk for pleasure nowadays, however, and sadly hiking is an activity that seems to have become the domain of visitors rather than local people. There are exceptions, of course, and a number of local hiking clubs do run regular outings, but it is generally true that few Dominicans explore and know their island as well as you may do by the time you leave.

Dominica has hiking trails that suit all interests and levels of ability. Most are cleared forest, river or mountain paths with wooden steps, *fougère* (tree fern) logs, or simply tree roots for those places where the trail ascends, descends or passes over sodden ground. Given the climate, the number of trails and the lack of budget and resources, it is all but impossible for trails to be maintained and cleared as often as they ought, but if they are fairly commonly hiked by guides and visitors they are usually in good enough condition to follow, despite a lack of useful signage. Trails that come to an end at waterfalls often require a rather slippery scramble over boulders and cascades to reach the foot of the falls and the bathing pools. Safe routes over these boulders are not always obvious and change during periods of very heavy rainfall when the rivers flood; local guides who know the terrain, or who are used to picking the best route, are worth their weight in gold in such circumstances.

'Unofficial', more obscure trails are less developed and are only maintained by the people who use them. Very few of these trails have any kind of signage at all, save perhaps for a ribbon or a piece of cloth tied to a tree, and you really need to walk with a good, experienced guide. Where there is a clear path this is not really a problem but when paths fork, cross rivers or pass through open clearings and scrubland, it is very easy to become disorientated or lost. In subsequent chapters this book will describe most trails in detail, others where a guide is essential, less so. I don't want to get you lost. And please don't forget that things change. A *gommier* tree that marks a trailhead or a turning today might well be a Kalinago canoe tomorrow.

DIFFICULTY RATINGS For each of the hikes described in this guide I have assigned a difficulty rating. This rating is based on a model devised by me and does not relate to any grading standards used by the Ministry of Tourism, the Discover Dominica Authority, or any other source relating to Dominica. Instead it is based on personal experience of these hikes, made many times over several years, and it takes account of feedback from hikers who used the previous editions of this guide. It is simply intended to be a basic indication of difficulty that may assist you with your selection and planning. Naturally, what may be tough for one person may be less so for another. There will always be variation, it can't be helped, and no system will ever be perfect, so please bear this in mind when you get back to your hotel and search for my email. The ratings are relative, so once you have completed one hike, you will hopefully have a better understanding of the numbers when selecting a hike for your next outing. Hopefully.

(TRED) Hike Ratings

Terrain	Unchallenging	Easy	Moderate	Challenging	Severe	Hazard!
Score	0	1	2	3	4	H

River X	No crossings	Easy	Moderate	Challenging	Severe	Hazard!
Score	0	1	2	3	4	H

Elevation	Flat	Easy	Moderate	Challenging	Severe	Hazard!
Score	0	1	2	3	4	H

Duration	< 1 hour	1–2 hours	2–4 hours	4–6 hours	> 6 hours
Score	0	1	2	3	4

Here are some tips about the kind of hiking gear that is good for Dominica.

FOOTWEAR Footwear has to be rugged, able to stand up to tough terrain, get muddy and wet, keep you upright, and then be able to do it all over again the next day, without fail, and without falling apart. Because of the diversity of terrain, Dominica is very tough on footwear and this should be an important part of your preparation. Try to avoid heavy boots, and especially with hard plastic soles. Heavy footwear will weigh you down and hard plastic soles are treacherous on wet rocks and wooden steps. Remember, unless you are walking the National Trail, we're talking day hikes – you don't need trekking boots. Something light and with a little give is better, and look for shoes with Vibram soles which I find excellent on wet and slippery boulders. Closed toes are also important. Hiking sandals are fine but avoid anything with an open toe design. You need to protect your feet. I like to wear low-cut Merrell all-terrain hiking shoes. A pair of trainers can work fine, but be prepared to dispose of them at the end of your trip. They may be a little soggy and have a rather unpleasant smell!

CLOTHING Clothing should be lightweight. T-shirts are just fine, though don't wear your best ones, and purpose-made hiking shirts with UV and mosquito protection are great, though more expensive, options. Lightweight shorts that you can swim in and that dry out quickly are good. If you plan on climbing some of Dominica's peaks then you should also bring long hiking trousers to protect you from areas of razor grass. Long-sleeve shirts are also good for this and have the added benefit of affording you more protection from mosquitoes, chiggers and so on (see pages 40–1). A hat to protect you from both rain and the hot sun is advisable, as is a pair of sunglasses. And bring a rain jacket – you will need it.

ACCESSORIES A waterproof rucksack (or rucksack bag) is a good idea, but failing that bring along a waterproof bag that you can carry inside a regular rucksack

Each hike is rated against four categories: terrain (T), river crossings (R), elevation (E) (the severity of the ups and the downs) and duration (D) (the time it takes to complete the hike). A score is given for each category with 0 being the lowest and 4 being the highest. The total is added up and then divided by the maximum possible score (16) and multiplied by 10 to give a final rating out of a maximum score of 10. The hazard (H) symbol is added to the score and final rating if the hike involves a particularly difficult section such as rock or tree root climbing. Clear as mud? Here is an example:

Morne Anglais: Terrain: 3H; River X: 0; Elevation: 4; Duration: 3. TRED rating: (10/16) x 10 = 6.3H. The hazard symbol is added because of the tree root climbing towards the summit. The duration relates to the whole hike – up and then back down again. By breaking the rating up into these four factors, I hope it makes things a little more meaningful than a simple 'easy', 'moderate' or 'difficult' description.

The most difficult hike possible would incur a rating of 10H. Fortunately, none of the hikes in this guide is that tough! *Appendix 2* on pages 254–5 lists all the hikes included in this guide together with details of their TRED ratings.

to protect valuables and sensitive items such as cameras, phones and other handheld devices. Your rucksack should be comfortable to wear, have padded straps and some degree of protection for your back. Keep the size small but functional. Outer webbing to carry water bottles and clips for walking poles are very useful.

A water bottle or a wearable hydration system is a must-have. Some modern day packs and rucksacks have hydration systems built in, and some water bottles have filters that enable you to use tap water (which is usually safe to drink on Dominica) rather than buy bottled spring water each time you go out. If you are trying to minimise your environmental impact, and keep your costs down, then a reusable solution such as this is ideal.

Walking poles do help. Telescopic poles also allow you to stash them when they are not needed. They are a great aid to your legs on long forest trails, they provide support and stabilisation on steep descents, and they are also really useful on river crossings, especially if you are not quite sure how deep the water is! I take my walking pole everywhere.

You should take a small medical kit with you that includes antiseptic solution or swabs, gauze, bandage, tape and painkillers. Bring mosquito repellent that contains DEET (or a natural alternative) and also sunscreen. A combination knife may also come in handy.

GPS and compass are not really needed on Dominica though if you have one it is always fun to see where you have been and how high you reached afterwards over a cold beer. Most of the 'official' trails are simply day hikes and are fairly easy to follow; the Wai'tukubuli National Trail is sign-posted and has painted trail blazes. The forest canopy is fairly dense in some places meaning it is difficult to get a continuous GPS signal unless you have a more expensive device. This isn't long-distance trekking, so it's not an essential piece of kit.

SETTING OUT The degree of preparedness required for your hiking trip will naturally depend on the difficulty and duration of the trail itself. It is essential to make sure your departure time is early enough to make it back before nightfall. Always plan to return to the trailhead by 17.00 at the latest, and inform someone of your plans and when you expect to return.

Take plenty of water with you; at least one or two litres each. It is very easy to dehydrate in the humidity of the rainforest and the heat of the tropical sun. Rivers and streams may provide handy refills if supplies run low, but only when you are sure there are no farmlands or houses upstream. If you are not sure, ask your guide. Water purification tablets and filters are a good option if through-hiking the Wai'tukubuli National Trail. Wear sensible footwear such as walking shoes, trainers or strong sandals (see *Hiking Gear* box, above). Flip-flops are really not a very good idea, and neither is walking barefoot – unless you are used to it.

Walking in Dominica's rainforest can often mean getting wet and dirty. A towel and a change of clothes either to take along or to leave in your car at the trailhead is a very sensible idea. If you take a change of clothes with you on the hike, be sure to put them in a waterproof or plastic bag. It is also a nice idea to have drinks and food waiting in a cooler on your return. As trails can become muddy and slippery

3

and some of them require climbing through tree roots, you should take along a small first aid kit for any cuts, knocks or scratches you may pick up as souvenirs along the way.

Generally speaking, it is not a good idea to go to waterfalls or cross rivers if there has been heavy rain, or if heavy rain is expected. Flash flooding is not theoretical, it happens, and people have been killed by it on Dominica. Notable places to avoid hiking during periods of high rainfall are the Sari Sari Falls, the Victoria Falls, the Jacko Steps, and any other hike that involves significant river crossings or river hiking. Use common sense and a reasonable degree of caution when deciding where to go in inclement weather. If local people advise against a hike due to heavy rainfall or swollen rivers, listen to them and do not go.

HIKING GUIDES Good hiking guides know which way to go when routes become unclear, they are usually trained in first aid, and they can provide interesting information about the history of the trail, and the flora and fauna that may be seen along the way. Hiring guides also provides a source of income to local people and, by extension, their families and communities. There is absolutely no substitute for local knowledge and, by increasing the demand for trained guides, you are creating development opportunities for Dominicans. The reassurance a good guide can provide when a trail is new to you is also invaluable.

Most hotels and guesthouses will be happy to arrange hiking tours for their guests using local tour operators or independent guides. It is always worth asking. Some may even employ their own certified guides. If you hire a guide, make sure you do a little homework and try to find one who has been recommended. You'll often come across 'guides' hanging out by trailheads; they are often more interested in getting paid than giving you a good time.

Here are some guides I know personally or who have good reputations. This list is by no means comprehensive and it is definitely worth asking at your hotel for a recommendation. You could also contact a local travel agent such as Decide On Dominica (page 35) or Dominica Tours (page 35) who only deal with experienced guides.

First Nation Taxi & Tours ☏767 614 0418; e firstnation365@gmail.com. Ali Auguiste is an experienced tour & hiking guide & has his own minibus. A Kalinago, he is an expert on the Territory but also many hiking trails around the island including Morne Diablotin, the Boiling Lake & many others.

Peter Green (Bushman Tours) e gbushmantours@hotmail.com. Peter is a very popular guide for the Boiling Lake Trail, which is his speciality, as well as for others in the Morne Trois Pitons National Park.

Devon Greenaway ☏767 317 7238; e dg_tours@hotmail.com; ⓕ. Popular hiking guide Devon also offers island tours. He does the Boiling Lake, Morne Diablotin, Wavine Cyrique, La Chaudiere, Sari Sari & many others.

Hiking Dominica ☏767 312 5459; e hikingdominica@gmail.com. Mike Rabess

is an extreme hiker & has walked most of Dominica's major trails. He is also an expert on the Wai'tukubuli National Trail & offers a whole range of trekking services including guiding, transportation & provisioning.

Eric Hypolite ☏767 276 4252; www.naturelink. dm. A conservation biologist, Eric knows many of Dominica's hiking routes & is an expert on the Wai'tukubuli National Trail which he helped to build. At the time of writing he is also a member of the WNT maintenance team.

Octave Joseph ☏767 245 3556; e seedatriva@ yahoo.com. Octave is a very experienced guide specialising in trails in the Morne Trois Pitons National Park & the south. He has a wealth of plant knowledge & is a good choice for the Boiling Lake, Perdu Temps & Victoria Falls.

Jungle Trekking Adventures & Safaris (JTAS) ☏767 440 5827 or 767 616 5827;

e jtasexperience@gmail.com; www. experiencescaribbean.com. Michael Eugene has expert knowledge of the Wai'tukubuli National Trail & offers guiding, transportation & provisioning services. He also knows many other trails including the Boiling Lake.

JustGo Dominica ☍767 245 4328 or 767 277 8360; e justgodominica@gmail.com; www. justgodominica.com. Nahjie is an experienced hiking guide & professional canyoneer. He has been professionally trained in rescue skills, CPR & first aid. He specialises in the Boiling Lake Trail but also knows many other hiking trails. Together with driver Addi, JustGo also offers numerous island-wide tours.

KHATTS (Ken's Hinterland Adventure Tours) ☍767 448 1660; ☍866 880 0508 (toll-free); e info@khatts.com; www.khattstours. com. Ken Dill & his team are very well respected & experienced tour guides offering both transportation to & guided hiking on the majority of Dominica's hiking trails. They have a tour desk at Fort Young Hotel (page 97).

Mirage Inc ☍767 440 8222 or 767 612 2400; e relax@rodneyswellness.com; www. rodneyswellness.com; ⓕ. Bevin Lewis of Rodney's Wellness Retreat is an experienced & knowledgeable guide, specialising in the trails of the south & the Morne Trois Pitons National Park.

Nature100percent ☍767 275 8424; e nature100percent@me.com; ⓕ. English-, French- & German-speaking guide Christine has over 25 years' experience exploring Dominica's trails. With a good knowledge of local culture & plant life, she offers transportation & guided hiking to both popular sites and as more remote, off-the-beaten-path places. Ask about her guest

bungalow (sleeps up to 6 with awesome views of Douglas Bay & the Cabrits).

Jenna Robinson ☍767 276 4659; e jenna23dm@yahoo.com. Jenna is an experienced guide offering a range of services including guided hiking & island bus tours. He has island-wide knowledge, but specialises in the north & northeast.

Sea Cat Tours www.seacattours.com. Sea Cat offers a range of tour & yachting services. He is a regular on the Boiling Lake Trail & with his own transportation is a very good choice for groups wishing to explore the Roseau Valley & Morne Trois Pitons National Park.

Elvis Stedman ☍767 225 1971. Elvis is a very experienced hiking guide & plant enthusiast with knowledge of many of Dominica's hiking trails, especially in the Morne Trois Pitons National Park which is his backyard. You will often see him on the Boiling Lake Trail & he's a good choice for student groups.

Tana's World ☍767 265 3760 or 767 315 7979; e tanaquilpfund@gmail.com; www.enjoy-dominica.com. French- & English-speaking guide Tana offers a range of hiking & jeep tours. She likes to get off the beaten path & has great knowledge of the southeast.

Ti Nath Kanion ☍767 616 7118; e ccdom@ canyonspeleo.com; www.canyonspeleo.com & www.canyoning-dominica.com. When she isn't on the end of a rope, expert canyoneer Nathalie Dalboussières can often be found on the Boiling Lake Trail.

David Victorin ☍767 449 3449 or 767 225 0006. David is an experienced hiking guide with transport & island-wide knowledge, specialising in the Boiling Lake, Middleham Falls, Wavine Cyrique, Heart of Dominica trails & many others.

HORSERIDING

Horseriding tours usually begin with a short training session for beginners, and include all equipment. They are fully guided and last around one hour. There is normally a maximum weight for each rider and tours may be cancelled in very wet weather.

Brandy Manor Riding Center Brandy, Bornes; ☍767 235 4871 or 767 612 0978; email: brandymanor@ymail.com; www.brandymanor. wix.com/ridingcenter; ⓕ. Whether you are a novice or a seasoned rider, ride through semi-

deciduous woodland & rainforest around Brandy Estate & Wai'tukubuli National Trail segment 11 or around Sugarloaf Mountain, where you can enjoy superb views of Prince Rupert Bay & the Morne Diablotin National Park. It costs around US$20 per

30mins per horse for either trail riding or lessons & you can go out for around 3hrs at a time. Either ask for a picnic or BBQ ride or alternatively enjoy refreshments at Brandy Manor when you return. **Rainforest Riding** Portsmouth; 767 445 3619 or 767 265 7386; e rainforestriding@yahoo.com; www.rainforestriding.com; . Canadian & long-time Dominica resident Valerie Francis offers accompanied horseriding around the Cabrits National Park trails, on part of WNT segment 14, & also along Purple Turtle Beach. She will also teach you how to ride & has a training ring at her farm near Douglas Bay. Accompanied tours are usually US$45–100 & lessons are US$40/hr. Rides are suitable for complete beginners as well as people with more experience.

RIVER TUBING

River tubing has become a very popular activity, particularly as a shore excursion for people visiting Dominica by cruise ship. Sit yourself in a large inflatable tube, shoot gentle rapids, and drift sedately along a river through Dominica's beautiful forest. Suitable for all ages, life jackets are provided and trained guides are on hand to tell you about the area and to assist in case of difficulties. Operators have vehicles to take you to the entry point and collect you at the exit.

Adventure Safari (Antours) 767 245 0886 or 767 316 2258; e antours@yahoo.com; www.dominicarivertubing.com. Book a river tube trip or turn it into a full day of tubing, waterfalls, beach or hot volcanic spa. Primarily aimed at cruise ship passengers during the high season, travellers are welcome to join existing organised group tours. **Hibiscus Valley Tours** Concord, Marigot; 767 445 8195; e info@hibiscusvalley.com; www.hibiscusvalley.com. Hibiscus Valley offers tubing on the Pagua River as well as a selection of tubing & adventure packages.

SCUBA DIVING

Dominica has gained an international reputation for excellent scuba diving and it is a popular destination for marine biologists, oceanographers and underwater photographers. Conditions are usually quite easy, with little or no current and rarely any surface chop, visibility is normally excellent, and there are lots of small marine creatures, fish, hard and soft corals, as well as spectacular underwater topography to see.

These conditions also make it a great place to take a certification course or to do an accompanied try-dive. Most dive centres have in-house professional instructors offering a range of recreational and speciality dive courses. All scuba diving on Dominica must be undertaken via one of the island's dive centres and is usually from a boat. You cannot independently rent tanks and drive yourself to a dive spot.

Certified divers must remember to bring their certification card. Few operators will ask to see log books given the relatively easy conditions of diving here. If it has been a while since your last dive trip, do the sensible thing and take a short refresher and local orientation dive with an instructor before jumping off a boat. Some operators may insist on this. It will make your diving both safer and, with renewed confidence, much more enjoyable.

Typically a two-tank boat dive will cost around US$80–90 plus 10% VAT and marine reserve fees, if applicable, which are US$2 per diver.

DIVE SITES
Southern dive sites On the south coast of Dominica there are several dive sites that require either intermediate or advanced diving skills or experience. This is because conditions in the Atlantic can sometimes be a little rough and strong

currents occasionally pick up during the dive. Interesting sites along this coast include **Suburbs**, a wall dive that drops to a shelf at around 40m before dropping again into the abyss; **Village**, another very dramatic wall dive; and **Condo**, which is a huge volcanic boulder at a depth of 18m. These sites tend to attract larger fish and the occasional migratory pelagic. Visibility is usually excellent here. **Des Fous**, **Mountain Top** and **Lost Horizons** are advanced sites that are only visited by special request due to both location and degree of difficulty.

At the tip of Scotts Head there are some excellent dive sites. **Swiss Cheese** and **Scotts Head Pinnacle** are particular favourites with a spectacular swim-through archway at 14m where you will come across lots of blackbar soldierfish. These two sites are part of the same formation and can be combined to make a great first or second dive. They should definitely be on your list. At the heart of the Soufriere Scotts Head Marine Reserve is a vast underwater volcanic crater. On the western edge of this crater is a wonderful wall dive called **Cachacrou**, the Kalinago name for the isthmus off Scotts Head village, and just beyond this site is a beautiful wall dive called **Scotts Head Point**. This site starts fairly shallow above a large patch of sand and reef before dropping spectacularly into the crater. Myriads of fish, in particular Creole wrasse, can fill your entire field of vision. On the northern edge of Scotts Head, within the shelter of Soufriere Bay, is the very popular **Scotts Head Drop-Off**. This site stretches to the east and west of the mooring and so can be experienced in two different ways. It is a nice sheltered site that combines the spectacular topography of Dominica's reefs with a wide variety of corals, sponges, fish and many other sea creatures. The three sea mounts of **Soufriere Pinnacles** on the north of the crater, within sight of the beautiful Soufriere Church, is a nice pinnacle dive and you will often encounter juvenile hawksbill turtles here.

La Sorciere, or Witches Point, lies directly below a tall cliff to the north of Soufriere and is a great wall dive. Turtle sightings are almost guaranteed, both along the wall as well as on the shallow reef above. A short distance to the north of La Sorciere is **L'Abym**, or the abyss, a dramatic wall dive located very close to the steep cliffs of the shoreline and dropping into the depths of the volcano. An interesting dive is along the cliff face between La Sorciere and L'Abym; ask your divemaster about it. Another one for your list of must-do dives is **Danglebens Pinnacles**, a series of beautiful sea mounts on the northern edge of the Soufriere crater. There are two moorings for this site, both hooked to the tops of tall pinnacles at a depth of around 10m. The site drops to around 40m and is alive with a variety of corals and fish. Hawksbill turtle sightings are also common here. **Danglebens North** is a broad expanse of reef that runs from the shore until it ends in a steep wall. It is a very nice site with plenty to see in both the shallow areas close to the shore and along the deeper formation to the west.

Coral Gardens is a large flat reef system at a depth of around 15m that connects both Danglebens sites. Nurse sharks are commonly seen resting on the sand beneath coral shelves around the western edge of this reef formation. **Pointe Guignard** is a small site that runs around a rocky headland. It has some caves and a fun swim-through on the way back to the mooring. To the north of Pointe Guignard is **Champagne Reef**, a large flat formation that extends from the shore until it reaches a drop-off. Because of its popularity, this dive site has three moorings. Champagne has become best known for the submerged fumaroles located very close to the shoreline, that blow a constant stream of bubbles from the sea floor. To the southwest of the bubbles lie some encrusted cannons and chains, and to the east of the reef system are two small shipwrecks. The *Debbie Flo* is a wooden boat that was sunk in 1994 and the *Dowess* is the scattered remains of a steel vessel. Both wrecks

3

lie at a depth of around 30m, have no fixed mooring and are rarely visited by dive operators. An interesting dive, however, is to drop down to the wrecks, explore them for a while, and then make your way up the Champagne Reef system to the bubbles, off-gassing naturally as you reach the shallows. Operators in the south also tend to visit Champagne Reef as a night dive. **Solomon Reef** is an unusual and rarely visited site located rather incongruously beneath the very ugly quarry face between Loubiere and Pointe Michel. Despite its location, this reef formation is interesting and teeming with a rich variety of marine life.

Southern dive centres

ALDive Loubiere, Roseau; 767 440 3483 or 767 275 3483; e aldive@aldive.com; www.aldive.com; f. Billy Lawrence is one of Dominica's most experienced scuba diving instructors & he & his dedicated team of dive professionals offer boat diving, PADI & NAUI dive training. You can rent equipment & the team is happy to accommodate requests for advanced dive sites such as Mountain Top. A small boat with a personal service means you avoid overcrowded dives.

Anchorage Whale Watch & Dive Centre Anchorage Hotel, Castle Comfort, Roseau; 767 448 2638 or 888 790 5264 (toll-free); e reservations@anchoragehotel.dm; www.anchoragehotel.dm; f. Catering for large or small dive groups, Anchorage offers daily 2-tank boat diving & PADI dive instruction. You can also rent dive equipment.

Buddy Dive Loubiere, Roseau; 599 717 5080 or 866-GO-BUDDY (toll-free); e dominica@buddydive.com; www.buddydivedominica.com. Operating out of Fort Young Hotel, Buddy Dive offers daily 2-tank boat diving, PADI tuition & equipment rental.

Dive Dominica Castle Comfort Dive Lodge, Castle Comfort, Roseau; 767 448 2188; e dive@cwdom.dm; www.castlecomfortdivelodge.com, www.divedominica.com; f. Dive Dominica is one of the island's most established & well known dive operators. The company has 5 fully equipped boats & offers daily boat diving, enriched air (Nitrox), equipment rental, & PADI dive training. Castle Comfort Lodge is also a popular place to stay with visiting scuba divers.

Champagne Reef Dive & Snorkel Champagne Reef; 767 440 5085 or 767 275 2001; e underwater@champagnereef.com; www.champagnereef.com; f. Located right on Champagne Beach, enjoy 1- or 2-tank scuba diving from the shore. You can rent equipment & also book a night dive.

Nature Island Dive Soufriere 767 449 8181 or 767 276 1505; www.natureislanddive.com. Nature Island Dive offers daily boat diving for small groups from the shores of the Soufriere Scotts Head Marine Reserve. Located within 10mins of all the SSMR dive sites, you can also rent equipment & book dive packages.

Central dive sites To the north of Roseau, near Canefield Airport, lies the wreck of the **Canefield Tug**. The 20m tugboat that sank in 1979 following Hurricane David is rarely visited by divers these days due to high turbidity and poor visibility. Unfortunately, run-off from the Boeri River has been supplemented by the heavy silting from a nearby cement factory, resulting in the decline of marine life on, and accessibility to, this dive site.

Central dive site topography is perhaps a little less dramatic than in the south, though the sites have excellent expansive coral reefs, steep vertical walls and diverse marine life. Long shore currents do occasionally come into play, but more often than not these dives will suit beginner and intermediate divers alike. A recent development at some of the central dive sites is the arrival of large groupers feeding on invasive lionfish (interestingly, the lionfish population has been less hunted by fishermen here). Another advantage of diving central dive sites is that you are unlikely to encounter other divers. Just south of the coastal village of Tarou is **Rodney's Rock**, a volcanic outcrop with a shallow reef at a depth of about 15m (see page 214 for the story of the rock). Off the beach at Mero are two sites, **Maggie's Point**, a series of thin coral formations and sand patches, and **Castaways Reef**, a flat expanse of reef formations and sand that go down to 24m. Both sites are suitable for novices. A little further out is **Barry's Dream**, a nice wall dive that descends to around 35m. Close to the village of Salisbury, off the coast of Grand Savanne, are six dive sites, including four wall dives. **Lauro Reef** is a wall dive that drops quickly to 35m close to the shore; **Brain Coral Reef**, **Nose Reef** and **Whale Shark Reef** are stunning walls that are adorned with barrel sponges, hard and soft corals and a variety of marine life including seahorses, rays and the occasional nurse shark. North of Grand Savanne is **Coral Gardens North**, a flat reef that starts shallow close to the shore and descends gradually to around 35m.

Central dive centres

East Carib Dive Salisbury; 767 449 6575 or 767 612 0028; e eastcaribdive@gmail.com; www.dominicadiving. East Carib Dive is a small, independent dive centre, speaking English, German & French, & offering boat & shore diving, & dive training. You can rent equipment & enjoy a great lunch when you get back to shore. Budget accommodation is also available.

Sunset Bay Club Dive Centre Coulibistrie; 767 446 6522; e sunset@cwdom.dm; www. sunsetbayclub.com. This resort dive centre offers daily boat diving, equipment rental & PADI dive training. See page 205 for more information about Sunset Bay's accommodation.

Northern dive sites Just like the west coast, the beauty of diving in the north of Dominica is that not so many people do it, and so it can really feel like you have the place to yourself. Just north of Pointe Ronde is **Ffutsatola Reef**, a rarely visited site on the southern edge of Prince Rupert Bay near Portsmouth; write the name backwards and you'll see what people think of it. **Sulphur Springs and Bubbles** is an unmarked region of diving that encompasses different diving options above submerged fumaroles. Much of the drama of this region lies below recreational diving limits, though some areas are as shallow as 6m. There are four main dive sites around the Cabrits peninsula. **Shark's Mouth** on the southern edge is a series of large boulders encrusted with corals and sponges. The site extends from the shoreline to a depth of 40m. **Anchor Point** is also made up of boulders and extends from the shore. On the western tip of the peninsula is the boulder reef of **One Finger Rock** and to the north of this site, **Five Finger Rock**. On the northern edge of the very pretty Douglas Bay is the steeply sloping reef of **Douglas Bay Point**. Around the corner in Toucari Bay are the twin sites of **Toucari Bay Point** and **Toucari Caves**, which are often combined into a single dive. Toucari Caves is a series of small, shallow caverns at a depth of around 12m. This is a very pretty site with an abundance of coral and fish life. There is also a submerged fumarole. At the tip of the island is **Point Break**, a spectacular though rarely visited wall dive with very strong currents, and only for advanced, experienced divers.

Northern dive centres

JC Ocean Adventures Cabrits National Park; 767 449 6957 or 767 295 0757; e jorgama60@ gmail.com; www.jcoceanadventures.com; . Located in the Cabrits National Park, just beyond

the cruise ship jetty, JC Ocean Adventures offers daily boat diving, PADI training & equipment rental. English & Spanish spoken.

SNORKELLING

There are some nice sites around the coast for snorkelling. Shallow reefs are alive with hard and soft corals and an abundance of colourful fish. Conditions along the west coast are usually very calm, making snorkelling a fun activity for both those who have done it before and those trying it for the first time. Snorkelling can be undertaken independently from the shore or from a boat with all of the island's scuba diving operators (see pages 80 and 81). Popular sites accessible from the shore include the sheltered drop-off at **Scotts Head** and the shallow fumaroles at **Champagne Reef** just to the south of the village of Pointe Michel (see pages 140–1). Along the west coast near **Salisbury** and Sunset Bay Resort there are shallow reefs for snorkelling, and in the north snorkelling is good around the **Cabrits** and in the sheltered **Toucari Bay**.

WELLNESS *with Terri Henry*

Terri is an eco-wellness mentor at Onelove Livity providing nature-based wellness experiences that satisfy our innate need to be connected to the earth. For further information visit: www.onelovelivity.com.

Imagine being surrounded by a lush tropical rainforest as you immerse yourself into a pool of hot sulphur-spring water and enrich your body with vital minerals emerging from the core of the earth. You alternate this luxurious soak with daring plunges into cold showers or rivers for a powerfully healing hydrotherapy treatment. Then you enjoy a 'mud scrub' with volcanic clay to cleanse your skin and emerge with your mind, body and spirit tingling with uplifted rejuvenation. If you are looking for optimal wellness in harmony with nature then Dominica is your holistic prescription.

Dominica is home to many qualified healing arts therapists and there is a diverse selection of treatments to choose from around the island. Local herbalists with knowledge passed down from generations have indigenous herbal remedies renowned for both preventative health care and curative measures. Dominica's unique health offerings often merge wellness activities with the natural environment. Yoga classes are available in the rainforest, on the beach, in tropical gardens and under the moonlight. Massage can be enjoyed overlooking a river, in cabanas nestled in tropical gardens and in expansive tree-top verandas with views and sounds of the crashing ocean waves below. Eco-therapy practices that help decrease stress and increase creativity take participants on winding trails to enjoy a sensory connection with nature whilst getting in tune with their own 'true nature'. Even facials use locally sourced botanical ingredients and pedicures soothe hard-working feet using coffee and cocoa blends that smell good enough to eat.

Locally grown foods are an integral part of this natural prescription for health – crammed with nutrients and vibrant tastes that are born from the combination of equatorial sun, abundant rain, rich soil and their just-picked freshness. Superfoods naturally available on the island include cacao, acerola cherries, soursop, sorrel, coconut water and coconut oil, alongside many other tropical fruits and vegetables that are filled with vitamins and flavour.

As you unwind, relax and energise on Dominica, you will want to capture the essence of these experiences in a bottle to take home. The closest thing to doing this is to purchase some of the local natural products made with plant extracts and essential oils. Skin-care soaps, creams and oils that offer aromatic fragrances and healing properties, are widely available. You will also find herbs and spices for both culinary and health purposes, packaged and ready to fly home with you.

Even if a 'wellness vacation' is not the main intention of your visit to Dominica, you will still feel the positive healing effects of nature – the reviving rainforest air, the cleansing clear rivers, the exhilarating rhythm of waterfalls or the awe-inspiring views of panoramic pristine landscapes – are all aspects of the island that rejuvenate the soul. And of course, just walking up and down a few hills on Dominica's rugged terrain is comparable to an hour in the gym – just a lot sweatier and vastly more enjoyable.

Dominica goes far beyond what a typical wellness destination can offer. You will find specialised treatments, infused with joy and a touch of wildness, that are a refreshing change from the norm. Indulge yourself in the adventure of outdoorsy, earthy spa activities and experiences for a vacation that is as good for you as it feels.

WELLNESS PRACTITIONERS Many of the larger hotels and resorts either have their own massage or yoga services or can put you in touch with one of the island's professional practitioners. Should you wish to contact a practitioner directly, here is a small selection. You could also check further listings on the Dominica Spa, Health & Wellness Association's website (*www.dominicawellness.com*).

Amethyst Holistic Therapy with Cindi John ↘767 225 0557; e amethyst@cwdom.dm. Cindi offers massage, reflexology, seated acupressure massage, Indian head massage, & hot stone massage.

Ingmari Roug (Body Harmony) ↘767 315 6452. Based at Zion Valley near Victoria Falls (page 152), Ingmari offers a range of meditation & body healing sessions.

Ariane Magloire ↘767 616 8687. Ariane offers personal massage & physiotherapy island-wide.

Beyond Vitality ↘767 613 8972; e sara@ beyondvitality.com; www.beyondvitality.com. Holistic nutritionist, Sara, offers a range of consultations & programmes for individuals & families. For more information, see pages 150–1 & check the website for details.

Onelove Livity with Terri Henry www.onelovelivity.com; f. Terri offers ecotherapy, holistic nature & wellness retreats,

health & wellness consultancy, & massage workshops. Check her website for details.

Quantum Leap with Dr Janet Taylor Wotten Waven;↘767 440 3118, 767 616 0173; e quantumleap@cwdom.dm. Janet offers holistic chiropractic care.

Rainbow Yoga Trudy ↘767 245 2474, Elise ↘767 315 0915, Silk ↘767 616 1703, Ellen ↘767 317 8806; www. rainbowyogaindominica. wordpress.com; f. Rainbow Yoga offers both scheduled & bespoke yoga classes island-wide (check Facebook page for latest schedules). Also offered are cooking & herbal classes & workshops, day tours, yoga in the rainforest, yoga by the sea, yoga for hikers, divers etc. Complete beginners & all fitness levels catered for.

Transcendental Meditation Centre Goodwill, Roseau;↘767 449 8154; e tmcentre@cwdom.dm. Transcendental meditation.

WHALE WATCHING

Sperm whales breed in the waters around Dominica and therefore sightings of these magnificent creatures are common. Pilot and humpback whales are also frequently encountered, as are large playful pods of spinner, Atlantic spotted and bottlenose dolphins. Though dolphins can sometimes be seen from the shore, a boat excursion increases the likelihood of sightings, and close encounters with dolphins and whales are experiences treasured by many. Nevertheless, before opting for a whale-watching trip, you should be aware that there are absolutely no guarantees when it comes to sightings. Operators reasonably claim success rates of over 80% but it is possible for a whale-watching excursion to become simply a rather expensive boat ride. Be ready for this. Your boat captain and his crew will do their best, but if whales are not around or are travelling fast, it may just be one of those days. Excursions usually take three to four hours and include refreshments. Sea conditions along the west coast are usually calm but if you are prone to seasickness, please take some *with marine biologist and underwater photographer, Arun Madisetti*

Eight kilometres apart, off the coast of Dominica, two sperm whales – sisters within a matrilineal group – synchronise their echolocation clicks to determine their location. Then, for the next 45 to 50 minutes they will descend to depths of up to 1,200m to feed on squid. This dive, one of many these two whales will make in a 24-hour period, is almost balletic, for after feeding – and though separated by distance – they will rise to the surface together.

Proximity to deep water trenches and ideal feeding habitats make Dominica the whale-watching capital of the Caribbean, where some 14 species of marine mammal can be seen in the waters off the west coast throughout the year.

Dominica's resident sperm whale pods are the most studied in the world and every year they give up new discoveries to researchers. We now know that each pod has a distinctive 'coda', or series of clicks, which identifies them as being part of the group; it is also now known that whales have an identifying click that only they make, effectively identifying themselves as individuals. Whales from other groups make different codas and have on a global basis been found to have different 'dialects'.

Sperm whales are very sociable and, when not travelling or feeding, they spend time in close physical contact with each other. This takes the form of rubbing their bodies together, which helps to establish closer social ties as well as to remove dead skin which whales shed in sheets.

Calves are born every four to eight years, making them the slowest reproducing mammal. Females remain within the pod for their whole life, which can be up to 60 years, while males remain with the pod for 12 to 14 years and then leave to become solitary global wanderers. Males are up to three times larger than females. A large bull sperm whale can be more than 21m in length; by comparison, the average female is 10 to 12m. Despite their size and (to us) imposing physical presence, sperm whales are actually very shy and somewhat skittish creatures. Their numbers are slowly increasing, having been decimated to fuel the wheels of the industrial revolution and despite still being killed for food. They have no predators other than humans and two species of whale (orca and pilot), which will target and kill calves.

Dominica is the most reliable place on earth to spend an afternoon in the company of the largest toothed creature on the planet and the largest brain in the animal kingdom. Being in the water with whales is an awe-inspiring feeling. It's a magical experience being alongside such large, powerful yet shy and gentle creatures. Sometimes I forget that I'm holding a camera with a job to do and I just hang in the water metaphorically open-mouthed.

medication ahead of your trip. Whilst prices vary, adults should expect to pay up to US$50. There is usually a reduction for children. Most operators have at least a couple of scheduled whale-watching days each week.

ALDive Loubiere, Roseau; ☎ 767 440 3483 or 767 275 3483; e aldive@aldive.com; www.aldive. com; ▮. Enjoy a personal & friendly service on ALDive's 'deep sea expedition' searching for whales & dolphins off Dominica's west coast.

Anchorage Dive Centre Anchorage Hotel, Castle Comfort, Roseau; 767 448 2638 or 888 790 5264 (toll-free); e reservations@anchoragehotel.dm; www.anchoragehotel.dm; f. Anchorage operates 2 large whale-watching catamarans, 1 of them sail-powered.

Dive Dominica Castle Comfort, Roseau; 767 448 2188; e dive@cwdom.dm; www.

castlecomfortdivelodge.com, www.divedominica. com; f. Dive Dominica offers regular whale-watching trips aboard 2 fully equipped boats.

Island Style Fishing Fortune, Roseau; 767 265 0518 or 767 613 9935; e islandstylefishing@gmail. com; www.islandstylefishing.com. Experienced & knowledgeable captain Jerry offers chartered whale-watching trips.

WORK EXCHANGE AND VOLUNTEERING

It's refreshing to see that some creative Dominican businesses are encouraging work exchange and volunteering programmes. Usually work exchanges will be offered during the low season when things are a bit slower and there is more time to work on improvements. At the time of writing, the following places are actively involved in organic farm work, permaculture, landscaping and building with natural materials: **Beyond Vitality** (pages 150–1), **Eden Heights** (page 151), **Rodney's Wellness Retreat** (page 131), and **Zion Valley** (page 152). Get in touch with them to find out more.

Part Two

THE GUIDE

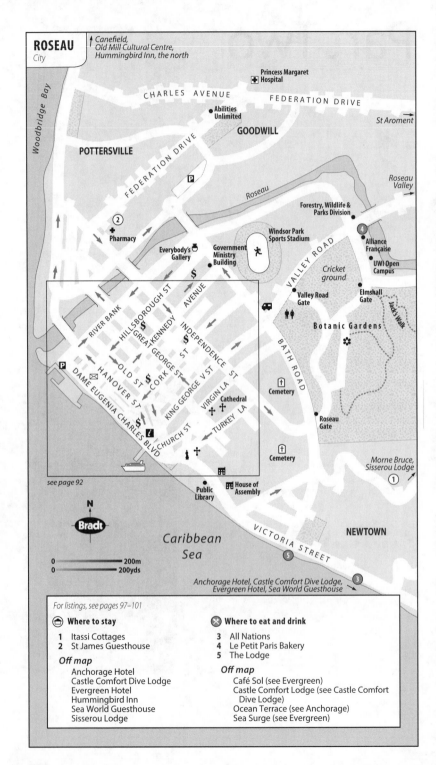

ROSEAU
City

↑ Canefield,
Old Mill Cultural Centre,
Hummingbird Inn, the north

Princess Margaret
✚ Hospital

CHARLES AVENUE

FEDERATION DRIVE

St Aroment

Abilities
Unlimited

GOODWILL

Woodbridge Bay

POTTERSVILLE

FEDERATION DRIVE

🅿

Roseau

Roseau
Valley

Forestry, Wildlife &
Parks Division

✚
Pharmacy

② Alliance
Française

Everybody's 👁
Gallery

Government
Ministry
Building

Windsor Park
Sports Stadium

UWI Open
Campus

VALLEY ROAD

Cricket
ground

Elmshall
Gate

RIVER BANK

HILLSBOROUGH ST

GREAT KENNEDY

AVENUE

INDEPENDENCE ST

Valley Road
Gate

Botanic Gardens

Jack's Walk

$

BATH ROAD

🅿

OLD ST

HANOVER ST

CORK ST

KING GEORGE V ST

VIRGIN LA

Cathedral
✝ ✝

✉

DAME EUGENIA CHARLES BLVD

CHURCH ST

TURKEY LA

🛈

Cemetery

Roseau
Gate

Cemetery

Morne Bruce,
Sisserou Lodge
①

see page 92

N

Public
Library

House of
Assembly

Bradt

Caribbean
Sea

VICTORIA STREET

NEWTOWN

⑤

0   200m
0   200yds

Anchorage Hotel, Castle Comfort Dive Lodge,
Evergreen Hotel, Sea World Guesthouse

③

For listings, see pages 97–101

⊖ Where to stay

1   Itassi Cottages
2   St James Guesthouse

Off map
    Anchorage Hotel
    Castle Comfort Dive Lodge
    Evergreen Hotel
    Hummingbird Inn
    Sea World Guesthouse
    Sisserou Lodge

✖ Where to eat and drink

3   All Nations
4   Le Petit Paris Bakery
5   The Lodge

Off map
    Café Sol (see Evergreen)
    Castle Comfort Lodge (see Castle Comfort
       Dive Lodge)
    Ocean Terrace (see Anchorage)
    Sea Surge (see Evergreen)

4

Roseau and Environs

Roseau is Dominica's capital and also its major seaport. It is located on the southwest coast of the island at the foot of a broad river valley. The central shopping, administrative and business district of Roseau is to the south of the river, and the residential neighbourhoods of Pottersville, Goodwill and St Aroment are situated to the north. At the southern edge of the central district is the old French Quarter, where the original European settlement was built (the Kalinago were already here). To its south is the coastal road and the neighbourhoods of Newtown, Citronniere and Castle Comfort.

First impressions of Roseau are generally mixed. For a capital, the town is very small, rather cluttered and often busy; habitually jammed with cars, people and buses. It can be noisy, sometimes rather smelly (open gutters and a propensity for some to urinate anywhere), and it is always very hot and sticky. A lack of proper footpaths and all those open gutters frequently force pedestrians out into the road amongst the traffic. This can make both driving and walking around town quite a precarious and frustrating business. The buildings of Roseau are a seemingly unplanned jumble of the old, the new and the downright ramshackle. Walk with your head down, dodging vehicles, trying not to fall down through holes in the pavement, dodging an increasing number of beggars, and getting steamy under the collar, and the town can feel ugly and oppressive. Take your time, walk slowly, look up at the jalousie windows, the ornate fretwork verandas and the mountainous backdrop, and it can be a different town altogether. But whatever you make of it, Roseau is really not a place for the traveller to dwell; for the beauty, intrigue and natural attractions of this wonderful Caribbean island lie beyond its diminutive and claustrophobic capital.

Ambitious plans to beautify Roseau and make it more visitor friendly have been talked about for many years and were on the cusp of being implemented before the financial setback of Tropical Storm Erika (page 4). The enhancement plans included boardwalks along the Bay Front, river paths, water taxis, pedestrian zones and more green spaces. A main bus terminus has also been suggested, which would help to alleviate traffic in the town as well as simplify things for those who don't have several years available to spend trying to figure out where on earth to catch a bus.

Whether you love it or hate it, Roseau is inescapably the administrative engine room of the island, the hub and the hubbub, where government, financial institutions, communications and transport services find their nucleus, where merchants trade and where farmers turn up from the countryside to sell their produce. It is also where the majority of visiting cruise ships put in.

A BRIEF HISTORY OF ROSEAU

Chief Ukale's Kalinago settlement on the flat lands around the river mouth was called Sairi. During the French occupation of Dominica in the early 1700s, the settlement was renamed Roseau after the preponderance of tall river reeds

(*Arundo saccharoides*) that still grow wild in the Roseau Valley, particularly in the area between Wotten Waven and Trafalgar. The town almost had to endure a third name change during the British occupation when King George III decided to call it Charlotteville after his wife, but unfortunately for the royal couple the name did not stick and the town reverted to Roseau.

Foresters from Martinique arriving on Dominica's south coast began building houses in the area alongside the Kalinago in the early 18th century, and a French settlement in the vicinity of Sairi was soon established. A church and small wooden fort were erected, and, when the British arrived in 1761, the town of Roseau was developed still further and the Kalinago were forced to retreat to the east. In 1805, during a French attempt to recapture the island, the entire town was engulfed and destroyed by fire. Everything had to be rebuilt. Roseau has subsequently endured damage from a number of hurricanes and tropical storms, and so a large part of the original settlement has either disappeared or been reconstructed.

GETTING THERE AND AWAY

BY BUS Buses to and from Roseau run throughout the day. Most buses do not run in the evenings, though it is possible to catch one up to around 21.00 on the west coast highway. Do not depend on it, however, and expect a wait. Although a bus terminus has been suggested, at the time of writing bus stops to and from different parts of the island are dotted around Roseau. See box on page 50 for a directory of Roseau bus stops and sample fares.

BY CAR Roseau has a one-way system that can be a little confusing at first, but you will get used to it. The town is not large and looking at the direction of parked cars will help you in places where signage is poor or non-existent. There are no traffic lights, but during the morning rush hour to work there are sometimes traffic police on duty, often compounding the mayhem.

If you are entering Roseau from the west-coast highway you will cross a single-lane bridge over the Roseau River and land on Independence Street, which is one-way and goes in a straight line all the way through the capital to the south. It will cross Kind George V Street, which, if you make a left turn along it, will take you up to the Botanic Gardens and up the Roseau Valley.

If you are entering Roseau from the south, you will usually pass along Victoria Street (unless cruise ships are in port, when you'll be diverted past the Old Market and up King George V Street), and at the small traffic island near the Fort Young Hotel and the cenotaph (look for the Neg Mawon statue; see page 95), the left-hand lane brings you on to Bay Front (Dame Eugenia Charles Boulevard), commonly known as the Bay Front. Please note you cannot turn right on to Turkey Lane at this traffic island. If you are entering Roseau from the south and wish to bypass the heart of it, especially during busy periods, take a right turn just before the House of Assembly (the big pink building opposite DBS Radio) and then take a left at the end on to Bath Road. If you wish to go up the Roseau Valley, head into the Botanic Gardens at the Roseau Gate. Exit the gardens to the left at the Elmshall Gate and turn right at the next road junction near the Alliance Française. If you wish to head north, continue along Bath Road, cross over the bridge, take a right at the traffic island and go up into Goodwill. In Goodwill, a left turn at the traffic island in front of the Princess Margaret Hospital will bring you down to the west-coast highway.

If you are approaching Roseau from the Roseau Valley you will come to a junction just over the Roseau River bridge. Left will take you past the Alliance

Française and UWI Campus into the Botanic Gardens via the Elmshall Gate, where you can bypass Roseau for the south (this is also a good way of getting back to Fort Young – just take a right when you see the DBS Radio station on Victoria Street). A right turn will take you past the Forestry & Wildlife Division office and around the back of the Windsor Park Stadium to the bridge that leads up to Goodwill. This is a good way of bypassing the heart of the capital if you are heading north along the west-coast highway. Straight on at the initial Valley Road junction brings you to the top of King George V Street (you should see the Police Headquarters) where you must turn right on to Bath Road.

Great George Street is one-way and runs northwest out of town over the Roseau River. Once across the bridge, an immediate left turn will get you on to the west-coast highway and straight on will take you to Federation Drive, Goodwill, the Princess Margaret Hospital, and St Aroment. A fourth bridge, often referred to as the 'Chinese Bridge', crosses the Roseau River at the northern end of Hanover Street by the new market. You can cross it from Roseau, heading north, and you will be on the west-coast highway. You can also cross it from the north, but the one-way system will send you up along River Bank and around in circles unless you know the back streets, where it is possible to get through on to the Bay Front. I suggest you are better off coming into town from the north over the bridge on to Independence Street, described above. It's far more straightforward.

ORIENTATION AND GETTING AROUND

DOWNTOWN ROSEAU The best and most practical way to get around Roseau is on foot, but even that can be a challenge. The town is small and nowhere is very far but a lack of proper footpaths, holes, extended porticoes and open gutters make walking quite troublesome, and it is important to keep a sharp lookout for traffic when you are inevitably forced on to the roads. Finding your way round the central area is fairly straightforward, as the layout is a grid system with all roads running in a straight line north to south or east to west. In the old French Quarter, the road layout is a little more interesting. Look out for small street signs on corners to help you find your way round and refer to the maps on pages 88 and 92.

Central Roseau Along the riverbank, at the northern tip of the Bay Front, is the **New Market**. Here fresh fruit and vegetables, ground provisions, flowers, seasonings, red meats and poultry are sold. The market is open every day except Sunday, but the majority of farmers and hucksters arrive to sell their goods on Friday and Saturday. From early in the morning, the Saturday market in Roseau is a very lively affair, in fact almost a social occasion, where people buy and sell, meet up and chat with their friends, or continue the party from the night before. Around the margins of the market Haitian women sell produce along the roadside, and along the riverbank you can often buy fish, jelly coconuts, even barbecue coals. In the covered areas you'll find flowers, clothing, local produce, crafts, a meat market and a smattering of bars and simple eateries.

It is the largest market on Dominica and you should certainly pay it a visit. Prices are not cheap, however, so be prepared for a few surprises. Also note that many market vendors have become particularly sensitive about having their photograph taken. Ask for permission and be prepared to receive a curt brush-off. Do not take it personally. If you would like to take photographs of produce only, this is usually fine, but be sure to ask first to avoid any kind of unpleasantness. Resist trying candid shots; someone will spot you and a fuss may ensue (see also page 64.) For information on the types of fruits and vegetables you may find here, see pages 56–7.

Located on the western edge of the new market along the Bay Front is the Roseau **fish market**, where you can buy fresh fish daily except on Sundays. The fish market is quite basic but also quite lively, especially on Saturdays; and it is always interesting to see fish steaks being chopped up with a wooden mallet and large machete. A little further along the Bay Front is the Roseau **ferry terminal** where you can catch the Express des Iles high speed catamaran service that operates between Guadeloupe, Dominica, Martinique and St Lucia (see page 38).

The Roseau City Council buildings, located opposite the fisheries complex and the ferry terminal, are some of the oldest still standing in the town. This was once the location of the town's **barracoon**, where slaves were temporarily

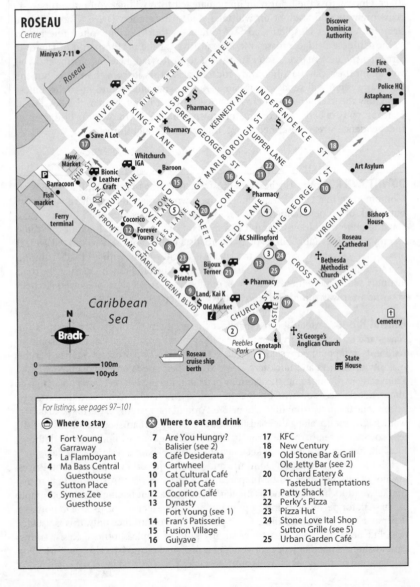

ROSEAU
Centre

For listings, see pages 97–101

🛏 **Where to stay**

1 Fort Young
2 Garraway
3 La Flamboyant
4 Ma Bass Central
   Guesthouse
5 Sutton Place
6 Symes Zee
   Guesthouse

🍴 **Where to eat and drink**

7   Are You Hungry?
    Balisier (see 2)
8   Café Desiderata
9   Cartwheel
10 Cat Cultural Café
11 Coal Pot Café
12 Cocorico Café
13 Dynasty
    Fort Young (see 1)
14 Fran's Patisserie
15 Fusion Village
16 Guiyave

17 KFC
18 New Century
19 Old Stone Bar & Grill
    Ole Jetty Bar (see 2)
20 Orchard Eatery &
    Tastebud Temptations
21 Patty Shack
22 Perky's Pizza
23 Pizza Hut
24 Stone Love Ital Shop
    Sutton Grille (see 5)
25 Urban Garden Café

barracked before being auctioned in the small courtyard beyond the archway on the south side of the building. The style of the barracoon is very similar to those constructed on the West African coast to house slaves prior to boarding ships for the West Indies.

To the south of the Roseau City Council buildings and also across from the ferry terminal is the main **post office**. From here the Bay Front (Dame Eugenia Charles Boulevard) runs along the shore to the Fort Young Hotel at its southern tip. Along the Bay Front are a couple of bars and cafés, boutiques, souvenir and duty-free shops, the tourist information building, the Dominica Museum (see page 95), the Royal Bank of Canada and the Garraway Hotel. In the centre of the Bay Front is the registry and court house. The Bay Front is also the current location of the Roseau **cruise ship jetty**, though every now and again we hear of plans to construct a new jetty and 'cruise ship village' further to the north.

From the Bay Front, Roseau moves inland in blocks of shops, eateries, banks and other businesses. Most shops are quite small and functional with little to attract visitors who are accustomed to large shopping malls and a plentiful supply of just about everything. There is an increasing number of cheap Chinese import shops, all of which seem to sell pretty much the same items. Nevertheless, there are one or two interesting places in this part of town if you are prepared to look for them. **Fields Lane** is a rather quaint, narrow street with some traditional old and colourful buildings. It is often rather peaceful here too, which is a welcome surprise in the ruckus of the town centre.

The **Windsor Park Sports Stadium** is located on Bath Road at the end of Kennedy Avenue. It was funded by China and constructed around the clock by an imported Chinese workforce in 2008. With a capacity of around 12,000 spectators, the stadium hosts occasional football and cricket matches as well as other cultural and music events. The annual World Creole Music Festival takes place here, and there have also been a number of international cricket matches as well as World Cup qualifying football.

King George V Street and the French Quarter
King George V Street runs in a straight line from the Bay Front right across the town to the entrance of the Roseau Valley. South of King George V Street is the area where French settlers developed a small village in the early 18th century. Referred to these days as the French Quarter, this area retains the character of a more historic Roseau which, despite the impact of hurricanes and conflagration, is still palpable when walking its meandering streets.

Like much of Roseau, King George V Street is a thoroughfare of hustle and bustle. At varying times of the day it is busy with either traffic, shoppers, street vendors or schoolchildren, and at lunchtimes all of them at once. The eastern end is dominated by the Astaphans department store and the rather foreboding battleship-grey Police Headquarters building. To the west of the junction with Independence Street there are a number of small shops, restaurants, snackettes and bars located in old buildings of stone and wood, and displaying some good examples of Caribbean colonial architecture. Upper-floor jalousie-style windows are framed by heavy wooden shutters and iron and wooden verandas are decorated with ornate fretwork. To appreciate this street from an architectural perspective you must walk it looking up, rather than down, for that is where you will see these interesting features and get a better feel for the history of the island's capital.

At the western end of King George V Street is the **Old Market**. This used to be a place where food produce and other wares were traded, where slaves were auctioned, and where public executions of captured runaways were carried out,

In all likelihood the first Catholic church in Roseau was an open-sided wooden hut with a roof made of river reeds, and it would have been in such an inauspicious setting that Bishop Dom Gervaise administered the sacrament of confirmation to French foresters in 1727. French settlers arriving from Martinique established themselves along the south coast and began to concentrate in the Kalinago village of Sairi. In 1730 Father Guillaume Martel arrived and began work on a solid timber church for his growing congregation. The new church had a stone floor and was approximately 12m long by 5m wide. Located in the same area as the present cathedral, this timber structure survived for almost a hundred years until it was destroyed by a hurricane in 1816. It was not until 24 years later that a replacement was completed, only for everyone to decide it was far too small. Emancipation meant that former slaves were now also free to worship in Roseau's church, and so a programme of enlargement began that did not reach its conclusion until around a hundred years later.

In 1855 the main steeple was erected and in 1865 the Kalinago offered a hand by cutting and transporting timber from the *simaruba* tree, from the northeast down to Roseau. For around three months, the Kalinago camped on the edge of town at night and installed a wooden ceiling in the cathedral by day. Around that time a huge stone pulpit carved by prisoners in the notorious Devil's Island penal colony arrived in Roseau from Cayenne in French Guiana. In 1873 the Chapel of St Joseph was constructed on the southeast corner with a crypt beneath it for deceased bishops and priests, and in 1878 Father Auguste Fort extended the aisles and had the east steeple built. Another hurricane inflicted considerable damage in 1883, but in its aftermath funds were collected to repair it along with other damaged churches around the island. It was during this period that the stained-glass windows were added. In 1902 new stone pillars were installed and new pews carved, and in 1916 the west steeple was added, the stones for which came from the old church at Pointe Michel. This balanced the external appearance of the cathedral. In 1925 the cathedral was consecrated by Bishop James Morris.

There have been few changes since 1925, though one or two small, modern additions such as electric lighting, a clock and an address system have been installed. Originally named L'Eglise de Notre Dame du Bon Port du Mouillage de Roseau, the cathedral has developed its presence and stands majestically overlooking the town today as Our Lady of Fair Haven. Its size is deceptive. From the outside it seems quite small, but once inside it feels very spacious, light and airy thanks to the stained-glass and the open windows that run along both east and west walls from the main entrance to the altar.

In recent times the cathedral has spent a good deal of time off limits having its roof renovated. At the time of writing there was no published deadline for completion of this work.

particularly during the early 1800s under the tyrannical governorship of Major General Robert Ainslie. Today, in rather stark contrast, it hosts a craft and souvenir market. It is interesting to note how the old streets laid by the French settlers radiate out from this central point. King George V Street goes straight up to the Roseau Valley, Hanover Street goes in a straight line to the Roseau River, and Church Street leads to the Roseau Cathedral (see opposite). Located within the Old Market Square is a cast-iron fountain where a well once stood, and the Dawbiney hucksters shelter which is still used today. The well was abandoned when the water was believed by many to have been tainted by the blood of so many brutally executed slaves. Between the Old Market and the Bay Front is the town's former post office building, constructed in 1810. Today it houses the **tourist information** office (☉ *08.00–17.00 Mon, 08.00–16.00 Tue–Fri, on w/ends for cruise ships*) on the ground floor and the **Dominica Museum** above (☉ *09.00–16.00 Mon–Fri, 09.00–12.00 Sat; entrance fee EC$3 adults, EC$1 students*). The entrance to the museum is up a flight of steps on the Bay Front side of the building.

At the southern tip of Bay Front (Dame Eugenia Charles Boulevard) is **Fort Young Hotel**. On a slightly elevated position above the original French settlement, a small wooden fort was constructed in 1720 to protect Roseau's inhabitants from attack. A sturdier stone structure was built in 1770 by Sir William Young, the first British governor of Dominica. Between 1778 and 1805 the French attempted to recapture the island from the British and the fort was the scene of much fighting. It was as a direct result of this warfare that in 1805 the settlement of Roseau caught fire and was razed to the ground. From the 1850s the fort was used as a police station and a hundred years later, in 1964, it was converted into a hotel. The hotel had to be rebuilt following Hurricane David 15 years later. The original battlements and ramparts of the fort can still be seen beneath its more modern additions.

Next to the Fort Young Hotel is **Peebles Park** which, even when cruise ships are in port, somehow seems to retain a peaceful serenity away from the excitement of the Bay Front and the Old Market. With its colourful flamboyant trees, wide benches, lawn and bandstand, it is often an oasis of calm. Take a seat and relax before heading back into the ballyhoo of town. On the small enclosed triangular lawn opposite the park is the **cenotaph**, a memorial to Dominicans who lost their lives fighting in World War I and II. The smaller memorial next to the cenotaph is in honour of the Free French who came to Dominica in 1940 from Martinique and Guadeloupe following the fall of France to Germany. Those islands supported the Vichy regime until US naval blockades forced them to switch their allegiance to the Free French.

On the southern side of Fort Young is the **Public Library**. Designed by Dominica's first Crown Colony administrator, Hesketh Bell, and funded by philanthropist Andrew Carnegie, the library was constructed in 1906. It is a beautiful building with a Georgian-style veranda around the south side overlooking a small lawned garden and the sea. The library contains a good selection of reference books, particularly on Dominica.

Across Victoria Street, opposite the library, is the gated entrance to the grounds of the old and new **State House**. The old state house is the building on the left; the new, very much larger and unconscionably expensive replacement is the one taking centre stage on the right. Considered by many a testament to ego rather than function, necessity, and appropriate use of finances on an island where poverty and unemployment are high, the State House was an extremely controversial and divisive construction project. Next to the State House is the very colourful **House of Assembly**, Dominica's parliament building. It was originally constructed in 1811, but in 1979 it was destroyed by arsonists and had to be rebuilt.

On the corner of Victoria Street, opposite the cenotaph and Fort Young, is the **St George's Anglican Church** of the Diocese of the North Eastern Caribbean and Aruba. Built in the 1820s, the church was yet another victim of Hurricane David in 1979 and had to be reconstructed.

4

This route will take between two and three hours at a leisurely pace. Take plenty of water.

Start in front of the Roseau cruise ship berth facing the old post office building, now home to the tourist information centre and Dominica Museum. Take the road between the museum and the Royal Bank of Canada and head northeastwards away from the sea up King George V Street. To your right is the Old Market. Continue straight on up King George V Street, taking note of the traditional architecture of the upper floors. At the junction with Great George Street, on your left, is Norwood House, one of the last surviving 19th-century town houses built almost entirely of wood. Continue along King George V Street right up to the junction with Bath Road. The Police Headquarters building will be on your left.

Straight ahead is Valley Road, gateway to the Roseau Valley. A short distance up this road on the right is an entrance to the Botanic Gardens (Valley Road Gate). Enter the gardens and walk alongside the cricket ground, which should be on your left. At the intersection, go left and then follow the signs for Jack's Walk, which will be on your right. Climb the steep footpath to the top of Morne Bruce and look out across the town from the viewpoint. Return back down Jack's Walk. At the bottom, take a left and then a right down the steps. The path emerges by the parrot sanctuary where it is possible to see sisserou parrots. A jaco parrot aviary is located nearby.

From the sanctuary head left at the junction and follow the path past the fallen giant baobab tree and the crushed school bus, and then exit the gardens through the Roseau Gate. Walk straight ahead at the road junction. Be careful because there is no footpath here. The Catholic cemetery is on your left. Take the second road on the left. This is Virgin Lane and it runs past the Bishop's House and main entrance of Roseau Cathedral. Continue along Virgin Lane to the junction. The Bethesda Methodist Church is on your left. Turn left and then take the second right along Turkey Lane and walk to the end. At the junction with the small traffic island, turn left. St George's Anglican Church is on your left-hand side followed by the grounds of the State House and then the House of Assembly. Cross the road and turn full circle, heading back towards town. The Public Library is on your left followed by the Fort Young Hotel. On the north side of Fort Young is Peebles Park with its flamboyant trees and bandstand. Cross the road to the cenotaph. On the far side of the cenotaph is the pretty Fort Lane. Walk down this old cobbled street. At the bottom of Fort Lane turn left on Church Street and head back to the Old Market and the Bay Front, where your walk began.

The quaint Fort Lane, located between the cenotaph and Church Street, is a good example of how Roseau perhaps once appeared. The cream-and-red painted house on the corner is typical of the town's historic vernacular architecture. On the corner of Cross Street and Virgin Lane is the **Bethesda Methodist Church** which is situated in close proximity to the **Roseau Cathedral**. To the east of the cathedral is the **Bishop's House**, which was constructed in the late 1800s.

NORTH OF DOWNTOWN ROSEAU On the northern outskirts of Roseau are the districts of **Pottersville**, **Goodwill**, and a little further along the coast, beyond the port and the cliffs, **Canefield**. Above Goodwill, at the end of Federation Drive, is **St Aroment**. These areas are mostly residential, interspersed with small businesses and the occasional guesthouse. Dominica's Princess Margaret Hospital is located on Federation Drive in Goodwill.

Canefield used to be one of the largest sugar-and-lime producing estates on the island. Some of the original works buildings were restored, and in 1988 the **Old Mill Cultural Centre** was opened, housing the offices of Dominica's Cultural Division. The centre hosts a theatre, art gallery and dance studio. It is a good place to call in and find out about events that may be taking place during your stay.

SOUTH OF DOWNTOWN ROSEAU To the south of Roseau along the coastal road are the residential communities of **Newtown**, **Citronniere** and **Castle Comfort**. Life in Newtown seems to revolve around the main thoroughfare, Victoria Street, which can be a lively place, especially in the evenings when locals can be seen sitting out on their stoops, discussing local affairs, listening to music, braiding hair, spilling drunkenly into the road, or just watching the world go by and shouting out to people they recognise in passing vehicles. The playing field on the northern edge of the two joined-up communities is Newtown Savannah, where football matches are played and live music events are occasionally hosted. Castle Comfort is a community to the south of Citronniere. Aside from some hotels on the waterfront, most of Castle Comfort is residential and located on the hillside beneath the heights of Giraudel village and Morne Anglais.

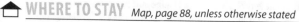

WHERE TO STAY   *Map, page 88, unless otherwise stated*

🏠 **Fort Young Hotel**   [map, page 92] (72 rooms) Victoria St; ☏ 767 448 5000; e fortyoung@cwdom.dm; www.fortyounghotel. com; 🄵; see ad, page 106. Probably Dominica's best-known resort & business hotel, Fort Young has ocean-front rooms & suites, all with AC, en-suite bathrooms, telephone, TV & internet access. The hotel has 4 bars, 2 restaurants & a boardwalk café. There is a spa, gym, duty-free shopping, a private jetty, an infinity pool, sun terrace & jacuzzi. The hotel offers a wide range of tours, scuba diving, wedding, honeymoon & family packages. It is a very popular choice & is in a convenient location for the capital & exploring the south. **$$$–$$$$**

🏠 **Anchorage Hotel Whale Watch & Dive Centre** (32 rooms) Castle Comfort; ☏ 767 448 2638; e reservations@anchoragehotel.dm; www. anchoragehotel.dm; 🄵. This long-established, family-owned & -run hotel offers 12 standard & 20 ocean-front rooms with en-suite bathrooms, private veranda, AC, TV, telephone & Wi-Fi. There is a large covered terrace restaurant, & a spacious lounge bar & swimming pool – all enjoying sea views. The hotel has its own jetty, 2 whale-watching catamarans, dive shop & dive boat, & it offers PADI dive courses. **$$$**

🏠 **Evergreen Hotel**   (17 rooms, 1 detached bungalow) Castle Comfort; ☏ 767 448 3288; e info@evergreenhoteldominica.com; www. evergreenhoteldominica.com; 🄵. A very pleasant family-run hotel on the seafront south of Roseau. All rooms have AC, en-suite bathrooms, TV, telephone. Some have a balcony & sea view. There is also a detached bungalow for extra privacy. The hotel has a fine dining restaurant, Café Sol lounge bar & grill, sun deck & swimming pool. Located right on the water, there is a small beach, mini dock & sun patio. In less than 1 min you can be snorkelling on the house reef. This is a very friendly hotel with good service & is well located for hiking & scuba diving excursions. **$$$**

🏠 **Garraway Hotel**   [map, page 92] (31 rooms) 1 Bay Front (Dame Eugenia Charles Blvd); ☏ 767 449 8800; e garraway@cwdom.dm; www. garrawayhotel.com. This business-style hotel is located on the Roseau Bay Front close to the Old Market & the historic French Quarter. It has a combination of dbls & suites, all with en-suite bathroom, internet access, AC, TV, fridge & telephone. Executive suites also available with business facilities. Rooms have either ocean or mountain views & there is a conference centre

Roseau and Environs   **WHERE TO STAY**

4

with essential business services. The Ole Jetty Bar overlooks the Roseau Bay Front, there is an open-air rooftop terrace, & the restaurant serves continental b/fasts, Creole & international lunches & dinners. Full packages including tours, honeymoon & dive are available. **$$$**

🏠 **Sisserou Lodge**　Reigate; 📞767 277 8714; e fsawers@gmail.com; www. dominicaaccommodation.com. Modern family-owned &-managed SC lodge with bedroom, lounge, kitchen, TV, internet, veranda & great views of Roseau. Other facilities include swimming pool, deck & gardens. The owners' property is within the same grounds & they can provide assistance with guides, tours & getting around. The location is good for access to Roseau, the south & the main trails of the Morne Trois Pitons National Park. **$$$**

🏠 **Castle Comfort Dive Lodge**　(14 rooms) Castle Comfort; 📞767 448 2188; toll free: 📞1 888 414 7276; e dive@cwdom.dm; www. castlecomfortdivelodge.com, www.divedominica. com; 🖪. This is a well-established family-run lodge & dive centre with gardens, private jetty & 5 fully equipped boats offering daily 2-tank scuba diving, snorkelling & whale-watching trips. Each room has en-suite bathroom, AC & fans, telephone, TV & Wi-Fi. There is waterside & restaurant dining, PADI scuba instruction, & a wide range of dive & accommodation packages available. Check website or call for details & special offers. **$$–$$$**

🏠 **Hummingbird Inn**　(6 rooms, 1 suite) Morne Daniel Cliffs, Rockaway, Canefield; 📞767 449 1042 or 767 285 4285; e hummingbirddominica@ gmail.com; www.thehummingbirdinn.com. With an emphasis on being eco-friendly, Hummingbird Inn is comprised of hardwood chalet-style accommodation in an elevated woodland setting above the main highway between Roseau & Canefield, in the area of Rockaway Beach. Standard rooms have en-suite bathrooms, fans, veranda & garden views. The suite has a large 4-poster bed, small kitchen & living area. The kitchen restaurant provides local cuisine by request & island tours can be arranged. *Rooms* **$$**, *suite* **$$$**

🏠 **Sutton Place Hotel**　[map, page 92] (8 rooms) 25 Old St; 📞767 449 8700 or 767 448 4313; e sutton2@cwdom.dm; www. suttonplacehoteldominica.com. Aimed primarily at the business traveller though suitable for anyone looking for a base in Roseau, Sutton Place

is an historic hotel in the heart of the capital with 5 standard rooms & 3 suites. All rooms have en-suite bathrooms, AC, TV & Wi-Fi. Rooms are traditionally decorated, some with 4-poster beds. Suites have a living area, dining table & kitchenette. The Sutton Grille restaurant on the ground floor is serviced by the popular Pearl's Cuisine & offers traditional Creole lunches. The Cellars Bar in the basement was once a rum store. It has AC & TV. **$$–$$$**

🏠 **Itassi Cottages**　(1 2-bed cottage, 1 1-bed cottage, 1 1-bed studio apt) Morne Bruce; 📞767 448 4313; e sutton2@cwdom.dm; www. avirtualdominica.com/itassi. Located on the slopes of Morne Bruce, near the Botanic Gardens, Itassi has 2 simple SC cottages in the grounds of the owner's home. The lower cottage sleeps 4 & is a traditional wooden building that was once the maid's quarters. The upper cottage with studio room below sleeps 2 & is a little more modern with veranda, hammocks, louvre shutters & wooden floors. All accommodation has private bathroom, TV & fans. **$$**

🏠 **La Flamboyant Hotel**　[map, page 92] (16 rooms) 22 King George V St; 📞767 440 7190 or 767 616 7191; e mail@laflamboyanthotel. dm; www.laflamboyanthotel.dm. La Flamboyant is a colourful business-style hotel located in downtown Roseau. Its standard rooms have en-suite bathroom, AC, TV & Wi-Fi. Its executive rooms also have fridge & business facilities. There is a bar & restaurant serving both traditional Creole & international food, & in the basement there is a conference room. **$$**

🏠 **Ma Bass Central Guesthouse**　[map, page 92] (12 rooms) 44 Fields La; 📞767 448 2999 or 448 9331. A basic but very clean & well-run guesthouse down a quiet lane just off Independence St. Ma Bass has 12 rooms with shared bathroom & kitchen facilities. Top 3 rooms have private bathrooms. All rooms have fans. Verandas overlook the rooftops of the town with nice views of mountains & sea. This is a decent option for travellers on a limited budget who don't mind sharing. **$**

🏠 **St James Guesthouse 1 & 2**　(11 rooms) Federation Dr & Church La, Goodwill; 📞767 448 7170; e stjamesguesthouse@hotmail.com; www. avirtualdominica.com/st-jamesguesthouse. This well-established budget accommodation option consists of 2 pleasant guesthouses located very close to each other & just a few mins' walk from downtown Roseau. Sgl, dbl & trpl rooms have ceiling fans, TVs, Wi-Fi, mosquito nets. Most rooms have en-suite bathrooms, some are shared, some have AC. Everything is very clean & tidy. There is also a small restaurant & bar for guests. This is very good value, well-run accommodation. B/fast inc. **$**

🏠 **Sea World Guesthouse** (14 rooms) ➘767 448 5068; **e** seaworlddominica@yahoo.com; www.avirtualdominica.com/seaworld. Budget accommodation is offered in this large & colourful seafront guesthouse on the coastal road in

Citronnier, between Newtown & Castle Comfort. All rooms have en-suite bathrooms, TV & fans. Some rooms have AC. Sea World has a bar & grill, yacht servicing & private jetty. It is popular with visitors from the French islands. **$**

🏠 **Symes Zee Guesthouse** [map, page 92] (15 rooms) 34 King George V St; ➘767 448 2494. Mr Symes offers rooms for rent above his bar & restaurant on a lively street near French Quarter. All have private en-suite bathrooms & fans, AC is also available. Some rooms can sleep up to 4 people. This is a handy downtown location, especially for the carnival & Creole seasons. **$**

✕ WHERE TO EAT AND DRINK *Map, page 92, unless otherwise stated*

CREOLE AND INTERNATIONAL

✕ **Balisier Restaurant & Ole Jetty Bar** Garraway Hotel, Bay Front (Dame Eugenia Charles Blvd); ➘767 449 8800; ⏀ daily. The Balisier Restaurant serves a range of local & international cuisine, with more casual dining & drinks on offer in the Ole Jetty Bar & the open-air rooftop terrace. Just turn up. **$$$**

✕ **Café Desiderata** Old St; ➘767 448 6525; **f**; ⏀ closed Sun. Located in the French Quarter near the Old Market, Desiderata's diverse, high-quality b/fast & lunch menu changes daily according to what is fresh. This fusion of Creole & international cuisine is complemented by the laid-back Fri & Sat evening tapas lounge where wine & conversation rule. Just turn up. **$$$**

✕ **Ocean Terrace Restaurant** [map, page 88] Anchorage Hotel, Castle Comfort; ➘767 448 2638; **f**; ⏀ daily. Dine in the Ocean Terrace restaurant overlooking the sea or relax in the poolside bar & lounge. The menu includes Creole & international fusion dishes as well as lighter bites & buffets. Just turn up. **$$$**

✕ **Sea Surge Restaurant & Café Sol** [map, page 88] Evergreen Hotel, Castle Comfort; ➘767 448 3288; ⏀ daily. The Evergreen Hotel Sea Surge restaurant & Café Sol lounge bar both enjoy sea views & sunsets. The restaurant is noted for its gourmet international & Creole dining & Café Sol serves lighter bites all day & until late. The weekly Lazy Sunday Buffet is a fixed price offering, often accompanied by music. Just turn up. **$$$**

✕ **Fort Young Hotel Restaurant & Bars** Victoria St; ➘767 448 5000; **f**; ⏀ daily. This well-known hotel has 4 bars (Ballas, Warner's, Palisades

& Sea Breeze) & a fine dining restaurant (Palisades) which serves a range of Creole & international dishes. Regular events include Fort Young Fridays (live music, BBQ food, discounted drinks) & Unwine Wednesday (kebabs, wine & more). Just turn up. **$$–$$$**

✕ **Fusion Village Restaurant & Bar** Old St; ➘767 440 9595; **f**; ⏀ daily. As the name suggests, this spacious & popular restaurant combines local ingredients with international fare which includes pizza, panini, salads, burgers & pasta dishes – all reasonably priced. Just turn up. **$$–$$$**

✕ **Sutton Grille Restaurant featuring Pearl's Cuisine** Old St; ➘767 448 8707; ⏀ closed Sun. Traditional Creole lunches are on offer downstairs at the Sutton Place Hotel. Prepared & served by Pearl's Cuisine, one of Dominica's oldest & most traditional culinary businesses, the food is always fresh & very reasonably priced. Just turn up. **$$–$$$**

✕ **Castle Comfort Lodge** [map, page 88] Castle Comfort; ➘767 448 2188; **f**; ⏀ daily. Creole & international lunches & dinners are served in the terrace restaurant & on the covered waterside deck. Try the popular Sunday BBQ & look out for regular food & music events. Just turn up. **$$**

✕ **The Lodge** [map, page 88] Victoria St; ➘767 440 4660; ⏀ Mon–Sat. Located opposite the Newtown Savannah, The Lodge offers a diverse selection of international lunches, snacks & dinners. Indoor & outdoor drinking & dining. **$$**

✕ **Old Stone Bar & Grill** Castle St; ➘767 440 7549; **f**; ⏀ closed Sun. Located in the French

4

Quarter, Old Stone Bar & Grill has a reputation for high-quality Creole & international dinners at reasonable prices. Just turn up. $$

✗ Urban Garden Café 8 Castle St; 767 317 8888; ☒; ☉ 07.00–17.00 Mon–Thu & until late Fri, closed w/end. Located in the historic French Quarter, Urban Garden Café serves value-for-money healthy, organic & great-tasting b/fast, lunch, all-day snacks & drinks. Just turn up. $$

✗ Cocorico Café Bay Front (Dame Eugenia Charles Blvd); 767 449 8686 ; ☉ closed Sun. Cocorico serves local & international b/fasts, lunches & refreshments & is popular with both locals & visitors – especially on cruise ship days or when the inter-island ferry is due. Just turn up. $–$$

✗ Guiyave Cork St; 767 448 2930; ☉ closed Sun. This is a long-established traditional Creole restaurant located above a popular patisserie. Dine on the veranda overlooking the street. Just turn up. $–$$

✗ Le Petit Paris Bakery Off Valley Road nr Alliance Française; 767 317 3333; ☒; ☉ until late Fri, closed Sat & Sun. Located on the east side of the Botanic Gardens next door to Alliance Française, Le Petit Paris bakes daily fresh breads, baguettes, quiche & more. The alfresco, covered dining area is a great spot for morning coffee & croissant, & the popular & extensive lunchtime menu includes wood-oven pizza. Just turn up. $–$$

✗ Cat Cultural Café King George V St; 767 265 9796; ☒; ☉ closed Sun. Combining delicious crêpes, chocolate mousse, smoothies & a range of sandwiches with astronomy presentations, workshops & … cats, this is perhaps one of the capital's most adventurous casual eateries. $–$$

✗ Pearl's Cuisine Hanover St; 767 448 8707; ☉ daytime only. In addition to catering at the Sutton Hotel, Pearl's, a long-established Dominica tradition, also has a small take-out service where you can get juices & snacks of all kinds including very good roti. $–$$

✗ All Nations [map, page 88] Victoria St, Newtown. All Nations is a popular late-night bar & eatery serving good local food & takeaway. The fish & chips is worth a try. $

✗ Cartwheel Bay Front (Dame Eugenia Charles Blvd); 767 448 5353; ☉ daytime only. Located in an old stone & wood building on the Bay Front near the cruise ship jetty, Cartwheel

serves coffee, tea, juice, cakes, sandwiches & traditional lunches. $

✗ Orchard Eatery & Tastebud Temptations Great George St; 767 448 3051. Orchard is a thriving catering service (they run the eatery at Douglas-Charles Airport) & specialises in traditional Caribbean fare. Opposite Orchard Eatery is Orchard Tastebud Temptations which serves ice creams, sandwiches, juices & other snacks. $

✗ Fran's Patisserie Independence St; 767 440 8275. Frans is a long-established & very popular patisserie serving great cakes & fruit tarts (you have to try them). Take away or eat in with coffee or fresh juice. $

CHINESE

There are several Chinese restaurants in Roseau but listing them is rather risky because they tend to either disappear or change name on a fairly regular basis. Here are a few that, even though their names may occasionally alter, at least seem to stay in the same building.

✗ Are You Hungry? Church St; 767 295 1859. Eat in, out on the veranda, or take away. Located in the French Quarter. $$

✗ Dynasty King George V St; 767 440 3021. Fairly established Chinese restaurant, bar & take out. $$

✗ New Century Cnr Cork St & Old St; 767 448 8808. Chinese restaurant & take out. $$

VEGETARIAN AND VEGAN

Many restaurants & take-aways will accommodate vegetarians or have vegetarian options on the menu. Here are a couple that specialise.

✗ Coal Pot Café Woodstone Shopping Mall, Cork St. Vegan, vegetarian & fish lunches, wholewheat bakes. $

✗ Stone Love Ital Shop Cross St (off King George V St nr ACS Shillingford); ☉ 08.00–17.00 Mon–Fri. Hole-in-the-wall eatery serving vegetarian & vegan food & drink to take away. $

FAST FOOD

✗ KFC Riverbank. Located by the New Market, this Kentucky Fried Chicken franchise with drive-in is extremely popular with locals.

✗ Patty Shack King George V St; 767 440 8150. Jamaican patties with a variety of fillings.

✗ Perky's Pizza Independence St; ☎767 448 1628. Florida pizza chain outlet serving pizza, chicken wings, sodas & beer.

✗ Pizza Hut Delivery Cork St; ☎767 617 7777. US pizza & pasta franchise, delivering only.

BARS AND NIGHTLIFE

Roseau's nightlife tends to focus around events, public holidays and parties and is usually a spontaneous event rather than something that takes place regularly at a particular venue. For drinks, most of the restaurants listed above are good options, other than that, simply pick a roadside bar, rum shop or snackette and mix with locals – but be careful, they are often known for very hard drinking and can stay open through the night. A good way of finding out what may be happening during your time on the island is to check the ◼f **Dominica Events Facebook page**.

SHOPPING

FOOD AND ESSENTIALS Roseau has many small convenience stores selling household essentials as well as food and drink. There are also a few larger supermarkets that are usually fairly well stocked. Shopping is quite expensive on Dominica; at least compared to the US and UK. For fresh produce, the **New Market** along the Roseau River is the best place to shop, especially on Friday nights and Saturday mornings, when most vendors set up their stalls and hucksters arrive selling from the back of pick-up trucks. You will also see plenty of Haitian women selling fresh produce in the streets around the market. Depending on what is in season, the market is usually a lively and colourful place, though it is also quite deceptive. Travellers who are used to the hubbub and shouting out of prices and bargains in English market towns, for example, may be surprised to find that the vendors, or hucksters, here all seem to sell their produce for the same price. Undercutting and yelling out your prices is unheard of here, indeed it seems many of the hucksters would prefer to return home with their goods rather than sell them at a cheaper price. Trying to haggle over prices will also take vendors by surprise and may cause an unexpected reaction. But if you are buying a lot of produce don't be afraid to ask for a discounted price nor be fearful of the hard stares such a request may generate! This is supposed to be a market after all, so why not treat it as such?

AC Shillingford King George V St. Supermarket & general store. Also look for the ACS 7–11 on High St (opposite the Inland Revenue building) & on Steber St in Pottersville.

Astaphans King George V St. Supermarket downstairs, department store upstairs. Astaphans has a dedicated car park to the side which is free if you shop in the store. Just show your parking voucher to the cashier. The entrance to the car park is via the last left-hand turn off Independence St before you reach King George V St. It is a short narrow road & the car park entrance is at the end on the right.

Green's Supermarket Wallhouse. Small, modern supermarket with a good selection of items. Located just off the main west-coast

highway between Castle Comfort & Loubiere. Parking.

Miniya's 7–11 Pottersville. Located on the northern bank of the Roseau River next to a filling station, this shop is part of a small family chain (the others are located in Canefield & the Roseau Valley). They are usually well stocked by Dominica standards & are extremely convenient, especially late at night & on w/ends.

Save A Lot River St. Small department store. Supermarket on ground floor, toiletries & household goods on upper floor. Open Sun.

Whitchurch IGA Old St. Popular & well-stocked supermarket with deli counter. There is parking at the front & to the side of the store though it is not restricted to Whitchurch shoppers.

ART, CRAFTS AND SOUVENIR SHOPS Most craft and souvenir stalls are located in or around the main tourist areas such as the Bay Front and the Old Market. The Old Market hosts the highest concentration of souvenir stalls though much of what they sell is mass-produced and imported rather than made on the island. If you take a tour bus up to Morne Bruce, to Trafalgar Falls or the Emerald Pool, you can expect to see exactly the same type of souvenir stalls (and the same souvenirs) in those places too – especially during the cruise ship season. If you can find it, do make an effort to buy authentic Dominican art and crafts. Here is a list of places in and around the capital where you could start. Also refer to the artist and artisan listings on pages 26–7.

Abilities Unlimited (Workshop for the Blind) Federation Dr, Goodwill; ☎ 767 448 2203. Craft workshop for the blind & disabled. All sales income from this high-quality work goes to fund the workshop. Mats, basketwork & other souvenir items.

Art Asylum Independence St. The art gallery of one of Dominica's best-known painters, Earl Etienne, is located near the Kairi FM building at the southern end of Independence St, just beyond King George V St. It contains an impressive selection of Earl's work.

Bionic Leather Craft Kennedy Av. Handmade leather shoes & sandals.

Cocorico Bay Front (Dame Eugenia Charles Blvd). A selection of authentic local crafts, jewellery, cards, Kalinago crafts & souvenirs.

Everybody's Gallery Hillsborough St. Located near the Windsor Park National Stadium, a small gallery containing paintings for sale by local artists including Ellingworth Moses.

Forever Young Bay Front (Dame Eugenia Charles Blvd). Assorted crafts & souvenirs.

LOCAL PRODUCTS

Try to support Dominica's cottage industries and buy local products if you can. By no means a comprehensive list, here is a selection that is worth looking out for when you go shopping. You will find some of these products at the big supermarkets, others (and more) you may also find in souvenir or duty-free shops. One place worth seeking out is **Zeb Kweole**, which is located in the covered section of the Old Market.

Aunty's Agro Processing Hot pepper sauce & seasoning pepper sauce.

Belfast Estate Dominica rum including Soca, Bois Bandé & Red Cap.

Bello & Co Ltd Jams, Café Dominique (local coffee), cocoa tea, pepper sauce, bay rum tonic.

Benjo's Sea Moss Flavoured health drinks made from seaweed.

Busy's Pure Honey Honey made near the village of Colihaut.

Café Local Arabica coffee from the mountain village of Giraudel.

Coal Pot Products Handmade soaps & massage oils made from natural ingredients in the village of Grand Bay.

Dominica Brewery and Beverages Ltd Beverages such as Loubiere Spring Water, Kubuli beer & Kairi Malt drink.

Karl's Hot Sauce Hot pepper sauce.

Macoucheri Rum Locally distilled & aged rum from sugarcane crops on the historic Macoucheri Estate on the west coast between Mero & Salisbury.

Natural Botanicals Soaps & shampoo made from natural products.

Nature Isle Volcanic Noni Medicinal noni (Morinda citrifolia) syrup from the northeast.

Rejuvananda Oil of Ojas Herbal healing oils from Toulon Agencies of Roseau.

Sico's Herbal remedies for colds & fevers from the west-coast village of St Joseph.

Talie's Pot A selection of organic jams by 100%Green founder Nathalie Roland.

LIFESTYLE BOUTIQUES AND DUTY FREE

Archipelago Wine & Spirits Long La. Located behind Land Duty Free, selling wines, spirits, tobacco etc.

Baroon Kennedy Av. Jewellery, watches, clothing & souvenirs.

Bijoux Terner Hanover St, Roseau. Located near the Ruins & the Old Market. Bags, accessories etc.

Cocorico Boutique & CocoChic! Cnr Bay Front (Dame Eugenia Charles Bvd) & Kennedy Av. Local crafts, souvenirs, spirits, tobacco, bags, sunglasses & more.

Land Duty Free Emporium Bay Front (Dame Eugenia Charles Blvd). Leather goods, alcohol, tobacco, sunglasses, local crafts & souvenirs.

Jewellers International Waterfront, Fort Young. Jewellery.

Kai K Bay Front (Dame Eugenia Charles Blvd). Located next to the Cartwheel Café, selling high-quality clothing & accessories. Duty free.

Pirates Long Lane. Sunglasses, spirits, wines, cigars, chocolates, cheeses.

OTHER PRACTICALITIES

MONEY AND BANKS Most shops and vendors in Roseau will accept US dollars. Fewer will accept UK pounds or euros, the main reason being that the exchange rate fluctuates with these two currencies whereas there is a fixed rate with the US dollar (US$1=EC$2.67). The number of shops and restaurants that accept credit cards is increasing but do not make any assumptions. Check first. There may also be a transaction charge.

The price of goods from most shops and vendors will include local (VAT) tax. The exceptions to this rule are duty-free shops, of course, and some hotels and restaurants. Again, check first by asking if the price quoted is tax inclusive.

Banks usually open between 08.00 and 14.00 Monday–Thursday and 08.00–16.00 Friday. All have ATMs that you can use to get local currency only (Eastern Caribbean dollars). Banks will also exchange currency and travellers' cheques.

$ First Caribbean International Bank Roseau branch Old St; ☎767 255 7900

$ National Bank of Dominica Head office Hillsborough St; ☎767 255 2300

$ Royal Bank of Canada Bay front (Dame Eugenia Charles Blvd); ☎767 448 2771

$ Scotiabank International Hillsborough Street; ☎767 448 5800

MEDICAL The **Princess Margaret Hospital** is the island's main medical facility and is located on Federation Drive in Goodwill. The hospital has a 24-hour casualty unit. For assistance: ☎767 448 2231.

Roseau's **pharmacies** are usually fairly well stocked and are open six days a week from 08.00–17.00 Monday–Friday and 08.00–14.30 Saturday. For assistance on Sundays, you should contact the Princess Margaret Hospital. If you are taking medication, please remember to bring it with you.

✚ Bulls Eye Pharmacy Federation Drive, Goodwill; ☎767 449 8600

✚ Garden of Eden Pharmacy Hillsborough St; ☎767 440 6651

✚ Harlsbro Pharmacy Hillsborough St; ☎767 448 8111

✚ Jolly's Pharmacy 36 Great George St & 8 King George V St; ☎767 448 3388.

✚ New Charles Pharmacy Cork St; ☎767 448 3198.

✚ Today's Pharmacy Hillsborough St; ☎767 277 2950

SAFETY Roseau is a very small capital and it is a safe place to be most of the time; you certainly shouldn't fear it. Sometimes Dominicans can appear quite serious, but break the ice with a smile and they are usually very happy to help you out.

Walking the streets late at night is when you are most likely to encounter any kind of threat, though it is uncommon. If it does happen, focus on getting through it rather than fighting back. Make a mental note of the thieves and report the incident to your hotel (get them to contact the police immediately). It is very important that you report thefts otherwise the problem goes unnoticed. Do not expect to see uniformed policemen on the beat at night. It simply doesn't seem to happen here.

POST OFFICE There are two post offices in Roseau. The main one is located towards the southern end of the Bay Front (Dame Eugenia Charles Boulevard), opposite the Roseau ferry terminal, and is open 08.00–17.00 Monday, 08.00–16.00 Tuesday–Friday. The second post office is located within the grounds of the Government Headquarters building on Kennedy Avenue and is open 08.00–17.00 Monday, 08.00–16.00 Tuesday–Friday.

INTERNET Access to the internet is rarely a problem on Dominica and Roseau's **Botanic Gardens** (pages 104–5) is a free Wi-Fi zone. Most cafés and bars also have Wi-Fi, as does the Roseau Library (page 95).

PUBLIC TOILETS There are two public toilets on Roseau. One is located at the side of the Tourist Information building on the Bay Front, just near the Old Market. The other is located just inside the Valley Road gate of the Botanic Gardens. You will need an EC dollar.

WHAT TO SEE AND DO

THE BOTANIC GARDENS ✳ On the east of the town are the tranquil, historic and very beautiful Botanic Gardens (also called the Botanical Gardens). Planting of the 16ha land, formerly a sugar plantation, began in 1890. The original idea for the gardens was an economic one, propagating crop seedlings for the island's farmers. The ornamental gardens of today are the result of the lifelong work of Joseph Jones, who managed their development from 1892. Botanists from Kew Gardens in England supplied a profusion of tropical species that they had collected from all over the world, thereby transforming the gardens from a purely functional nursery to an attractive landscape of exotic trees and flowering shrubs. Ornately decorated wrought iron gates were erected, ponds were created, and over 80 species of palm were also added. Part of the gardens was later lawned and set aside for a cricket ground and small pavilion.

Hurricane David wrought havoc on the gardens in 1979 and much was lost. With a strong resolve, however, the gardens were cleared of debris and, insofar as was possible, replanted. Today Roseau's Botanic Gardens are a tropical haven of peace and colour.

The gardens are still divided into an economic section and an ornamental section. The ornamental section on the western side is the most visible; the economic section is on the eastern side. Division of Agriculture, veterinary and laboratory buildings are located between the two sections in the southeast corner. The northernmost buildings are home to the two parrot aviaries where it is possible to see Dominica's endemic Amazonian parrots, the sisserou and the jaco.

In front of the Agricultural Division buildings are the crushed remains of a school bus. A giant African baobab tree fell on the empty bus during Hurricane David and it was left there, exactly as it fell, in memory of this great, destructive storm. The tree was cut, but lateral off shoots grew and produced the tree you see today.

A walk through the gardens is a nice way to spend a couple of hours. The Forestry, Wildlife & Parks Division, located just off Valley Road, opposite the Alliance Française, sells *An Illustrated Guide to Dominica's Botanic Gardens* which is a great source of information if you are interested in the local and exotic plants and trees that grow here. Just enter the old stone building, turn right and ask for the book at the reception desk. It costs about EC$15.

Highlights of the gardens include: the *bwa kwaib* (*Sabinea carinalis*), Dominica's national flower (look for it between the Roseau Gate and the crushed bus); the Canonball tree (*Couropita guianensis*), a South American species with unusual round fruits; Colville's glory (*Colvillea racemosa*), a really beautiful tree when in bloom; a gorgeous saman tree (*Samanea samaan*) that grows on the margins of the cricket ground; the golden shower (*Cassia fistula*), with fragrant golden flowers when in bloom; the velvet tamarind (*Dialium indum*), an evergreen with a tangy edible fruit; balsam (*Copaifera officinalis*), of which there is a huge specimen growing by the sisserou aviary; and the roucou (*Bixa orellana*), whose seeds were used as a food colouring and a dye for Kalinago body painting (see box on page 6).

There are also several species of palm including: the royal palm (*Roystonea oleracea*), the sago palm (*Cycadaceae*), the bottle palm (*Mascarena lagenicaulis*), the gouglou palm (*Acrocomia aculeate*), the century palm (*Corypha umbraculifera*), and the scheelea palm (*Attalea butyracea*).

In addition to cricket matches, the gardens are used for a range of activities including steel-pan competitions, parades, independence celebrations and Creole in the Park, forerunner to the annual World Creole Music Festival. You may see people practising stilt-walking (*bwa bwa*) here in the weeks before carnival, or groups of children out with their school teachers on a walk (*belle marché*) and a picnic. During the cruise season the gardens can get a bit crowded with tourists and buses, or even a rather bizarre yellow train (you'll know it when you see it), particularly in the mornings.

The Botanic Gardens are within easy walking distance of downtown Roseau. Simply walk up King George V Street from the Bay Front and, at the junction with Valley Road and Bath Road (by the Police Headquarters), go straight on. The Valley Road Gate is just a couple of hundred metres on the right.

MORNE BRUCE AND JACK'S WALK Situated on the eastern side of the Botanic Gardens is the steep pinnacle of Morne Bruce. From the summit of this low peak there are expansive views of the town and the sea beyond. Named after James Bruce, a captain of the Royal Engineers who designed many of the island's original fortifications in the 18th century, the site was selected by the British as the location for a military garrison. Today there is still a cannon overlooking the town, as well as the original barracks and officers' quarters. The buildings on the summit are now used by the government and the police. The giant cross was erected in the 1920s.

There are two ways to reach the summit of Morne Bruce. One is by road, taking the first turning on the left after the Anglican cemetery on Bath Road – simply follow the road up to the top. The more adventurous may wish to take a 20-minute walk to the top up a footpath called **Jack's Walk**, located on the northeastern side of the Botanic Gardens near the Elmshall Gate. The footpath is quite steep so take good care as well as plenty of water. The views of Roseau from the top are really worth the climb.

During the height of the cruise ship season it can get quite crowded at the viewing point on Morne Bruce as it is a popular stop-off for bus tours. There are

4

also a number of souvenir vendors here at this time of the year. A nice time to go is later on in the afternoon, say around 17.00, when the heat of the day is waning and the sun is thinking about setting over the Caribbean. If you go by road rather than via Jack's Walk, look out for Mountain View Snackette and Bar, a very small, colourful place set back from the apex of a bend (you may only see it on the way up). It is a nice place to have a drink, enjoy the view, and watch the sun go down on a lovely Dominica day.

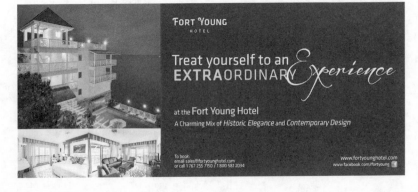

5

Roseau Valley and Morne Trois Pitons National Park

The town of Roseau lies on a plain of flat pyroclastic (volcanic lava) flow where a broad river valley meets the Caribbean Sea. **The Roseau Valley** stretches eastwards until its steep sides converge in the heights of Trafalgar and, above it, Laudat. From the crowded residential suburb of Bath Estate just beyond the Botanic Gardens, the Roseau Valley embraces several small hamlets and villages. On the southern ridge at a height of 460m is the elevated farming community of Morne Prosper. On the northeastern ridge, at a height of 600m, is the hamlet of Laudat, gateway to several of the natural attractions of the Morne Trois Pitons National Park. In the valley below Laudat are the very popular twin waterfalls of Trafalgar and the village of the same name. Below Trafalgar are the residential settlements of Shawford and Fond Cani. On the southern edge of the valley is the village of Wotten Waven with its hot sulphur springs and volcanic fumaroles.

The Morne Trois Pitons National Park was established in 1975, and in 1997 it was designated a UNESCO World Heritage Site. It is approximately 7,000ha in size and contains a high concentration of volcanoes. The park's vegetation zones include deciduous and semi-deciduous forest, secondary and mature rainforest, montane forest, and elfin woodland at the volcano summits. Volcanic activity can be seen within the park. The **Valley of Desolation,** one of the island's active volcanoes, is a fascinating landscape of violently steaming fumaroles, hot-water rivers and cascades, boiling mud and a thin crust of rocks and boulders that have been stained in multi-colours by the chemicals and the gases that are released from the magma chamber below. The **Boiling Lake** (pages 118–20) is a flooded fumarole with both a diameter and a depth of around 60m, reputedly making it the second-largest of its kind in the world (the largest is Frying Pan Lake in New Zealand).

Of the volcanoes within the park boundary it is the dominant three-peaked **Morne Trois Pitons** itself, at 1,342m that is the highest (pages 126–7). From the summit there are spectacular views of lush and dense rainforest all around. To the south are the peaks of **Morne Micotrin** (1,221m, pages 124–6), **Morne Watt** (1,224m) and **Morne Anglais** (1,123m, pages 142–3). To the north is a vast blanket of green covering the area from the Central and Northern Forest Reserves to the distant summit of Morne Diablotin (1,447m) and the Morne Diablotin National Park (page 207).

In addition to the Boiling Lake, the Morne Trois Pitons National Park has two other large freshwater lakes. The 2ha **Boeri Lake** (pages 120–1) is the highest mountain lake on the island at an elevation of 853m. A little beyond the Boeri Lake, though very difficult to get to, are two much smaller lakes. Located very close to the Boeri Lake, though at a slightly lower altitude of 762m, is the 4ha **Freshwater Lake** (pages 122–3). Within the park are several waterfalls that are worth visiting. The tallest is the **Middleham Falls** (pages 123–4), which can be found to the west of Morne Micotrin. To the north of Morne Trois Pitons is the very popular **Emerald Pool** waterfall (pages 215–16), which has become a firm favourite for day visitors.

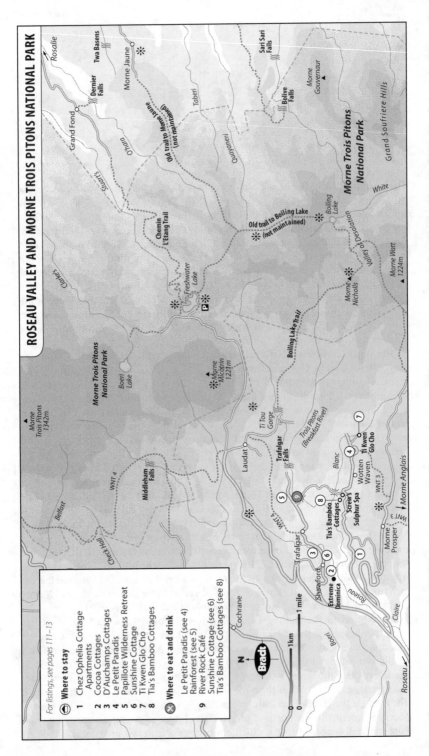

ROSEAU VALLEY AND MORNE TROIS PITONS NATIONAL PARK

For listings, see pages 111–13

Where to stay
1 Chez Ophelia Cottage Apartments
2 Cocoa Cottages
3 D'Auchamps Cottages
4 Le Petit Paradis
5 Papillote Wilderness Retreat
6 Sunshine Cottage
7 Ti Kwen Glo Cho
8 Tia's Bamboo Cottages

Where to eat and drink
Le Petit Paradis (see 4)
Rainforest (see 5)
River Rock Café
Sunshine Cottage (see 6)
9 Tia's Bamboo Cottages (see 8)

Morne Trois Pitons National Park

Perhaps the least visible, especially for the non-swimmer, is the waterfall located within the water-filled **Ti Tou Gorge** (page 115) near the village of Laudat, also a popular attraction for cruise visitors who file in and out on floatation rings. There are many other waterfalls located above and below Ti Tou Gorge and the Breakfast River which can only be accessed via a canyoning trip (page 70).

The Morne Trois Pitons National Park's main habitat is rainforest. Common vegetation includes trees such as *chatanier* (*Sloanea dentata, Sloanea caribaea* and *Sloanea berteriana*), *gommier* (*Dacryodes excelsa*), *mang blanc* (*Symphonia globulifera*), *karapit* (*Amanoa caribaea*), *maho cochon* (*Sterculia caribaea*) and *bwa bandé* (*Richeria grandis*). There is an abundance of tree ferns and epiphytes such as bird's nest anthuriums, orchids and bromeliads. In the montane forest the vegetation becomes shorter and the trees have a noticeably smaller girth. *Palmiste moutan* (mountain palm), hibiscus and a wide variety of ferns are common. At the summit, mossy covered, low-growing elfin woodland is dominated by plants such as the *kaklen* (*Clusia mangle*), *z'ailes mouch* (*Asplundia rigida*) and *kwé-kwé* (*Miconia mirabilis*). Fumarole vegetation is found in the Valley of Desolation. Plants able to withstand hot and sulphurous gases include *kaklen*, bromeliads and grasses.

Birds that can be seen and heard throughout the park are numerous and include the bananaquit, all four species of hummingbird, thrashers, tremblers, warblers, vireos, and the unmistakable mountain whistler (rufous-throated solitaire). You will also come across the jaco, one of Dominica's two endemic species of Amazonian parrot. (For more on Dominica's birds, see page 7.) In the wet montane forests, particularly where the ground is very sodden, you may be lucky enough to hear the grunts of feral pigs, though they are extremely elusive and more commonly known to live within the Northern Forest Reserve. Other mammals that are found here include the agouti and several species of bat. Lizards include the endemic zandoli (page 8), and amphibians such as the Antillean tree frog (page 9) are common throughout the park. You may also come across the boa constrictor (page 9), though such encounters are rare.

GREAT DAYS OUT

Here are some suggestions for great days out in the Roseau Valley and Morne Trois Pitons National Park. You will find details of all the places mentioned in this chapter.

THE BOILING LAKE, TI TOU GORGE AND HOT VOLCANIC SPA Hike to the Boiling Lake and back from Laudat and take a swim up Ti Tou Gorge. Head down to Wotten Waven and soak those weary muscles in a hot volcanic spa.

THE FRESHWATER LAKE, THE BOERI LAKE, LUNCH AND GARDENS Park up at the Freshwater Lake and hike the trail in an anticlockwise direction. When you emerge on the road, head right and hike to the Boeri Lake. Hiking over, drive down to Papillote Wilderness Retreat for a late lunch, a walk around the gardens and perhaps even a soak in a hot pool.

MIDDLEHAM FALLS, LUNCH, THE TRAFALGAR FALLS Hike to the Middleham Falls and back from Laudat and then head down to Trafalgar for some lunch at River Rock Café. Afterwards, visit the Trafalgar Falls.

5

WHEN ARE THE CRUISE SHIP DAYS?

You can actually find this information online (it changes each year, of course), but failing that you can check at the Whitchurch Travel Agency (see page 35) in Roseau (they manage the majority of cruise ships calling at Dominica). At the bottom of the steps leading up to the travel office is a notice board giving cruise ship information for the coming week. Alternatively, try the tourist information office on Bay Front.

GETTING THERE AND AWAY

Given their proximity to the capital, the natural attractions of the Roseau Valley are very accessible and certainly worth seeing. A trip to the twin falls at Trafalgar, a visit to the volcanic fumaroles along the River Blanc, a wander around the tropical gardens of Papillote Wilderness Retreat, and a soak in a hot sulphur spring at Wotten Waven make for a fun day out. Please note that because of their accessibility these attractions can become crowded on days when cruise ships are calling at Dominica; as can the narrow roads leading to them. At the time of writing the Trafalgar Falls is actually out of bounds to everyone but official cruise tours up to 12 noon on such days. This ill-conceived decision was the result of bus congestion on the narrow road leading to the visitor centre. It seems no-one gave much thought to simply better organising the scheduling of these tours. Incredibly, this 'ban' also applies to Dominicans.

The road to Laudat is also a little busier on cruise ship days; floating through Ti Tou Gorge, hiking to Middleham Falls and kayaking on the Freshwater Lake are popular activities.

BY BUS See page 50 for information on where to catch buses from Roseau. As the Trafalgar Falls are a little way up from Trafalgar village itself, bus drivers may request a little extra to go all the way. Alternatively, just get out and walk, though be prepared: the approach road is very steep. Buses will rarely go beyond Laudat village to the Freshwater Lake, Ti Tou Gorge and so on. You could offer to pay extra, but failing that you must walk there or hitch a ride.

BY CAR By car, head east along King George V Street and at the junction with Bath Road (with the Police Headquarters to your left), go straight across on to Valley Road. The route passes the Botanic Gardens and then crosses a bridge over the Roseau River. Beyond the small residential suburb of Bath Estate, the road continues eastwards into the Roseau Valley. The Valley Road forks just beyond Bath Estate near the settlement of Fond Cani. The road to the right goes to Wotten Waven with a further right-hand fork a little further on that goes up to Morne Prosper. The road to the left heads towards Trafalgar and Laudat. The junction is clearly signposted.

After taking a left at this junction, you follow a winding road until you come to a second fork. The road to the left goes up to Laudat, Ti Tou Gorge, the Freshwater Lake, the Boeri Lake trail, the Boiling Lake Trail, Morne Micotrin, and the Chemin L'Etang trail. The fork to the right goes to Trafalgar. Again this junction is well signposted.

Pass through the village of Trafalgar to get to the waterfalls. A junction to the right goes across the valley to Wotten Waven, straight on goes up to Papillote Wilderness Retreat, and the Trafalgar Falls visitor centre and car park.

If heading up to Laudat, stick to the main road all the way and be sure to use your horn on the numerous blind corners. You will pass a sign on your left and a narrow road that goes down to the Middleham Falls trailhead. A little further on is a junction where you may meet a park warden checking site passes. The concrete road straight ahead goes to the Freshwater Lake, the Boeri Lake trail, Morne Micotrin, and the Chemin L'Etang trail. The road to the right goes to Laudat village and, before it, a left-hand turn-off to Ti Tou Gorge and the Boiling Lake trailhead. If you are heading for one of these, keep going to the left of the hydro plant and balancing tank until you come to a dead end. Park up around here and walk.

If you are heading for Morne Micotrin, the Freshwater Lake, Chemin L'Etang and the Boeri Lake, follow the concrete road at the Laudat junction all the way into the Morne Trois Pitons National Park. This road eventually splits with a left-hand fork going to the Boeri Lake and Chemin L'Etang trailheads, and the right-hand road going to the Freshwater Lake visitor centre and car park. See page 124 for the exact whereabouts of the Morne Micotrin trailhead.

WHERE TO STAY

Papillote Wilderness Retreat [map, page 108] (2 apts, 3 rooms) Trafalgar; 767 448 2287; e papillote@cwdom.dm; www.papillote.dm; ; usually closed Sep & Oct. See ad, page 2. Papillote has long been a firm favourite with visitors to Dominica, especially with those who enjoy tropical gardens. Unfussy & relaxing accommodation is set in 2ha of beautiful, immaculate & mature rainforest gardens with 3 hot volcanic pools, 1 cold-water pool & 2 waterfalls. (See page 114 for more about Papillote Gardens.) The SC apts each have 2 bedrooms & are spacious with lounge, fully equipped kitchenette, fans, mosquito nets & porch. The rooms have private en-suite bathrooms, lounge, veranda, mosquito nets & fans. All enjoy free Wi-Fi. If you are travelling as a family or group of friends, you can also rent out the whole building as 1 villa. Papillote has a large restaurant overlooking the gardens serving a high standard of Creole & international cuisine. Massage & yoga are available, as are guided tours of the gardens. Ask about the popular Interlude Package, which includes a garden tour, lunch & use of the hot pools. A 15min walk to the Trafalgar Falls & a 15min drive to Roseau make it an ideal location. *Apts* **$$$**, *rooms* **$$**, *whole villa* **$$$$$**

Cocoa Cottages [map, page 108] (6 rooms, 1 'treehouse') Shawford, Roseau Valley; 767 276 2920; e cocoacottage@gmail.com; www.cocoacottages.com; . Very attractive, laid-back & stylish accommodation in forest & tropical garden surroundings. The cottage rooms are rustic, cosy & romantic. All have en-suite bathrooms. There is a communal kitchen restaurant serving fresh local dishes & an open lounge & music area

with a 'TV' window on to nature. The 'treehouse' SC accommodation sleeps up to 6. In an idyllic natural setting, & with easy access to the Morne Trois Pitons National Park's major trailheads, Cocoa Cottages offers comfortable, relaxing accommodation for those looking to unwind or explore. For adventurous travellers interested in a canyoning trip, Extreme Dominica (page 70) is next door, and for those with a sweet tooth, the homemade Coco-Jazz chocolate is worth a try. *Rooms* **$$$**, *treehouse* **$$$$**

Chez Ophelia Cottage Apartments [map, page 108] (5 bungalows) Roseau Valley; 767 448 3438 or 767 615 6518; e chezophelia@cwdom.dm; www.chezophelia.com; . Located within pleasant gardens on the road to Wotten Waven in the Roseau Valley, all cottages have en-suite bathroom facilities, free Wi-Fi & fans. There is a communal lounge, TV & restaurant area where b/fast & dinners are served. Cuisine is traditional Creole & is sometimes accompanied by the voice of 'Dominica's Lady of Song', Ophelia Marie, who is the owner of the cottages. French also spoken. **$$**

Roxy's Mountain Lodge (16 rooms) Laudat; 767 448 4845; www.roxymountainlodge.com. Roxy's is a stone & wood mountain lodge located on the outskirts of Laudat on the margins of the Morne Trois Pitons National Park. The scenery is dramatic & the location good for hikers looking to explore the park's trails. Simple rooms have private bathrooms & Wi-Fi, & there's a restaurant & bar for food & refreshment. Bring something warm to wear at night – it gets cold at this kind of elevation, even in the Caribbean! **$$**

5

⌂ **Sunshine Cottage** [map, page 108] (2 bedroom cottage) Shawford, Roseau Valley; 📞 767 285 6399; e sunshinedca@gmail.com; www.sunshinecottagedominica.com; f. Sunshine is a peaceful & private cottage set in tropical forest & garden surroundings in Shawford, on the road to Trafalgar. It has 2 comfortable bedrooms, bathroom with stylish shower, fully equipped kitchenette, living area & spacious veranda with hammocks. There is also free Wi-Fi. The owners live nearby & speak French, German & Italian. They also run the popular vegetarian & vegan Sunshine Restaurant (see opposite). **$$**

⌂ **Tia's Bamboo Cottages** [map, page 108] (6 cottages) Wotten Waven; 📞 767 448 1998 or 767 225 4823; e tiacottages@gmail.com; www.tiasbamboocottages.com. Tia offers rustic bamboo & wood cottages, hot pools, bar & restaurant set amid well-tended tropical flower & forest gardens. The cottages are comfortable & clean, each with their own private bathroom. There are 3 hot volcanic pools set alongside the river & another 2 within enclosed bamboo cabanas. The open-sided bamboo restaurant serves Creole food by reservation only. Tia's is very handy for National Trail hikers looking for budget accommodation & a place to soak weary limbs. **$$**

⌂ **D'Auchamps Cottages** [map, page 108] (3 cottages, camping) Roseau Valley; 📞 767 285 2117; e sarahonychurch@msn.com; www.dauchampscottages.com; f. D'Auchamps Cottages are located on Honychurch family land in the heart of the Roseau Valley. They are surrounded by forests, colourful flower, fruit & vegetable gardens, & residents can enjoy near 180° views of the volcanoes of the Morne Trois Pitons National Park. Tree Fern Cottage is made of stone & wood & has 1 bedroom, spacious living area, fully equipped kitchen, shower & toilet, mosquito nets & private porch with garden view. Hog Plum House has 2 bedrooms (1 dbl, 1 twin), mosquito nets, a fully equipped galley kitchen, lounge area, writing desk, porch & garden views. Firefly is a sgl-room wooden cabin with dbl bed, mosquito nets, kitchenette & private outdoor toilet & shower.

The camping area has space for around 4 tents. It also enjoys great views & has a communal toilet, shower, kitchen & laundry shed. D'Auchamps is great value accommodation in a wonderful setting; perfect for budget travellers, hikers, researchers & even work-exchange horticulturalists! **$–$$**

⌂ **Le Petit Paradis** [map, page 108] (5 apts) Wotten Waven; 📞 767 440 4352 or 767 276 2761; e lepetitparadis200@hotmail.com; www.lepetitparadisdominica.com. Located in the heart of Wotten Waven village, Le Petit Paradis has budget apts & a bamboo restaurant decorated in traditional madras. Apts accommodate hikers – WNT Segment 3 emerges opposite (see pages 229–31) – couples & families. All have private bathrooms. The restaurant serves traditional Creole fare. There is free Wi-Fi & a gift shop. **$**

⌂ **The Secret Garden** (5 rooms) Wotten Waven; 📞 767 448 8712 or 767 225 7711; e sg_dominica@yahoo.com. The Secret Garden is a rustic wooden house with 5 rooms & 4 bathrooms, living area, kitchen, mosquito nets, fans & shared veranda. It has a garden trail down to the volcanically active River Blanc, where there is a hot sulphur spa. This is simple but clean & comfortable accommodation that would suit a group of travelling friends or an outdoors-loving family travelling on a budget. **$**

CAMPING

⌂ **D'Auchamps Cottages** [map, page 108] Roseau Valley; 📞 767 285 2117; e sarahonychurch@msn.com; www.dauchampscottages.com; f. Around 4 pitches are available enjoying awesome views & pretty garden surroundings. There is a shared toilet & shower, kitchenette & laundry. **$**

🏕 **Ti Kwen Glo Cho** [map, page 108] Wotten Waven; 📞 767 440 3162. Ti Kwen Glo Cho has beautiful natural gardens, hot & cold pools, a waterfall, small bar, & toilet facilities. Local food can be prepared on request. Garden pitches are available. Situated near the end of Segment 3, this is handy camping for WNT hikers. **$**

✖ **WHERE TO EAT AND DRINK** *Map, page 108*

✖ **Rainforest Restaurant** Papillote Wilderness Retreat, Trafalgar; 📞 767 448 2287; ⊕ usually closed Sep & Oct. Papillote consistently serves

excellent Creole & international cuisine in the open-sided Rainforest Restaurant overlooking the gardens (page 114). It is a beautiful & relaxing setting. Try the dasheen puffs! Dinner reservations are essential but you can just turn up for lunch. **$$–$$$**

✗ **Le Petit Paradis** Wotten Waven; ☎767 440 4352; m 767 276 2761; ⏰ daily. This Creole-themed bamboo restaurant serves local lunches & dinners. There is no menu, they cook whatever is fresh in. It is handy for WNT hikers seeking refreshment. Confirm prices & currency before dining. **$$**

✳✗ **River Rock Café & Bar** Trafalgar; ☎767 225 0815. Located close to Trafalgar Falls serving Creole lunches, sandwiches & dinners on a covered veranda overlooking the river valley, River Rock Café is a popular stopping-off point for travellers. In a handy location & panoramic riverside setting,

River Rock is open daily & a great place for all-day food & drink. All the food is good here & the passionfruit rum punch a knockout. Dinner is by reservation only. **$$**

Sunshine Cottage Shawford, Roseau Valley; ☎767 285 6399; e sunshinedca@gmail.com; www.sunshinecottagedominica.com. ❙f❙; ⏰ opening times may vary so call ahead. Enjoy a selection of vegetarian & vegan dishes with wood oven pizzas a speciality. **$$**

✗ **Tia's Bamboo Cottages** Wotten Waven; ☎767 448 1998 or 767 225 4823. At the entrance to Tia's is a rustic, open-sided bamboo & wood restaurant overlooking tropical gardens, forest & hot volcanic pools. The restaurant doesn't really cater for walk-ins so you need to call ahead. **$–$$**

WHAT TO SEE AND DO

VILLAGES OF THE ROSEAU VALLEY Following the 1805 **Battle of Trafalgar** between the British and the French fleets, the estate at the head of the Roseau Valley was named in honour of Nelson's famous victory by the English landowners who had settled there. The estate produced coffee and sugar. Following emancipation in 1838, the liberated slaves established a settlement and grew vegetables and ground provisions, supplying fresh produce to the townspeople of Roseau; this became Trafalgar village. At the head of the valley, above the village, are the famous twin waterfalls, also called Trafalgar (see pages 115–16). Nearby is a hydro-electric plant that uses water that runs down from the Freshwater Lake, via Ti Tou Gorge and the waterfalls. The cascading water and rapids that descend from the falls below the village and along the valley floor eventually become the Roseau River. This river is often a visible measure of how much rain is falling in Dominica's interior. In times of heavy downpours it quickly floods and runs brown with mud. During Tropical Storm Erika in August 2015 the river tore into the land, expanding its banks and flooding low-lying areas. The shanty village of Silver Lake was completely swept away along with riverside dwellings and gardens of Copthall and Bath Estate. If you are on this river or exploring the waterfalls during periods of unsettled weather, you should always take note of conditions. The moment you see forest debris and brown water you should exit and give the area a wide berth. Just because it isn't raining where you are doesn't mean it isn't or hasn't been pouring down in the heights of Dominica's mountaintops.

Trafalgar village is small, steep and mostly residential with a few small bars and snackettes. A favourite with visitors is the River Rock Café on the way to the falls (see above), but you should also check out some of the smaller, local eateries in the village itself. River Rock Cafe's veranda deck has lovely views of the river and next door is a staircase down to the river where there is a great pool. As well as the waterfalls, Trafalgar is home to the delightful **Papillote Gardens** (see overleaf).

The village of **Wotten Waven** is located in the southeastern corner of the Roseau Valley and is (usually) connected to Trafalgar by a road that crosses the River Blanc and the Roseau River (the river crossings were completely destroyed during Tropical Storm Erika in 2015).

Beneath the ground in this area the active volcanic magma layer is believed to be relatively close to the surface, perhaps within 10km, and for this reason escaping gases are still hot when they reach the surface. Ground water, rivers and streams are on the receiving end of these hot gases and innovative locals have tapped these mineral-rich, hot volcanic water sources and created some rather nice spas (see pages 116–18).

At ground level the original estate lands once produced coffee, sugar and ground provisions. Following emancipation, liberated slave workers established a small settlement on the estate and much of the land in the area was sold off. Today it is still a community of farmers but is fast becoming better known for its volcanic spas. Look out for the very quaint **Brenda's Shop** at the junction between Tia's and Screw's. It's a great little place for homemade confectioneries and a cold drink. Wotten Waven has a tourist information centre but it hardly ever seems to be open. If you get lucky, let me know if you discover anything interesting inside!

The village of **Morne Prosper** is perched on the top of a ridge on the southern side of the Roseau Valley. It is known for its farmlands and agricultural produce. You should take a trip up there. The road is a little narrow and winding, but once you eventually get to the top, keep going until you reach the farmlands and then get out of your car and walk. The views all around are lovely. Say hello to the farmers and perhaps even buy some produce. Where you are standing is part of Wai'tukubuli National Trail Segment 3 (pages 229–31), with an optional (and very difficult) route heading off into the foothills of Morne Watt to emerge just above the Valley of Desolation on the Boiling Lake Trail (pages 118–20).

Laudat is Dominica's highest village and came about as a stay-over point when people used to use the Chemin L'Etang track (page 121) to cross the island from east to west and back again. Today it is a very quiet place, rural and mostly engaged in farming. It is also one of the principal gateways to the natural attractions and hiking trails of the Morne Trois Pitons National Park.

CANYONING ❋
For the adventurous and fun-loving, a canyoning trip along a section of the river between Ti Tou Gorge and the Trafalgar Falls is a great way to spend a day. Once you have been shown how to rappel and are fully kitted out, you ease your way down the side of a waterfall at a river section just below Ti Tou Gorge. Once inside, you hike, rappel and jump your way downriver until you reach the exit point. The canyon formations are spectacular, the river pools deep and beautiful. Other routes in this area for more advanced canyoneers are above Ti Tou Gorge, along the Breakfast River and down the Father Falls at Trafalgar, or down the obscure but very pretty Ravine Dejeuner on the Chemin L'Etang trail (page 121). For more on canyoning and canyoning operators, see page 70.

PAPILLOTE GARDENS
First started in 1967, and then substantially repaired following the devastation that was wreaked by Hurricane David in 1979, Papillote is Dominica's best known private tropical garden. It is a 2ha oasis of rainforest plants and flowers, natural hot springs and pools, waterfalls, hummingbirds, butterflies, stick insects and much more; a delight for gardeners, photographers, horticulturalists and botanists. A 60-minute accompanied or self-guided walk takes in a variety of tropical flora including tree ferns, bromeliads, orchids, heliconias, gingers, breadfruit and calabash trees, jade vines and rare aroids. The sparkling river, terraced walkways and rest areas all complement this garden beautifully and make it a must-visit for anyone with a hint of green in their fingers. At the end of your walk, luxuriate in a hot spa, have an outdoor massage, or enjoy some fine local cuisine in the Rainforest Restaurant. Local crafts and souvenirs are available for purchase at the Butterfly Boutique. For details of opening times, fees, restaurant and accommodation go to www.papillote.dm or check out their Facebook page.

TI TOU GORGE Ti Tou Gorge is a very popular attraction, especially during the cruise ship season and at weekends.

Located between the Freshwater Lake and Trafalgar Falls, at the head of the Roseau Valley, there is a deep river gorge. At a point near the village of Laudat, near the start of the main Boiling Lake Trail, a short section of this gorge is accessible to swimmers. Through the narrow cleft in the rock it is possible to swim through the deep, cold water to reach a small waterfall. The name 'Ti Tou' is Creole for 'small throat', a perfect description of the narrow rock funnel through which the river runs from the waterfall to emerge at a small, manmade pool.

Ti Tou Gorge was one of the set locations for the film *Pirates of the Caribbean* and, during the height of the season it may be busy with day visitors swimming up and floating downstream in very colourful buoyancy belts. Tour guides may be leaping from the cliffs above into the deep pools, or ascending the waterfall as part of the show. If you prefer to enjoy the gorge in a little more peace and serenity, it may be wise to come in the late afternoon once the crowds have died down, or early in the morning before they arrive (see page 110 for information on cruise ship days). Ti Tou Gorge is definitely worth a visit, so try not to let the prospect of cruise ship hordes put you off.

See page 50 for bus information from Roseau. Public buses will not take you all the way to the gorge, however. The walk there from the village of Laudat takes around 15–20 minutes and is easy-going.

If you are heading to Ti Tou Gorge by car, take the Valley Road out of Roseau (at the eastern end of King George V Street), taking a left at the forks for Wotten Waven and then Trafalgar, and following the signs to Laudat. Park up just by the wooden bridge and follow the wide track and river crossing.

For the most part, the water inside the Ti Tou Gorge is too deep to stand up in and the walls on each side are smooth and slippery. Around halfway into the gorge there is a short, shallower section and an opportunity to stand and walk a while. It takes around five minutes or so of fairly gentle swimming to reach the waterfall at the end of the gorge though you will be swimming against a weak current. It is deep at the end, but you can work your way around the perimeter to the waterfall. Taking some kind of flotation aid is a great idea and allows weaker swimmers to experience the fun and excitement of passing through this lovely natural formation to see the waterfall. When it is crowded, keep a watchful eye out for people jumping in from above. The water in the gorge is very cold and the waterfall at the end can be quite powerful. Unless equipped with something waterproof, leave cameras behind. Do not swim up the gorge in periods of heavy rainfall. Flash flooding does occur here. If the water is very high and brown with lots of floating debris, do not go.

TRAFALGAR FALLS (*Site pass required*) The Father Falls, with a drop of around 85m, and the Mother Falls, with a drop of around 40m, make up the Trafalgar Falls. As you face them, the Father Falls are on the left-hand side and the Mother Falls on the right. The Father Falls used to cascade down a tall face of smooth rocks alongside a natural hot spring, but in 1996 there was a huge landslide and this unusual hot and cold water cascade was lost. Tropical Storm Erika in August 2015 moved many of the landslide boulders away and so the Father Falls now partially resembles its former state. The waterfall is still quite lovely, however. It has a deep pool and there are warm water pools and springs nearby. The source for the Father Falls is a river that runs from the Freshwater Lake via Ti Tou Gorge in the Morne Trois Pitons National Park.

The Mother Falls are the more accessible of the two waterfalls, though it can still be a very tricky scramble over large and often slippery boulders. Taking its source

Dominica has nine active and dormant volcanoes – one of the highest concentrations in the world. They are: Morne Diablotin, Morne Aux Diables, Morne Trois Pitons, Morne Micotrin, Morne Watt, Morne Anglais, Morne Plat Pays, Grand Soufiere Hills, and Valley of Desolation. Though scientists and seismologists study and monitor them, much of what lies beneath is still relatively unknown. The island has a history of large, explosive eruptions, including the largest in the Caribbean in the last 200,000 years which generated about $58km^3$ of material. It produced pyroclastic (volcanic lava) flow deposits over 200m thick in central Dominica and blanketed nearby Caribbean islands and the Caribbean Sea in ash.

Dominica's volcanic landscape is made up of a series of domes that form a 'spine' down the island. Scientists believe that beneath them is a series of magma chambers that lie at different depths and have different effects on the visible landscape at the surface. At Morne Aux Diables, for example, the fumarole of Cold Soufriere (page 195) is, well, cold, whereas those at Wotten Waven and in the Valley of Desolation are piping hot. This is because the magma chambers in the Morne Trois Pitons National Park are closer to the surface so the hot gases they produce do not have time to cool down.

The main gases that are released from magma chambers are carbon dioxide, sulphates, and hydrogen sulphide, the last being the gas that has the 'rotten eggs' smell. When this gas dissolves in water it becomes a weak hydrosulphuric acid which, although initially clear, develops a cloudy white colour as it reacts with oxygen dissolved in the water. If metal ions are present, the reaction with hydrogen sulphide creates a dark colour.

Despite their appearance, there is no water involved in the creation of fumaroles. They are gas vents rising from the magma chamber and, because the gases are so

from the Morne Trois Pitons River (better known locally as the Breakfast River), which is crossed by hikers on the Boiling Lake Trail (pages 118–20) from Ti Tou Gorge, this thundering waterfall also has a great pool.

The Trafalgar Falls visitor centre has a large car park with souvenir stalls, toilet and changing facilities, snack bar and a display room with examples of flowers and birds that may be seen in the area. It is also the entrance to the waterfall trail and where a forestry officer will ask for site passes. The Trafalgar Falls has a wooden viewing platform just ten minutes or so along an easy trail where you can get photographs of both falls. This area is a rainforest habitat and it is possible to see several species of fern, epiphyte and bromeliad. Look out for large land crabs scrambling for cover as you pass. Certified guides can be hired at the visitor centre to escort you either along the trail to the viewing platform or all the way to the foot of the falls.

HOT SULPHUR SPAS Look around the mouths of these volcanic fumaroles and you may see yellow deposits of precipitated sulphur which some believe provides positive benefits to the body including detoxification of skin cells and as a natural remedy for infection, inflammation and fungal conditions. Hot sulphur springs are also said to assist with skin rehydration, joint and muscle pain, and in replenishing the body with naturally occurring minerals. For these reasons, many also claim sulphur-rich treatments such as hot baths and mud wraps aid in the anti-ageing process.

It is through the creative exploitation of this naturally occurring phenomenon that both Trafalgar and Wotten Waven attract visitors to their hot sulphur hot, they superheat any ground water or streams they come into contact with to create steam. Look around the mouth of fumaroles and you will see the yellowy deposits of precipitated sulphur which some consider effective in the treatment of skin disorders – this is why hot volcanic spas are lauded by wellness therapists.

The road between Wotten Waven and Trafalgar crosses the Roseau River and the smaller River Blanc. From the River Blanc bridge crossing you can see at least two fumaroles. This is where the hot gases have escaped the magma chamber, breached the surface and superheated the river bank, forcing up boiling water and steam. A trek up the River Blanc reveals more fumaroles as well as hot water pools.

The Boiling Lake is an extremely large, deep fumarole. Gases rise from a magma chamber and superheat the ground water, turning it into steam and forcing it up to the surface where it condenses to water and is trapped within a volcanic crater. The lake is also fed by streams and spills out on its eastern lip to form the White River. This activity is largely consistent but there have been episodes when activity has subsided resulting in no steam being forced to the surface and the lake's level settling to that of the surrounding water table, thus 'emptying' the lake. The Boiling Lake is actually at a higher level than the surrounding water table thanks to the superheated steam that forces it up, and so when it empties due to rare lulls in volcanic activity, the water is simply finding its natural level. The last time this happened, as the lake was refilling, the water was actually cold and took around two years to get back to normal temperature.

Tropical Storm Erika in August 2015 caused some minor damage to the Boiling Lake. The lip where it spills out to form the White River was reduced in height, resulting in the lake being around 1m lower than before the storm. For a detailed description of the Boiling Lake Trail, see pages 118–20.

spas, which combine the beauty of their natural surroundings with relaxation, rejuvenation, and of course, great fun. Take an after-hours soak under the stars in a hot sulphur pool, watching the steam rise against the moon and stars above, accompanied by the music of the river and the songs of the tree frogs, and it is easy to appreciate the attraction and natural mystique of this area.

Most – but not all – sulphur spas have an entry charge of US$10 for non-residents.

Bongo Baths Wotten Waven; ☏ 767 295 2233. Unfinished at the time of writing, this hot spa appears to be by prior reservation only (this may change, of course). You will find it on the right-hand side of the road to Wotten Waven, just before you get to the village.

Da-Scape Hot Sulphur Spa Wotten Waven; ☏ 767 616 6800; da-scape@da-scape.com or da-scape@gmail.com; ⓕ. Located just off the link road between Wotten Waven & Trafalgar, Da-Scape is one of the Roseau Valley's latest hot spa offerings. It has 3 small outdoor & 2 indoor hot pools, changing room & toilet facilities.

Papillote Wilderness Retreat Trafalgar; ☏ 767 448 2287; e papillote@cwdom.dm; www.

papillote.dm. Papillote is well known for its immaculate & mature tropical gardens where you will also find several hot volcanic pools & waterfalls. The pools are small & intimate & the surrounding gardens lush & exotic. It's a lovely setting. Massage & yoga are also offered. Facilities include changing & wash rooms, bar & restaurant, & accommodation (page 114).

Screw's Sulphur Spa Wotten Waven; ☏ 767 440 4478. Reflecting the owner's unfaltering creative & artistic ambition, Screw's has transitioned from a very simple & natural hot volcanic spa to something resembling a theme park. With several large pools, hot & cold water cascades & an elevated water slide, it is very popular & often rather crowded with cruise ship visitors during the high season. Without doubt an extremely ambitious & laudable achievement, unfortunately the steel fence, locked gate, rather unwelcoming staff, & higher entry price (double that of other spas in the area) mean that it has lost some of its original natural simplicity & charm. But you should make up your own mind about Screw's. It is without question unique & you may well love the place. Facilities & services include changing rooms, washroom, food & drink.

✳ **Ti Kwen Glo Cho** Wotten Waven; 📞767 440 3162. Set in wonderfully natural garden surroundings, 2 hot pools & a series of very original bamboo shower-filled bathtubs are all great places to soak. There's a waterfall, a volcanic mud pool,

changing facilities & a rustic wooden bar serving refreshments. Owners & hosts Henry & June are relaxed, friendly & welcoming. You can also camp here when it isn't too wet.

Tia's Bamboo Cottages Wotten Waven; 📞767 448 1998 or 767 225 4823; e tiacottages@gmail. com; www.tiasbamboocottages.com. At the foot of lush & well-tended tropical gardens, Tia has created 3 delightful hot pools alongside the river. 2 additional pools are set within bamboo cabanas for those who would prefer not to share with others, one of which is very accessible by wheelchair. Facilities include changing area, washroom, restaurant & bar, & rustic bamboo cottages.

HIKES

THE BOILING LAKE (FROM TI TOU GORGE) ✳ (*Site pass required. Difficulty: T: 3; R: 2; E: 3; D: 4; Rating = 7.5; Guide strongly recommended*) Dominica's Boiling Lake is considered to be the second-largest of its kind in the world (the largest is Frying Pan Lake and the connected Inferno Crater Lake in the Waimangu Volcanic Rift Valley on the North Island of New Zealand).

It is an extremely large and deep fumarole whose gases rise from a magma chamber and superheat the ground water turning it into steam and forcing it up to the surface where it condenses to water and is trapped within a volcanic crater (see box, pages 116–17).

Though Amerindians no doubt came across it earlier, the first recorded sighting of the Boiling Lake was in 1870, when a magistrate from the east-coast village of La Plaine, Mr Edmund Watt, attempted to find an alternative route across the interior of the island. After several days spent in the depths of the forest he finally arrived at the village of Laudat and reported sighting a boiling volcanic crater. Mr Watt was later accompanied by Dr H A A Nicholls and a number of porters and bush cutters to the location of his sighting, along the same route that the main hiking trail follows today. The mountains of Morne Watt and Morne Nicholls bear the names of the two men.

The Nicholls–Watt route, the primary trail that is used to access the lake today, begins at Ti Tou Gorge and climbs up to Morne Nicholls before descending into the Valley of Desolation and then to the lake itself. The Valley of Desolation is one of Dominica's active volcanoes and is a wide valley, or caldera, containing hot streams, bubbling mud and violent steam vents. Touch the ground in some places and it is hot. The fumarole vegetation in the valley consists of lichens, mosses, bromeliads and *kaklen* (*Clusia mangle*). Subjected as they are to sulphurous gases and a heady concoction of heat and chemistry, the rocks of the valley are painted in whites, browns, yellows and oranges. The trailhead for this hike is located at Ti Tou Gorge.

The Boiling Lake Trail has changed considerably over the years and continues to do so, indeed Tropical Storm Erika reshaped it yet again, making some stretches a little more precarious than before. Nevertheless the trail is easier than the tough, muddy scramble it once was, along a very roughly hewn track with large steps made of mud and ropes to pull you up and help you down. Today the path is much improved and far more accessible to a broader range of hikers, though it is not without its challenges and at least 2 hours of walking there, and the same back (sometimes more), with several steep ascents and descents, mean this trail can still take its toll and should not be taken lightly. The passage through the Valley of Desolation is much as it used to be: tricky, rough and, if you are not paying attention, quite difficult to follow. Straying from the beaten path here can result in serious injury and should be avoided if you are not with an experienced guide. I recommend a guide on this trail (see pages 76–7 for some suggestions or ask at your hotel). Avoid engaging one of the men you may see at the Laudat village junction; they are usually not trained, certified nor especially reliable. They can also be rather aggressive in their pursuit of business.

There is a concrete road and refreshments building at Ti Tou Gorge – built to cater for cruise ship visitors visiting the gorge rather than Boiling Lake hikers. Look for the stone steps to the right of the wooden shelter at the edge of Ti Tou Gorge and follow the path up into the forest. These steps are usually slippery even when it isn't wet; remember them when you return as many tired hikers end up on their backsides just here; so happy to have made it back, they forget how slippery these steps are. The first section of the trail is wide and fairly easy-going for the first hour, climbing gently and making its way deeper into the rainforest. You will see lots of examples of magnificent rainforest trees such as the gommier and the buttress-rooted chatanier. Listen out for the unmistakable call of the mountain whistler (page 8) as you get deeper into the interior. After an hour or so, you will descend sharply down to the Breakfast River, completing the first third of the walk to the lake. Often at this point you begin to detect the unmistakeable aroma of sulphur dioxide. You are getting closer to volcano country.

It is better not to dwell for long at the Breakfast River for there are always plenty of troublesome mosquitoes around here and your challenge is hard enough as it is. Find a route across the river and take care crossing – it was affected by Tropical Storm Erika, but does not present much of a problem. The temptation always is to keep feet and shoes dry but I guarantee that on the return leg you will just walk right through it, your shoes muddy and sodden from the journey, so why not just get it over with now? As you are facing the Breakfast River you may be interested to know that if you follow it to your right, downstream, you will end up at the top of the Mother Falls at Trafalgar (I don't recommend trying this as it is extremely dangerous) and there are a number of waterfalls along the way (if you fancy this adventure, contact one of the canyoning operators on page 70).

Once on the other side of the river, the trail gets tougher as it climbs steeply to the top of Morne Nicholls. The route up is often a good place to listen and look out for jaco parrots. After about 45–60 minutes you will reach the top of the mountain and find yourself in a circular clearing where, on a bright day, you can enjoy spectacular views across the Morne Trois Pitons National Park. To the west is Roseau and the Caribbean, to the north Morne Micotrin and behind it Morne Trois Pitons itself. To the east is the ridge of the Grande Soufriere Hills and beyond it the Atlantic Ocean, and to the south is the foreboding peak of Morne Watt (there is no trail to the top of this one). If you look to the east you should also spot the steam rising from the Valley of Desolation and the Boiling Lake.

At the top of Morne Nicholls you are about halfway to the lake and at the highest point of the hike. From here you must negotiate a long series of steep steps that descend into the Valley of Desolation. Be careful, these steps are really slippery and often waterlogged or broken. The descent is in sections, the final one being more of a climb into one of the rivers that runs through the valley. This is a tricky section; ease your way down the rocky river slope – on your backside if necessary – until you are able to pick up the trail again on the other side. At the time of writing, this was a high, narrow shelf that gave the impression it would give way at any time – perhaps it will have done by the time you read this – so take care on this stretch. It is more of a mental than a physical challenge and if you do find it too much, the alternative is to negotiate yourself down to the bottom of the river cascade and enter the valley that way. Follow the advice and lead of your guide if you have one.

Once in the valley the trail isn't obvious at all – unless there are other hikers ahead of you – and it's even trickier to figure out on the return leg, but it is there, meandering across the rocks alongside the stream, the fumaroles and the hot bubbling pools, and exiting at the far side along the river. If you have chosen to do this hike without a guide, now is a good time to look back at where you have just come from so you can remember it on the return journey.

At the end of this first section of the Valley of Desolation the trail follows the river then crosses it to the right where it becomes a narrow path. Along the way you will see small cascades of water and hot pools down to your left. This is where you could choose to bathe on the return leg of your hike. It is worth it. Follow the river and cross again until you reach a short but steep scramble up and over a rock face followed by an undulating hike through the forest with further river crossings – one with a steep climb down. After 30–45 minutes or so, the trail enters the second part of the Valley of Desolation. Take care as you enter; the trail is high and narrow. Follow the track as it winds around the left-hand side to the river. Cross over it carefully and then start climbing up the steep, rocky ridge ahead of you. Once at the top, take a breather and smile – you just have a few minutes to go. Follow the clear trail to the lake.

THE BOERI LAKE (*Site pass required. Difficulty: T: 2; R: 1; E: 2; D: 1; Rating = 3.8; Guide not essential*) At an elevation of 853m and with a surface of 2ha, the Boeri Lake is the highest mountain lake on the island. It is a crater lake located between Morne Micotrin and Morne Trois Pitons. The lake is thought to be around 40m deep and is fairly devoid of subsurface vegetation or life. Surrounded by large boulders and upper montane thicket, overlooked by the cloud-covered summit of Morne Micotrin, and with the only sound coming from the mountain whistler (rufous-throated solitaire), the lake is exquisitely serene.

Beyond the lake, to the west, there are two much smaller lakes. Without a guide and a sharp machete you should consider them inaccessible. From these two lakes, however, the river eventually makes it to the Middleham Falls (page 123).

To get to the Boeri Lake, follow the same directions to the Freshwater Lake (above), but turn left at the fork instead of right. The Boeri Lake trailhead is at the end of the road.

Follow the clearly marked trail uphill for around 30 minutes until the wooden steps give way to a path of rocks and boulders. Before reaching this point, if the weather is clear, there should be fine views across to the Freshwater Lake in the south and the village of Grand Fond in the east. Head down the hill and then take great care over the rocky path; this walk is often very wet underfoot and these stones can be quite slippery. Cross over the narrow and shallow Clarke's River and then two more streams including an outlet for the Boeri Lake itself. Negotiate a further rocky path that leads right up to the lake. You will come to a fork; to the right is the lake, and straight ahead the remains of a wooden viewing platform. You now find yourself in a crater between Morne Micotrin, which is above and beyond

above left Fairtrade bananas — Dominica's banana trade has faced severe difficulties in recent years (PC) pages 19–20

above right *Crab back*, a traditional Creole dish made with black crab (CS) page 55

right Fresh fruits, vegetables and ground provisions are grown islandwide (CS) pages 6–7

below Fishermen at Fond St Jean — every coastal village has a community of fishermen (PC) page 20

above   The annual World Creole Music Festival takes place during the last week of October (PD) page 59

left   Dominica's Rastafarians are proud of their African heritage and live in harmony with nature (PC) page 23

below   Traditional Creole *bélé* dancing (CS) page 25

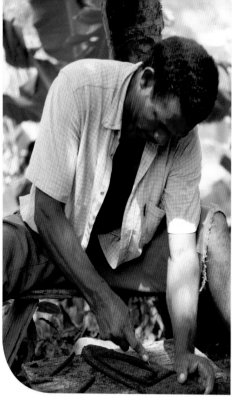

above   Kalinago craft includes masks carved from giant tree ferns (*Cyathea arborea*) (both PC) page 154

right   Master Kalinago canoe builder, Merlin Stoute (PC) page 149

below   Basketware is made from the *larouma* reed (*Ischosiphon arouma*) in the Kalinago Territory (PC) page 155

above left   The *bwa kwaib* (*Sabinea carinalis*) is Dominica's national flower (PC) page 6

above right   The sisserou (*Amazona imperialis*), Dominica's national bird (SS) page 7

far left   Purple-throated Carib (*Eulampis jugularis*), one of four hummingbirds recorded in Dominica (CS) page 7

left   Torch ginger (CS) page 6

below left   75 species of orchid have been recorded in Dominica (PC) page 6

below   The boa constrictor (*Constrictor nebulosa*), or *tête chien* (PC) page 9

above — The hawksbill turtle (*Eretmochelys imbriocota*) is the most common of the four turtle species observed in the waters around Dominica (OL/D) page 12

right — The longlure frogfish (*Antennarius multiocellatus*) is one of the more unusual fish species found around Dominica (S/D) page 11

below — The longsnout seahorse (*Hippocampus reidi*) (OP/FLPA) page 11

below right — Sperm whales (*Physeter macrocephallus*) can be seen all year round (AM) page 12

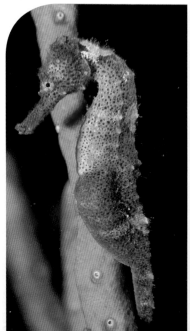

above left   Scuba diving in the Soufriere Scotts Head Marine Reserve (DS/S) page 133

above right   Canyoning beyond Ti Tou Gorge — the waterfalls, pools and rock formations in the canyons are quite breathtaking (ED) page 70

left   Tubing on the Layou River — sit yourself in a large inflatable tube, shoot gentle rapids, and drift sedately along a river through Dominica's beautiful forest (PC) page 78

below   Hiking through primary rainforest on segment 8 of the Wai'tukubuli National Trail (PC) pages 240–2

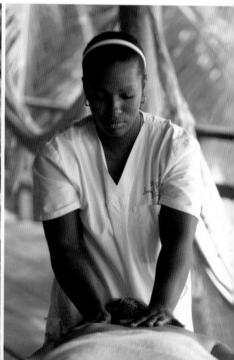

Discover the Caribbean.
The *Slow* way.

It's been said that if Columbus could explore the Caribbean again today, Dominica is the only island he'd still recognise. And now you can discover the Caribbean's 'nature island' walking through its lush and exotic landscape on a *Slow Holiday* with Inntravel.

Inntravel.co.uk
The *Slow Holiday* people

AITO assured · ABTA Travel with confidence

below Take a short drive from the capital to see the waterfalls, rivers and hot volcanic springs of the Roseau Valley (PC) pages 107–27

the ridge behind you, and Morne Trois Pitons, which is above and beyond the ridge in front. You can almost hear a pin drop, it is so still. Take a swim to cool off; the water is refreshing, but very cold, and more than a little eerie.

CHEMIN L'ETANG *(Difficulty: T: 2; R: 0; E: 2; D: 2; Rating = 3.8; Guide not essential)*
The Chemin L'Etang trail is thought to have originally been used by Amerindians to cross the island and was later used by villagers from east and west before roads were constructed. Together with rough sea routes, this path was once an important method of cross-island transportation for people and their produce. Meaning 'lake road', the trail passes the Freshwater Lake in what is now the Morne Trois Pitons National Park at an elevation of 762m. Originally people would have walked from the mouth of the Rosalie River up to the lake, then down the Roseau Valley to the capital, and vice versa. The village of Laudat was created by people needing to overnight on the journey. Thanks to road access, today's Chemin L'Etang trail is considerably shorter and more forgiving than that, with one end at the village of Grand Fond and the other at the Freshwater Lake itself.

The hike is very scenic with great views of the interior and the Atlantic coastline. At each end of the hike there is an interesting and beautiful natural feature. At the western end of the trail is the exquisite serenity of the 4ha Freshwater Lake. At the eastern end of the trail, at the top of the village of Grand Fond, is a short but steep trail down to the Dernier Falls (pages 168–9).

The trailhead at the Freshwater Lake end is just off the Freshwater Lake circular trail (pages 122–3). Enter the trail from the road that runs to the Boeri Lake trailhead and follow it for about ten minutes. You will come to a trail junction; straight on is the Freshwater Lake Trail, left is Chemin L'Etang. The trailhead at Grand Fond is right at the end of the paved road at the top of the village. Follow the wide track to the right of the building and then right again as it transitions to rough vehicle track.

Between 30 and 45 minutes from the Freshwater Lake you will come across a tall cascading waterfall. This is Ravine Dejeuner. The cascade has three small pools that are often teeming with crayfish. A little beyond this point heading towards Grand Fond, look down below the river crossing and see it form another tall waterfall that tumbles down into the valley. Be careful near the edge.

Just over an hour or so from the Freshwater Lake you will come across large boulders on the path. This is the beginning of a rather tricky section. The boulders are from a previous landslide and have settled. There's a fairly obvious route over them, but this is often obscured by vegetation so finding a solid place to put your feet isn't easy. Negotiate these rocks and boulders carefully for the next 20 minutes or so. After that, the trail is fairly clear again.

Eventually the narrow forest trail spills out into a river. This is a tributary of the Stuart's River and there was a small bridge before Tropical Storm Erika. Perhaps it has been rebuilt. If not, head downhill to your left and look across the river to your right where you'll see a wider track. Cross the river and head up the trail. It is now easy going all the way to Grand Fond, which you'll reach in approximately another 20 minutes.

If you wish to continue to the Dernier Falls, follow the paved road for about ten minutes until you see the sign. The trailhead is off to the right.

You can do this as a there-and-back hike but remember that the way back to the Freshwater Lake is uphill and a bit of a slog. I would suggest saving your energy for the Dernier Falls and then finding transportation – either catch a bus or hitch a ride – down to the main east-coast road at Rosalie.

THE FRESHWATER LAKE CIRCULAR HIKE ✳ (*Site pass required. Difficulty: T: 2; R: 0; E: 3; D: 1; Rating = 3.8; Guide not essential*) The Freshwater Lake is located in a valley between Morne Micotrin and Morne Nicholls, and from the heights of its perimeter trail you can also see Morne Trois Pitons, Morne Watt, Morne John and Morne Anglais. It has a surface area of approximately 4ha and is at an elevation of 762m above sea level. This area receives some of Dominica's highest rainfall, almost 900cm a year, making it just about the wettest place on the island. It is often cloaked in cloud and can be subject to strong easterly winds. Sometimes it feels more like Scotland than the Caribbean. Due to the weather it receives and its location, the area around the lake is a combination of upper montane and cloudforest. The vegetation is fairly low-growing, consisting of ferns, mosses, *kaklen* (*Clusia mangle*) and mountain palms. Bromeliads, colourful gingers, heliconias and orchids can also be found growing around the lake trail. Aside from a mythical monster, living in the lake are tilapia, a tropical freshwater fish species belonging to the cichlid family that were introduced some time ago. Although not blessed with an abundance of clear and sunny days (though when they do come, this place is stunning), the serenity of the Freshwater Lake and the natural beauty of the volcanic peaks and unspoilt environment all around are breathtaking. As they are located so close to each other, it is also a nice idea to combine a hike around the Freshwater Lake with the Boeri Lake, if you have the time and energy.

The Freshwater Lake is located beyond the village of Laudat, and within the Morne Trois Pitons National Park. (See page 50 for bus information.) Please note, public buses will not go beyond Laudat to the lake. You must either pay extra if the driver agrees to go the extra distance, take a taxi, hitch a ride, or walk. The walk from the junction to the lake is about 30–45 minutes along a paved road. It has great views on a clear day though so it's not that bad!

By car, follow the Boeri Lake directions (pages 120–1) and at the signposted fork take a right to the Freshwater Lake visitor car park.

I think the best way to do this hike is in an anticlockwise direction. This means that you descend rather than ascend the steepest parts. It also works best if you wish to go on to the Boeri Lake.

The trailhead is beyond the visitor building and across the dam wall. It is a clear path that winds its way around the lake and up and down the peaks and ridges along the way. From the top of these ridges there are nice views of the lake and the village of Grand Fond, with Rosalie Bay and the Atlantic Ocean beyond it to the east. On a clear day it is also possible to see the island of Marie-Galante further to the northeast.

You will make a gradual ascent to the top of a ridge from where you can enjoy the views. Further around the loop you will find yourself on the top of a sharp peak where there is a bench to have a rest. The climb down this peak is very steep, but thankfully the steps are mostly made of tree fern rather than wooden logs. Again, take your time and take in the awesome views across the interior. In front of you is Morne Micotrin and a little to the right, beyond it, is Morne Trois Pitons. To the left you will see two prominent volcanoes: Morne Anglais to the west facing the Caribbean, and Morne Watt a little further to the east. Whenever you see Morne Watt, think Valley of Desolation and Boiling Lake – they are located to the northeast of this volcano.

Descend to a flat ridge and then climb up to the next peak. You will come to a small circular clearing with a rough trail heading down to the east. This is the Chemin L'Etang trail to the village of Grand Fond. Straight ahead is the continuation of the loop trail and to the left is the Freshwater Lake itself. You will emerge on the paved road that links the Freshwater Lake to the Boeri Lake. To the right is the Boeri Lake trailhead and to the left is the Freshwater Lake and car park.

At the visitor centre you can get drinks and good food. You can also rent kayaks.

MIDDLEHAM FALLS (*Site pass required. Difficulty: T: 2; R: 1; E: 2; D: 1; Rating = 3.8; Guide not essential*) When plans were being developed to create the Morne Trois Pitons National Park in the 1970s, the then owner of the Middleham Estate, Mr John Archbold, an American millionaire, donated the land in its entirety to the World Wildlife Fund in an effort to encourage the formation of the park. The estate covered in excess of 400ha and was transferred to the government of Dominica when the national park was created in 1975. The rainforest vegetation in this area includes fine specimens of the buttress-rooted *chatanier* tree, *gommiers*, tree ferns, epiphytes and bromeliads. Jaco parrots, one of two endemic Amazonians, also inhabit this region and are frequently heard if not actually sighted.

The main trail to the waterfall actually runs all the way between the villages of Cochrane and Laudat, and the WNT now also connects the Middleham Falls with Pont Cassé and Sylvania. The most common route used by visitors is the trail from Laudat, which is fairly easy and takes around an hour each way. This route is also part of the Wai'tukubuli National Trail Segment 4. The trail from Cochrane is less frequently used though it is a little less steep and passes through very undisturbed areas of rainforest. This route takes a little more than an hour each way and runs past Tou Santi or 'Stinky Hole', a natural volcanic rock fissure that is home to bats. The stench of their droppings gives the place its name. Both routes require small river and stream crossings (the route from Cochrane more so) and they converge at a junction just above the waterfall. The last section of the trail to the falls is steeper. The pool at the bottom is very deep and well worth the scramble down for a refreshing dip. Be careful getting in and out. This waterfall changes quite noticeably between seasons. When it is dry, the falls are narrow and the pool tranquil and pleasant. In the height of the wet season the waterfall is full and thunderous, throwing out vast clouds of spray and making access to the pool almost impossible.

The trailhead from the Laudat side is well signposted, particularly as it also forms part of the Wai'tukubuli National Trail. You will see the signs on the left, just before you reach Laudat. Turn off and follow the narrow road until you come to the end. There is a small parking area and a changing facility (with lots of mosquitoes so don't hang around here for too long).

For the Cochrane trailhead, follow the road next to the Old Mill Cultural Centre in Canefield, just off the west-coast highway, and keep going until you reach Cochrane. Drive up the very steep road all the way through and to the top of the village. At the junction, turn right, and then left. Follow the road until you come to a second junction where you turn left again. Keep going until you reach the end of the road when there is a small area to park up.

See page 50 for information on where to catch public buses to Cochrane and Laudat from Roseau. Please note that Cochrane buses do not run very often and will only take you to the village itself. From there, you must walk.

Middleham Falls from Laudat

Follow the clear path through the forest and across the shallow river. The trail works its way gradually uphill and though it is steep in places, it does not become particularly severe. After about 30–45 minutes (a bit longer if you are puffing and wheezing) you will reach a signposted junction. Straight ahead leads to the village of Cochrane, the right-hand track is the continuation of Segment 4 of the Wai'tukubuli National Trail (this leads to Sylvania and Pont Cassé), and to the left is the route down to the waterfall.

From this point the trail heads downhill via a series of switchbacks and then comes to a wooden staircase. At the bottom, be careful crossing over slippery rocks and streams, especially in the wet, and look out for a point where the trail passes over a boulder on your right. You should be able to see the viewing platform and waterfall from this point. Clamber over the boulder and make your way along the path and then around to the wooden platform. It's fun to head down to the pools to bathe, but be careful negotiating the rocks and boulders; some can be rather sharp. And be warned: the water is extremely cold!

Middleham Falls from Cochrane
This is a nice alternative to the more oft trodden route from Laudat. The trail is a little more unkempt, but good enough, and the forest dense, lush and tranquil. You will often hear jaco parrots, you may even see agouti, and Tou Santi (see below) offers the promise of bats.

Getting to the trailhead can be a little tricky. At the time of writing, the road (a narrow feeder road) was rather rough and you certainly needed a 4x4. Drive to the very top of Cochrane village and you come to a junction; head right and then left at the next junction. Stick to the main road from here and you should find the trailhead OK (it's where the road comes to an end). From the trailhead, follow the path down into the forest. This route involves crossing a number of small rivers. They are fairly straightforward challenges, but the climb down and then up the riverbanks, as well as negotiating slippery rocks and boulders, can be challenging if you are not used to this kind of terrain. These rivers, though small, are scenic, with cascades and pools.

Twenty minutes or so into the trail is **Tou Santi** or 'Stinky Hole'. Should bats be a subject of interest to you, this is an interesting place to be at dusk when they emerge from the cave in a dense cloud and fly out into the forest. Please don't try to climb down into Stinky Hole for a better look; in my opinion there are more interesting things to see and do on this island, and most of them smell a little better.

After around an hour of gently undulating trail, interrupted only by more those river gullies, you should reach a signposted junction. Straight ahead is the route to Laudat (another 45 minutes or so), to the left is part of Segment 4 of the Wai'tukubuli National Trail to Pont Cassé and Sylvania, and to the right is the trail down to the waterfall (see directions above).

MORNE MICOTRIN
(*Difficulty: T: 3H; R: 0; E: 4; D: 3; Rating = 6.3H; Guide highly recommended, though few know it*) At 1,221m Morne Micotrin is Dominica's fourth-highest mountain after Morne Diablotin, Morne Trois Pitons and Morne Watt (which is inaccessible to hikers). It is located very close to and immediately south of Morne Trois Pitons. Morne Micotrin is also known as Morne Macaque which is a very confusing name as there are no monkeys on Dominica. Perhaps there once were; introduced in a similar way to the mona monkey (*Ceropithecus mona*), also known as macaque, which can still be found in the elevated interior of Grenada, though no records exist to support this notion. It has also been suggested that the mountain is so named because you have to be able to climb like a monkey to reach the top. Well, if you take it on, you will see for yourself. I have actually walked behind friends who were making the entire descent on their backsides, so perhaps there is something to it.

The climb is undoubtedly steep and, technically as well as physically, challenging. There are some large boulders to negotiate but the real effort is in avoiding concealed holes. Micotrin is a volcano that collapsed in on itself and there are places where rocks and boulders that fell together left gaps between them. These deep holes are often masked by grass and other foliage, so it is absolutely paramount that when you are hiking the upper section of the mountain you pay attention to this fact. Though steep and certainly demanding, it is more a technical and mental challenge to get up and down this mountain. No twisted or broken ankles please; you have to really watch out for this.

Despite this hazard, Morne Micotrin is a great mountain to climb. Unlike the others, it is very open, especially towards the top, where rocky crags and ferns make the terrain seem more like the highlands of Scotland than the tropics. There are two peaks; one higher than the other. Both have communications masts at their summit and the views are excellent on a clear day.

To get to the trailhead, follow the same directions to the Freshwater Lake (pages 122–3) but look out for a ladder on your left-hand side, propped against the steep embankment, halfway between the steel bridge and the road junction that separates the Freshwater Lake from the Boeri Lake trailhead.

At the top of the ladder, the track goes immediately to your left and then you will find a fairly wide path ahead of you. The terrain here is a little tricky; lots of loose rocks, so be careful with your footing. The first hour or so is simply a straight uphill slog and there are not many views through the trees. After that it becomes more interesting. You are rewarded with wonderful vistas, including a bird's-eye view of the Freshwater Lake. From now on the climb is much more open, there are some large boulders to negotiate, and you have to look out for those troublesome holes. It is more a climb than a hike at this point, but the open surroundings more than make up for your growing tiredness and paranoia about slipping down a dark fissure, never to be seen again.

MORNE PROSPER TO MORNE NICHOLLS

When they were creating the Wai'tukubuli National Trail, the project team had the rather nice idea of opening up an old, abandoned route to Morne Nicholls from the farming village of Morne Prosper. If you are hiking Segment 3, just beyond the Morne Prosper farmlands you will see a sign offering you this option. My recommendation is to ignore it, pretend you never saw it, and simply head down the hill to Wotten Waven, a cold beer and a hot volcanic spa.

The old track passes through the forests and along the slopes of Morne Watt (and if you spot it, there's a small lake on the Du Mas Estate) before arriving at a long and arduous section of steep, muddy ridges and gullies that erode and wash away in the heavy rains this part of the interior receives. The last time I hiked here I was fairly convinced I would never be able to climb back out of one of them, so muddy, steep and slippery was it. When I did finally emerge on the main Boiling Lake Trail and bumped into a group of hikers, it must have looked like I had been lost in the forest for months. This trail is no longer maintained (the WNT team have enough to do with the main trail) and there is a real risk that you could get yourself stuck, lost or both.

As pretty as the forest section is (and it really is), this trail simply isn't worth it right now. If you do actually make it to Morne Nicholls, it will have taken you around 3 rather exhausting hours; then it's another 2 to the Boiling Lake, and then another 3 or 4 back to Laudat.

If you are absolutely determined to try it, however, please make sure you tell someone where you are going.

You will eventually reach a junction, though you may not notice it as it is often very overgrown. At the junction, the trail to the left goes to the lower peak and is usually very overgrown; the trail straight on goes to the higher peak. Both will take about a further 20 minutes. The terrain continues to be challenging and the trail hard to follow, so please take care and take regular note of your route.

When you reach the summit you will come to a junk yard. Yes, really. It is the debris left behind from communications people and lightning strikes and it really needs a good clean up. But, hey, who is going to pay for that? So here it will probably remain. Do not attempt to climb the masts nor any of the structures, they are rusty and dangerous. I prefer to pick a spot a little further down from the peak and embrace the absolute stillness and serenity of it all.

MORNE TROIS PITONS (*Site pass required. Difficulty T: 4H; R: 0; E: 4; D: 3; Rating = 6.9H; Guide strongly recommended*) At 1,342m, Morne Trois Pitons is the second-tallest mountain on Dominica. Named after its three-peaked summit, this magnificent volcano dominates the southern landscape and includes three main vegetation types: rainforest, montane thicket and cloudforest, or elfin woodland (see page 5). It is also possible to see all four species of endemic hummingbird on this hike (see page 7), especially as you get closer to the summit.

It is a strenuous climb to the first summit of Morne Trois Pitons, but great fun and really worth the effort if the weather is good and the skies clear. It is possible to continue to the middle summit (add at least another two hours to the hike), though not recommended at all. The trail from the first peak is in very poor shape and quite treacherous. It is not a place to become stuck or indeed lost. Satisfy yourself with your achievement to reach and enjoy the awesome views from the rocky crag of the first piton.

The trail itself is clear and very easy to follow. In a couple of places towards the summit it is steep and the ascent involves climbing up and over rocks, tree roots and branches. Many of the steps you have to climb are round wooden logs rather than the tree-fern trunks which offer greater traction. These wooden logs are slippery, especially in the wet, and on descent. There are also three places where you have to scale short but steep slopes using ropes. All of these factors, plus some not insignificant trail erosion from Tropical Storm Erika, combine to give the terrain its hazard rating. One or two sections are quite precipitous so vertigo sufferers may wish to think carefully before taking on this hike. A clear day makes for the best views, of course, so check the weather before starting out. Regardless of the forecast, it is always a good idea to carry a light waterproof to protect you from the elements. Depending on conditions, the summits of Dominica's mountains can sometimes be very cold places.

The trailhead is located a short distance along the road from Pont Cassé to Castle Bruce and Rosalie. From the Pont Cassé roundabout, look for a sign on the right-hand side of the road.

The first 15 minutes of the hike is a steady ascent through rainforest. After that the climb becomes much more severe and you have to cope with what are often very slippery wooden steps, so be careful. After around 45–60 minutes there is a tricky little traverse across a narrow rock followed by more steep steps and rock scrambles.

About halfway up you will notice that the environment transitions from montane thicket to elfin woodland, and you are rewarded with your first clear sight of the summit. There are also magnificent 180° views of the west, north and east. To the west, you can see the ridge of Warner and beyond it the Caribbean Sea. Directly to the north is the cloud-covered summit of Morne Diablotin, Dominica's highest peak. On a clear day you can even see as far as the island of Guadeloupe. Down below and in front of you is the roundabout of Pont Cassé, the Layou Valley, Bells and the particularly pointed summit of Morne Laurent (also known as Morne Negres Mawon after the Maroon camp that was once there), which is located on the fringes of the Central Forest Reserve.

Your next challenge is to negotiate three quite short though very steep and slippery rock faces. Use the ropes and take your time. These rocks have very few good foot holes and they are often running with water, so take care. Tree roots on either side can help, but check that they are secure before trusting them with your weight.

Once you have successfully negotiated these rock faces in one piece, the final stretch is a tough but fun climb through *kaklen* (*Clusia mangle*) trees. Take it very slowly and test each branch before risking your full weight. The trick here is careful and thoughtful movement rather than a rush to get through it. Part of this last section is very steep, sodden and muddy. It deserves your full attention. Your reward is the view, which is fantastic along this stretch.

You should get to the summit in around 2½–3 hours. It is a crag of moss-and-*kaklen* covered rocks. Hopefully the skies are clear for you. If not, be patient and wait for a window to appear in the clouds. Break out your picnic and enjoy being where you are.

Roseau Valley and Morne Trois Pitons National Park HIKES

5

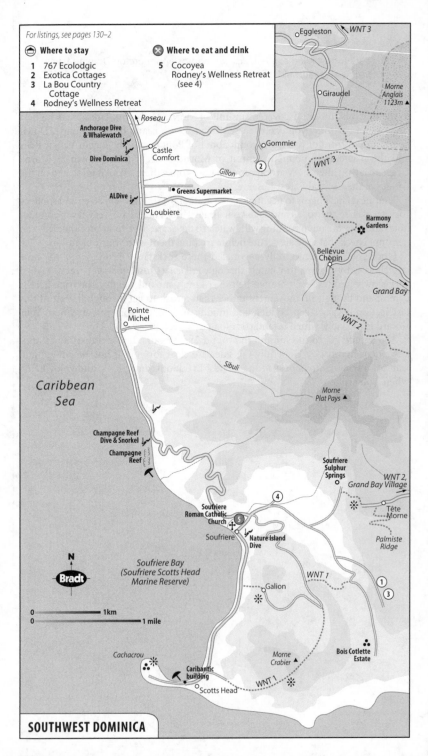

For listings, see pages 130–2

Where to stay
1 767 Ecolodgic
2 Exotica Cottages
3 La Bou Country Cottage
4 Rodney's Wellness Retreat

Where to eat and drink
5 Cocoyea
Rodney's Wellness Retreat (see 4)

Eggleston

WNT 3

Giraudel

Morne Anglais 1123m ▲

Roseau

Anchorage Dive & Whalewatch

Gommier

Castle Comfort

Dive Dominica

Gillon

WNT 3

2

ALDive

Greens Supermarket

Loubiere

Harmony Gardens

Bellevue Chopin

Grand Bay

Pointe Michel

WNT 2

Caribbean Sea

Sibuli

Morne Plat Pays ▲

Champagne Reef Dive & Snorkel

Champagne Reef

Soufriere Sulphur Springs

WNT 2, Grand Bay Village

4

Tête Morne

Soufriere Roman Catholic Church

5

Palmiste Ridge

Soufriere

Nature Island Dive

1

3

N

Bradt

Soufriere Bay (Soufriere Scotts Head Marine Reserve)

Galion

WNT 1

0 — 1km
0 — 1 mile

Cachacrou

Morne Crabier ▲

Bois Cotlette Estate

Caribantic building

Scotts Head

WNT 1

SOUTHWEST DOMINICA

6

The South

When Tropical Storm Erika dropped around 30cm of rain in 12 hours in August 2015, it was the south of Dominica that suffered the most. The steep slopes of the Foundland volcano lost their grip and slid down in deadly waves of mud and boulders the size of vehicles into the surrounding communities, and its rivers became unimaginable torrents ripping away the landscape. Homes, businesses and lives were lost.

The worst hit were the communities of Petite Savanne and Dubique, both of which were eventually evacuated. The road beyond Bagatelle was torn away and buried along with much of Petite Savanne, and the countless giant landslide scars that were left on the mountainside serve as visible reminders of the storm.

This chapter will explore the south, from Loubiere on the west coast, around to Stowe and Bagatelle on the southern coastline. But it will stop there. It may well be that, in the months and years after this edition of the guide is published, things change for the better on the south coast and that the road is fixed up and you can once again drive all the way around to Delices. Fingers crossed.

GETTING THERE AND AWAY

BY BUS Information about public bus stops in Roseau can be found on page 50. There is a good service between Roseau, Pointe Michel, Bellevue Chopin, Grand Bay, Soufriere, Scotts Head, Eggleston and Giraudel, but beware that buses operate less frequently between the morning and late afternoon rush-hour periods and hardly at all in the evenings.

BY CAR The road to the two mountain villages of **Giraudel** and **Eggleston** is a loop with both ends located on the coastal road south of Roseau. Head south from the capital down Victoria Street, and pass through Newtown until you come to a junction with a road heading up to the left (you will see a painted sign on a wall that says Kaibel, a Creole word meaning the 'house of Bell', which is a common family name in these parts). This steep winding route passes through the community of Fortune (pronounced 'fort-né') and then up the side of a steep ridge overlooking the Roseau Valley. There are good views from here. Drive carefully as the road is narrow and there are numerous blind corners. Remember to use your horn. After around ten minutes or so the village of Eggleston appears. Continuing through Eggleston the road climbs further (more great views to the north) and curves back around towards the south. After a short distance the road passes through the flower village of Giraudel before turning to the west and beginning a steep descent down the mountainside. The road bisects the residential community of Castle Comfort before emerging on to the main coastal road once more.

To get to **Pointe Michel**, **Soufriere**, and **Scotts Head**, take the southern coastal road from Roseau that passes Fort Young, the Public Library, State House and the

Here are some suggestions for great days out in the south. You will find details of all of the places mentioned in this chapter.

GARDEN OR FARM TOUR, LUNCH AND SNORKELLING Contact the Giraudel Flower Growers (see box, page 133) or the Bellevue Chopin farmers (see box, page 135) to arrange a morning tour and then head down to the coast for a light lunch at one of the roadside stalls in Pointe Michel, followed by some snorkelling at Champagne Reef.

MORNE ANGLAIS HIKE, LUNCH AND A SWIM OR HOT SPA Hike up to the top of Morne Anglais and enjoy the awesome views before heading down to Scotts Head for a fish lunch at Chez Wen or Roger's. Afterwards, enjoy a relaxing swim at Cachacrou or a hot sulphur bath at Soufriere – either in the hot springs or on the Bubble Beach.

MORNE CRABIER HIKE, LUNCH AND SNORKELLING Hike up to Morne Crabier via Galion and then enjoy a seafood lunch in Scotts Head. Drive north along the coast to Champagne Reef and spend the late afternoon snorkelling in the bubbles.

House of Assembly. Continue through Newtown and at the junction over the small bridge in the village of Loubiere, continue straight ahead along the west coast (the road to the left goes to Grand Bay). The road is quite narrow through Pointe Michel so look out for oncoming vehicles. When you eventually arrive in Soufriere, there is a junction with little or no signage. The road immediately to the left goes to Soufriere Sulphur Springs (page 141), the road next to it goes up to Galion, the road ahead just goes into the back of the village, and the somewhat hidden road to the right goes down through the village and continues along the coast to Scotts Head. At the bottom of this road is Slow Corner where a right turn takes you over a small bridge to the very pretty Soufriere church (page 133) and Bubbles Beach Spa. A sharp left turn takes you south along the coast.

To get to **Bellevue Chopin**, **Grand Bay**, **Fond St Jean** and **Petit Savanne**, take the southern coastal road out of Roseau through Newtown and Castle Comfort. Immediately over the small bridge in Loubiere is a road to the left. This road goes to Grand Bay via Bellevue Chopin and Pichelin. Just after Loubiere the road passes through Fond Baron, the Everton Estate and Snug Corner, home of Kubuli beer. After around 15 minutes the road reaches the high elevations of Bellevue Chopin before descending again through the small village of Pichelin towards the coast. Upon reaching the only major junction, the road to the left goes east along the south coast past the Geneva Estate, Dubique, Stowe, Fond St Jean and eventually to what is left of Petite Savanne. The road to the right goes to Grand Bay Village and on to Tete Morne.

WHERE TO STAY

La Bou Country Cottage
[map, page 128] (2 cottages) Soufriere; ☏ 767 265 7826; e laboucottage@gmail.com; www.

laboucountrycottage.com; 🅵. Set in an acre of private gardens, La Bou Cottage is certainly one of Dominica's most uniquely designed &

original places to stay. Sleeping 2, with kitchen, bathroom & a great outdoor shower, La Bou is also comfortable, peaceful & romantic. Within the grounds, diminutive 'Birdhouse', popular with honeymooners, also sleeps 2 & has its own facilities. For those who want to sleep under the stars there are hammocks & there is also outdoor dining. Private, with Wi-Fi throughout, & just 5mins from the village of Soufriere, this countryside retreat comfortably accommodates up to 6 friends. **$$$$$**

🏠 **Zandoli Inn** [map, page 136] (5 rooms) Stowe; 767 446 3161; e reserve.zandoli@yahoo. com; www.zandoli.com; 🅵 see ad, page 145. Perched on a cliff side overlooking Grand Bay & the ocean, Zandoli Inn offers extremely comfortable accommodation. The rooms are tastefully furnished with en-suite bathrooms, fans, mosquito nets, Wi-Fi, jalousie windows & verandas with awesome ocean views. The restaurant serves haute cuisine on request & caters for resident guests only, either outside on the patio or indoors in the dining room & bar area. A number of trails run through the coastal forest belonging to the hotel, including a path to a small sun deck & pool, which continues down to the rocky shoreline where the snorkelling is fabulous. Your host, Jenn, grew up on the south coast & is a mine of knowledge about the Grand Bay area & is happy either to take you on or to arrange very authentic tours. Zandoli is a peaceful escape in an ideal location for exploring the south. **$$$**

✳ 🏠 **Rodney's Wellness Retreat** [map, page 128] (2 cottages, camping) Kanawa, Soufriere; 767 440 8222 or 767 245 4725; e relax@ rodneyswellness.com; www.rodneyswellness.com; 🅵. Set in just under 2ha of gardens on an old lime estate near the fishing village of Soufriere, Rodney's quaint cottages each have 1 bedroom, living area, refrigerator, kettle, coffee maker, microwave, Wi-Fi, TV, fans, outside patio. Also within the landscaped fruit & flower gardens are fixed tents that sleep 2 plus flat pitches where you can set up your own – known as the Big Banana Campground. There's also a communal Big Banana Pool for cottage & camping guests. All facilities are available & there is a restaurant & bar on site. Owner & host Bevin is also a knowledgeable & experienced hiking guide. This is a great budget option for young groups looking to do some hiking & explore the south. Al packages available. *Cottages* **$$$**, *camping* **$**

🏠 **Exotica Cottages** [map, page 128] (7 cottages) Gommier, Giraudel; 767 448 8839; e exotica@cwdom.dm; www.exotica-cottages.com. Exotica offers attractive, spacious & comfortable wooden cottages in the natural hillside surroundings of Gommier near Giraudel. Each cottage has a living area with sofa bed, a bedroom, en-suite bathroom & kitchen, TV, Wi-Fi, fans & verandas overlooking the ocean & gardens. Organic produce is grown on the grounds & owner, Mrs Fae Martin, will prepare excellent Creole meals for you on request. This is very comfortable & authentic accommodation in a cool mountain setting enjoying great views. Roseau is just a 15min drive away. **$$–$$$**

🏠 **767 Ecolodgic** [map, page 128] (2 cottages) Soufriere; 767 615 6253; e 767ecolodgic@ gmail.com. Designed & constructed by the same gentleman who created La Bou Country Cottage, 767 Ecolodgic consists of 2 unique SC 'eco' cottages suitable for couples or groups of friends. Located in private grounds behind the fishing village of Soufriere, the setting is pastoral & serene. Handy for WNT segments 1 & 2, whale watching, scuba diving & snorkelling. **$–$$**

🏠 **The Hide-Out Cottage** [map, page 136] (1 cottage) Geneva Over River, Grand Bay; 767 446 4642, 767 277 8750; e seedatriva@yahoo. com; www.hideout.ch. The Hide-Out is a rustic wooden cottage hidden away in beautiful natural surroundings beside the Geneva River on the south coast near Grand Bay. Off-grid, it comfortably sleeps 2 & has bathroom & kitchenette. Owner Octave is a seasoned hiking guide with an impressive knowledge of local plants. An authentic & comfortable option for budget travellers. **$**

🏠 **Ocean View Apartments** (3 apts) Scotts Head; 767 449 8266; e oceanview_apts@ hotmail.com; www.avirtualdominica.com/ oceanview_apts. Located high in the village of Scotts Head & enjoying sweeping views of the Atlantic & Martinique, Ocean View has 3 SC ground-floor apts with combined living & sleeping areas, kitchen & bathroom. Each apt is equipped with ceiling fans, mosquito nets, Wi-Fi, & private terrace. A nice SC option for budget travellers looking to experience village life. **$**

🏠 **Stowe Ocean Vista** [map, page 136] (2 bed apt) Stowe; 767 446 4777 or 208 884 1425 (UK); e tonywalsh473@gmail.com; www.dominicavista. com. Located just above the road in Stowe, with great ocean views, this is a 2-bed SC apt with spring-fed water, bathroom, lounge area, fully equipped kitchen, veranda & Wi-Fi. Long- & short-term rentals available. **$**

🏠 **Villa Christina** (2-bed apt) Soufriere; 📞 767 285 7536; e loubiere@hotmail.co.uk. Villa

Christina is a 2-bedroom SC apartment with lounge, fully equipped kitchen, dining area, bathroom, fans, Wi-Fi, a veranda with mountain views & a roof terrace for stargazing. Long- or short-term rentals available. **$**

✗ WHERE TO EAT AND DRINK

✗ **Cocoyea** [map, page 128] Slow Corner, Soufriere; 📞 767 285 7536; f; ⏲ lunch & dinner, closed Mon. Located within a walled courtyard near Soufriere Church & attracting both locals & visitors, Cocoyea serves a wide range of Creole & international dishes. Seafood is always a speciality but everything tastes good here. Just turn up. **$$**

✗ **Chez Wen** Scotts Head; 📞 767 448 6668; ⏲ daily. Anna & her staff offer fresh local cooking & extremely good seafood in the simple waterside eatery in the fishing village of Scotts Head. Call ahead for lobster, otherwise just turn up. **$–$$**

✗ **Rodney's Wellness Retreat** [map, page 128] Soufriere; 📞 767 440 8222 or 767 245 4725; f; ⏲ daily. Rodney's offers alfresco dining in extensive garden surroundings. The food is authentic Creole using home-grown produce,

freshly caught fish from the village, chicken & pork. The one-pot *braf* is a speciality. Just turn up. **$–$$**

✗ **Roger's** Scotts Head; 📞 767 448 7851. Roger's is a small eatery on the main road in Scotts Head. The cuisine is local, & fresh fish dishes are a speciality. Just turn up. **$–$$**

✗ **Melvina's** Champagne, Pointe Michel; 📞 767 440 5480. Melvina's is a large wooden bar & eatery on the south side of Pointe Michel, just before Champagne Beach. Known for its very busy Fri night 'lime', you can also get simple but good food here. Try the fish & bakes. **$**

✷✗ **The Fish Spot** Pointe Michel. Don't miss this hole-in-the-wall eatery on the northern tip of Pointe Michel. They show you the fresh catch, ask you to pick your own, & how you would like it cooked. Sides inc provisions, fried plantain & salad. **$**

WHAT TO SEE AND DO

VILLAGES OF THE SOUTH The south coast is where European settlers first gained a foothold on Dominica. Despite an agreement between Britain and France concluding that the island should remain the possession of the indigenous Kalinago, prospectors from Martinique soon began to venture across the channel to begin small lumber enterprises in what is now known as Grand Bay. These settlers succeeded in living alongside the indigenous people and they soon spread around the coast to the Kalinago settlement of Sairi, now known as Roseau.

The influence of France has always been strong in the south, indeed it was with the co-operation of villagers from La Pointe (now Pointe Michel) that the French were able to mount an invasion in 1805, sacking Roseau and forcing the outnumbered British to retreat all the way to Fort Shirley at the Cabrits. Today people from Grand Bay, Pointe Michel and the tiny hamlets around are fine exponents of Creole traditions, particularly in music and dance.

Farming and fishing play an important part in the life of these southern villages. Fond St Jean, Soufriere and Scotts Head are noted for their fishermen, and Bellevue Chopin is known as a centre for organic farming.

Eggleston and **Giraudel** are small mountain villages located at an elevation of around 450–500m on the western slopes of Morne Anglais. Looking down on Roseau and the Caribbean Sea, the height of the villages usually means temperatures are a little lower and beautiful panoramic views along the west coast are guaranteed. Eggleston runs along a narrow ridge between two river valleys and is a small community of residential

This small community group is responsible for the organisation of the Giraudel and Eggleston flower show and is also involved in the growing and selling of plants and flowers in the area. The group is also involved in community tours of gardens as well as Creole cooking classes. If you would like to take a garden tour, contact the group via its Facebook page (**f** Giraudel/Eggleston Flower Group) or call in at the Giraudel Flower House on a Wednesday morning and make arrangements.

houses. Giraudel is also a small village, located to the southeast of Eggleston. Both communities come alive with colour in May when the flower show usually takes place. Giraudel is also known for its traditional jing ping music (see page 25).

Loubiere is a small village south of Castle Comfort on the southern coastal road. It is the home of Kubuli beer and Loubiere mineral water, which are produced using natural spring water at Snug Corner – a little further inland along the road to Bellevue Chopin and Grand Bay.

The original Kalinago name for **Pointe Michel** was Sibouli, the name of a fish presumably caught in abundance in the area. The French settlers of the early 18th century who arrived from Martinique named the area La Pointe and a number of estates growing coffee, sugar and limes were established on the hillside of Morne Plat Pays behind the village. The Union Estate still has one of the last surviving wooden estate houses.

The Pointe Michel of today is a lively community of farmers, fishermen, and returnees. The coastal road becomes very narrow as it winds through the village and close to the water's edge, where its residents can be seen socialising or mending fishing baskets and nets. Standing at the centre of the village above the cemetery, and looking out across the sea, is the picturesque Roman Catholic Church of St Luke. The coastal road passes the cemetery and several more seafront houses, convenience stores and bars.

Soufriere is a seaside village located between Pointe Michel and Scotts Head. Soufriere Bay, home to the **Soufriere Scotts Head Marine Reserve**, is a submerged crater formed by the eruption of a large volcano millions of years ago. The steeply sloping hillside behind the village, with active hot springs and sulphur deposits, is testament to this formation.

Soufriere's Roman Catholic Church of St Mark is perhaps one of the most photographed landmarks in the south and is particularly pretty when viewed from the sea or from around the bay towards Scotts Head. Completed in 1880, the interior walls of the church are decorated with pretty murals depicting simple village life. On either side of the altar there are colourfully painted scenes of villagers dancing the *bélé* and men fishing from small wooden boats. Along the sides of the church are wooden louvre windows and decorated arches. Outside are the convent and presbytery buildings, and at the foot of the cliffs, where the church grounds meet the shoreline, is a cave where it is believed the original settlers may have sheltered. Above the cave is a shrine and in front of it an altar for open-air services.

On the shore in front of the church is **Bubble Beach Spa**. A submerged fumarole in the shallows beyond the beach warms up the sea and creates a natural hot volcanic spa. Two pools have been fashioned with rocks – one warmer and smaller than the other – and payment is voluntary. There is a beach bar, sun lounger rentals, and you can also get a massage. At weekends there is usually a

The South   WHAT TO SEE AND DO

6

barbecue and live music. Also along this stretch of beach you may see examples of the very simple *pwi pwi* fishing rafts of those not yet able to upgrade to a wooden or fibreglass boat. These basic wooden rafts hark back to the past and the kind of vessels some of the earliest settlers may have used to catch fish from inshore waters. Though many fishermen have boats, you will still see *pwi pwi* rafts being used for fishing in inshore waters.

Soufriere Bay is a place where both Amerindian and French settlers found haven and home. In the 1970s archaeological excavations at a number of sites around Soufriere uncovered artefacts dating back to the earliest Amerindian settlers, as well as to their Arawakan successors. Carved *zemi* stones and conch shells depicting earth spirits were also found here. In more recent times, archaeological work by researchers from Northwestern University, Illinois, has uncovered a slave village dating back to the 1800s, along with artefacts that suggest a strong and wide network of communications may have existed between slaves of different estates and the Maroons (runaways) who lived in forest camps and traded food (wild yams) for guns and ammunition.

In the heart of the village are the ruins of Rose's lime factory. Established in Scotland in the 1860s, the L Rose and Lime Company, manufacturer of Rose's Lime Juice Cordial and lime marmalade, was a prominent business on Dominica in the early part of the 20th century. Several estates in the west of the island were purchased by the company for the production of lime products, including Bath Estate, Picard Estate, St Aroment Estate, Canefield Estate and, in 1950, Soufriere Estate. Economic and social circumstances forced the company to withdraw from Dominica in the late 1970s and the estates were either sold off or presented to the Dominican government.

In July Soufriere hosts the denouement of the island's annual Dive Fest. Traditional Kalinago canoe races are held here on the final Sunday of the festival. Anyone can take part, but be prepared to get wet. The prize is usually a crate of beer and there is lots of street food and music. If you are on the island at this time, it's definitely worth a visit.

The village of **Scotts Head** is named after Colonel George Scott, who was lieutenant governor of Dominica from 1764 to 1767. Scott was part of the British invasion force that captured Dominica from the French in 1761 and was responsible for the construction of some of the island's military installations, including a fort on the prominent isthmus beyond the village. This headland

THE SOUFRIERE SCOTTS HEAD MARINE RESERVE (SSMR)

The Soufriere Scotts Head Marine Reserve was established by an Act of Parliament to manage and balance the demands placed on the natural resources of Soufriere Bay by recreational watersports and local fishermen. The SSMR is managed by the Local Area Management Authority (LAMA), which has its office along the shore in Soufriere. The LAMA employs wardens to monitor the reserve, its marine life and reefs, as well as maintain moorings and collect user fees. The SSMR is sectioned into four zones: the fishing priority zone, which is the largest of the four; the scuba area; the nursery; and the recreational area. Encompassing the submerged vents at Champagne Reef all the way through to the dramatic drop-offs at Scotts Head, the SSMR attracts scuba divers from around the world. For more about the dive sites of the SSMR see pages 78–81.

BELLEVUE CHOPIN ORGANIC FARMERS GROUP

The Bellevue Chopin Organic Farmers Group was founded in 2004. It offers a range of organic farm products and also has its own organic composting facility. As part of a drive to develop the new agrotourism sector on Dominica, this community group also offers a variety of short tours to visitors interested in this subject.

The **Broad Meadows Tour** takes you on a trip around Mr Gordon Royer's vegetable and herb garden, and a tour of the organic composting facility; there are also nice views of the surrounding area and if you want to stay overnight, the hammocks in his rustic cabin enjoy fabulous mountain and ocean views. The **Harmony Garden Tour** is a walk around Mr Roy Ormond's organic herbal farm where you can also learn about the traditional uses of herbs and natural medicines. Harmony Garden also welcomes camping and is very handily placed for WNT through-hikers. On the **River Farm Tour** you can see Mr Petronel Green's organic pineapple and anthurium gardens as well as enjoy the river and beautiful scenic views. Mr Delroy Registe's **Mountain Creole Garden Tour** gives you an insight into traditional planting methods and natural landscaping. You can also see organic vegetables, citrus fruits and bananas.

For more information: ☎ 767 316 2710 or 767 315 1175.

also bears his name, as well as the original Kalinago one, **Cachacrou**, whose literal meaning is thought to be 'hat which is being eaten', presumably by the surrounding swells of the convergence of Atlantic Ocean and Caribbean Sea. Scott's fortifications on top of Cachacrou have mostly slipped down the cliffs beneath the waves, though some ruins remain visible today.

Predominantly a fishing village, you cannot fail to notice the number of brightly painted wooden and fibreglass fishing boats resting along the shore or moored in the bay. Towards Cachacrou is a colourfully painted building where fishermen keep their tackle and boat equipment, and all around this area it is possible to see people sitting along the shoreline mending nets and fish traps. The sound of a conch shell being blown is a signal to the village that a fisherman has brought his catch ashore and is ready to sell. Depending on the fisherman, his boat and the tactics he has employed, this catch may be anything from a string of small snapper to a large tuna, mahi mahi or marlin.

The village of Scotts Head is nestled on the slopes of Morne Crabier and is a delightful labyrinth of narrow, twisting alleyways and small roads. On a clear day, either from the heights of the village, or from the shoreline, it is possible to see the outline of Martinique some 30km to the south.

Located at the beginning of the Cachacrou isthmus is the **Caribantic**. This building marks the starting point of Dominica's Wai'tukubuli National Trail (see *Chapter 10*). Used as a meeting place and interpretation centre, but more commonly a bar, the Caribantic also has a shower, toilet and changing facility

Visiting snorkellers heading to the seaside cove beneath Cachacrou should theoretically pay a US$2 per person **Marine Reserve Fee**. This fee is collected on a rather ad hoc basis by fisheries wardens. On the Cachacrou headland there is a rough and somewhat overgrown path leading up to the ruins where there is a small cannon. Just along the wall by the radio mast is a further trail that goes right up to the very top of Cachacrou where there are excellent views of the bay. At the bottom, along the Caribbean shoreline, there is a path to the right leading to a sheltered

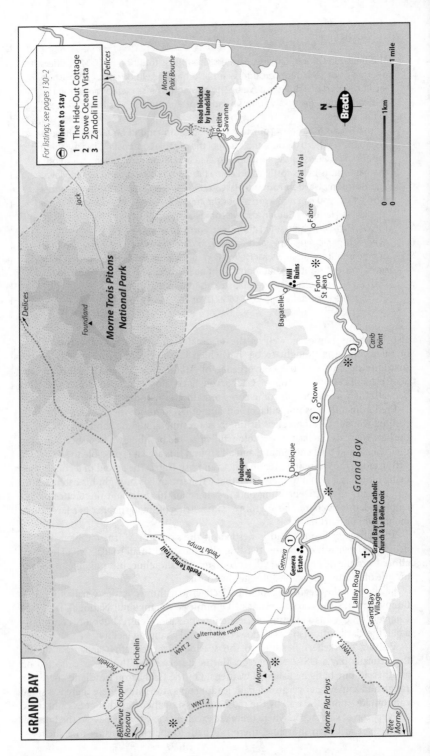

For listings, see pages 130–2

Where to stay
1 The Hide-Out Cottage
2 Stowe Ocean Vista
3 Zandoli Inn

Morne Trois Pitons
National Park

Foundland

Jack

Delices

Delices

Morne
Poix Bouche

Road blocked
by landslide

Petite
Savanne

Wai Wai

Fabre

Mill
Ruins

Fond
St Jean

Bagatelle

Carib
Point

Stowe

Dubique
Falls

Dubique

Grand Bay

Geneva

Geneva
Estate

Perdu Temps Trail

Perdu Temps

Pichelin

Pichelin

Bellevue Chopin,
Roseau

WNT 2

(alternative route)

Morpo

WNT 2

Morne Plat Pays

Tête
Morne

Grand Bay Roman Catholic
Church & La Belle Croix

Lallay Road

Grand Bay
Village

Brandt

N

1 mile

1 km

cove. This is a popular spot for bathers and snorkellers, with the Scotts Head Drop-off dive site within easy swimming distance (the dive buoy marks the spot).

The village of **Bellevue Chopin** is located on a ridge between the peaks of Morne Anglais, Morne Canot and Morne Eloi. Morne Canot was the source of minor earthquake swarms in 1998, when tremors were felt throughout the south of the island.

Located high above Roseau and Grand Bay, the area around Bellevue Chopin was a place of Maroon encampments during the 18th and 19th centuries. Today it is a small farming community and, with the assistance of EU funding, is very gradually developing an agrotourism offering. You can take a tour to learn about and gain first-hand experience of organic farming in Dominica (see box, page 135).

The bus stop area at the top of the ridge is a nice place to stop and take a break. There are a couple of small shops selling drinks, cooked food, snacks and fruits, and the view down to Roseau is fabulous.

The community of **Grand Bay** stretches between Pointe Tanama and Carib Point and is surrounded by the peaks of Morne Vert and Morne Plat Pays to the west, Morne Anglais to the north and Foundland to the east. The Amerindian settlers who arrived in this natural bay on the south coast are thought to have named the area Bericoua, a name which survives today though is often written 'Berekua'. This is also the area where the first French settlers arrived from the neighbouring island of Martinique, and set up small plantations and timber works. Jeannot Rolle was a free black man from Martinique who purchased land and established the first significant plantation here. He invited Jesuits to the area and erected a large stone cross, known as **La Belle Croix**, which can still be seen standing in the cemetery today.

Often referred to as **Grand Bay Village** or **South City**, the settlement of Berekua is to be found on the western edge of the bay. When approaching from Roseau via Bellevue Chopin, a right turn at the junction a little beyond the Perdu Temps trailhead takes you into the heart of Grand Bay Village. The junction is well signposted. The road passes through a residential area before joining the main thoroughfare of Lallay. This is the very lively main street of Grand Bay Village and is lined with small shops, colourful bars and snackettes.

The Lallay road runs from the seafront all the way up through Grand Bay Village to **Tete Morne**. The road is steep, narrow and full of hairpin bends so take care and use your horn on blind corners if driving. As you enter the hillside community of Tete Morne, the road becomes lined with small wooden houses as it nears the heart of the village and there are pleasant views across the valley as well as down to the bay below. The village is located on a ridge between Morne Plat Pays and Morne Vert. From Tete Morne there is a trail across the Palmiste Estate to the summit of Morne Vert (pages 143–4). Segment 2 of the Wai'tukubuli National Trail also passes through this village (pages 227–9).

At the foot of the Lallay road where it meets the sea there are several small wooden houses, some ruins and the impressive Grand Bay Roman Catholic Church. The church is large and quite beautiful, built from stone with a bright galvanised-steel roof. Tall stone arch windows are opened to let in the Atlantic breeze and above them are modern stained-glass windows decorated in a kaleidoscope of abstract colour. The church is situated beneath the cemetery, within which stands the 18th-century La Belle Croix, and a tall stone bell tower that stands proud on the hill above.

At the heart of the Grand Bay area, between the village and the Geneva River, is the **Geneva Estate**. Once a very large estate originally owned by Jesuits and then by a family of Swiss Huguenots who named it after their home town, it produced sugar, rum and molasses. In the early 19th century it was sold to the Lockharts, the family of novelist Jean Rhys's mother. In her 1966 novel, *Wide Sargasso Sea*, the

6

Beyond Bagatelle, the narrow road winds around the steep slopes of the southern coastline until it reaches the small village of Petite Savanne. In August 2015 this area experienced terrible destruction from Tropical Storm Erika. Countless landslides tore down the steep mountain sides, ripping away sections of road, utilities and homes – some with people trapped inside them. At the time of writing, 18 people had been declared dead, though only six bodies had been recovered. The rest are presumably still buried beneath many feet of mud, rocks and boulders.

The government decided the village had to be evacuated since no-one could guarantee that the land had stabilised, and the homes that were still standing were considered too dangerous to inhabit. Villagers made their way down the slopes to the shoreline where they were collected by boats and taken to Roseau and given temporary shelter and housing. Most are still living in temporary housing and the government has decided Petite Savanne should be abandoned and that it will create homes for the displaced in the nearby village of Bellevue Chopin. None of this has happened yet.

Those who still have homes in the village go back there regularly to clean, tidy, fix up the garden. But no-one really knows what the future holds.

At the time of writing, it is possible to drive to the western outskirts of the village but then you have to walk to get any further into what remains of the community. At present you cannot pass through the village and then on to Morne Paix Bouche and the village of Delices as you once could. There is much debate about this road, and what should happen next.

What *has* been happening, however, can best be described as 'disaster tourism'. The curious (Dominicans as well as overseas visitors) have been gradually making their way to the village to take a look. Whether this is right or wrong is not for me to say. I understand the curiosity, but I would like to think that anyone making this trip would be prepared to give something back in some way. But that is your decision to make. If you do go there, please be respectful and mindful of what happened and the loss and trauma that many of the survivors are still experiencing.

Geneva Estate features as 'Coulibri' and, just as with the estate of the book, Geneva has experienced periods of uprising, arson and violence in each of the last three centuries. Today the estate is owned jointly by the state and by private holdings and is the location of the **Geneva Heritage Park**, which seems to spark rather sporadically into life from time to time and is worth looking out for if you are in this area. The main building displays local artworks and handmade products.

Also within the grounds of the former Geneva estate is **The Coal Pot**, a local cottage industry producing soaps and oils for domestic consumption as well as for export. The Coal Pot is one of several cottage industries producing scented soaps. Find them in the main supermarkets and pharmacies of Roseau.

On the northern edge of the Grand Bay and set in a narrow valley between the cliffs is the tiny settlement of **Dubique**. This village suffered considerably during Tropical Storm Erika; there were fatalities and the village had to be evacuated. Beyond the village is a series of cascades known as the **Dubique Falls**. Dubique is also known for its cultural group who are wonderful exponents of traditional *bélé* dancing (see page 25). If you are on the island during Creole and Independence celebrations (late October and early November), you may have an opportunity to see them perform. To the east of Dubique is **Stowe**, a large estate that once produced sugar and rum. Stowe Estate was also the site of a gun placement defending one of the few accessible landing places in the bay. The stretch of coastline between Stowe and Carib Point is very scenic, with great views to the south across the Martinique Channel and to the rugged Morne Fous across the bay to the west.

To the east, between Carib Point and Point Retireau, is the small fishing community of **Fond St Jean**. It is a quaint village with a long tradition of fishing and is one of the south's main sources of fresh fish caught by intrepid fishermen using hand lines from small boats in the choppy seas of the Martinique Channel. Watching the fishermen returning in the afternoon and unloading their catch is fascinating. Most of the catch is sold to hotels and restaurants before it reaches the shore, though it is also possible to buy them directly from the fishermen if they have enough to spare.

The narrow road to Fond St Jean runs alongside a beautiful terracotta-coloured cliff face that has been shaped by weather and sea. The road enters the village and passes the small stone beach behind the buildings on the right-hand side where the brightly painted fishing boats are lined up along the water's edge. It then exits the village and winds its way steeply up to **Fabre**, from where there are super views of Fond St Jean and the coastline all the way westwards to Point des Fous. This area is picturesque, with steep hills, deep valleys and lush greenery. The hillsides are dotted with bay trees and along the road in Fabre there is a bay distillery shed, one of several in the area. At the end of the road is a small coconut-lined rocky beach where the waves of the Atlantic roll ashore creating a deep thundering sound as the smooth rocks are tossed around beneath the surface. The isolated valley between Fabre and Fond St Jean is **Wai Wai**, a former Kalinago settlement.

Bagatelle is a small village running alongside the main road, located just above Fond St Jean. Midway through the village is a small road that runs down to some houses above the Malabuka River, ending at the ruins of an old mill. Fittingly, the road is called the **Bagatelle Old Mill Road** and the ruins are really worth visiting. They are accessed via some large, brightly painted wrought-iron gates and include a number of pieces of machinery and a large waterwheel that would have powered the cane-crushing machinery in the production of sugar and molasses for rum. The Bagatelle village council has been very keen to develop the mill in an attempt to retain and promote the area's cultural heritage. The council has also talked of developing a heritage walking trail that would incorporate the mill and several bay distilleries in the area around Fond St Jean and Bagatelle.

BAY LEAF PRODUCTS

The leaves of the bay tree, or *bois d'Inde*, are strongly scented and are used to season foods, aromatise Bay Rum and produce essential oils. Village farmers harvest their bay leaf crops on the slopes of the mountains, then bind the branches together and send them rolling down to the bottom. These bundles are then assembled and taken to a distillery. A fire is set beneath a large vat and the bay leaves are cooked until they release their oil. It is a basic, yet productive system. The organic manufacture of bay oil has traditionally been one of the prime income sources for the farmers of the villages in the southeast of Dominica. The methods remain very simple and traditional, and bay farmers can often be seen transporting their crops to small village distilleries for oil production in this area.

The **Cool River Shop and Bar** can be found on the apex of a bend above Bagatelle. Located next to a small river, in a wide river bed – thanks to Tropical Storm Erika – it is a nice place to stop for some refreshments and perhaps watch the domino games that occasionally take place here.

ACTIVITIES AND SPECIAL INTERESTS

SCUBA DIVING IN THE MARINE RESERVE (*SSMR fee payable*) Operators in the south offer daily boat-diving tours of sites within the marine reserve, as well as to more advanced sites on the Atlantic side of Scotts Head. Dive site tours are led by qualified divemasters or dive instructors. In addition to basic dive rates, operators in this area must also charge a Marine Reserve Fee of US$2 per diver. (See pages 78–80 for information about dive sites and dive operators in this area.) Diving within the marine reserve is easy; there are rarely any strong currents and the visibility is usually excellent. Underwater photographers can expect to see plenty of reef fish, frogfish, sea horses, banded shrimp and a wide range of other 'critters'. Hawksbill turtles are very common sightings and you may also see batfish, squid, nurse sharks, spotted eagle rays and barracuda. Operators also offer regular night diving on reefs within the marine reserve.

SNORKELLING AT CHAMPAGNE REEF (*SSMR fee payable*) One kilometre south of Pointe Michel, at the very first bend in the coastal road, is Champagne Beach. Operating a snorkel and dive service here is **Champagne Reef Dive and Snorkel** (\767 440 5085 or 767 275 7001; e *underwater@champagnereef.com; www.champagnereef. com;*). You can rent snorkelling and scuba diving equipment here and you can book accompanied snorkelling tours and scuba diving. You can also take a PADI scuba diving certification course here, as well as enjoy snacks and refreshments. (See page 80 for other scuba dive and snorkelling tour operators in this area.)

Continue down the path to the shore and along the boardwalk and track to the end of the beach. Right at the very southern end of the beach, before a small rocky volcanic outcrop, is the inshore area of Champagne Reef. It is a broad formation that starts at the shore and continues out into deeper water. In the shallow area at the end of the volcanic outcrop, near a white marker post, is a submerged active fumarole. All around this area bubbles emerge from vents in the rock creating an impression of champagne bubbles in a glass. If you are snorkelling here without a guide and cannot find the bubbles, you are probably looking for them too far out. They are very close to the shore at the end of the outcrop. The vents themselves are warm, and in places quite hot. It is really quite beautiful when the sea is clear and the sun reflects off the streams of bubbles.

Although the best corals are deeper, the shallow area along the shore is often alive with fish and other marine creatures. You should see parrotfish here as well as smaller reef fish such as damselfish, blue tang, bluehead and surgeonfish. It is also possible to see hawksbill turtles cruising by. Take care not to touch black sea urchins or fireworms. Both cause skin irritation that will require attention. Located beyond the bubbles and a little to the south are the encrusted remains of cannon and iron chains. You will probably need a guide to find this; they are very hard to spot.

The reef is very popular with snorkellers and scuba divers, and when cruise ships are in it can be quite a busy place. Try to arrive here later in the afternoon when the crowds have gone and the low sun illuminates the reef. Due to its popularity it is really important to take care of the area and not damage it. When snorkelling or scuba diving please do not stand on nor touch the bottom. Be careful not to damage yellow tube sponges or any other marine life with your fins.

To snorkel at Champagne Reef visitors must pay a US$2 per person Soufriere Scotts Head Marine Reserve (SSMR) fee. This is usually collected by staff at Champagne Reef Dive and Snorkel.

You can also try snorkelling at **Scotts Head**. Walk to the Cachacrou isthmus and take the wide track to the right along the shoreline and into the sheltered cove. Alternatively, just head into the water from the narrow section of the isthmus where people park their vehicles. The dive buoy you can see a little distance offshore is the mooring for the Scotts Head Drop-Off dive site. This also marks the dramatic drop off. There is a line of corals and sponges all along the top of the wall and you may even see the occasional barracuda, eagle ray or school of jacks in the deep. Snorkellers and bathers swimming out to the drop-off should take note of prevailing currents which, though rare in this area, are likely to run along shore towards the open ocean, making the swim back a little more taxing than the swim out to the reef itself. Please bear this in mind, particularly if you are not an especially strong swimmer.

Visitors snorkelling at Scotts Head should pay a US$2 per person Soufriere Scotts Head Marine Reserve (SSMR) fee. This fee is collected by fisheries wardens on a rather ad hoc basis.

SOUFRIERE SULPHUR SPRINGS (*Site pass required*) At the four-way junction at the top of the village of Soufriere is a sign indicating the road to the Sulphur Springs. It's the first road on your left if you are coming from the north. The road heads inland towards the valley for a short distance before coming to an end at the Sulphur Springs car park and reception centre. Visitor passes can be purchased at the site itself.

From the car park there is a tree-lined path to the reception building, a stylised wooden cabin, where a forestry officer will usually collect your pass. These trees have name plates and the reception centre has an imaginative and informative display describing the history and geological formation of the area. From here the path crosses a warm-water cascade to a small junction. To the left is a large sulphur pool and to the right is a path leading to three further pools and a trail that takes you to scarred areas of hillside where volcanic activity creates steaming, pungent deposits of sulphur. Straight ahead at the junction is a changing facility, a covered picnic area and refreshments building.

The path leading to the three higher pools also takes you to the trailhead of the climb to the top of the Soufriere ridge and across to the village of Tete Morne (pages 227–9). Like the hot sulphur springs in the area of Wotten Waven (pages 116–18), bathing in the mineral-rich waters is considered to be a rejuvenating and healthy activity.

BOIS COTLETTE ESTATE The Bois Cotlette Estate was established by French settlers in the early 18th century and is considered to be the best-preserved example of plantation buildings existing on Dominica today. The estate is named after the Bois Cotlette tree (*Citharexylum spinosum*) that grows in this area. Thanks to ongoing preservation work, the results of which are quite beautiful, the planter's house and surrounding land and buildings paint a vivid picture of the past when coffee, sugar, limes, rum and molasses were produced there – by slaves, of course.

To the south of the estate is the windmill tower. When functioning, it would have faced the trade winds which powered its sails, enabling it to turn the rollers and crush the sugarcane. This windmill tower is the only one of its kind on Dominica. At the centre of the grounds is the attractive wooden planter's house and on either side are industrial buildings such as the boiling house and distillery where sugar, rum and molasses were produced, and the coffee house where the dried coffee was stored and prepared for shipping.

The South   ACTIVITIES AND SPECIAL INTERESTS   **6**

South of Bois Cotlette is **Morne Rouge Estate**, another of the first French estates established in the south. It produced sugar, cocoa, coffee and limes and until the mid 20th century was still owned by the original French family. The estate building stands today and is thought to be one of the oldest surviving on the island. A privately owned house, it is quite beautiful, located on the cliffs above the sea with a view across to Martinique.

Although restoration continues, which is great, Bois Cotlette is private rather than state owned. There are tours for cruise ship visitors during the peak season, but if you are an independent traveller and want to have a look around this impressive heritage site, you have to call ahead and book (↘ 767 440 8805; e *boiscotlette@gmail. com; www.boiscotlette.com*).

CACHACROU VIEWPOINT A steep uphill walk and a rather tricky scramble over loose scree, the views of Soufriere Bay from the top of Cachacrou are worth the effort. On the isthmus dividing the Atlantic Ocean and Caribbean Sea, a path to the right along the water's edge takes you to a tiny sheltered cove that is good for bathing and snorkelling. The other path goes straight up to the top of the point. Follow it through the clusters of wild lemon grass until you reach the rather unsightly communications mast that has been unceremoniously planted almost on top of a shrine to lost mariners. The path to the right, away from the mast, runs to an old stone wall and to the right of this is a short, often overgrown track to a viewpoint with a cannon overlooking the bay. Just above and behind the painted wall at the entrance to the communications facility there is a narrow track that runs all the way to the very top of Cachacrou. The climb is steep and a little slippery on the crumbling ground, so take it steady, but the views from the summit are wonderful and definitely worth the effort of getting there. On a clear day you can also see Martinique to the south.

HIKES

MORNE ANGLAIS ✳ *(Difficulty: T: 3; R: 0; E: 4; D: 3; Rating = 6.3; Guide recommended)* This is a steep walk and in places quite a tricky climb through deep mud, over and around trees and roots, but it is the easier of the main volcano hikes and the views are awesome. You can see from Roseau all the way up to Salisbury on the west coast, Grand Bay in the south, and even Delices in the east – all from one spot.

The trailhead is in the village of Giraudel (see page 50 for information on buses and page 129 for driving directions) and is a little tricky to find. The best route to take up to Giraudel is directly up through Castle Comfort from the Rubis petrol station on the west-coast highway. When you enter the village, one of the first buildings you meet is the small schoolhouse (it has a mural painted on the side). There is a small parking area here. You can either hike from here or you can try to drive a little higher and save yourself some legwork. If you do want to drive further, take the narrow concrete road that runs up above the school. When you reach the top, turn left at the junction and follow the road around until you come to the Giraudel water catchment (look for a concrete road to the right and then a large concrete water tank next to it). Park up here and begin your hike by walking up the road next to the water tank.

If you are parking up by the school, look for a rough, steep and narrow road to the left of the school (the second left). It will pass a couple of houses – don't worry about the dogs. Follow it all the way up until you reach a junction with the village back road. Follow this road to the left and look for the concrete road and water tank on your right.

Walk up this steep road, past the tank right up to a large disused water catchment, surrounded by a wire fence. As you face it, head for the bottom left-hand corner. Standing at the bottom left-hand corner of the old catchment, follow the fence all the way to the top left-hand corner. The bush on your left may be a little overgrown and there may also be one or two rather curious goats on your path, but keep going. Ignore spur trails to the left and stick to the fence right to the end.

When you get to the top of the catchment you should see a trail heading up and away from the corner. Follow it through the woods. It can be steep and rather slippery here and sometimes the trail disappears a bit, but keep going until you come out at the bottom right-hand corner of a large open field.

Make your way up to the top right-hand corner. You may be able to make out a faint trace through the grass. Halfway up, cows permitting, turn around and take in the view.

When you reach the top right-hand corner, look for a trail running up and away from the field. It may be difficult to spot in the bush, but it is there. When you find it, follow it up through the forest. The trail is now a lot easier to see but you should still pay attention. There are some areas where the path seems to disappear around a sharp corner or behind a tree. You are climbing a narrow ridge that curves around towards the summit, so you cannot go too far wrong. It has some steep and narrow stretches and you will be able to enjoy a couple of good viewpoints. To your right (the south), the village you can see in the distance is Bellevue Chopin; the smaller one before it is Pichelin. To your left (the north), you can see Morne Micotrin and occasionally Morne Trois Pitons and the sun reflecting off Freshwater Lake if the weather is clear.

The trail goes downhill for a stretch and it is from this point that the terrain becomes a little more challenging. Once you reach the bottom of this incline, you climb again, all the way to the top. It is usually muddy and you have to use your upper-body strength from time to time to help you climb up a few steep sections. Eventually you reach the top and, as you do so, you may be greeted by razor grass. Lovely. The path through the grass may be a little overgrown, but it is there. Pick your way through it as carefully as you can, trying not to get too cut up by it, and aim for the radio mast in front of you. Watch out for occasional hollows in the trail beneath your feet.

You will come out at a clearing, the lower summit of the two, where there is a solar panel and ham radio equipment. The trail to the upper summit ahead of you is not worth the risk; it is dangerous, eroded and slippery. Enjoy the fabulous views and please don't sit on the solar panel!

PALMISTE RIDGE (*Difficulty: T: 2; R: 0; E: 3; D: 21; Rating = 3.8; Guide not required*)
This is a there-and-back hike that begins and ends at Soufriere Sulphur Springs. It climbs up to the village of Tete Morne and then on to the Palmiste Ridge, which is part of Morne Vert. The views of Grand Bay from the top are fabulous – you could easily sit here for hours and it's a great place to take a picnic. End the hike with a hot sulphur spa or a refreshing dip in Soufriere Bay.

The first half of the route simply follows Wai'tukubuli National Trail Segment 2 from the Soufriere Sulphur Springs to the village of Tete Morne (see pages 227–9 for a trail description). In Tete Morne, walk a short distance down through the village and look for a partially ruined stone building on your right. There is a track just beyond it. Walk along the side of the building, through the small clearing and then up the steep mountainside via a series of long switchbacks. Ignore any spurs – just keep going up. It is a fairly easy track to follow because farmers use it regularly and some of them even bring their cows up here.

When you emerge at the top, walk along the grassy ridge and find a spot to sit and relax on the slope. Enjoy the view.

Beyond this ridge are farmlands and the Morne Vert summit. There is an old track that runs extremely steeply down the other side of the mountain to Bois Cotlette Estate; it was always in danger of disappearing from natural erosion but at the time of writing it seemed to have been deliberately blocked near the bottom and was impassable. A great shame as it is thought to be an historic trace used by Kalinago.

So once you have had your fill of the view and perhaps your picnic, head back down to Soufriere the way you came.

GALION AND MORNE CRABIER (*Difficulty: T: 2; R: 0; E: 3; D: 2; Rating = 4.4; Guide not required*) This hike takes you from Scotts Head up to the village of Galion where you can enjoy great views of Soufriere Bay. After passing through the village, you pick up the Wai'tukubuli National Trail Segment 1, but do it in reverse, all the way down to Scotts Head again, where you can reward yourself with a swim, a fresh fish lunch and a cold drink.

The trailhead is located near a small stone building with a red galvanised steel roof on the side of the long concrete road between Scotts Head and Soufriere. Look for a small public convenience; it is near there. To the left of this building is a wide track heading uphill. This is the start of the walk. If you are in a car, I would suggest leaving it in Scotts Head village (on the Cachacrou isthmus) and either walking or catching a ride to this point.

Follow the track all the way up to the village of Galion. It can be a little loose underfoot so take care. It takes around 30 minutes of steep switch-back walking to reach the top, where there is a wonderful view of Soufriere Bay.

Walk through and then out of the village, following the main road for about 15–20 minutes. Note the volcanic nature of the landscape beyond the village. The escarpments to your right have volcanic activity and you may notice the distinctive smell of sulphur dioxide from time to time. Look at the ridges around you; you are clearly inside a crater. This road is also lined with cashew trees.

As the road begins to climb, you will reach a sharp hairpin bend. Look for the National Trail shelter and signs. You are now going to follow part of Segment 1 in the opposite direction all the way to Scotts Head – see pages 226–7 for a trail description.

When you finally make it back down to the village, take a dip in the sea and enjoy a great local seafood lunch at either Chez Wen or Roger's (page 132).

PERDU TEMPS (FROM PICHELIN) (*Difficulty: T: 3; R: 3; E: 2; D: 3; Rating = 6.9; Guide essential*) This beautiful rainforest hike was quite badly affected by Tropical Storm Erika. Beginning on the main road between Pichelin and Grand Bay, and ending up near the village of Delices on the southeast coast, it follows a trail once used by people in the south to cross the island before roads were constructed. Near Pichelin there used to be a small settlement called Perdu Temps and a paved road leading to it. In 1979 Hurricane David forced people to abandon the settlement after the Pichelin River Bridge was washed away and houses were destroyed. In 2015, more devastation followed.

Due to poor signage and numerous confusing river crossings, a guide was always essential on this hike. Following the beating it took from Erika, the trail became even trickier to follow.

A good contact is **Octave Joseph** of the Hide-Out Cottage in Geneva (✆ 767 245 3558); he knows this trail well but his availability may be limited. Otherwise, try the guides listed on pages 76–7.

The trailhead is located between the hamlet of Pichelin and the Grand Bay junction. Look for the sign. Use a Grand Bay bus to get here (see page 50), or by car, following the directions to Grand Bay described on page 130.

The beginning of the trail used to involve a pleasant forest walk with a few easy river crossings. Now the route follows the wide river bed that was carved by the torrents of the tropical storm, until it eventually turns back into the forest to pick up the Jack River and forested northern slopes of the Foundland volcano. The riverbed terrain is tough going and, without a guide, really difficult to follow. In the forest there are some fairly steep ups and downs but you will come across a number of interesting plant species native to this kind of habitat, such as the *chatanier*, with its buttress roots, the *gommier*, tree ferns, mountain palms, *zel-mouch*, *bwa riviere*, wild anthuriums and several varieties of orchid. The ground on either side of the trail is covered in an emerald blanket of *pawasol agouti*, and if you are lucky enough, you may even disturb an agouti and see it scuttling off into the forest. Jaco parrots may also be heard calling from high up in the canopy here, especially in the vicinity of *gommier* trees. A good guide, with knowledge of forest plants and animals, can really enhance this hike for you; and, for the next stretch, will spare you the stress and embarrassment of getting lost, which is very easily done.

The trail makes a series of river crossings and the route becomes even more difficult to follow until it turns out of the dense forest to a ridge with views across a river valley to **Jacks Falls**, which is particularly impressive in the wet season (sadly it has no pool). Across the Jack River the trail heads uphill towards a flat area of woodland, pasture and bay trees. To the south you will see the summit of Foundland, the tallest mountain in the southeast. The trail then begins its final descent towards the White River. Crossing the White River can be tricky as it is fast-flowing and quite deep in places. The source of this river is the Boiling Lake (pages 118–20). Once on the other side, you will meet the trailhead for the Victoria Falls, which forks to the left and is another 30–45 minutes upriver (see pages 170–1). The trail straight on emerges at a clearing and Zion Valley, a 'rastarant' and gardens owned by the very friendly Moses (see page 153). It is a nice place to stop for a drink and something to eat. The vehicle track takes you uphill to the main road south of Delices.

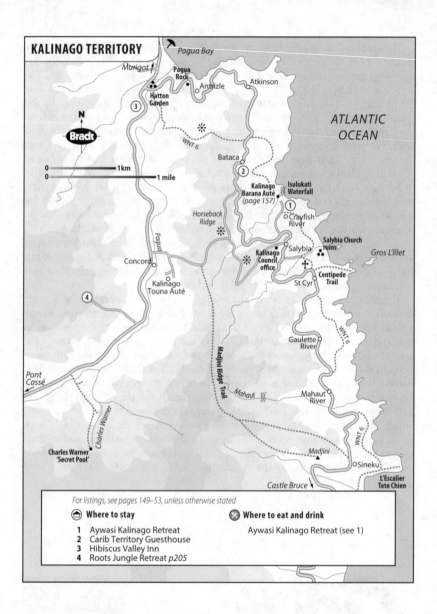

KALINAGO TERRITORY

Pagua Bay

Marigot

Pagua Rock

Antrizle

Atkinson

Hatton Garden

N

Bradt

3

WNT 6

Bataca

2

Kalinago Barana Auté *(page 157)*

Isulukati Waterfall

1

Crayfish River

ATLANTIC OCEAN

Horseback Ridge

Salybia Church ruins

Salybia

Gros L'Illet

0 ——————— 1km
0 ——————— 1 mile

Concord

Pagua

Kalinago Touna Auté

Kalinago Council office

St Cyr

Centipede Trail

4

Gaulette River

WNT 6

Pont Cassé

Madjini Ridge Trail

Charles Warner

Mahaut

Mahaut River

Charles Warner 'Secret Pool'

WNT 6

Madjini

Sineku

L'Escalier Tete Chien

Castle Bruce

For listings, see pages 149–53, unless otherwise stated

⌂ **Where to stay**

1 Aywasi Kalinago Retreat
2 Carib Territory Guesthouse
3 Hibiscus Valley Inn
4 Roots Jungle Retreat *p205*

✕ **Where to eat and drink**

Aywasi Kalinago Retreat (see 1)

7

The Kalinago Territory and the East

THE KALINAGO

'Carib' is a word you may hear often both, before and during your visit. It was the name used by Europeans to describe the Amerindian people of the Greater and Lesser Antilles island chain. Very controversially, and without any factual grounding, this name had connotations of cannibalism and it is just one of the reasons why many of Dominica's indigenous people do not like it very much. Indian tribes travelled by dug-out canoe from South America and arrived in islands such as Dominica as early as 5000BC. They migrated to and populated large parts of Central and North America, as well as the islands and lands in between. Much of what happened is derived from archaeology and anthropology. What was written down in later years was done so by colonising Europeans and the Roman Catholic Church. Amerindians transcribed very little of their own history, and so they have been forced to accept and believe in a version of history and an identity that was written by others. This leads to controversy and misunderstanding; some would argue that it also served as a one-sided justification for the brutal enslavement and annihilation of indigenous people.

The Taino people settled in the Greater Antilles and the Igneri in the Lesser Antilles. The Kalinago were also an Arawakan-speaking people from South America who, it is believed, arrived in the Lesser Antilles in the 12th and 13th centuries, eventually displacing the Igneri. When the Spanish arrived in the Greater Antilles in the 15th century they set to work enslaving and killing the Taino people until none remained. The Kalinago who had settled on Dominica fought against the Spanish and, quite incredibly, resisted all attempts to take the island for around 200 years. Unfortunately this constant battle had a high price and the number of Kalinago living here seriously declined. By the time the first French settlers arrived in the early 18th century, it seems likely that the Kalinago realised they had little choice other than to share **Wai'tukubuli**, the name they gave Dominica, with these new people. Perhaps they thought they would leave.

Though the first settlers were interested in logging, eventually land for growing sugar became a valuable commodity in the region and, though the British and the French had agreed to leave the island to the Kalinago, it was inevitable that European colonialists would eventually arrive, creating small sugar estates and claiming more and more land as their own. The Kalinago were consequently forced further and further into the more remote reaches of the island. West African slaves brought from other islands to work on the French and subsequently British estates often escaped into the rainforest, where they either clashed or collaborated with the Kalinago against the Europeans. Following emancipation in 1838 and the later arrival of more West Africans from slave ships, many of the estates declined and new settlements were created in their place. The population of liberated slaves grew and farming and fishing villages were established throughout the island.

Here are some suggestions for great days out in the east. You will find details of all of the places mentioned in this chapter.

WAVINE CYRIQUE, TWA BASENS AND LUNCH Hang on to tree roots and rope ladder down the cliff and back up again to see one of Dominica's most spectacular waterfalls. It's a hike for the brave! Soak and cool off at Twa Basens before heading to the Riverside Café at Citrus Creek for some great food.

VICTORIA FALLS, LUNCH AND 'RASTA' GARDEN TOUR Victoria Falls is an adventurous river hike with great scenery and pools to enjoy along the way. The waterfall itself is magnificent. Follow it up with an ital lunch at Moses James's Zion Valley 'Rastarant' and then a tour of his garden.

CHARLES WARNER SECRET POOL, LUNCH AND KBA Cross the Pagua River and head into lush rainforest on the northern margins of the Kalinago Territory to this exquisite pool. Follow it up with some lunch at, and then a tour of, the Kalinago Barana Auté.

During this time Kalinago numbers were in serious decline and in 1903, Crown Colony administrator Hesketh Bell secured a reservation for them on the east coast. This land became known as the Carib Reserve and, more recently, the Carib Territory. The people currently living in this territory are descendants of the Kalinago. Though racial and social integration, together with the influences of North America, Europe and Africa, have significantly affected the development of the Kalinago, there is a contemporary movement that aims to arrest the decline of their cultural heritage, and rediscover their warrior spirit.

Throughout this book I refer to Dominica's indigenous people as Kalinago and do not use the word Carib. You will hear Kalinago themselves use the word Carib occasionally – some may even reject the term Kalinago outright – but they are in the minority. Kalinago consciousness is a movement that should be encouraged to grow and I urge you also to use the name that most now prefer.

The sporadic and fragile development of tourism on Dominica offers the Kalinago people an opportunity to elevate the profile of their cultural heritage as well as generate an income from it. Throughout the territory you will see many stalls selling traditional crafts and two innovative projects, the Kalinago Barana Auté and the Kalinago Touna Auté, complement each other as showcases for both historic and contemporary Kalinago life and culture.

GETTING THERE AND AWAY

BY BUS Buses run here from Roseau. Please remember that buses tend to stop running in the early evening and that you should be prepared for longer waits in more remote places such as Saint Sauveur, Petite Soufriere, and Delices.

BY CAR To get to the Kalinago Territory by car you either approach it from the north at Hatton Garden junction or from the south near Castle Bruce. From Roseau it is easier to get there via Castle Bruce. Take the Imperial Road from Canefield up to Pont Cassé and then take the right-hand exit, following the signs to Castle

CANOE BUILDING

The Kalinago were master canoe builders, carving out vessels from single tree trunks, usually *gommier* (*Dacryodes excelsa*), and using them to catch fish, to migrate between islands and for inter-island trade. Unfortunately the art of canoe building is no longer as strong as it once was, though there are still one or two builders in the Kalinago Territory who are trying to keep the tradition alive.

The method of creating a canoe has changed a little with the introduction of modern tools, but the process itself is still very much the same. The hull of the canoe is carved out from a large *gommier* tree – either in the forest, or after it has been dragged out to the workshop, depending on how big it is. Sometimes fire is used to speed up the hollowing-out process, together with simple hand tools. In former times, sharp volcanic rock would have been the cutting tool of choice. Hot rocks and steam are also used to stretch out the canoe, with tree branches acting as props. The bordage along the top of the canoe is also made from the *gommier* tree and is sealed using soft *gommier* sap blended with black sand to produce a tough, water-resistant sealant and resin that the builders refer to as *putty*. The ribs, bow and rowlock pins are usually made from white cedar. As a finishing touch, canoes are painted in bright colours according to the wishes of the customer.

Bruce. About ten minutes down this road you will come to a second junction. Take the road to the left past the Emerald Pool and, at the end of the long Castle Bruce stretch, just before you reach the coast, take another left.

If you are heading to the rest of the east coast from Roseau you have two options. The first is to go via Pont Cassé as described above, but instead of turning left towards Castle Bruce and the Emerald Pool, go straight. This will take you to Rosalie, Riviere Cyrique and beyond.

To get to Good Hope and Saint Sauveur you take the road that runs next to the playing field and across the river in Castle Bruce.

WHERE TO STAY

Rosalie Bay Resort [map, page 160] (28 rooms) Rosalie; 767 446 1010; e info@ rosaliebay.com; www.rosaliebay.com. This high-end luxury eco-resort is located beside the Rosalie River & the black volcanic sands of the Atlantic coastline where turtles are known to come ashore & nest. The 28 rooms & suites cater for all preferences, each very stylishly designed & furnished offering comfort & privacy. They have king & queen beds, en-suite bathrooms with organic products, shower & tub, Wi-Fi, TV, fridge, safe, fans & verandas with either ocean, river or garden views. The restaurant offers a full service of haute Creole & international cuisine, there is a fully equipped gym, a spa offering a range of wellness services, a unique freshwater bathing pool, cabana bar & colourful tropical gardens. A state-of-the-

art conference centre has audio-visual facilities, stage, bar & other amenities. Eco sensitivity is demonstrated by the large wind turbine & the promotion of leatherback turtle nesting site & education activities. Rosalie Bay is a good choice for romantics, business retreats or those who simply wish to escape & indulge. Additional offerings inc nature tours, weddings, retreats, airport transfers. **$$$$$**

Banana Lama Eco Villa [map, page 160] (1 villa, 2 cottages) Newfoundland Estate, Rosalie; 767 446 1183; e bananalamaecovilla@mailbox. as; www.bananalamaecovilla.com. Located along the Cacao River off the road to Rosalie from Pont Cassé, Banana Lama is an awesome place to stay. Accommodation consists of a luxurious 2-bedroom & 1 suite villa with large open-plan living, dining

149

& covered deck area, & a fully equipped & stylish kitchen. The villa is very artistically designed yet also casual & relaxing. You can either rent out the whole place or just the self-contained & very romantic Bougainvillea Suite. Located either side of the villa are 2 spacious, comfortable & very private 1-bedroom self-contained cottages. Both enjoy open-plan living areas, deck, kitchen, bathroom & surrounding gardens, with the river just a few steps away. Owners & hosts Andy & Melissa live on the property & have sailed around the world on superyachts. The diverse world cuisine that can be prepared for you is a reflection of their exotic voyages. Set within 3 acres of private riverside, farm & forested land & completely off-grid, Banana Lama is fully self-sustainable & there is Wi-Fi throughout. If you are renting a car, you'll need a 4x4 to negotiate the access road, ford & bridges. *Cottages & suite* **$$$**, *villa* **$$$$$**

🏠 **Beau Rive** [map, page 160] (8 standard rooms, 2 cottage rooms) Castle Bruce; 📞767 445 8992; e info@beaurive.com; www.beaurive. com. Beau Rive is an elegant & intimate hotel with a traditional feel set in tranquil gardens with beautiful ocean views. Each tastefully designed & decorated room sleeps 2, has en-suite bathroom, ceiling fan & veranda looking out on the Atlantic Ocean. There is a lounge & library, free Wi-Fi, restaurant, bar & open terrace, swimming pool & sun deck. Cool sea breezes & a perfect balance of design & comfort gives this hotel its distinction. It is very popular & has an excellent reputation for high standards & personal service. **$$$$**

🏠 **Aywasi Kalinago Retreat** [map, page 146] (6 cottages & several *ajoupas*) Crayfish River, Kalinago Territory; 📞767 235 4455; e info@ aywasiretreat.com; www.aywasiretreat.com. This is a lovely place, right in the heart of the Kalinago Territory – on the same road to the Kalinago Barana Auté – on a coastal bluff & bay called Aywasi. Traditionally crafted, romantic wooden cottages combine the rustic with the modern, with all the amenities you need; bedroom, living area, veranda, bathroom & shower. The Atlantic breeze takes care of cooling. Backpackers & Wai'tukubuli National Trail through-hikers will love the traditional *ajoupas* where a hammock can be set up for you. Alternatively, pitch your tent in the forest gardens. All facilities are available. The restaurant serves a combination of traditional Kalinago, Creole & international cuisine. Tours

& excursions can be arranged for you. Aywasi is a socially conscious & environmentally friendly retreat; Kalinago staff from the local community are an integral part of the business. Perfect for exploring the Kalinago Territory & learning about the island's indigenous people. **$$$**

☀️🏠 **Citrus Creek Plantation** [map, page 163] (8 cottages & villas) Taberi, La Plaine; 📞767 446 1234; e riverside@citruscreekplantation. com; www.citruscreekplantation.com; 📘. Citrus Creek is nestled alongside the Taberi River, within a 20-acre protected valley, & within easy reach of natural attractions such as Sari Sari Falls, Wavine Cyrique, Twa Basens & Bout Sable Beach. There are no pretentions here & a relaxed & comfortable ambiance make you feel at home. Wood & stone cottages & villas, part of a rental pool programme, fit perfectly into the forest, garden & riverside setting. Fresh b/fast ingredients are delivered daily to your door each morning, & airport transfers & tours can all be arranged for you. **$$$**

🏠 **Sunrise Farm Cottages** [map, page 160] (10 cottages) Richmond, Castle Bruce; 📞767 446 0000 or 767 275 5600; e info@sunrisefarmcottages.com; www.sunrisefarmcottages.com. Set on the ocean-facing slopes of Richmond Estate, between Castle Bruce & the Kalinago Territory, the locally designed wooden cottages each sleep 2 people & have kitchen, living area, bathroom, covered veranda, TV, AC & Wi-Fi. Within the manicured grounds there is a pool, restaurant & bar (reservations preferred) as well as local farm produce. Located between WNT segments 5 & 6, Sunrise Farm Cottages is handily placed for through-hikers as well as travellers wishing to explore the Kalinago Territory. **$$**

🏠 **Vanil Vaness** [map, page 163] (1 lodge) Citrus Creek Plantation, Taberi, La Plaine; 📞767 265 3760 or 767 315 7979; e tanaquilpfund@ gmail.com; www.enjoy-dominica.com; 📘. This accommodation is a spacious loft in the pretty Vanil Vaness stone lodge, located beside the Taberi River within the Citrus Creek Plantation. The lodge has a dbl bed & 2 sgls. There is a private bathroom, kitchen, garden, terrace & riverside BBQ, & Wi-Fi throughout. Tana, the owner, lives on site & is an experienced & knowledgeable hiking & 4x4 guide. English & French spoken. **$$**.

🏠 **Beyond Vitality** [map, page 160] (3 cabins, hammocks & camping) Belle Fille, Castle Bruce; 📞767 613 8972; e sara@beyondvitality.com; www.beyondvitality.com; 📘. Set in 6 acres of riverside forest & farmland, this family-run off-grid nature camp also serves as a practical extension for holistic health, fitness & nutrition courses. Each cabin sleeps 2 – there are plans to extend accommodation options to cob cottages – and there are communal cooking, shower & toilet facilities, all very thoughtfully designed. Sleep outdoors in a hammock or pitch a tent in the camping ground (a good option for WNT Segment 5 through-hiking). Food is wholesome & healthy. Cook your own or order dinner. B/fast inc. Work exchange programmes are offered at certain times of the year when you can swap field labour for food & accommodation. Very pleasant & friendly hosts Sara & Stephan will also take you on island tours & help you organise other activities. $–$$

⌂ **Hibiscus Valley Inn** [map, page 146] (3 bungalows) Concord; ☎ 767 445 8195; e info@ hibiscusvalley.com; www.hibiscusvalley.com. Located near the village of Concord, Hibiscus Valley Inn consists of 3 rustic wooden 2-room bungalows. Each bungalow has private bathroom facilities, fans, hammock & veranda. The restaurant serves meals by request & a wide variety of tours & adventure packages can be arranged. Near the end of WNT Segment 6. $–$$

⌂ **Mermaid's Secret** [map, page 160] (3 cabins, 2 Mongolian yurts, camping pitches) Newfoundland Estate, Rosalie; ☎ 767 446 2147 & 767 295 6299; e mermaids.secret@gmail.com; www.mermaids-secret.co.uk. Mermaid's Secret offers a selection of riverside accommodation including 2 self-contained wooden cabins that have bedroom, private bathroom, kitchenette, lounge area, covered deck, fans & Wi-Fi. 1 cabin can comfortably sleep 3; the other 2. A camp bed & travel cot are also available. Mongolian yurts add a colourful twist for those looking for a little camping luxury. The Sun (sleeps 4) & Moon (sleeps 2) yurts have detached but private kitchen & bathroom facilities. Bring your own tent & camp – bathroom facilities are available for campers. The Mermaid's Tale is a bar & restaurant where guests can relax with drinks & a 'pot luck supper' (whatever is fresh & available) on a spacious deck overlooking the river. The pretty Mermaid's Pool is accessed via a short track from the gardens. This friendly, fun, family-run accommodation offers a very personal service. Land & sea tours can be organised for you. *Cabins & yurts* $$, *camping pitch* $

⌂ **Eden Heights** [map, page 160] (2 cabins) Fourmi, Castle Bruce; ☎ 767 616 4031; e edenheightsdominica@gmail.com; www.edenheightsdominica.wordpress.com; ▊. Set in 1ha of fabulous hill & riverside land near Castle Bruce, Eden Heights offers a very simple, close-to-nature experience with 2 rustic cabins, rambling gardens & a chance to join in & work for your supper! The quaint Kalinago Hut sleeps 2 & has a vetiver-thatched roof, outside toilet & shower, kitchenette & solar-powered lighting. The Coconut Cabin also sleeps 2 & has a kitchenette, toilet, shower & solar lighting. Both enjoy fabulous views of St David's Bay & the islets. Eden Heights offers a work trade; bring your skills to help develop the accommodation or gardens & in return get a place to stay & 3 (vegetarian) meals a day. In the planning is a wooden bothy for volunteers, but you can also camp in the gardens. Eden Heights suits young, outdoor- & nature-loving people. Permaculture workshops are also planned. Min 2 night stay; prices inc b/fast. $

⌂ **3 Rivers Eco Lodge** [map, page 160] (cabins, treehouses, camping) Newfoundland Estate, Rosalie; ☎ 767 446 1886; e info@ 3riversdominica.com; www.3riversdominica. com. 3 Rivers offers rustic, back-to-basics accommodation. Self-contained wooden cottages enjoy forest & ocean views & have cooking & bathroom facilities. Rudimentary wooden cabins & treehouses are near monastic in their simplicity & would suit anyone with a strong urge to retreat from the world & get back to nature. Camping pitches are also available. $

⌂ **Carib Territory Guesthouse** [map, page 146] (8 rooms) Crayfish River; ☎ 767 445 7256; e charlohotel@yahoo.com; www. avirtualdominica.com/ctgh.htm. This guesthouse offers basic dbl rooms with fans, 3 of which have en-suite bathrooms. There is a shared terrace on the upper floor with ocean views. The bar & restaurant – also with ocean view – serves b/fast & dinner to guests by reservation only. There is Wi-Fi & a shared lounge with TV. Convenient for WNT through-hikers on Segment 6. $

⌂ **Domcan's Guesthouse & Restaurant** [map, page 160] (6 self-catering suites) Castle Bruce; ☎ 767 445 7794; e domcanrestaurant@hotmail.com; www.domcansguesthouse.com. Each SC suite sleeps 2 & is equipped with galley-style kitchen, living &

dining area, bedroom & en-suite bathroom. Roll-out cots are available for an extra adult or children. Each suite has ceiling fans, TV & verandas at the front & back, with ocean views to the rear. There is Wi-Fi & a restaurant serving local food on request. Not far from WNT Segment 5. $

🏠 **Gingerlily Cottage** [map, page 163] (2 bedroom house) Riviere Cyrique; 📞 41 32 724 2607; e gingerinfo@hotmail.com; www.ginger-lily.com. Gingerlily is a fully furnished & equipped 2-bed house located in Morne Aux Frégates, just above Riviere Cyrique. It has a large balcony with great mountain & ocean views. Meals can be ordered from Restaurant Bar Ti-Suce Paradise, just a short walk away. Very good value & would suit a family or small group. $

🏠 **Sea Breeze Inn** [map, page 160] (8 rooms) Castle Bruce; 📞 767 446 0269; e info@seabreezedominica.com; www. seabreezedominica.com; 📘. Sea Breeze Inn offers seafront accommodation right on Castle Bruce Beach. Rooms sleep 2–4 & have en-suite bathroom, TV, Wi-Fi & ceiling fans. There is also a restaurant serving all-day local cuisine. B/fast included. Handy for WNT Segment 5. $

🏠 **Zion Valley** [map, page 163] (1 cottage, hammocks, camping) Fond Toufai, Delices; 📞 767 612 7587; e lngmari@roug.se; 📘. Moses James & his family offer a warm welcome to travellers wishing to learn about & live the Rasta way during their Dominica trip. Located alongside the White River at the head of the Victoria Falls & Perdu Temps trails, the rustic wooden cottage has 3 simple rooms & a shared outside washroom. There are covered shelters for hammocks & a riverside campground

where you can either pitch your own tent or rent 1. For an additional charge, meals can be cooked for you. Activities inc learning about herbal medicines, hiking to the waterfall, garden tours & holistic therapies such as mindfulness yoga & meditation. Moses has reached near celebrity status & often features in documentaries about the island. French is also spoken here. This is for open-minded travellers who are interested in getting back to nature & learning about Rastafarian living. $

CAMPING

🏕 **3 Rivers Eco Lodge** [map, page 160] Newfoundland Estate, Rosalie; (see entry on page 151). Riverside & forest camping pitches with tents to rent. Basic facilities. $

🏕 **Aywasi Kalinago Retreat** [map, page 146] Crayfish River; (see entry on page 150). Ajoupas, hammocks & camping pitches in a coastal woodland setting, located on WNT Segment 6. Facilities. $

🏕 **Beyond Vitality** [map, page 160] Belle Fille, Castle Bruce; (see entry on pages 150–1). Hammocks & camping ground in a forest & farm setting, located on WNT Segment 5. Facilities. $

🏕 **Mermaid's Secret** [map, page 160] Newfoundland Estate, Rosalie; (see entry on page 151). Fully equipped Mongolian yurts & camping pitches (bring your own tent) in a riverside setting. Bathroom facilities for campers. $

🏕 **Zion Valley** [map, page 163] Delices; (see entry opposite). Hammocks & riverside camping. Rent a tent or bring your own. A great location for hiking the Victoria Falls & Perdu Temps trails. Facilities. $

🍴 WHERE TO EAT AND DRINK

CREOLE AND INTERNATIONAL RESTAURANTS

🍴 **Zamaan Restaurant** [map, page 160] Rosalie Bay Resort, Rosalie; 📞 767 446 1010. Dining both indoors & alfresco, the restaurant at this luxury eco-resort is open to the public & serves a fusion of fine international & Creole cuisine. Reservations are recommended but you can just turn up. $$$

🍴 **Aywasi Kalinago Resort** [map, page 146] (see entry on page 150). Incomplete at the time of writing, but a restaurant is promised. Look for it on the steep road down to the Kalinago Barana Auté in Crayfish River. $$–$$$

🍴 **Islet View Restaurant** [map, page 160] Castle Bruce; 📞 767 446 0370. This is a long-established & popular restaurant with both visitors & locals. Host & chef Rudy cooks up traditional Creole dishes & is the creator of an unparalleled range of homemade rum fusions. Festooned with bamboo & banana leaves, this wooden restaurant has a great deck with awesome views of St David's Bay. Budget travellers & WNT through-hikers could also ask Rudy about his cottage, next door. Just turn up. $$

✳🍴 **Riverside Café** [map, page 163] Citrus Creek Plantation, Taberi, La Plaine; 📞 767 446

Kanki is a traditional Kalinago dish made from cassava roots (*Manihot esculenta*). The roots are peeled and grated then soaked in water before being strained through muslin. The water is left to settle in a bowl until a starchy residue has collected at the bottom. The excess water is poured away and the starchy residue mixed up with the grated cassava, sugar and a variety of spices until it becomes sticky. Portions of the mixture are wrapped in banana leaves and tied up with string before being boiled in a pot of water. After around 15 minutes the *kanki* is ready to serve.

1234. This is a lovely laid-back riverside restaurant serving high-quality French & Creole lunches & all-day snacks. They have fresh juices, wines, espresso coffee & more. There is also Wi-Fi. The menu board changes daily. Just turn up & enjoy. $$

✕ Sea Breeze Restaurant [map, page 160] Sea Breeze Inn, Castle Bruce; ✆ 767 446 0269. Perched on the margins of Castle Bruce Beach, this restaurant serves local Creole food & snacks. Located at the end of WNT Segment 5 it's a convenient spot to flop down for refreshments. Just turn up. $$

✕ Zaboka Restaurant [map, page 160] Sunrise Farm Cottages, Richmond, Castle Bruce; ✆ 767 446 000 or 767 275 5600. This restaurant specialises in traditional Creole using ingredients from the farm as well as locally caught fish. Advance reservations are preferred. $$

✕ Domcans Guesthouse & Restaurant [map, page 160] Castle Bruce; ✆ 767 445 7794. This budget guesthouse located above the village of Castle Bruce & not far off WNT Segment 5 also has a small restaurant & bar that serves local dishes. Calling ahead is recommended. $–$$

✕ Kalinago Barana Auté [map, page 157] Crayfish River; ✆ 767 445 7979. The KBA has a basic eatery that serves traditional lunches in calabash bowls. It's a handy place for a bite & refreshments if you are exploring the Kalinago Territory (there are not many places to eat in this area) or if you are through-hiking WNT Segment 6. Just turn up. $–$$

✳✕ Zion Valley 'Rastarant' [map, page 163] Fond Toufai, Delices; ✆ 767 612 7587. Traditional one-pot ital food & fresh juices are served by Rastafarian Moses James & his family at this colourful & rustic riverside eatery. It's a great spot to eat, relax & chat after exploring the southeast & hiking to the Victoria Falls. Just turn up; larger groups should call ahead. $

WHAT TO SEE AND DO

THE KALINAGO TERRITORY The Kalinago Territory covers 1,530ha on the east coast of Dominica, from the village of Bataca in the north to the village of Sineku in the south. It was established in 1903 by Dominica's first Crown Colony administrator, Hesketh Bell, who governed Dominica between 1899 and 1905. The Kalinago Territory is administered by the Kalinago Council, which is headed up by the Kalinago Chief. Both council and chief are democratically elected by residents of the villages within the Kalinago Territory every five years. The Kalinago Territory and its people are represented in government by the Ministry of Kalinago Affairs.

By law, the Kalinago Territory is communally owned. No one person can buy or sell part of the territory nor use it as collateral at a bank for a loan. This is often cited by Kalinago as a hindrance to both personal and business development and for this reason some are calling for statutory modifications or specific financial allowances to be enacted for Dominica's indigenous people. Any Kalinago resident may stake a claim to a vacant portion of land, however, and so long as no-one else has already claimed it, and the Kalinago Council approves the claim, then that resident may build a house there and work the land. Any land which has been left untended for more than a year may theoretically be claimed by someone else, subject to approval by the Kalinago Council.

There are eight hamlets within the Kalinago Territory: Bataca, Salybia, Concord, Crayfish River, Mahaut River, St Cyr, Sineku and Gaulette River. In appearance these hamlets resemble any other rural settlements on Dominica, consisting of small houses of wood and concrete, flower gardens and vegetable plots, yet there is perhaps a more visible appearance of poverty here. Along the roadside you will see wooden stalls selling traditional *larouma* basketwork and various other hand-crafted gifts. Much of the interior of the territory is uninhabited, stretching from Sineku westwards across a high ridge and up to the banks of the Pagua River in the area of Charles Warner.

The administrative centre of the Kalinago Territory is **Salybia,** which is home to the Kalinago Council and the main police station. Heading north through Salybia there is a road to the right that goes down to the Salybia Catholic Church, which was built in 1991. Its steeply pitched roof and the anchor poles that are driven deep into the ground are designed to protect the church from hurricanes. Both the exterior and interior have murals depicting Kalinago life and the arrival of Europeans. The church altar is a small hand-carved canoe.

Continue down the path towards the Atlantic coast and you will discover the original Salybia Church in an area that was once a settlement called St Marie and the subject of a community restoration project.

Located in Salybia Bay are two islets referred to as either the Salybia Isles or **Petit L'Ilet** and **Gros L'Illet**. According to Kalinago legend, each islet was once a ship that was used to transport the spirits of dead Kalinago out to sea. It is said that on at least one of the islets there is a large steel anchor chain emerging from the rock down to the ocean floor.

On a high ridge overlooking the hamlet of **Bataca** and the Pagua River Valley is **Pagua Rock**. This volcanic rock formation, some 20m in height, is said to be the home of a benevolent spirit and the steps leading up to it were once used by the people of Bataca in search of good fortune, which could be found in the form of charms on the top of the rock itself. According to legend, if you are very lucky, you may find a small white flower that only blooms one day of the year. If it is in bloom, you should rub it into the palm of your hand and then point your palm at any person you wish to command. Upon calling their name, that person will do as you wish. There is a catch, however. The rock has a number of cracks and if you were ever to catch sight of the spirit living within, you could be sure someone you knew was going to die.

Kalinago Barana Auté (*Crayfish River;* ☎ *767 445 7979;* e *kbamanager@cwdom. dm; www.kalinagobaranaaute.com;* ⊕ *daily (Kalinago guides are available by*

The Kalinago are excellent basket weavers. Their beautiful products can be purchased from stalls and craft shops around the island. Traditionally, basketwork would have been used to carry food, store clothing and supplies, and to catch fish and crustaceans. Today a variety of wares are available, including beautifully shaped baskets, bottles, mats and 'finger traps'.

They are made from the *larouma* reed (*Ischosiphon arouma*), which was probably brought by Amerindians from the Amazon River basin several thousand years ago and planted as a crop. The Kalinago word for the reed was *oualloman*, but it underwent a transition to French Creole and became *l'arouman*. It is a tall reed which, after harvesting, is split and the pith removed. The strips of reed are laid out in the sun to dry and turn a reddish brown. Some reeds are coloured black by covering them in mud and leaving them for a few days. White reeds are created simply by using the underside of the reddish-brown reeds that have been left out in the sun. Some baskets were traditionally lined with the leaves of the *z'ailes mouches* (*Caludovica insignis*) plant, which is found growing in the rainforest and provides a natural waterproofing.

Traditionally, *larouma* baskets are made by Kalinago women and you can see some of them at work at the Kalinago Barana Auté (KBA). Kalinago basketwork is sold at the KBA, at a number of roadside stalls and craft shops throughout the Kalinago Territory, and in gift shops and boutiques in Roseau.

request)) Kalinago Barana Auté (KBA) translates to 'Kalinago village by the sea'. Located down a very steep paved road in the hamlet of Crayfish River, the village is well signposted from the main road and therefore easy to find.

This showcase village was opened in April 2006. It is a representation of a pre-Columbian Amerindian village and attempts to recreate and promote greater awareness of the Kalinago tradition and former way of life. The KBA was made possible through funding by the government of Dominica and the involvement of local people within the Kalinago community. It is a very interesting place where visitors are able to experience and learn about the Kalinago traditional way of life as well as purchase crafts and souvenirs.

A circular trail begins at the reception centre where you pay an entrance fee. You can either choose to walk the trail by yourself or pay for a Kalinago guide to accompany you. The latter is absolutely the best way to make the most of your visit and to learn about Kalinago people and their culture.

Passing through a tall thatched archway there are craft stalls on the left where Kalinago women are busily creating *larouma* basketware. On the right are toilets and refreshment facilities. The **Old Mapou Tree Trail**, or Binalecaall Mapou Wêwê, takes you to the cliff side where there is a viewpoint, or Barana Neupatae, over the Atlantic. Curving back inland, the path crosses the Crayfish River before heading back to the coast again. There are further viewpoints of the rugged coastline as well as the **Isulukati Waterfall** as it cascades down the smooth rocks, through a pool and down into the sea. The pool beneath the falls is known locally as Basin Bleau and is a nice place to bathe. Signs along the route point out plants and trees that have been traditionally used by the Kalinago for both herbal medicine and shelter construction.

The trail ascends and passes a number of thatched huts called *ajoupas* and *mwenas*. On the way back towards the Crayfish River, the trail meets the impressive Karbet.

Cozier Frederick

The hamlet of Salybia, also known as St Marie, was at the heart of the Kalinago Territory long before the community's formal establishment in 1903. The region was referred to as the 'Carib Quarter', consisting of a few scattered houses along the Salybia River. In actual fact, the present-day Kalinago Territory was previously referred to as Salybia by the Colonial Office and the wider populace, and this settlement was the nucleus for all administrative affairs and social gatherings. Still evident is the ruin of the old Salybia Catholic Church, the presbytery, the health centre and the old Salybia Primary School compound, a playing field and a sheltered bay that was used as a local trading point for sailors making the journey to the French islands, and a key location for the indigenous peoples' subsistence fishing activities.

On the southern bank of the river is a monument dedicated to the last Kalinago resistance effort in 1930, which attempted to reject the decree by the colonial authorities prohibiting the free movement of freedom and goods, which was a long-standing tradition for the Kalinago people.

For a number of years, St Marie has been the final resting place for many of our ancestors as it is the location of both a Catholic and public cemetery. The Catholic Church also funded the construction of a new chapel.

The Wai'tukubuli National Trail runs through historic St Marie, which is still a residential area of around ten households.

The Salybia Heritage And Restoration Project (SHARP) has several aims: to provide the community with a solution to the evident land degradation and slippage; to establish systematic conservation of the area's flora and fauna; to undertake restorative works on the ruined church and school buildings; to create a campsite and heritage orchard; and to support and encourage alternative sustainable economic activities. This project matters to the entire indigenous community, as well as the rest of Wai'tukubuli, because it highlights the historic and cultural importance of the area to the indigenous Kalinago people.

Cozier Frederick (Kalinago name Chouboutouiba) is a postgraduate student of Kalinago history at the University of the West Indies, and development officer in the Ministry of Kalinago Affairs.

Traditionally, a *karbet* was a large thatched hut that was located in the centre of an Amerindian village, with the smaller *ajoupa* huts surrounding it. The word *karbet* is actually a French term that was used to describe this structure. The original Kalinago word was *taboui* but sadly it has been rather lost over the years. Only Amerindian men were allowed in the *karbet*, which would probably have been around 20m long and 10m wide. It was a place where they kept their weapons and slept in hammocks strung up between the beams. The women and children of the village slept in their *ajoupas*, which the men visited from time to time. The replica *karbet* in the KBA is used for presentations of Kalinago culture as well as for dance performances by groups such as the Carina Cultural Group and the Karifuna Cultural Group on cruise ship days.

The old coastal road brings you back across the Crayfish River to the reception building and the vendors. The basketwork crafts sold at the gift shops are great value for money and unique souvenirs of your visit. Try to support them if you can.

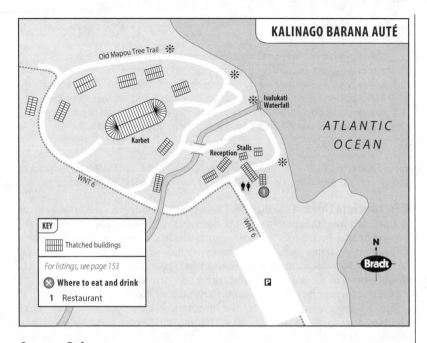

KALINAGO BARANA AUTÉ

Old Mapou Tree Trail

Isulukati Waterfall

ATLANTIC OCEAN

Karbet

WNT 6

Reception Stalls

WNT 6

KEY

Thatched buildings

For listings, see page 153

❌ **Where to eat and drink**

1   Restaurant

P

N

Bradt

Cassava Bakery (*Daniel's Cassava Bakery, Salybia* ☏ *767 617 5058*) Cassava (*Manihot esculenta*) was brought to the island by Amerindian settlers. It is extensively cultivated in many subtropical regions of the world where it is a food staple for both humans and animals. Also called **manioc**, the root must be cooked thoroughly to rid it of its toxins. It is very rich in starch but is quite bereft of protein and other nutrients. It can be cooked in many ways; as puddings (*tapioca*) or sweet cakes (*kanki*), but it is more commonly used to make a basic bread. The Cassava Bakery is functional as well as a visitor attraction. If it is operating when you are there, stop and see how it is made, then try some.

Kalinago Touna Auté   Meaning 'Kalinago village by the water, or river', Touna (*www.ouaitoucoubouli.com*) is the smallest of the Kalinago Territory's communities and also one of its most original. Some years ago, former chief and village elder, Irvince Auguiste, came up with the idea of showing travellers how Kalinago live today, rather than how they lived in the past. He convinced some of the villagers to open up their houses and gardens to visitors, to demonstrate some of the things they do, the vegetables they grow and the animals they rear, and to talk about Kalinago village life. Located alongside the Pagua River, it is a pretty setting, and the community erected traditional *ajoupas* (thatched shelters) and a *karbet* (a much larger structure usually located at the centre of a village where meetings would take place and men would sleep) for their overseas guests.

On the cruise ship itinerary for some time, the village became a popular tour excursion, but in recent times, mainly due to the poor health of Irvince, momentum has waned. But Irvince is thankfully on the mend and his enthusiasm for the project is still as strong as ever. Expect to see a resurgence of Touna Auté, including a campsite, homestays and traditional Kalinago skills workshops.

Look for the sign in Concord or reach it via a relatively new road across the Horseback Ridge, connecting Touna to Salybia. You can also contact Irvince by phone and email (767 285 1830; e *onenicepeople@gmail.com*). Alternatively, get in touch with Ali Auguiste, Irvince's nephew (e *firstnation365@gmail.com*).

L'Escalier Tete Chien L'Escalier Tete Chien is an impressive lava dyke that emerges dramatically from the sea to the foot of the coastal cliffs in Sineku. These dykes are formed by lava forcing its way up through cracks in a volcano and then hardening to form impermeable rock. Water cannot push its way through this rock at all and so the dyke becomes increasingly impressive and prominent as the rock around it is slowly eroded by the ocean. Locals who have tried free-diving down the formation report that they see it plunging to depths beyond their breath-hold limits.

The Kalinago legend that gives the formation its name tells of a giant snake climbing up the volcano from the deep, churning up the rock along the way. Upon reaching the top of the cliff, the snake made its way to a mountain called **Madjini** overlooking Sineku, where it now resides in a large cave. The snake was said to resemble a boa constrictor, hence the French Creole name Tete Chien. The lava dyke has become the boa's staircase and the snake itself is said to be one of three gods residing in the Kalinago Territory. The other two are a giant centipede in the area of St Cyr and a smaller snake locally called a *koulèv* in the Pagua Rock area near Hatton Garden. Legend has it that if you take a carved canoe paddle, some tobacco and a rooster to the snake god in his cave at Madjini, a man will appear and grant you a wish.

The track to L'Escalier Tete Chien has some interesting plants that have a number of medicinal uses in the Kalinago Territory. There are several types of bromeliad along the way as well as an endemic grass known locally as *bartad lapit*, which has a white powdery substance on its underside. According to the Kalinago, this powder may be used as an antiseptic, traditionally for the cut umbilical cord of a baby.

L'Escalier Tete Chien is located along the rugged Atlantic coastline off the village of Sineku. If you are coming from the south, look to the right-hand side when you are near the centre of the village, opposite a calabash tree. You should see a sign and a vehicle track running along the left-hand side of a bar.

If you make it as far as the parking area, it is a very short distance to the formation. Follow the track downhill until it reaches the rocky coastline and turns into a narrow, and rather steep, path. Take care here as it can be slippery. You will soon see L'Escalier Tete Chien and can therefore decide how far, if at all, you would like to go down to get a better look. If you do go down, be very careful if the sea is rough and people have been washed off the formation by high and powerful waves in the past.

EAST COAST VILLAGES Amerindians arrived on the black sandy shores of **Castle Bruce** some 2,000 years ago and built a settlement there. They named it **Kouanari** and probably lived off fish and shellfish caught from the bay and the brackish water

I do not recommend visiting L'Escalier Tete Chien alone. Indeed, it may be prudent to hire a Kalinago guide (see pages 76–7). This is not because the track to the formation is especially demanding, it is because this area has been a trouble spot for many years. Visitors have been hounded by some locals and even robbed. The bar on the main road is where trouble often begins.

If you are in a car, just drive up the track to the newly constructed reception building and park up there. If you feel threatened in any way I suggest you discreetly withdraw and report the incident to the police and the Kalinago Council in Salybia. You could also report any incidents to your hotelier and the DHTA (page 21). Try to avoid confrontation at all costs. There is no excuse for allowing visitors to continue to be hassled and threatened at L'Escalier Tete Chien, but nothing, unfortunately, ever seems to be done about it.

of the lagoon at the mouth of the river. On the fertile land of red soil they would have planted cassava and other root crops until the Europeans turned up and changed their existence forever.

When the French and British settled here, the flat and extremely fertile lands stretching inland from the bay became sugarcane and coffee plantations. In 1761, when the British captured Dominica from the French, the bay was named St David's Bay and Royal Engineer Captain James Bruce, who built some of the island's fortifications at the time, purchased all 600ha of the river valley and named the area after himself. Bruce imported over 150 West African slaves to work his cane and coffee plantations. After emancipation in 1838, the estate was abandoned and the slaves began to settle in the valley and further to the north in the area of Richmond Estate. A village eventually began to develop up the hillside overlooking the bay. Access to Roseau was by ship or on foot. People walked tracks from the village across the interior along what is now Segment 5 of the Wai'tukubuli National Trail.

The people of Castle Bruce have depended upon agriculture for their living ever since the estates broke up and free people began tending to their own smallholdings. The predominant crop for a long time has been the banana and, though you are presented with a wide corridor of dense banana plantations along the stretch of the valley to the shores of St David's Bay (known as the 'Castle Bruce stretch'), this is one of those communities that has been severely impacted by WTO (World Trade Organisation) rules affecting the banana trade. Many farmers have been forced out of agriculture and those remaining have had to rethink their whole approach to production, farm management and trade. Thanks in part to organisations such as The Fairtrade Foundation, Dominica's small banana producers still eke out a living from a crop that is now increasingly prone to diseases (a global phenomenon) such as black sigatoka, and new, less vulnerable varieties are now being introduced.

Before arriving at the shoreline, there is a school on the left and playing fields and a community entertainment centre on the right. The road ahead curves to the left into Castle Bruce village, the road before it goes north along the east coast through the Kalinago Territory, and the small road to the right winds south along the coast to the villages of Saint Sauveur and ultimately Petite Soufriere. Castle Bruce is a patchwork of dwellings perched along steep slopes overlooking the ocean below. The quaint Roman Catholic church stands at its centre.

The beach along St David's Bay is natural and wild. Smooth driftwood of all shapes and sizes litters the black sandy shoreline all the way to the mouth of the river.

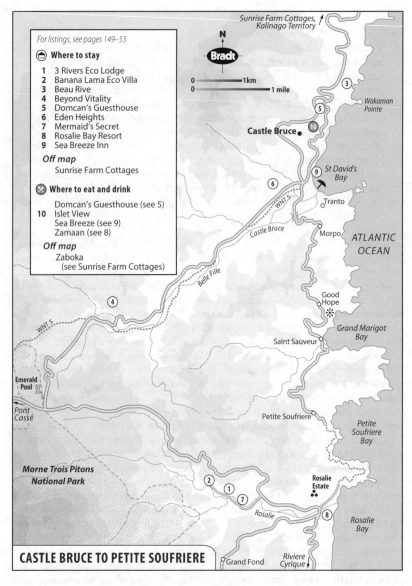

For listings, see pages 149–53

Where to stay

1 3 Rivers Eco Lodge
2 Banana Lama Eco Villa
3 Beau Rive
4 Beyond Vitality
5 Domcan's Guesthouse
6 Eden Heights
7 Mermaid's Secret
8 Rosalie Bay Resort
9 Sea Breeze Inn

Off map
   Sunrise Farm Cottages

Where to eat and drink

   Domcan's Guesthouse (see 5)
10 Islet View
   Sea Breeze (see 9)
   Zamaan (see 8)
Off map
   Zaboka
      (see Sunrise Farm Cottages)

Sunrise Farm Cottages,
Kalinago Territory

N

Bradt

0   1km
0   1 mile

Castle Bruce

Wakaman
Pointe

St David's
Bay

Tranto

WNT 5

Castle Bruce

Morpo

ATLANTIC
OCEAN

Belle Fille

Good
Hope

Grand Marigot
Bay

WNT 5

Saint Sauveur

Emerald
Pool

Pont
Cassé

Petite Soufriere

Petite
Soufriere
Bay

**Morne Trois Pitons
National Park**

**Rosalie
Estate**

Rosalie

Rosalie
Bay

CASTLE BRUCE TO PETITE SOUFRIERE

Grand Fond

Riviere
Cyrique

At the southern end of the bay are two islets and at the mouth of the Castle Bruce River is a brackish water lagoon where local families are often seen bathing in the late afternoons.

The journey south from Castle Bruce along the coast to Petite Soufriere is a scenic one. It passes through several settlements that capture the essence of both rural and coastal life on Dominica and there are also some excellent viewpoints of the rugged Atlantic coastline and photo opportunities along the way. The road is very narrow and winding, sometimes very high above the sea, other times down alongside it. There are many blind corners and very little by way of signage (Good Hope can be a little confusing) so take your time and ask the way if you are unsure.

The **Karifuna Cultural Group** and the **Carina Cultural Group** are dedicated to preserving and teaching the cultural heritage and traditions of the Kalinago people. You will see them performing at the Kalinago Barana Auté and at the village of Concord on cruise ship days, as well as at cultural events throughout the year. The groups also travel abroad occasionally, promoting and developing relationships with people sympathetic to or with a common interest in the perpetuation of Kalinago cultural heritage.

Despite government promises to construct a link to Rosalie and the southeast, the road still comes to an end a little beyond Petite Soufriere and – given the road and bridge repair challenges following Tropical Storm Erika – it seems unlikely this situation will change in the foreseeable future. Blocking the completion of the road is a huge, apparently immovable, rock. At the time of writing, a walking trail around this apparently unforeseen obstacle remains the only way to reach Rosalie.

The road to Petite Soufriere from Castle Bruce passes through fields crowded with banana plants, then crosses some marshland and goes over the Castle Bruce River. From the area of Tronto and Depaix and the cliffs of Pointe Zicac, the road climbs up towards the small settlement of **Morpo**. From here there are some beautiful views of St David's Bay, the Castle Bruce River and the twin islets on the southern tip of the bay. The journey continues along the cliff side towards the village of **Good Hope**, where it descends quite sharply down a narrow road lined with colourful crotons (an evergreen shrub). You may see evidence of the landslides that claimed lives during Tropical Storm Erika. From Good Hope there are nice views of Grand Marigot Bay and the pointed outcrop of L'Ilet just offshore along the southern tip of the cove. Near Good Hope there is a cassava-processing plant where ground manioc or *farine* is produced for island-wide consumption as well as for export. Also along this stretch are bay sheds for storing and drying bay leaves ready for boiling to extract their oil. Looking inland it is possible to see a number of young bay trees growing on the steep slopes of Morne Aux Delices. From Good Hope the road continues its descent to the fishing village of Saint Sauveur.

Saint Sauveur is located along the shore in the southwest corner of Grand Marigot Bay. Upon entering the village, the scene is dominated by the new school and Roman Catholic church sitting on a rare piece of flat ground next to the ocean. It is thought that over 2,000 years ago this area was the site of a pre-Kalinago Amerindian settlement. The church was rebuilt following a hurricane in 1916 and is undergoing refurbishment. A narrow stone road opposite the school passes between some residential properties until it reaches the village cemetery. If the word 'beautiful' could ever be considered appropriate for a cemetery then it would be for this one. Volcanic rocks protruding from the ground, surrounded by colourful plants and flowers, complement makeshift wooden crosses and headstones to create a scene of simple but stunning beauty in this place of rest. Hummingbirds in large numbers dart between flowers alongside the narrow path up to the cemetery.

A road between the new school and the church leads down to the bay. At the end of the road is the heart and soul of Saint Sauveur. Fishing has been a tradition in this village ever since the first settlers arrived here. From the **Bay Bar** (sadly, rather often closed these days) at the end of the road, villagers await the return of the fishing boats each afternoon (usually between 14.00 and 15.00). The spectacle of their return and of the villagers eagerly awaiting them is a snapshot of tradition

Vaval is the spirit of Carnival and Téwé Vaval is the symbolic burial or burning of an effigy representing the spirit of Carnival that takes place on Ash Wednesday. In the west-coast village of Dublanc and also in Bataca in the Kalinago Territory, these effigies are paraded through the streets before being burned at sunset. This ritual symbolises the end of Carnival and the beginning of the Lent period. These days, instead of marking the end of festivities, Vaval appears to be a good excuse to make the Carnival jump-ups last one more day, for those who still have any strength left, that is.

and history. 'I cooking chicken tonight, oui!' calls a woman to a boat captain with a disappointing catch. When the dorado, tuna and marlin are running, these men can easily bring back over 20 fish apiece in their brightly painted boats, which look so fragile and small against the powerful waves of the Atlantic Ocean as they round L'Ilet and return home across the bay. The Bay Bar is a good vantage point to witness this scene each afternoon throughout the year. And you can also buy fish should you so wish.

Heading south from Saint Sauveur the road climbs again until it reaches the rural farming hamlet of **Petite Soufriere**. Due to the severe terrain, it was never part of a working estate but instead developed as a peasant farming community. Today you can see the villagers of Petite Soufriere tending to their root crops on the vertiginous slopes above the ocean.

Some of Dominica's most captivating coastline is to be found from Rosalie south to Delices and Carib Point. The drama of rugged cliffs, rocky islets, crashing waves, sea stacks, hidden coves and volcanic outcrops is breathtaking. Settlements of pretty wooden houses cling to the steep hillsides above the cliffs, and rivers running from deep in the interior plummet down to the ocean as coastal waterfalls.

The Rosalie River is formed by the convergence of several other rivers (the Clarke's River, the Cacao River, the Stuart's River and several smaller tributaries) that find their source deep within the Morne Trois Pitons National Park. It is along this river that one of Dominica's largest estates was once located. Covering an area of over 840ha, the Rosalie Estate produced sugar, limes, cocoa, bananas and coconuts. In the 1780s, during a period of conflict with bands of well-organised Maroons (runaway slaves), the estate was attacked and plundered. Chief Balla, one of the most prominent Maroon leaders of the time, led an assault during which several estate workers were killed, including its manager, and much of the estate was burned down. This action led to a greater intensity and focus by Governor George Robert Ainslee to capture and kill the bands of marauding Maroons. Thanks to tip-offs from captured Maroon women, several leaders were taken, including Balla, who was shot and then exposed on the iron frame of a gibbet, taking, it is said, a week to die. (For more on the Maroons see pages 15 and 208.)

Today, the ruins of the estate buildings can still be seen near to the river mouth, including an aqueduct and sugar works. The church has been restored and is now the Rosalie Diocesan Centre.

Immediately to the south of the Rosalie River bridge, opposite the Rosalie Bay Resort, is a road that runs steeply up into the interior and the elevated village of **Grand Fond**. At a height of around 400m, the small settlement lies on a narrow ridge with deep river valleys to the north and south. The village is known to travellers and hikers for the **Dernier Falls** (pages 168–9) and the **Chemin L'Etang trail** (page 121) that climbs

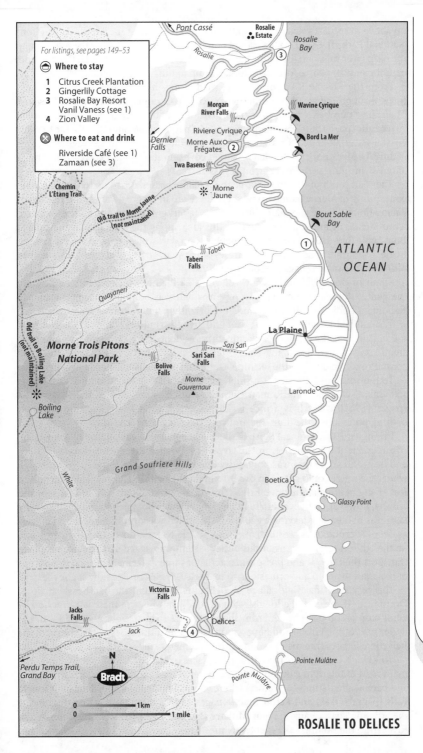

For listings, see pages 149–53

Where to stay

1 Citrus Creek Plantation
2 Gingerlily Cottage
3 Rosalie Bay Resort
  Vanil Vaness (see 1)
4 Zion Valley

Where to eat and drink

Riverside Café (see 1)
Zamaan (see 3)

Pont Cassé

Rosalie Estate

Rosalie Bay

Rosalie

Morgan River Falls

Wavine Cyrique

Riviere Cyrique

Bord La Mer

Morne Aux Frégates

Dernier Falls

Twa Basens

Chemin L'Etang Trail

Old trail to Morne Jaune (not maintained)

Morne Jaune

Bout Sable Bay

ATLANTIC OCEAN

Taberi

Quayaneri

Taberi Falls

La Plaine

Morne Trois Pitons National Park

Old trail to Boiling Lake (not maintained)

Sari Sari

Sari Sari Falls

Bolive Falls

Morne Gouvernaur

Laronde

Boiling Lake

White

Grand Soufriere Hills

Boetica

Glassy Point

Victoria Falls

Jacks Falls

Delices

Jack

Perdu Temps Trail, Grand Bay

Bradt

Pointe Mulâtre

Pointe Mulâtre

N

0   1km
0   1 mile

ROSALIE TO DELICES

up above the Stuart's River valley to the Freshwater Lake in the Morne Trois Pitons National Park. The road up to Grand Fond has some scenic views of the interior and the deep river valley on the south side of the ridge. As buses rarely reach Grand Fond, expect plenty of people to ask you for a ride up to the village if you are driving.

From the Rosalie River bridge, the road along the southeast coast twists and turns through the small communities of **Riviere Cyrique** and **Morne Aux Frégates**. There are a number of interesting natural features in this area including the **Morgan River Falls** (page 166) **Twa Basens** river pools (pages 165–6) and the **Wavine Cyrique** coastal waterfall and cliff trail (pages 171–2). South of the trail to Wavine Cyrique is **Bord La Mer** or **Secret Beach** a secluded cove and dark-sand beach – think twice about swimming as there are strong cross currents.

The road south of Riviere Cyrique to La Plaine passes a road up to the mountain community of **Morne Jaune**, from where there are more great views, and the **Taberi Estate**. Once a large sugar and lime estate, Taberi got its name from the Kalinago word *taboui*, meaning 'house'. Also in this area, along the shoreline, is the rugged **Bout Sable Bay**. This bay of smooth pebbles and dark volcanic sand is a recognised turtle nesting site where, at certain times of the year, giant leatherbacks can be seen returning to lay their eggs (see pages 11–12).

South of Bout Sable Bay is the village of **La Plaine**, which gets its name from the gently sloping area of flat land upon which it is built. The original Kalinago settlement here was called *Koulirou*. The brightly painted Roman Catholic church with small bell tower, galvanised roof and arched windows stands at the centre of the village near the school. Predominantly residential, La Plaine has a number of small convenience stores and snackettes (check out **Turtle Bay Café** on the main coastal road), and is also the location of the **Sari Sari Falls** trailhead (page 170).

To the south of La Plaine is a small village called **Boetica**, also once a Kalinago settlement. Opposite the Roman Catholic church is the start of the **Glassy Trail** (pages 169–70), which is a nice walk to the cliffs and the interesting saltwater bathing pools along the dramatic and very rugged eastern coastline.

In August 2015, Tropical Storm Erika caused major devastation, not to mention considerable inconvenience, in this area. The Boetica River runs through a deep and beautiful gorge that was previously filled up – save for a large culvert through which the water could pass – in order to build the road to Delices. This was quite a feat of engineering at the time. Erika's torrential rains built up behind this dam and culvert, however, until eventually the weight of water became too much. The entire dam was obliterated, leaving a gap in the road that was over 30m wide and at least as deep. A crude track was cut, allowing people to walk down into the gorge and up the other side, and an ingenious pulley system was rigged up to enable people to transport their goods and possessions across, as well as farmers to send their crops of bananas, plantain and provisions to market. A Bailey bridge now spans the gap.

The very quiet farming village of **Delices** is located at the southeastern tip of Dominica. At the end of a long stretch of road from Boetica there is a junction by a bus stop and a pay phone. From the north, the road straight ahead goes to the upper part of the village and beyond to the very beautiful coastal farmlands of the Belvedere Estate. The small Roman Catholic cemetery in this area, located on a high narrow ridge, is one of the most beautiful places of rest you could ever imagine. The main road to the right runs down to the lower village and then past arrowroot, bay and banana plantations to Victoria where you will find the trailhead for the **Victoria Falls** (pages 170–1) and **Perdu Temps** (pages 144–5) hiking trails. The road meets the Atlantic coast again at Point Mulâtre Bay and River (this is where the White River from the Boiling Lake eventually meets the ocean). It is quite a nice beach and there are some pleasant bathing pools along the river. Beyond the bridge the road climbs steeply up to the peak of Paix Bouche, part of the Foundland volcano, and then heads steeply down to the lost village of Petite Soufriere (page 162).

THE PAGUA RIVER VALLEY The Pagua River is one of Dominica's longest and runs northeastwards from the area of D'Leau Gommier in the Central Forest Reserve (page 207), all the way to the east coast, where it meets the Atlantic Ocean at Pagua Bay just south of Douglas Charles Airport. The river also marks the western boundary of the Kalinago Territory. It is a very picturesque river and has a number of accessible bathing pools and cascades.

Both river and road pass through the small village of **Concord** on the northern edge of the Central Forest Reserve. From the main road you should see a sign to **Kalinago Touna Auté** (pages 157–8), where you can experience a little of contemporary Kalinago life. The tall ridge you can see to the southeast of the village is Horseback Ridge in the Kalinago Territory and you can drive up to the top and then down into the village of Salybia via a narrow road that runs through Touna Auté.

To the north of Concord, where the Pagua River meets the sea, is **Hatton Garden**. As the name suggests, this was once a British-owned estate that produced sugar, rum and limes. It had a water wheel and was worked by around 200 slaves. The ruins of the factory are now part of the former Silks Hotel (closed at the time of writing). When you emerge from the interior to meet the sea at Hatton Garden, you are greeted by the beautiful and dramatic Pagua Bay. At the junction before the bridge, the road to the right goes south along the coast through the Kalinago Territory and the road straight ahead follows the coast to Marigot, Douglas Charles Airport and the beaches and villages of the northeast.

On the northern edge of Pagua Bay is Marigot (page 188) and on the southern edge is the village of **Atkinson**. The original Kalinago name for this village was Warawa, but it was renamed in the 1760s after William Atkinson, a British landowner in the area. It is a small farming community overlooking the bay on the northern boundary of the Kalinago Territory. Right next to Atkinson is the tiny hamlet of Antrizle. Look for a bus stop and (occasionally) a sign down to Antrizle Beach, another very pretty Dominican secret.

On the road between the village of Concord and the northern boundary of the Central Forest Reserve is an area called **Deux Branches**. Along the side of the road there are several colourfully painted and rather overgrown signs for the **Sisserou Falls** (sometimes also called Diamond River Falls, sometimes something else entirely). Occasionally the bush is cut back and someone may ask for a 'contribution' for passing over private land and trail maintenance, other times it is completely overgrown and there is no-one around. In actual fact, these falls are a series of large river rapids and pools rather than a waterfall, but it is a scenic and interesting natural site nevertheless, if you can be bothered to beat your way through the bush. The tallest river rapid can be seen from the road if the weeds aren't too high, but a track (if you can find it) just beyond the signs leads to a great river pool. It may well to be too overgrown to find, but it is worth a try. Be careful of traffic if you decide to park up and take a look.

ACTIVITIES AND SPECIAL INTERESTS

TWA BASENS This is a series of three pools and cascades located on a shallow river near the village of Riviere Cyrique. The first pool is very accessible and follows a short walk. The pools above it require a short but wet and slippery climb up each cascade. All three pools are fairly deep, very pretty and make an excellent spot for a refreshing river bathe, especially if you have just been climbing Wavine Cyrique (pages 171–2).

To get to Riviere Cyrique from Roseau, take the Imperial Road via Pont Cassé and follow the signs to Rosalie and La Plaine. For bus information see page 50.

On the south side of Riviere Cyrique, right next to the sign for the village and a road bridge that crosses a river, you will find the rather overgrown trailhead for this short walk. The track is next to the concrete block, heading inland. Walk it for a very short distance until you reach the stream. Simply follow it. You will come to the first pool and cascade in no more than five minutes. The track runs along the left-hand side of the first pool right up to the cascade, which you must then climb if you wish to go up to the two higher cascades and pools. It is slippery but it's not high. I would suggest leaving your bags and towel at the bottom, getting into swimming gear and just getting wet and having a bit of fun climbing up. I like the second and third pools best.

MORGAN RIVER FALLS Few seem to have heard of this waterfall (perhaps it goes by other local names) but it is impressive and very accessible. There's just a short scramble up boulders and cascades to negotiate. You'll get a bit wet, but it's a tall cascading waterfall, especially worth seeing in the wet season when it is flooding a bit more. There is a short, rather overgrown track, with no sign (yet) on the apex of a bend just before you enter the village of Riviere Cyrique from the north. If you reach the sign for Wavine Cyrique, then you have gone a little bit too far. Go back to the last sharp bend crossing a river and look on the inland side of the road. As you look inland, the track is to the right (don't wander down the drainage gulley, you may never get out again!).

Walk along the track until it meanders down to the stream; ignore any track that goes uphill or into the bush as they are just farmers' trails. Criss-cross the stream until you come to boulders and climb up the left-hand side. You'll see the waterfall within 10–15 minutes of the road. It is slippery and wet, but that's part of the fun.

TURTLE WATCHING At certain times of the year (usually from late March to October) it is possible to see endangered giant leatherback turtles coming ashore to lay their eggs (March and April), and then baby turtles returning to the sea (September/October). Turtles arrive at night, but organised releases of young turtles usually take place during the day.

Head for Rosalie before nightfall, giving yourself time to set up a tent on the beach (I know, it isn't strictly allowed but it is 'unofficially accepted' when it comes to turtle watching). There is a trail with access to the beach on the right of the Rosalie Bay Resort (please don't wander through their grounds). Look for a painted hut (The Ark) and a sign. It's actually a nice little track and it will bring you out on the beach next to the mouth of a small river. Head to the right and find a spot. At the height of the season when turtles come ashore, the beach is patrolled through the night. This is a service offered to guests of Rosalie Bay Resort, but the warden will alert you (or wake you up) if turtles come ashore. Just befriend him and he'll be happy to share his knowledge. It's a good idea to bring along a flashlight with a red filter as this gives you light without confusing the turtles.

Please be sure to view these creatures as unobtrusively and respectfully as possible. There is a period after digging and laying eggs when the turtle rests; this is the time for a photograph or two, but the warden will advise you. For information about the best times to go, you could contact the Forestry, Wildlife and Parks Division (☏ 767 266 3817).

BORD LA MER 'SECRET BEACH' Locally known as Bord La Mer, meaning 'beside the sea', a short downhill walk brings you to a secluded sandy cove. It is pretty, bounded by littoral woodland and coconut palms. It has black sand and rolling waves and is a nice spot to relax with a picnic. Unfortunately the sea has a strong undertow and rather unpredictable cross-currents making it unsuitable for bathing safely.

There is a sign for the trail on the main road passing through the east-coast village of Riviere Cyrique. It is a little to the south of the sign for Wavine Cyrique. Follow the paved road down to the playing field, where you will see a second sign at the top of the trail on the right-hand side of the field.

Follow the clear, wide track downhill for 20 minutes or so until you reach the beach.

HIKES

CHARLES WARNER 'SECRET POOL' ✳ (*Difficulty: T: 2; R: 2; E: 1; D: 2; Rating = 4.4; Guide suggested*) This is a fairly easy, though quite often waterlogged and muddy, trail through lush rainforest in a region called Charles Warner, on the south side of the Pagua River, near the village of Concord. It takes about an hour to reach a rather idyllic and 'secret' rainforest pool and cascade.

Charles Warner was a British landowner, descendant of Sir Thomas Warner and relative of Kalinago Chief Thomas 'Indian' Warner, who was murdered by his half-brother in the infamous massacre of 1764 (see page 214). Charles Warner purchased a number of properties on Dominica, his main estate being in the parish of St Paul on the west coast between Mahaut and Layou, and now called Warner.

The trailhead for this hike is quite difficult to describe and find (perhaps someone should put up a sign). You have to look for it about halfway between the Deux Branches (where you exit the Central Forest Reserve) and the village of Concord. If you are travelling from the Heart of Dominica towards Concord, it is on the right-hand side, opposite a utilities pole, just after a concrete drainage culvert. There is a small, stony area where you could park a vehicle off the road, and beyond it, lots of red ginger lilies. The narrow track runs through low vegetation, past the gingers, towards the river. It is often waterlogged and there are stepping stones.

You will reach the Pagua River in just a few minutes. Look for the trail on the far bank (it climbs and curves steeply up and around a large boulder) and find a place to cross. Though fairly shallow around the margins, the river does get quite deep, especially if it has been raining. The river is lovely and bathing here is irresistible on the return journey.

On the far side of the river, climb up the bank (take it easy – it's narrow and steep) and then follow the track. Ignore any spurs you see going down to the left. This is pretty much the rule of thumb for the rest of this hike too. It's tempting to follow the track that looks like it goes down to the river but stick to the main trail and it will take you right to the pool.

You will pass occasional plots of farmed land and, after about 20 minutes, you'll pass a small wooden farmhouse down to your right. Climb up the bank (try not to destroy the carved-out mud steps) and keep going up and over a couple of small ridges until you come to more dense forest. You'll hear the river running down to your left and it will soon come into view.

The trail follows the right-hand bank of the Charles Warner River, quite often fairly high above it, and the trail is a little steep, eroded and challenging in places. Carefully negotiate tree roots and rocks as you gradually descend to river level. The trail can be rather waterlogged, muddy and slippery at this point, but you are nearly there.

You will emerge at the rocky margins of the pool, which is deep and suitable for bathing. Surrounded by typical rainforest vegetation, it is a very picturesque and peaceful place. It's possible to climb up the cascade (the right-hand side is best), but please be careful. There are a couple of nice pools up above.

MADJINI RIDGE TRAIL *(Difficulty: T: 4; R: 0; E: 4; D: 2; Rating = 6.3; Guide essential)* This rather obscure and difficult ridge trail was being developed at the time of writing and was part of an initiative aimed at reviving and rehabilitating old heritage trails within the Kalinago Territory. Formerly used by Sineku farmers to carry produce – in particular bananas – to the village of Touna (Concord) on the Pagua River, where there was a boxing station, it follows one of many sharp ridges emerging from the diminutive yet legendary Madjini Mountain (where the snake that created L'Escalier Tete Chien is said to reside). Should this trail have no signage by the time you read this book, I recommend you contact either Kent Auguiste or his son Ali via email (see First Nation, page 76) and hire one of them as your guide.

Begin the trail at Salybia, where the trailhead can be found just off the link road between Salybia and Touna on the Horseback Ridge. Having passed a small farmstead, the trail climbs the steep face of a mountain ridge through thick bush and then forest until reaching the spine. From this point onwards the trail follows the narrow back of Madjini Ridge in a southerly direction. The going is tough. You have to negotiate steep and slippery ascents and descents, clamber over tree roots and try not to let the vertiginous drop down the northern flank get into your head.

After around 2 hours you will reach the highest point of the ridge where you can enjoy great views of the territory and beyond. The trail splits at this point with one route leading to Madjini Mountain and the other making a sharp descent through the forests and into the farmlands of Sineku. You should emerge into Sineku village opposite the trailhead for L'Escalier Tete Chien after approximately 3 hours.

With a good Kalinago guide, you'll learn much about the history of trails such as this, about the legends of Madjini, about the trees and plants along the way, and how some of them are used in traditional Kalinago bush medicine.

CHEMIN L'ETANG (FROM GRAND FOND) *(Difficulty: T: 2; R: 0; E: 2; D: 2; Rating = 3.8; Guide suggested)* For details on this historic hike please see page 121. The trailhead in Grand Fond is at the very top of the village. Where the road ends and then forks, simply keep following the wide track to the right (use the communication poles as your guide). Now follow the instructions given in *Chapter 5*, but in reverse of course!

DERNIER FALLS *(Difficulty: T: 2; R: 0; E: 3; D: 1; Rating = 3.8; Guide not essential)* The Dernier Falls is an interesting waterfall within a circular cavern in a deep river valley to the south of Grand Fond. The trail down to the river is short but steep – it takes about 45 minutes each way. At the time of writing the trail wasn't in great shape; some of the steps had eroded or been washed away and it was muddy and slippery. It may have been fixed up again by the time you hike it. But this shouldn't put you off – it's worth the effort; just take your time going down, stick to the main track and ignore any narrow spurs heading off into farmers' fields at the top. On the descent you'll come across a few shortcuts that go straight down, otherwise follow the switchbacks of the original track. When you finally emerge at the bottom, turn around to take note of where you need to go on the way back, and then make your way upriver (to the right) over the rocks to the cavern. The waterfall is inside.

Buses to Grand Fond run very infrequently (see page 50 for information on where to catch a bus) and you will often see people at the bottom of the road, near the Rosalie River bridge, waiting and hoping for a ride up to the village. If you are travelling by car, head for Rosalie and La Plaine from Pont Cassé and, once you cross the Rosalie River, take a right straight away and follow the road all the way up to the village. Keep going all the way through the village (it's longer than you probably expect) until you see a signpost near the top on your left. The trailhead is just a couple of minutes up this little village road; there's a sign. Park by the sign or on the main village road without blocking anyone in.

An alternative way to get to the trailhead is to hike the Chemin L'Etang trail from the Freshwater Lake (pages 122–3).

THE GLASSY (GLASSIE) TRAIL (*Difficulty: T: 2; R: 0; E: 1; D: 1; Rating = 2.5; Guide not essential*) This is a fairly easy hike starting at the southeastern village of Boetica to a high clifftop and then down to a volcanic isthmus where there are three small saltwater pools. You should do it on a sunny, windless day because if the sea is rough you will not be able to access the pools safely. Besides, it looks a lot prettier in the sunshine.

Boetica is located on the east coast between Delices and La Plaine. To get there from Roseau, take the road from Pont Cassé to Rosalie and La Plaine. At the time of writing, due to Tropical Storm Erika landslides, it was not possible to take the southern route via the evacuated village of Petite Savanne. See page 50 for bus information.

Find the trailhead opposite the Roman Catholic chapel in Boetica; it is clearly signposted. Pass alongside farmlands and eventually through woodland towards the coast. There are views of the ocean and of L'Ilet, a rocky islet just offshore. The trail snakes back inland and descends at a gentle gradient through the woods into a gulley where it turns sharply back towards the ocean. Take care here as it is quite wet with loose rocks and fallen leaves making it a little greasy underfoot. Torrential rain has also eroded part of the track where it crosses the stream so you have to climb up a low bank. Check rocks are solid before giving them your weight. The trail makes two more full turns inland and at the second gulley you must actually follow the river bed before coming to the trail again on your right as you head back out towards the ocean. The cliffs come into view after around 30 minutes from the start and the trail reaches a point where it runs across a narrow ridge to the Glassy isthmus. Cliffs and ocean are now on either side of you, some distance down. Be careful. You will come to a viewpoint on your left where you look down towards a sea cave. Don't lean on the tree hanging over the edge! Follow the path down towards the sea. It will reach a point where it gets steeper and reaches sea level via a series of switchbacks. Take care here as the terrain can be rather crumbly underfoot. The path narrows considerably and continues around a rock face to a

> ### BOLIVE (BOLI) FALLS
>
> Keen hikers may come across references to the Bolive or Boli Falls. Honestly, if your time is limited, you should pass on it. The trail is very long (3 hours each way), usually very muddy and in places quite steep and overgrown; and the 'reward' at the end is a little disappointing. Bolive is a three-tier cascading waterfall which you never really see from any decent vantage point – there's simply too much forest. Instead the trail brings you to the middle pool, which is very lovely, it has to be said, but you do find yourself sitting there, scratching your head wondering whether it was really worth such a long trek. So I'd say Bolive is only for the dedicated hiker who has done everything else and has plenty of time to spare. The trailhead is unmarked beside a farmer's field in the community of Carse O Gowrie, between Taberi and La Plaine. You will definitely need a guide.

volcanic outcrop where, once you make your way down, you will find three saline pools, one of which is very small but quite beautiful. This kind of lava formation can be quite sharp so take care of hands and footing. Also, if the sea is rough, keep a watchful eye on it – people have been swept away here – 'Never turn your back on the sea!', the locals will yell at you. On a clear day there are nice views to the north and south along this unusual stretch of coastline.

PERDU TEMPS (FROM DELICES) *(Difficulty: T: 3; R: 3; E: 2; D: 3; Rating = 6.9; Guide essential)* This hike is described on pages 144–5. The route from Delices is exactly the same, but in reverse, of course. You must take a guide.

SARI SARI FALLS * *(Difficulty: T: 3; R: 3; E: 2; D: 2; Rating = 6.3; Guide suggested)* This is a very impressive waterfall located on the Sari Sari River behind the east-coast village of La Plaine. The hike to the waterfall is fairly challenging as half of it is in the river itself. You have to negotiate rocks, boulders, cascades and pools. Though it is not especially far, the terrain is difficult, making this a hike for the adventurous. Please do not attempt this hike when it is raining or if there has been recent heavy rain. The Sari Sari River is prone to flash flooding in these conditions and people have died here.

Due to landslides on the south coast caused by Tropical Storm Erika, La Plaine, is currently only accessible via the east coast and not from the south. See page 50 for bus information.

When you reach La Plaine on the main coastal road, keep going until you see the sign for Sari Sari Falls. Drive up through the village and keep going until you can get no further (ask for directions if you are unsure). The paved road ends at a vehicle track. If you are driving, park up here.

Follow the wide track to the end. It narrows and curves to the right, heading through farmland and then steeply down an old, well-worn track to the river. At the time of writing there was a landslide near the bottom and the final series of steps was muddy and slippery. This may have improved by the time you get here.

Cross the river and pick up the trail on the other side. It will lead you through light woodland with the river visible on your left. After a short distance you will reach the river again. Head straight across and find the trail on the other side. Again an old, well-worn trail, you will climb steeply upwards, high above the left bank before descending very sharply back down to the river again. The trail is narrow on this section and in places rather eroded so take your time as you are rather high up.

When you reach the river, the easy part of this hike is over. Now you have to make your way upstream along the river bed. Look ahead for cairns (piles of stones) or other similar markings that helpful hikers may have left to show you where to go next. It is challenging, but fun and not too difficult. The key to this is patience; take the time to figure out the best and safest route (if no signs are visible) – you could also look out for footprints in the sand. After about 30 minutes or so you should be able to see the waterfall. I found that access to the top was easier up the left-hand side of these final boulders. At the time of writing there was no pool directly beneath the waterfall; it had silted up and was full of rocks following Tropical Storm Erika, but the pools before it were deep and refreshing.

Take your time on the return leg; most accidents happen on the way back when you are tired and a little less careful.

VICTORIA FALLS * *(Difficulty: T: 3; R: 3; E: 0; D: 2; Rating = 5.0; Guide suggested)* If it is raining heavily, or has been, pick a different hike. Flash flooding does happen here and negotiating the White River's rapids, pools and enormous boulders can be tricky even in the dry season. But this is my favourite Dominica waterfall hike so do try it if conditions are good enough. Be prepared to get wet. Leave a change of clothes in your vehicle or with Moses at Zion Valley, take a dry bag for cameras and other valuables.

The Victoria Falls Trailbegins on the southern outskirts of the village of Delices. There is a sign; also look for a sign to Zion Valley (page 152). As the southern route to Delices is closed due to landslides at the time of writing, the only way to Delices is via Rosalie and La Plaine. See page 50 for bus details.

From the sign on the main road, either walk or drive down the vehicle track to the clearing at the bottom where you'll find the Zion Valley 'Rastarant' and cottage. You can hire a guide here if you'd like to be accompanied and it's also a great spot for refreshments and some ital food at the end of your adventure.

The trail begins by the 'Rastarant' and heads down to the river. You will see a spur almost immediately to your right. Take it.

This trail and the riverscape itself were transformed by Tropical Storm Erika, but actually for the better. It is even more beautiful than before, with lots of river pools and cascades. Access to the main waterfall pool at the end is also easier than it used to be (but then it could hardly be more difficult), though it does require a degree of boulder climbing.

Follow the trail along the bank and down to the river where you must make your first crossing. Look across to the far bank, towards the apex of the bend in the river. Head for the large rocks and boulder on the other side and try to find the route up to the top of the bank, where you will find a track through low-growing vegetation (mostly ferns). Follow this track until you reach the river again and cross over to the other side. Follow the riverbank and look for a path up above it through the trees. Don't worry if you can't find it; simply follow the right-hand bank. If you do find the track, you will emerge at the river again. Stick to the right-hand side until you can go no further, then cross to the left, make your way over the rocks and boulder and around the bend until the waterfall comes into view. I found the best way to reach the main pool was to negotiate the boulders, cascades and pools on the left, but it is tricky and slippery, of course. You'll definitely get wet, but that's all part of the fun!

WAVINE CYRIQUE ✳ (*Difficulty: T: 4H; R: 0; E: 4; D: 1; Rating = 5.6H; Guide strongly recommended*) Many people mistakenly refer to this site as the 'Secret Beach'. Actually the Secret Beach is a different place a little further south (see Bord La Mer, pages 166–7). If you see photographs of a waterfall shooting from the top of a high cliff down into the sea, you are actually looking at a place called Wavine Cyrique.

Whatever people may tell you, please be under no illusions: this is a challenging and potentially dangerous hike. But it is also unique and quite unforgettable. It requires a steep climb from the top of a cliff to the bottom using ropes, a rope ladder and tree roots. If you are afraid of heights, this may not be for you. It is a physically challenging hike because you have to use upper and lower body strength on the vertical climbing section, but moreover it is a mental challenge. Conquering your apprehension and fear is certainly half the battle. Taking a guide is a very good idea on this one for both reassurance and safety, and to show you the best way down and back up again.

To find the Wavine Cyrique trailhead, take a bus or drive to the small village of Riviere Cyrique on the east coast (see page 50 for bus information). There is a very clear sign on the main road towards the centre of the village. When you have found the sign, follow the narrow, croton-lined road through a pretty residential area until the paved road ends next to a brick house on the right. If you are in a car, find a spot that will not block the road or impede access for others. A short vehicle track takes you a short distance to the main trailhead. Just by the trail sign at the end of the vehicle track is a wooden house on the right. Sometimes you'll see a man there (Nicodemus 'Cokes' Lawrence) and, if you haven't already organised a guide, ask him to take you.

Walk for around 15 minutes along a ridge and then down a trail with rather worn tree-fern steps. It will bring you to the top of the cliff, where all you will see is the end of a rope tied to a tree. Make your way down and you will come to a second rope. The climb is vertical now and you must use a combination of rope, tree roots and branches to get down. Take your time. Going down is much harder than coming up because it is difficult to see where you are putting your feet and, as you have never been here before, your imagination is running riot. Be sure you have a firm footing and are secure before lowering yourself or letting go of anything! You will come to a rock face and a rope ladder. Most people think this is the hardest part because the rope ladder is a little wobbly and you do not have the security of lots of tree roots to hang on to. Just before the bottom of the ladder, shift yourself to your right across the rock face above and behind a small tree until your feet reach the ground. This is a bit tricky. Follow the ropes and breathe!

Almost immediately to your right is another short but tricky climb to a narrow track. And it is narrow. Hold on to the vegetation on your right; it can be slippery here, especially with fallen leaves in the wet. You'll come to another short climb and then a long and rather slippery route straight down towards the beach. Use the rope to help you walk down safely.

When you reach the bottom, take note of the ropes so you can find the trail on the way back. Now, facing the sea, go left over the coastal rocks until you come to a black-sand beach and the Wavine Cyrique waterfall. If conditions allow, go and stand underneath it, but keep a watchful eye on the waves, the surge and the currents.

Hopefully your legs have stopped shaking by now.

Remember to save a little energy as you have to climb all the way back up again. Take your time going back up, and pick your way carefully over the tree roots (I find using the tree roots rather than the rope is the best way to climb – I just use the rope as a directional guide). For some reason the rope ladder feels harder going up than down too.

When you make it to the top, hike back up the trail (was it really this steep when you came down?) and pat yourselves on the back. I like to go to Twa Basens (pages 165–6) to wash and cool off afterwards and then head for the Riverside Restaurant at Citrus Creek (pages 152–3) for a strong drink and something good to eat.

8

Cabrits National Park and the North

In this chapter we explore the historic Cabrits National Park. We head to the remote coastal villages of the north, crossing the Morne Aux Diables volcano, and we discover hidden waterfalls and volcanic springs. Then we travel to Calibishie and down to the sprawling community of Marigot, exploring beaches, river cascade, and dramatic coastal formations along the way.

GETTING THERE AND AWAY

BY CAR The west-coast road from Roseau gets you to Portsmouth in about an hour. After passing through the medical university campus and community of Picard, the road curves towards the sea at Glanvillia where you must take a right turn along the seafront and over the Indian River (page 196). At the small three-way junction when you arrive in Portsmouth, the road ahead goes through the town and on to Purple Turtle Beach, the Cabrits National Park, Douglas Bay and the villages of the northwest, where you can connect to a link road that takes you over Morne Aux

GREAT DAYS OUT

Here are some suggestions for great days out in the north of Dominica. You will find details of all of the places mentioned in this chapter.

CABRITS, BEACH AND INDIAN RIVER Spend a morning wandering the forest trails of the Cabrits National Park and follow it up with lunch on the beach (either a picnic at Douglas Bay – buy food from the market near Ross – or at the Purple Turtle Beach Club). After a swim, take a late afternoon boat ride up and down the Indian River.

SEGMENT 12 LOOP, VOLCANO DRIVE AND BEACH Park up where the final stretch of WNT Segment 12 leaves Vieille Case (see pages 248–9) and then wander along this pretty coastal track to Lower Pennville. Walk back to Vieille Case along the road and hike up to Bwa Nef Falls *en route*. Back at your car, drive across the Morne Aux Diables volcano via Cold Soufriere and then chill out by the beach at Toucari.

LA CHAUDIERE, LUNCH AND RED ROCKS Drive through Bense and along the Hampstead Ridge and then stroll down to La Chaudiere for a dip in the pool. Have lunch in Calibishie (Rainbow and Bamboo are good options), call in at the Pointe Baptiste Estate for chocolate and then enjoy the late afternoon sun on the Red Rock coast.

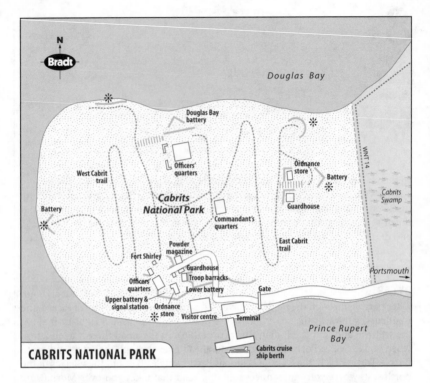

CABRITS NATIONAL PARK

Diables to Pennville. The road to the right links the west with Bornes, Vieille Case, Calibishie and the northeast coast.

To get to Marigot and Douglas Charles Airport from Roseau, take the Imperial Road through the interior, passing Pont Cassé and the Central Forest Reserve, emerging at the Atlantic coastline via Concord and Hatton Garden. Heading north along the coastal road, you pass through the sprawling hillside community of Marigot. Douglas Charles Airport is just a little further along the coast. It usually takes an hour or so to reach the airport from Roseau.

BY BUS See page 50 for information about buses in Roseau and Portsmouth.

 WHERE TO STAY

NORTHWEST

Map, page 182, unless otherwise stated

🏠 **Secret Bay** (6 units) Petite Baie, Portsmouth; ✆767 445 4444; e info@secretbay.dm; www. secretbay.dm; f. Secret Bay is undoubtedly Dominica's most exclusive (& expensive) eco-luxury resort. There are 6 units with a further 2 in progress, set amid coastal gardens overlooking Prince Rupert Bay & the Cabrits National Park. Artistically designed & constructed from Guyanese greenheart wood & local red cedar, each is completely private, fully self-contained & equipped with top-notch facilities &

appliances. All have AC, Wi-Fi, music systems, Apple TV, books & DVDs. The 2 villa units have private pools. Services include personalised cooking, private dining, massage, yoga, kayaking, snorkelling & boat rides. Staff will also organise all your island activities should you so wish. The gardens have viewing, dining & music decks & there is a path down to the small & secluded Ti Bay Beach where you'll also find the Souce Shack restaurant and bar. The remote & pretty Secret Beach is just around the bluff & can only be reached by kayak or boat. Min stay 5 days. **$$$$$**

🏠 **Manicou River** [map, page 185] (3 cottages) Tanetane, Portsmouth; ☏ 767 616 8903; e info@manicouriver.com; www.manicouriver.com; 🅵. Manicou River's hand-crafted wooden cottages, bar & bistro are completely off-grid & set within 4ha of forested hillside overlooking Douglas Bay & the Cabrits National Park. Each cottage has a dbl bed, bathroom, shower, SC facilities & deck with panoramic views. The property's expansive forest gardens have walking trails & the pretty Manicou River borders the property. The Manicou River Bar & Bistro also overlooks the Cabrits & Douglas Bay & serves French Caribbean dishes. Reservations are recommended though not essential. Manicou is a peaceful & private retreat with great views at the end of a partly unpaved & steep feeder road. A 4x4 is recommended. **$$$$**

🏠 **Picard Beach Cottages**
(18 cottages) Picard; ☏ 767 445 5131; e info@picardbeachcottages.dm; www.picardbeachcottages.dm; 🅵. This tranquil family-owned resort has private wooden cottages in pleasant & private beachside gardens. Each solar-powered cottage has en-suite bathroom, TV, AC, Wi-Fi, ceiling fans, private veranda with deckchairs, telephone & SC facilities. All cottages face the sea, with Prince Rupert Bay & the Cabrits National Park a picturesque backdrop; some are directly on the beachfront. Watersports, wellness activities & a range of island tours can all be arranged. Le Flambeau Restaurant (page 179) is just a short walk away. **$$$$**

🏠 **Hotel The Champs** (5 rooms) Picard; ☏ 767 445 4452; e info@hotelthechamps.com; www.hotelthechamps.com; 🅵. The Champs offers modern, well-furnished superior & garden room accommodation on a high hillside position above Picard, enjoying fabulous views of Prince Rupert Bay & the Cabrits National Park. The neatly furnished rooms have 1 bed, en-suite bathroom, balcony terrace, AC & free Wi-Fi. Leisure & pool decks are set in tropical gardens & have loungers, hammocks, hot tub, waterfall shower, restaurant & bar service. The Champs restaurant & bar offers panoramic vistas, very high-quality Creole & international cuisine, wood-oven pizza & a good selection of fine wines. The Champs is a popular accommodation choice for academics & families visiting Ross University students, but is also well positioned for independent travellers exploring the north of the island. As it is a university community,

Picard also enjoys a good selection of shops & eateries. **$$$**

🏠 **Sisters Beach Bar Restaurant & Lodge**
(5 cottages) Picard; ☏ 767 445 5211; e sistersbeachbarrestaurant@gmail.com; 🅵. Sisters offers clean & convenient self-contained lodge accommodation located within tropical gardens next to the beach at Picard. Each stone lodge has 2 dbl beds, en-suite bathroom, kitchenette, living area, ceiling fans, insect screens, & porch. The beachfront bar & restaurant specialises in seafood but everything is good – even the pasta is homemade. Sisters is good-value accommodation in a semi-private beachfront location & handy for exploring the north. A short walk into Picard offers even more dining options. **$$**

🏠 **Lilly's Guesthouse** Brandy; ☏ 767 317 4723; e lillysguesthouse@gmail.com; www.lillysguesthouse.com; 🅵. To get to Lilly's you ideally need a 4x4 as the terrain can be muddy & rough beyond Brandy Manor. Follow the road towards Brandy Manor from the main road near Bornes (there is a sign) & drive past it for a few hundred metres. Lilly has constructed a rustic wooden cabin, a treehouse & there is also an ajoupa-like structure where you can shelter with a hammock. This is back to basics, natural living. Lilly will cook for you – everything comes from his own garden & the sea (ask him about his charter sailboats – he may take you out in one). Solar panels provide the power, there is a communal toilet & the washroom is the river. Lilly's gardens are rich with herbs, flowers, vegetables, ground provisions & fruits. Lilly is happy to take you on tours or help you to arrange them. **$**

NORTHEAST
Map, page 191, unless otherwise stated

🏠 **Atlantique View** (35 rooms & suites) Anse de Mai; ☏ 767 445 6719; e sales@atlantiqueview.com; www.atlantiqueview.com; 🅵. Atlantique View is a large, resort-style hotel covering a steep hillside above the fishing villages of Anse de Mai & Anse Soldat. Rooms are en suite, some have jaccuzzi, all have private balconies with ocean views. The hotel's facilities include restaurant & bar, tiered infinity pool, tennis court, Wi-Fi, mini gym & massage services. **$$$$$**

🏠 **Pagua Bay House** [map, page 189] (4 cabanas, 2 suites) Pagua Bay, Marigot; ☏ 767 445 8888; e paguabayhouse@gmail.com; www.

paguabayhouse.com; **fi**. Pagua Bay is a chic boutique hotel overlooking the ocean, between the Kalinago Territory & Marigot. The cabanas are stylish with a large bedroom with king-sized beds, oversized en-suite bathroom & shower, AC, TV & Wi-Fi. The suites are similar in design but also enjoy their own plunge pool or sunken bathtub & private, spacious sun terrace. The restaurant is open to both guests & the public & enjoys panoramic ocean views as well as a large sun terrace with swimming pool. It serves b/fast, lunch & dinner – a fusion of American and Caribbean – with dinner reservations preferred. The owners & managers live on the premises & there is on-site security. Island tours & excursions can be arranged for guests. Up-market & exclusive, Pagua Bay suits romantics & vacationers simply wishing to recharge, but it is also well located for exploring the sights of the interior, north & east coasts. **$$$$$**

Villa Vista (3-bed villa, 1-bed apt) Hodges Bay, Calibishie; ☏767 235 5760, 767 275 1010; **e** villavistadominica@yahoo.com; www. villavistadominica.com; **fi**. Mediterranean meets Caribbean at Villa Vista, where stucco walls & terracotta tiles fuse with louvre windows & heavy wooden hurricane shutters, to create a modern & attractive 3-bed villa with lovely views of Hodges Beach & Bay. The villa has private bathrooms, a fully equipped kitchen, laundry, large terrace & sun deck with infinity pool & those great ocean views. There is a jacuzzi, Wi-Fi, ceiling fans, mosquito nets & TV. A trail alongside the villa leads down to the river & bay. Villa Vista is relaxing, peaceful, secure & private. It is a great self-contained accommodation option for couples, friends & families. The downstairs sgl-bed open-plan apt is also fully equipped & enjoys a garden deck. **$$$$$**

Villa Passiflora (3 bedroom villa) Calibishie; ☏(US) 423 718 1842; **e** parkneur@comcast.net; www.villapassiflora.com; **fi**; see ad, page 201. Located to the southeast of Calibishie, between Pointe Baptiste & Hodges Bay, Villa Passiflora is a beautifully designed home-away-from-home in a tranquil & private setting. Perched on a hillside enjoying both a cooling breeze & magnificent ocean views, the villa has 3 bedrooms each with en-suite bathroom, there is an open-plan living, dining & fully equipped kitchen area, a study & library, large veranda decks, an infinity pool, hammocks, 4-poster beds with mosquito netting, & those wonderful sea views. Housekeeping services include cooking if required & there is also

a visiting masseuse & yoga expert as well as on-site caretakers for additional peace of mind. Villa Passiflora is a great option for a family vacation or for a group of friends. **$$$$$**

Aria Sea Villa (4-bedroom villa) Calibishie; ☏767 445 8537 or 767 275 3362; **e** info@ calibishie-lodges.com; www.calibishie-lodges. com. Located on a high ridge above Calibishie village, Aria is a luxurious private villa that enjoys sweeping ocean views from its sun deck & swimming pool. It has a spacious open-plan living area, TV, Wi-Fi, a fully equipped kitchen & 4 comfortable 1-bed suites, each with high-quality furnishings & private bathroom with rain showers. If you don't fancy cooking, you could either have a private chef cook for you or just pop down the road to the Bamboo Restaurant at Calibishie Lodges (page 179). You can either rent individual suites or the whole villa. *Suites* **$$$$**, *villa* **$$$$$**

Pointe Baptiste Estate [map, page 185] (1 main house, 1 cottage) Pointe Baptiste, Calibishie; ☏767 225 5378, 767 445 7368; **e** manager@ pointebaptiste.com; www. pointebaptiste.com. This charming & historic estate house sleeps 6 & has 4 bedrooms, bathrooms, sitting room, kitchen, dining area, library, ceiling fans, mosquito nets & very large veranda. Home of the Napier family since 1930, the main house is a traditional design with antique furniture, books & artworks. Guests have included Somerset Maugham & Noël Coward. The small wooden cottage comfortably sleeps 2 & has kitchen area, bedroom, bathroom, ceiling fan, mosquito net & veranda. Located in 10ha of landscaped private grounds with herb & organic fruit & veg gardens, trails to Red Rocks (page 197), secluded black & white sand beaches & its own chocolate factory (see box, page 188). *House* **$$$$$**, *cottage* **$$$**

Calibishie Cove (2 suites, 2 rooms) Hodges Bay, Calibishie; ☏767 245 5231; **e** calibishiecove@ gmail.com; www.calibishiecove.com; **fi**. Calibishie Cove offers spacious rooms & fully SC suites overlooking Hodges Bay. The sea view & garden view rooms are en suite & have fridges & balconies, the rainforest suite has kitchenette, AC, large patio & views, the penthouse suite fills the entire top floor of the building & has kitchen, wrap-around balcony & plunge pool. There is free Wi-Fi throughout & staff will arrange in-room dining by request. Kayak & bike rental, yoga, massage & island tours can all be arranged. **$$$$**

⌂ Comfort Cottages [map, page 185] (4 cottages) Blenheim; ✆ 767 445 3245 or 767 616 3325; e comfortcottages@cwdom.dm; www.comfortcottages.com; ⓕ. Perched on a high hillside above Blenheim, just off the road to the village of Vieille Case, this gated residence of 4 modern, well-furnished SC cottages enjoys great views of the Atlantic Ocean & the northeast coastline. 3 cottages have 1 bedroom, 1 cottage has 2 bedrooms. All have alarm systems, TV, Wi-Fi, AC, DVD player, lounge, fully equipped kitchen, private deck with plunge pool. The manicured gardens have panoramic coastal views, BBQ area, & covered gazebo with hammocks. There is also a small restaurant & bar for guests only. There are discounted rates for long stays & Best Deal Rent a Car hire. **$$$$**

⌂ Calibishie Lodges (6 lodges) Calibishie; ✆ 767 445 8537 or 767 275 3362; e info@ calibishie-lodges.com; www.calibishie-lodges. com. With ocean & mountain views, just 20mins from the airport & within walking distance of the Red Rock coast, Calibishie Lodges' suites have bedroom, bathroom, living area with dbl sofa bed, kitchenette, fans, TV, insect screens, free Wi-Fi & private balcony. There is a small swimming pool & a restaurant with all-day dining (see Bamboo Restaurant, page 179). The owners are friendly & welcoming & there is an emphasis on providing guests with good service. **$$$**

⌂ Coffee River Cottages [map, page 189] (1 cottage, 1 apt) Melville Hall Estate, Marigot; ✆ 767 613 4696 or 767 614 5140; e coffeeriverdominica@ gmail.com; www.coffeeriverdominica.com; ⓕ. Coffee River comprises a lovely SC cottage & spacious apt in 1.5ha of beautiful gardens, working farm & river setting. Thoughtfully designed & fully equipped, the cottage comfortably sleeps a family of 4 but could also be a romantic hideaway for couples. It has a fully equipped kitchen, lounging area, bathroom & shower, & very creative attic bedrooms with walkway. The nearby apt sleeps up to 8 & is ideal for 2 families travelling together. It has 4 bedrooms (2 downstairs, 2 up in the very original attic), 3 bathrooms & showers, fully equipped kitchen & spacious semi-outdoors lounging area. The owners live nearby & are extremely helpful & attentive, taking care of your personal needs as much as they can. Off-grid, secure, peaceful & with all you need, this is a great SC option for both couples & families with kids. Stroll through the gardens, bathe in the river & explore the east coast with ease. Just mins from Douglas Charles Airport & Marigot village. **$$$**

⌂ My Father's Place Guest House [map, page 189] (GH rooms & 3 SC apts) Marigot; ✆ 767 445 7215 or (US) 201 620 5398; www. myfathersplaceguesthouse.com; ⓕ. Located just above Sandy Bay near Marigot Bay, My Father's Place is a large & pleasant family residence that has been converted into a guesthouse. Within the grounds are 3 SC apts. The main house is traditional with a shared lounge, verandas & Wi-Fi. 2 apts have 1 dbl room, the 3rd also has a sgl room. All have fully equipped kitchen & AC. There is a garden bar & restaurant; b/fast & dinner are available on request. **$$$**

⌂ Classique International Guest House (1 suite, 4 rooms) Marigot; ✆ 767 445 8486; e classiquedominica@gmail.com; www. classiqueinternational.com; ⓕ. Perched on a hillside above the northern community of Marigot with great views of the surrounding countryside & ocean, Classique is just 10mins from Douglas Charles Airport. Its rooms are en suite, with AC, TV, fans, free Wi-Fi & a small fridge. Set within manicured & colourful gardens, there are communal balconies & terraces (the suite has a private balcony), a bar & kitchen where meals can be prepared for you on request. Friendly host, welcoming, private & secure, this is a good option for those just landed, about to take off, or exploring the north on a budget. **$$–$$$**

⌂ Bay View Lodges (2 SC apts) Calibishie; ✆ 767 245 8705; e trevor.nerwal@gmail.com; www. bayviewdominica.com. Set in a large hillside garden, Bay View offers nicely designed, bright, airy & clean SC accommodation with awesome views of Hodges Bay. Each lodge has 1 dbl bedroom, dining & living area with sofa bed, bathroom, kitchenette, Wi-Fi & private veranda. **$$**

⌂ Calibishie Gardens Pillar house accommodation available at this popular restaurant (see page 179 for details). **$$**

⌂ Dominica's Sea View Apartments (5 apts) Calibishie; ✆ 767 445 8537; e info@ dominicasseaviewapartments.com; www. dominicasseaviewapartments.com. Located above the village of Calibishie &, as the name suggests, enjoying great sea views, 1-bedroom upper-floor apts sleep 2 people & the ground floor 2-bedroom apts sleep 4. All have en-suite bathrooms, dbl beds, fully equipped kitchens, living area, TV, fans & veranda. The upper floor enjoys especially good views. The apts are tastefully designed & furnished & they have Wi-Fi. If you prefer to have meals cooked for you, head down to sister accommodation Calibishie Lodges where you can enjoy b/fast, lunch & dinner at the Bamboo Restaurant (page 179). **$$**

🏠 **Jacoway Inn** [map, page 185] (2 rooms, 1 cottage) Calibishie; 📞767 445 8872, 767 613 2908; e jacowayinn@gmail.com; www.calibishie.net. Located amid the banana & plantain farmlands on the ridge above the village of Calibishie, Jacoway's 2 rooms have dbl bed, en-suite bathroom, fridge, microwave, dining & seating area. The upper room has a private veranda, the ground floor room has a private terrace, & there is Wi-Fi throughout. Enjoy ocean views, gazebo & gardens. The quaint & colourful SC garden cottage sleeps 2. Jacoway is a good option for couples or friends on a budget. **$$**

✳ 🏠 **Sea Cliff Cottages** (5 cottages) Calibishie; 📞767 445 7008, 767 445 8998; e seacliff@dominica-cottages.com; www.dominica-cottages.com. See ad, page 201. Sea Cliff Cottages has been accommodating travellers to the Calibishie area for longer than most & it is still a great place to stay. Its very pleasant self-contained cottages are located in expansive hillside gardens overlooking Hodges Bay. They sleep 2–7, & are fully equipped with en-suite bathrooms, kitchen, TV, Wi-Fi, seating areas & balconies where guests can enjoy panoramic sea & mountain views. Mobile phones provided to guests who need them & a nearby trail runs down to the beach & river at Hodges Bay. Within walking distance to Calibishie's shops & restaurants, Sea Cliff Cottages is excellent value SC accommodation in a scenic & practical location, suitable for both couples & families. **$$**

✳ 🏠 **Veranda View Guesthouse** (2 rooms) Calibishie; 📞767 445 8900; e reserve@lodgingdominica.com; www.lodgingdominica.

com. Veranda View is lovely guesthouse accommodation located right on the water in Calibishie village. Artistically designed & decorated by owner Hermien, it is colourful, fresh, relaxing & excellent value for money. Each room has bed, lounger, en-suite bathroom, a small kitchenette & a private veranda with gorgeous sea views. There is a covered terrace bar & restaurant where dinner can be cooked for you by reservation. European & Creole seafood dishes are Hermien's speciality. Just 20mins from Douglas Charles Airport & as close to the water as it is possible to be without getting your feet wet, Veranda View is well established, popular & highly recommended. **$$**

🏠 **Windblow Estate** (3 suites) Calibishie; 📞767 445 8198; e islandtwo@windblowestate.com; www.windblowestate.com; Skype: islandtwo. Located on a ridge overlooking Calibishie, Windblow is a villa with 3 individual fully furnished SC suites. 2 suites have 1 bedroom & the third has 2 bedrooms. They all have en-suite bathrooms, ceiling fans, Wi-Fi, TV, fully equipped kitchen & verandas with panoramic views of the Atlantic Ocean. Cool breezes keep the temperature comfortable. **$$**

CAMPING
Map, page 182

⛺ **Brandy Manor** Brandy, Bornes; 📞767 235 4871 or 767 612 0978. Located alongside the Brandy River & near to the end of Wai'tukubuli National Trail Segment 11, Brandy Manor offers camping pitches & shared kitchen & bathroom facilities. Bring your own tent. **$**

🏠 **Lilly's Guesthouse** Brandy; 📞767 317 4723; e lillysguesthouse@gmail.com; www.lillysguesthouse.com; 📘 . Close to the end of WNT Segment 11, Lilly's wooden cabin & treehouse are an option, or you could overnight in a hammock or pitch your tent in his garden. **$**

✖ WHERE TO EAT AND DRINK
NORTHWEST
Map, page 182, unless otherwise stated

Portsmouth has a handful of small snackettes serving local dishes, but the majority of restaurants are located in the university community of Picard & along the beach in Lagoon. Due to the international nature of the place, there is more diversity & choice in Picard. If you are looking

for great value take-away food then one of the best places to go is the food market next to Ross University School of Medicine in Picard. You will find local lunches, pizza, wraps, *rotis*, barbecues, subs, sandwiches, curries, salads, fresh fruit juices & much more. It's very popular with the students & is a good place to organise food for a picnic or a hike.

✖ The Champs Restaurant Hotel The Champs, Picard; ☎767 445 4452; ☐ ; ⊕ daily. Located on the hillside above Picard with fabulous views of Prince Rupert Bay & the Cabrits, The Champs Restaurant offers a wide range of excellent Creole & international dining. You can also enjoy wood oven pizza, vegetarian specialities & a good selection of wine. Dinner reservations are preferred but you can also just turn up. $$

✳ ✖ Iguana Café Michael Douglas Blvd, Portsmouth; ☎767 445 315 0471. Quirky-looking 'Rasta' restaurant serving excellent seafood & pasta dinners, with reservations preferred but not essential. Enjoy great food & a warm welcome from Jennifer & Cartouche. $$

✖ Le Flambeau Picard, Portsmouth; ☎767 445 5142; ☐ ; ⊕ daily. Actually part of the Portsmouth Beach Hotel, which predominantly serves as student accommodation, but also functioning as a restaurant for next door's Picard Beach Cottages, Le Flambeau is a popular & established beachside restaurant with great views across Prince Rupert Bay to the Cabrits. The restaurant serves a range of international & 'Creole fusion' dishes. Just turn up. $$

✖ Manicou River [map, page 185] (3 cottages) Tanetane, Portsmouth; ☎767 616 8903; ☐ . A restaurant with one of the best views (& the heaviest tables!) on the island, Manicou serves a delicious fusion of Caribbean & French cuisine with Douglas Bay & the Cabrits National Park as a stunning backdrop. The access road can be a little challenging without 4x4 so call ahead for both reservations & assistance. $$

✖ Purple Turtle Beach Club Lagoon, Portsmouth; ☎767 445 5296; ⊕ daily. Located right on the beach, Purple Turtle is a popular spot with travellers, yachties & locals. Dishes are a mix of international bites & traditional Creole lunches. $$

✖ Riverside Restaurant & Bar Picard; ☎767 445 5888. Located just off the west-coast highway (look for the sign), serving a variety of international dishes, but specialising in Chinese. $$

✖ Sisters Beach Bar, Restaurant & Lodge Picard; ☎767 445 5211; ☐ . Located on the beach, just off the Lizard Trail to the north of Ross University (look for the signs), Sisters is a very popular spot for dinner. Just turn up for great seafood, homemade pasta, sunsets & more. $$

✖ The Tomato Café Picard, Portsmouth; ☎767 445 3334. An American-style restaurant, café & bar serving a range of international dishes. $$

NORTHEAST

Map, page 185, unless otherwise stated

✖ Pagua Bay House [map, page 189] Pagua Bay, Marigot; ☎767 445 8888; ☐ ; ⊕ daily for b/fast, lunch & dinner. Pagua Bay House's restaurant enjoys awesome ocean views & has a large terrace & swimming pool for diners to enjoy (many choose to spend the day here). The food is high-quality American Caribbean. In the high season (roughly Oct–Jun) you can just turn up, but in the low season you should call ahead, especially for dinner. $$$

✖ Bamboo Restaurant Calibishie; ☎767 445 8537 or 767 275 3362. Calibishie Lodges' restaurant is open to hotel guests & the public & serves a range of local & international dishes. Drop in for b/fast, lunch & dinner (advanced dinner reservations preferred though not essential). $$

✖ Calibishie Gardens (Poz) Calibishie ☎767 612 5176 & 265 7915; ☐ . Also known as the 'Land of Poz – where pozitive people meet', the popular Calibishie Gardens restaurant offers international fare alongside swimming pool & wine bar. Pillar house accommodation available. Look for the signs. $$

✳ ✖ Rainbow Restaurant Calibishie; ☎767 245 9995 or 767 245 4838; ☐ . Located right on the water's edge & even incorporating a narrow strip of sand, Rainbow serves great French Creole food. Eat inside or upstairs on the deck. There are nice sea views to accompany lionfish, coconut chicken in pineapple, & other delicious lunches & dinners. Just turn up. $$

✖ Coral Reef Restaurant & Bar Calibishie; ☎767 445 7432; ⊕ daily. Out of sight behind the Coral Reef Supermarket on Main St, Calibishie, this waterside bar & restaurant serves good-value local & international food, from traditional Creole lunches to burger & fries. It's simple but tasty & affordable. Lovely sea views. Just turn up. $–$$

SHOPPING

Shopping in Portsmouth is a bit of a struggle. There are not many places geared towards travellers; everything is very functional – from building supplies to car insurance – but if you are prepared to look hard you should find the bare essentials (drinks, snacks, ice cream – that kind of thing). For many years the town has had rather a run-down feel to it though there is always talk of rejuvenation and investment, which will hopefully lift it from the doldrums. If the large hotels planned for the Cabrits actually materialise, perhaps they will help. Portsmouth certainly needs a boost of some kind. Three main streets run in parallel but it is only Bay Street (the one closest to the water) that has much to offer in the way of shops and services. If you cannot find what you are looking for in Portsmouth, then you should head for Picard, which benefits from the presence of the Ross University School of Medicine and has more to offer in terms of food and essentials shopping, dining and accommodation.

Just off Bay Street (Portsmouth's main thoroughfare), there are the fisheries, and on Saturday mornings you'll also find a fresh-produce market. Bay Street also has a couple of minimarts selling the bare necessities. Over the bridge in Lagoon – on the way to the Cabrits, before you reach Purple Turtle Beach – you'll find some small shacks selling art, crafts and souvenirs – but they may not be open.

In Picard there is an **HHV Whitchurch IGA** supermarket, which is the best place for general shopping in this area, and there are a couple of minimarts off the main drag, near the university.

On the east coast, the largest village is Marigot, where you can find small shops selling basic foodstuffs. There is also a small Saturday market.

OTHER PRACTICALITIES

BANKS

$ **National Bank of Dominica** Bay St, Portsmouth. Located on the south side of Portsmouth near the Indian River. Car parking & ATM.
$ **Scotiabank** Picard. Small banking unit with ATM located opposite Ross University School of Medicine.

Tourist information

ℹ **Calibishie Tourist Information** Look for a brightly painted building along the roadside as you enter Calibishie from the west. Accommodation, dining & tours information, local crafts, books, magazines, leaflets & general advice.

WHAT TO SEE AND DO

THE CABRITS NATIONAL PARK (*Site pass required*) The 525ha Cabrits National Park was established in 1986. The twin peaks of the Cabrits are thought to have been formed from the same volcano that collapsed and eroded over time. East Cabrit is 140m above sea level and West Cabrit stands at a height of 171m. Located within the park, and its most prominent feature, is the ruined 18th-century **Fort Shirley garrison**. The park is connected to the mainland by Dominica's largest wetland, the Cabrits Swamp, and it also includes some 421ha of marine environment. The name 'Cabrits' is derived from the French word *cabri*, meaning 'young goat'. It is said goats were brought here for food and allowed to roam freely around the headland.

In 1990 the government of Dominica established a cruise ship berth at the Cabrits on the site of the dockyard that would have served Fort Shirley garrison some 200 years before, and it has become the location for two large hotel projects. At the time of writing one of these projects had started and then stopped, the other was simply making the news headlines. Whether either or both are likely to become significant accommodation options or not, only time will tell.

On arriving at the Cabrits National Park there is car parking on the left along the waterside, just before the gate and cruise ship arrivals building. You will also find a gift shop here. Beyond this is the visitor centre, which houses an exhibition room and a snackette where you can get reasonably priced local dishes and drinks. The exhibition room displays an interesting and informative interpretation of the geological formation of the Cabrits as well as the history of the garrison.

A site pass is required for the Cabrits National Park, which can be purchased at the snackette. The stone archway and path in front of the visitor centre forms the entrance to the park and leads uphill to the restored main garrison and the woodland trails. The trails are very pleasant walks through the forested park and include several interesting garrison ruins. They also have excellent views of the surrounding area.

The Cabrits habitat is dry coastal woodland. Trees found here include teak (*Tectona grandis*), the silk cotton tree (*Ceiba occidentalis*), the bay tree (*Pimenta racemosa*), the naked indian tree (*Bursera simaruba*), the mahogany (*Swietenia mahogani*) and the savonnet (*Lauchocarpus latifolus*). In the grassy area above the Fort Shirley powder magazine you can see Dominica's national flower, the *bwa kwaib* (*Sabinea carinalis*).

The Fort Shirley garrison Despite the fact that Portsmouth was no longer an appropriate location for the island's capital, the natural harbour of Prince Rupert Bay still needed defending from invaders. British Governor Sir Thomas Shirley began the task of constructing a military garrison on the headland of the Cabrits, based on the plans of Captain James Bruce, who designed many of the island's fortifications at the time. All of the forest was cleared from the area, and a fully functional and quite impressive 80ha military stronghold of over 50 buildings was created.

Other than witnessing the Battle of the Saints in 1782, the fort experienced no military conflict. Due to its location next to a large swamp, many of the troops stationed there fell ill and died from malaria and other fevers. The garrison's problems were compounded by the escalating costs of defending an island that was producing little by way of income. The solution was to create regiments of African and Creole slaves who were more accustomed to the testing climate and who were also considerably cheaper. These troops formed what became known as the Black West India Regiments, or the 'Black Regiments'.

In 1802 soldiers of the 8th West India Regiment staged a revolt at the Fort Shirley garrison. Their commander-in-chief was Governor Andrew James Cochrane, who took it upon himself to use the regiment to work his private estates without pay. On 9 April the regiment took over Fort Shirley for a number of days, though troop reinforcements and attack from HMS *Magnificent* resulted in many deaths. Those who survived fled into the forest where they joined up with bands of Maroons (escaped slaves). Rather ironically, this internal conflict was the only battle ever to take place here.

In 1805 French forces attacked Dominica from the south and a fierce battle raged off Roseau. The French fleet gained ground in La Pointe (Pointe Michel) and cannon fire from Fort Young resulted in flames drifting on the wind towards the town. Roseau was burned to the ground and the remaining British troops under Governor Sir George Prevost retreated to the garrison at Fort Shirley, where they hid and hoped. Prevost refused to surrender and the French, perhaps no longer relishing the prospect of further fighting and knowing the garrison would be a tough egg to crack, withdrew from Dominica with their loot.

Following the ultimate defeat of the French, the requirement for military fortifications gradually receded and in 1854 the garrison of Fort Shirley was

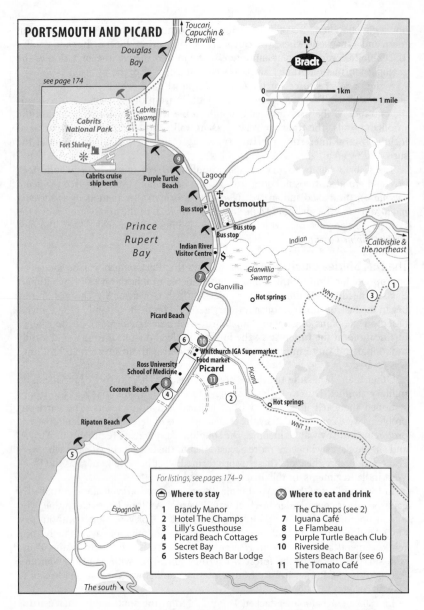

Toucari,
Capuchin &
Pennville

Douglas
Bay

N

Bradt

see page 174

Cabrits
Swamp

0 .... 1km
0 .... 1 mile

Cabrits
National Park

Fort Shirley

Cabrits cruise
ship berth

Purple Turtle
Beach

9

Lagoon

Portsmouth

Bus stop

Prince
Rupert
Bay

Bus stop

Bus stop

Indian River
Visitor Centre

Indian

Calibishie &
the northeast

$

Glanvillia
Swamp

7

Glanvillia

Hot springs

WNT 11

3

1

Picard Beach

6 **10**

Whitchurch IGA Supermarket
Food market
Picard

Ross University
School of Medicine

8

11

Coconut Beach

4

2

Picard

Hot springs

Ripaton Beach

WNT 11

5

Espagnole

For listings, see pages 174–9

Where to stay

1 Brandy Manor
2 Hotel The Champs
3 Lilly's Guesthouse
4 Picard Beach Cottages
5 Secret Bay
6 Sisters Beach Bar Lodge

Where to eat and drink

   The Champs (see 2)
7 Iguana Café
8 Le Flambeau
9 Purple Turtle Beach Club
10 Riverside
   Sisters Beach Bar (see 6)
11 The Tomato Café

The south

abandoned to nature. In 1983 restoration began and, whenever subsequent funding becomes available, is continuing primarily under the professional guidance of Dominica's renowned historian, Dr Lennox Honychurch.

From the clearing above the visitor centre, walk up the stone path to the fort. The entrance passes between two stone buildings. On your left is the **guardhouse** and on your right the **powder magazine**. The guardhouse has small windows through which guards would have been able to observe and fire at intruders entering the fort. To the left of the guardhouse are the **troop barracks**, beyond which is the restored **lower battery**, with seven cannons pointing out across Prince Rupert Bay. At the rear of the lower battery is the **ordnance store**, where you can see cannonballs, grapeshot and ordnance tools.

The garrison is thought to have had 35 cannon in all and 17 of them can still be found here. The cannon were 32 pounders, each with a range of around 2.4km and accuracy to 1.2km.

Continue up the path past the bottle palms to the upper section of the fort. This area is dominated by the restored **officers' quarters**. Beneath the large mango tree in front of the building is an iron pump. This is a **cistern**, one of three located in the garrison that would have provided the troops with fresh drinking water collected from rooftops and a water catchment. To the left of the officers' quarters is the **upper battery** and **signal station** with cannons pointing out across the bay.

The woodland walks around the Cabrits are described in the *Hikes* section (pages 197–201). From time to time wedding receptions, cultural events and small music festivals are held here.

PORTSMOUTH AND PICARD The broad and beautiful bay that stretches from the Cabrits headland south to Morne Espagnol was called **Ouyuhayo** by the Amerindian settlers who lived there and then later **Grand Anse** by the French. Today it is named after Prince Rupert of the Rhine, a Royalist commander during the English Civil War (1642–51) who is said to have taken refuge here in 1652. Following defeat by the Parliamentarians of Oliver Cromwell, the man he named 'Ironside' at the 1644 Battle of Marston Moor, Rupert took to piracy, attacking English shipping first in the Mediterranean and later in the West Indies.

Prince Rupert Bay was a natural harbour for ships, both military and commercial, and in 1765 the area along its eastern shoreline was laid out by the British as the

---

THE RESTORATION OF FORT SHIRLEY   *Dr Lennox Honychurch*

Fort Shirley and the Cabrits garrison, abandoned to the forest since 1854, has been undergoing significant restoration in recent years. A team of skilled carpenters and masons has been piecing together the ruined buildings. The focus has been on the garrison headquarters at Fort Shirley where cast-iron cannons that were once scattered in the forest are now pointing out to sea again on restored ramparts and gun carriages. The restored officers' quarters are popular for events such as weddings, small conferences and dinners. In the main hall is an exhibition of reproductions of 18th-century paintings of Dominican scenes, while old maps and artefacts are displayed in the Powder Magazines. The Troop Barracks have been converted into a hostel for groups on heritage and ecology study tours. The troops' kitchen has been restored and the former parade ground, where soldiers attended drill practice each day, has been cleared for recreation. For those who prefer ruins, a loop trail follows the military roads through the forest to make a circuit of the main army buildings in the valley. It includes a viewpoint towards the French islands overlooking the site of the Battle of the Saints, fought between the French and British fleets in 1782.

Dr Lennox Honychurch, DPhil, MPhil, is a historian and educator who takes an active role in the preservation of Dominica's architectural heritage. One of his many roles is to oversee the restoration of Fort Shirley and the Cabrits garrison. For more information: www.lennoxhonychurch.com.

8

island's capital. As it was to be a major seaport, it was named Portsmouth after the English naval town. Unfortunately large swamplands both to the north and to the south of this developing settlement resulted in too many cases of malaria and yellow fever for this to be a practical plan. Just three years later the project was abandoned and the settlement of Roseau in the south was made Dominica's capital instead.

To the east of Portsmouth is the large playing field of **Benjamin's Park** and beyond that there is a grid of residential housing. To the north of the town is the district of **Lagoon**. Prince Rupert Bay is a very popular anchorage for visiting yachts and cruisers, and the small bars, snackettes and restaurants along the beaches at Lagoon and Picard benefit from the arrival of these visitors. 'Yacht Chasers' can be seen heading out in their small boats, paddleboards or canoes from Lagoon to greet arriving vessels, offering mooring services, provisioning, even gifts and island tours.

Picard   A little to the south of Portsmouth, beside a long stretch of beach, is the rapidly growing community of Picard. This area has experienced a significant expansion over the years primarily due to the **Ross University School of Medicine** (*www.ross.edu/goMD*) that is located here. Ross is a US-based medical school and it is a major contributor to the economy of the island, particularly in the north, and mutual benefit arrangements with the government of Dominica mean that the island also receives medical assistance from the school.

Located next to the university is a small market area with stalls selling a wide selection of food and drinks. It is an excellent place to drop in for a take-away or to gather provisions for a hike or a picnic. The alluring smells of cooking fill the air and it is almost impossible to resist giving something a try.

Picard also has a selection of restaurants, small eateries, coffee shops, bars and minimarts. You will also find an ATM. I haven't listed all these places as they change rather frequently. So just turn up and see what takes your fancy. Up on the hillside to the east of the university is a hotchpotch of buildings that look like they have simply been dropped from the sky rather than planned; it's an entrepreneurial rush to cash in on the need for student housing that seems to have cast aside the need for proper roads and planning. This jumble of buildings mostly consists of single-bedroom apartments that are rented to students on a mid- to long-term basis. This area of 'little America' is usually busy and there is always another new building going up somewhere. But despite the apparent madness of it all, RUSM is an excellent and ever-growing campus, providing much needed income to this region.

THE TOP END   The very north of Dominica has rugged and interesting stretches of coastline as well as a very scenic and mountainous interior. A narrow road snakes its way up the west coast from Douglas Bay to the remote village of Capuchin. A road from Savanne Paille cuts across the interior and passes over a northern crater of Morne Aux Diables to the Delaford Estate and the elevated coastal community of Pennville. From the northeastern hamlet of La Haut, the road meanders along the east coast through the village of Vieille Case down to Thibaud, where it joins the main road from Marigot to Portsmouth.

To the north of the Cabrits is **Douglas Bay**, once called Malalia by Amerindian settlers, then renamed after Sir James Douglas, an 18th-century admiral of the British navy. With the twin peaks of the Cabrits to the south and the headland of Douglas Point to the north, this calm and tranquil bay is very picturesque. It also has a couple of very nice sandy beaches. Unlike the beaches further to the south, the narrow stretch of sand near **Tanetane** is rarely visited and a more secluded stretch just 5 minutes into the margins of the Cabrits Swamp on Wai'tukubuli National Trail

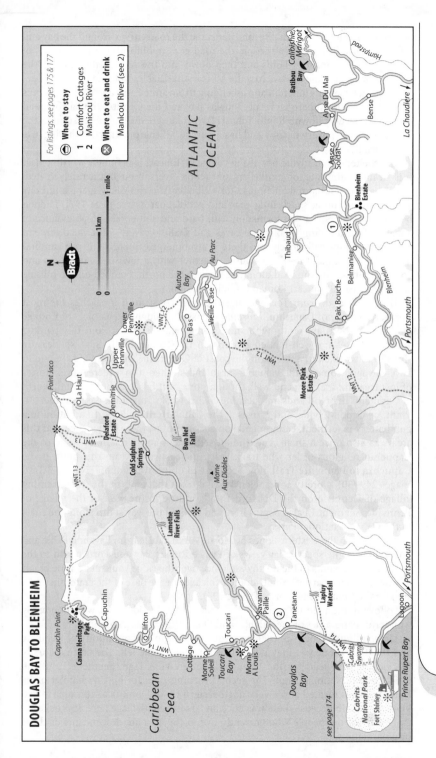

DOUGLAS BAY TO BLENHEIM

For listings, see pages 175 & 177

Where to stay
1 Comfort Cottages
2 Manicou River

Where to eat and drink
X Manicou River (see 2)

ATLANTIC OCEAN

Caribbean Sea

N

0   1km
0   1 mile

Bract

Point Jaco

Capuchin Point

Canna Heritage Park

WNT 13

O La Haut

Delaford Estate

Demitrie

Cold Sulphur Springs

Capuchin

WNT 14

Clifton

Cottage

Morne Soleil

Toucari Bay

Toucari

Morne A Louis

Savanne Paille

Tanetane

Lamothe River Falls

Morne Aux Diables

Bwa Nef Falls

Laplay Waterfall

WNT 14

Douglas Bay

see page 174

Cabrits National Park

Fort Shirley

Prince Rupert Bay

Lagoon

Cabrits Swamp

Portsmouth

Upper Penville

Lower Penville

WNT 12

En Bas

Vieille Case

Au Parc

Autou Bay

Thibaud

WNT 12

Moore Park Estate

Paix Bouche

Belmanier

WNT 12

WNT 11

Portsmouth

Blenheim

Blenheim Estate

Anse Soldat

Anse Du Mai

Batibou Bay

Calibishie, Marigot

Bense

Hampstead

La Chaudiere

Segment 14 is quite beautiful. Beyond Tanetane the road curves around the bay and offers a choice of routes. To the left, the road goes uphill through the hamlets of Savanne Paille, Morne A Louis and then down into the very pretty Toucari. The road to the right is the route across the Morne Aux Diables Volcano to Pennville.

Taking a left at this junction and ascending to Savanne Paille and Morne A Louis presents you with superb views of Douglas Bay and the Cabrits. The narrow road then heads steeply downhill into Toucari Bay. Take care during this descent as the road is very steep, very narrow and has a number of sharp corners. If driving, use your horn liberally.

The sheltered and idyllic bay at the village of **Toucari** is definitely worth a visit. It is an interesting site for snorkellers and scuba divers, though it is rarely visited. It also serves as a natural anchorage for sailboats. You can easily make a fun day of it here by renting snorkelling gear and paddleboards (see page 197). Hidden beneath its waters is a reef formation with hard and soft corals, an abundance of aquatic life and a number of small caves and shallow caverns. The northern end of the bay is especially lovely and there is a submerged fumarole, if you can find it. Small cottages and dwelling houses, together with a few snackettes, bars and coconut palms, line the road along the bay. To the north, perched on the hillside above the road, is Toucari Roman Catholic Church.

The road north from Toucari hugs the west coast until it reaches the most northerly village of **Capuchin**. *En route* it passes through the hamlets of **Cottage** and **Clifton**. Both are pretty with small convenience stores, colourfully painted wooden houses and well-tended gardens. In 1567, a number of Spanish treasure ships were wrecked in a storm off the coast of Capuchin. The Kalinago are said to have salvaged some of the valuable cargo and stashed it in a secret cave. Stories of lost treasure are alive and well, though none of it has ever been found. North of Capuchin the road ends and becomes a dirt track. This track passes Capuchin Point, or Cape Melville, and arrives at the **Canna Heritage Park**. In addition to a gun battery placement, cannon and some stone ruins, there is evidence that this area was also once a small Amerindian settlement and a missionary site of the Capuchin religious order. The track that runs eastwards from this point is the **Capuchin to Pennville Trail**, now Segment 13 of the Wai'tukubuli National Trail (pages 249–50), a pretty and ancient coastal track that ends in the small farming village of Demitrie on the Delaford Estate, a little to the west of the village of Pennville. Segment 14 also begins here and runs all the way south along the coast to the Cabrits National Park.

The road up the western slopes of Morne Aux Diables from Savanne Paille and Toucari has some spectacular views of Prince Rupert Bay and Portsmouth to the south, and the Saints to the northwest. Once over the ridge you enter a wide crater of what was once part of a multi-domed volcano. At the base of the crater there is a sign for the **Cold Sulphur Springs** (page 195).

Following the road up and over the crater's eastern ridge, you will soon enjoy wonderful panoramas of the Atlantic and Dominica's eastern coastline.

Descending Morne Aux Diables through the farming community of **Demitrie** and **Delaford Estate**,you may notice two turnings to the left. The first is actually the eastern trailhead for the Capuchin to Pennville Trail, Segment 13 of the Wai'tukubuli National Trail. The second turning goes to the tiny hamlet of **La Haut**, which is located at the very northeastern tip of Dominica. This area is also known as **Carib** because there was once an Amerindian village here. It is believed that many of the people who currently live in the area are descendants of those original settlers.

On the lower slopes of Morne Aux Diables you arrive at the coastal village of **Pennville**. The village is in two parts, Upper Pennville and Lower Pennville. Located on the main road between Lower Pennville and the small community of **En Bas** to the south is a short river trail to the **Bwa Nef Falls** (pages 197–8).

In 1646, Father Raymond Breton, a French priest of the Dominican order, gave the island's first Christian service at the Amerindian village of Itassi in the *karbet* of Chief Kalamiena. Unfortunately for Father Breton, it was not for another hundred years that Christianity gained a firm footing on Dominica. A mural of his first Mass is painted on the wall of the parish hall at the top of the village, now called **Vieille Case**.

In November 2004, an earthquake 27km north of Dominica, measuring 6.3 on the Richter Scale, shook the island and caused damage to several buildings in the north, including the Vieille Case Catholic Church. The quake was followed by a series of aftershocks and torrential rains. This very unusual church – completed in 1869, constructed from volcanic rock and with a beautiful Spanish façade and shingle roof – unfortunately could not be saved. A new, more modern replacement has been erected.

Vieille Case is built on a steep slope overlooking the bay at **Autou**. This charming but rugged cove serves as a landing place for local fishermen and is accessed via a steep and narrow road at the bottom of the village. The road emerges at a small pasture where cows or horses may be grazing. On the left-hand side is a wide grassy path leading to the boat landing. Watch the waves rushing into the bay from the open ocean and imagine how tricky it must be both to set out and land at this point. At the end of the pasture is a narrow track leading out to a rocky volcanic outcrop. There are great views along the coast from here. There was once a rite-of-passage challenge for the children of Vieille Case called '*decouvé l'église*'. The children, usually young boys, had to swim out from the shore at Autou until they could see the roof of the church high up above the village.

Along the coast from Autou is another nice cove called **Au Parc**.

South of Au Parc is the small farming and fishing community of **Thibaud**, named after a French settler who purchased land from the Amerindians here in the 18th century. The school and playing field are located on the shoreline of Sandwich Bay. This area is the site of the original village.

Before arriving at a junction with the main route between Portsmouth and the east coast, you will come across a sign to Blenheim along a small road to the right. From this road the views south across to Morne Diablotin and north towards Moore Park and Morne Aux Diables are fabulous. The road emerges at Belmanier, south of Paix Bouche. At the junction, the road to the right goes to Paix Bouche and Moore Park, the road to the left goes to the junction with the main Portsmouth road.

THE NORTHEAST COAST In the 1830s British plantation owners in the northeast imported slave labour from other English-speaking islands such as Antigua. They also provided a base for Wesleyan missionaries who began to have a significant influence in the area. The settlements that developed around the estates following emancipation contrasted to those that emerged elsewhere on the island. Here it was a Methodist rather than a Roman Catholic community which did not speak in French Creole, but rather an English form of Creole known as *kockoy*.

The settlement that developed around the former estates of Charles Leatham, such as the Eden Estate, was known as Wesleyville and later simply as Wesley. A little to the south of Wesley is the village of Marigot, also a settlement that developed with significant English influence due to imported Leeward Islands labour. Marigot Bay was also a busy place for the trans-shipment of cargo. It had a jetty and a small fort for protection.

In the 20th century, the northeast was a major area of banana production and received significant economic benefit from this trade. When world trade rules were changed, the area was on the receiving end of a devastating reduction in demand for small island bananas. Unable to compete with the huge banana-producing companies of the Americas, the outlook in this area appeared quite bleak. Villages such as Woodford Hill and Wesley, places that had just begun to develop on the back of a banana boom, suffered a reversal of fortune and became run-down. Thanks to the assistance of The Fairtrade Foundation, the small island banana producers in the Caribbean received a fragile lifeline. The ridges and elevated tracts of land behind the villages of the northeast are covered in banana farms and it still remains an important source of income for the people of this area.

The sprawling hillside village of **Marigot** developed around the plantation of John Weir, who brought in slave labourers from Antigua and the Leeward Islands. The modern village stretches from Pagua Bay to the Douglas Charles Airport and consists of several small districts, including one called Weirs after the former plantation owner. The main road runs through the heart of the village and is where most of the bars, shops and eateries are to be found.

Located on the southern edge of the village is an area called North End, which was once a small community in its own right. In 1795 there was fighting in North End between the British and the French and in the mid 19th century there was a small Kalinago village here. As the village of Marigot expanded southwards, the Kalinago crossed the Pagua River and settled in what is now the Kalinago Territory.

The impressive Marigot Fisheries complex on Marigot Bay was funded by Japan. (Though it is always denied, most fisheries funded by the Japanese in the Caribbean region have been linked with favourable voting at the annual Whaling Commission. Dominica used to abstain but now votes against commercial whaling.) You can purchase fresh fish here most days of the week and there is also a good local eatery called **Tickles** that serves great value Creole food.

There is a secluded beach and cove to the south of Marigot Fisheries called **Sandy Bay**. On a hairpin bend on the main road above the fisheries you will see a guesthouse called My Father's Place. Look for a nearby sign pointing to a beach track. Take care descending as it can be slippery. The beach here is beautiful and the sea is great for swimming and snorkelling as it is protected by a reef. There is a second beach around the corner and cave to the south (your right, as you look seawards).

North of Marigot is the expansive and dramatic Londonderry Bay, where waves roll along the sandy and rocky shoreline in front of **Douglas Charles Airport** (page 37).

POINTE BAPTISTE ESTATE CHOCOLATE

Historic Pointe Baptiste Estate is now also home to a chocolate factory. Having never found any chocolate to his liking, estate owner Alan Napier decided to make his own. He began simply with a makeshift wooden *boucan* (a traditional cocoa drying rack), fermentation and processing shed but quickly resolved to construct a proper factory in the estate grounds. Nibs, truffles and bars come in various strengths and flavours including 80% cocoa, mint, tangerine, ginger and many others. Now available island-wide, Pointe Baptiste Estate Chocolate also welcomes visitors on chocolate factory tours (☏ 767 225 5378; e chocolate@pointebaptiste.com).

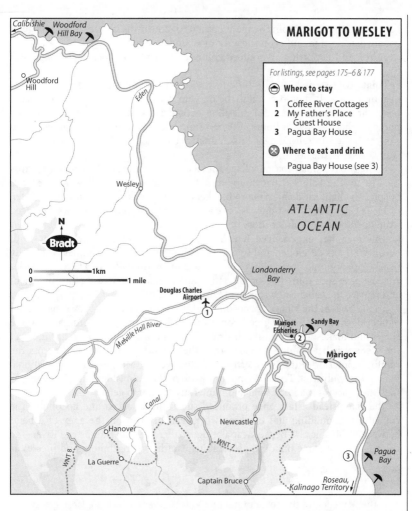

For listings, see pages 175–6 & 177

🏠 **Where to stay**
1   Coffee River Cottages
2   My Father's Place
     Guest House
3   Pagua Bay House

❌ **Where to eat and drink**
     Pagua Bay House (see 3)

ATLANTIC
OCEAN

Calibishie
Woodford
Hill Bay

Woodford
Hill

Eden

Wesley

N

Bradt

0 ————1km
0 ————1 mile

Londonderry
Bay

Douglas Charles
Airport

Melville Hall River

Marigot
Fisheries   Sandy Bay

Marigot

Canal

Newcastle

WNT 7

Hanover

WNT 8

La Guerre

Captain Bruce

Pagua
Bay

Roseau,
Kalinago Territory

The sea wall around the end of the runway is occasionally swamped by breaking waves when seas are rough.

The village of **Wesley** lies to the north of Marigot and Melville Hall Airport. Standing quite majestically above the predominantly residential village is the Our Lady of Assumption Roman Catholic Church. The church has commanding views of the village, the brightly painted Anglican church, and the ridges beyond, where bananas grow in abundance. On the northern edge of Wesley towards the Eden Estate, you may see people working on the production of *copra* (dried coconut kernels).

The banana-farming community of **Woodford Hill** is located in the area of a former sugar-producing estate, one of the largest on the island in the 19th century. The area also had a harbour and a small fort for protection. Before the Europeans arrived, it is believed there was an Amerindian settlement here. Behind the village there are large tracts of banana farms where the present-day villagers grow and sell the bulk of their produce via The Fairtrade Foundation. Along the shore is one of the nicest stretches of light-sand beach on Dominica; indeed it is comparable to any other in the Caribbean. Look for a small road running to the shore from the main coastal road near the centre of the village. It usually has no sign and is on the apex of a bend.

A little to the north of Woodford Hill is another pleasant beach at **Hodges Bay** (page 194).

Pointe Baptiste is located a little to the south of Calibishie and is a naturally beautiful place. It should certainly be on your agenda. It has a lovely white-sand beach and a quite wonderful coastline of **Red Rock formations** that will keep photographers happy for hours. The best time to come is late afternoon when you can catch the sun setting over this dramatic coastline and the foothills of Morne Aux Diables to the northwest.

Calibishie is a small coastal village with a pretty shoreline and great views across the sea to The Saints, Guadeloupe and Marie-Galante. A shallow reef extends beyond the light sand shoreline to breakers and the rock formation Port D'Enfer, or Hell's Gate. The formation was once a natural arch through which water surged from open ocean to calmer shore.

This area has experienced a consistent wave of overseas investment, with ocean-view lots developed and sold for guesthouses and second homes. The sandy beaches, panoramic ocean views, sea breeze and proximity to the Douglas Charles Airport have seen tourist accommodation and ancillary services both supplement and replace the banana as a source of local income.

To the back of the village are coconut palms and banana farms covering a series of tall ridges in a blanket of green. A network of farm feeder roads runs along these ridges and makes for a fun hike or drive. The roads are a little rough at times but the scenery is beautiful, with views over the ocean to the north, and across the rainforest interior of the Northern Forest Reserve and Morne Diablotin National Park to the southwest. Try the Windblow Road or the Calibishie Ridge Road and, as these farm access roads are long and numerous, try not to get lost!

The **Hampstead Estate** once produced sugar, limes, cocoa and coconuts. The ruined estate building and machine works can be seen on the apex of a bend between Calibishie and Bense, near a bridge that crosses the Hampstead River. The ruins consist of stone buildings, several items of heavy machinery and presses as

FROM COCONUT TO COPRA

The flowering of the coconut palm produces *drupes*, which are large green fruit growing in bunches high in the tree. Each fruit is surrounded by a tough fibrous husk up to 15cm thick which is called the *pericarp*. Beneath this is a thin, hard brown kernel containing the *albumen*, or coconut milk, which transforms itself into a white flesh as the fruit matures. Young coconuts are often referred to as *jellies*, in reference to the soft, sweet jelly-like flesh that is beginning to form. The albumen of these young coconuts is often called coconut water and is a refreshing drink.

Mature coconuts are harvested and their dried fibrous husks removed to extract the tough, thin shell of the kernel. This in turn is cracked in half to expose the white flesh of the coconut. Each coconut half is thoroughly dried either by exposure to the sun or by cooking in an oven for up to two days. The dried flesh is then extracted from the kernel. This dried flesh is *copra*.

The *copra* is bagged, sold locally or exported. *Copra* products include coconut oil and skin-care products. Low-grade *copra* is often used as fodder for fattening horses and cattle.

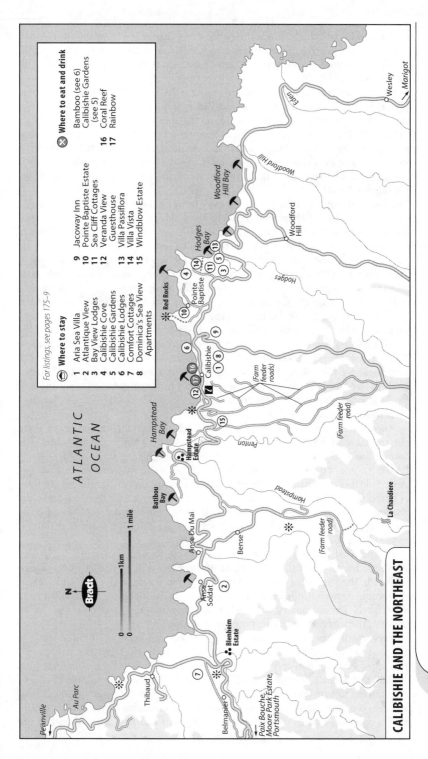

ATLANTIC OCEAN

For listings, see pages 175–9

Where to stay

1 Aria Sea Villa
2 Atlantique View
3 Bay View Lodges
4 Calibishie Cove
5 Calibishie Gardens
6 Calibishie Lodges
7 Comfort Cottages
8 Dominica's Sea View Apartments
9 Jacoway Inn
10 Pointe Baptiste Estate
11 Sea Cliff Cottages
12 Veranda View Guesthouse
13 Villa Passiflora
14 Villa Vista
15 Windblow Estate

Where to eat and drink

Bamboo (see 6)
Calibishie Gardens (see 5)
16 Coral Reef
17 Rainbow

CALIBISHIE AND THE NORTHEAST

well as a waterwheel which was driven by water channelled from the river. Along the side and to the rear of the ruins is a track that follows the Hampstead River into the depths of the former estate, through plantations of coconut palms that are still harvested for *copra*.

On the road from Calibishie, before reaching the Hampstead Estate ruins, there is a vehicle track that runs to **Hampstead Beach**. It is located on the seaward side of the road, oppostite the Windblow Road, on the apex of a bend. It may have a sign saying 'Number 1 Beach'. This track can become very muddy if it has been raining, it is quite narrow and vertiginous at the beginning and further along, and even in a 4x4 it can be a challenge. It only takes about 15 minutes to walk down. It is a long beach and was one of the iconic locations for the feature film *Pirates of the Caribbean: Dead Man's Chest*.

Beyond Hampstead Beach, heading away from Calibishie, you will see the ruins of a small Methodist church on the right-hand side of the road. A short distance along is another vehicle track running down to the sea which leads to **Batibou Beach**. Batibou is the original Kalinago name for the area and this beach is a good place for bathing. The vehicle track is very broken up and it may be a better option for you to walk down. It will take about 20 minutes. The landowner charges for vehicular access.

To the west of Batibou Beach is the signposted road to **Bense**. This small farming village is located on the slopes of a narrow ridge that extends inland towards the foothills of Morne Diablotin. Through the village the route makes the transition to farm feeder road and continues to the area of Ti Branches. *En route*, and probably much further along than you expect it to be, there is a small sign to **La Chaudiere Pool**. A rough road descends down the ridge to a river where there is a water catchment for the village. Before the end, there is a walking trail on the left that leads to La Chaudiere, an effervescent pool and a pretty cascade that is surrounded by dark rocks, giving it the appearance of a cooking pot. It is a nice spot for river bathing and a picnic (see page 198).

Anse is the Creole word for bay and, to the west of the junction for Bense, along the coastal road, are the two fishing villages of **Anse Du Mai** and **Anse Soldat**. The former has a concrete jetty, a pretty cove and beach, fishing boats and a customs house. It is one of three ports of entry for private boats and has a sheltered anchorage. Anse Soldat is quite beautiful, its tranquil bay perhaps one of Dominica's prettiest. A paved road leads into the village and the sheltered cove with its beach and clear shallow waters. There is a bar from where local people watch the fishing boats returning. The fishermen sell their catch from a table along the shore, near the end of the village road.

As the road leaves the coast and heads west towards Portsmouth it passes **Blenheim Estate**. You will see the ruins of the sugar mill on the left-hand side of the road. The somewhat overgrown ruins contain machine works, a sluice canal that would have controlled the flow of water from the Blenheim River, and a large waterwheel. The machinery, cogs and presses show how river water was channelled to rotate the wheel and turn the cane roller presses.

Very shortly after the ruins on the right-hand side, heading to Portsmouth, is the road to Vieille Case and Pennville. The next road on the right goes to the small hamlet of **Paix Bouche**, and above it **Moore Park**. Paix Bouche means 'shut your mouth' in reference, it is said, to walkers climbing up the steep hillside having to stop talking to save their breath. The road that runs straight up and through both hamlets is a nice drive or hike on a clear day. It continues beyond Moore Park, past a communications tower, before turning into a farm track and part of the Wai'tukubuli National Trail Segment 12 (pages 248–9). The road, though somewhat narrow, is in good condition and has panoramic views of Morne Destinee, Morne Aux Diables and Morne Diablotin.

The road between Portsmouth and the east coast passes through the villages of Dos D'Ane and Bornes. In Bornes, you will see a colourful sign for **Indigo** – the unique treehouse gallery and studio of artist Marie Frederick (page 27). Beyond Bornes there is a signposted feeder road to Brandy Manor (see *Horseriding,* pages 77–8). This road is a little rough beyond Brandy Manor and leads to an obscure trail to **Brandy Falls** (you'll need a guide – ask at Brandy Manor, pages 195–6). Also in this area you may come across the remains of the only **railway** the island has ever had. Rails used to run from Brandy Ridge to the Indian River, transporting timber for the 1910 Forest Company Ltd. From here the timber was taken by river to the coast. The company went bankrupt just three years after starting the endeavour and the rails were salvaged by construction workers for buildings in Portsmouth. The small steam train that transported the timber was sold overseas, though remains of discarded rolling stock can still be seen around Brandy Manor. The route of the railway is part of Wai'tukubuli National Trail Segment 11 (pages 246–8).

ACTIVITIES AND SPECIAL INTERESTS

BEACHES Though it is known more for its greenery than it is for its sand, Dominica has some lovely beaches, bays and sheltered waters that are great for bathing and watersports. Some of the best ones are located in the north. Here is a selection.

Anse Soldat Located on the northeast coast, this tiny fishing village is nestled on a pretty bay that is protected from the Atlantic by a shallow reef. A thin strip of white sand, calm, shallow waters and the occasional fishing boat coming in to land make this a gorgeous and very peaceful spot. Follow the main road through the village all the way to the shoreline.

Batibou Taking its name from the Kalinago word for 'bay', Batibou is accessed via a rough vehicle track on the main coastal road from Blenheim to Calibishie. Look for it on the seaward side of the road, close to the apex of a bend, near to the ruined Methodist church. The road down to the beach is very rough and it is better to walk down (the landowner also charges for vehicular access). It will take about 20 minutes. The bay is very pretty and the beach quite long and sheltered. You will find a rustic wooden restaurant and bar here that is especially popular on Sundays when locals come down for a cook-up and beach 'lime'.

Calibishie The village of Calibishie has a narrow but very pretty stretch of white-sand beach running its entire length and a little beyond. You can access it from a number of places. There is a reef system that protects the inshore waters, which are very shallow. At low tide you may see local people wandering around in the surf looking to catch a supper of octopus and sea eggs. A great spot is near the Coral Reef Supermarket where you can also enjoy good food and drink at the beachside restaurant at the back. This is a real gem. To the south of Calibishie is **Pointe Baptiste** (page 190), where the beach is also lovely.

Douglas Bay This very beautiful and tranquil bay (my particular favourite) is located on the north side of the Cabrits peninsula. It has a very narrow strip of sand with access just before the bridge and sea wall at Tanetane. Also near this point there is a picnic area on the northern edge of the Cabrits Swamp. If you follow Wai'tukubuli National Trail Segment 14 southwards for about 5 minutes you will come to a small and secluded stretch of sand. It is a gorgeous spot for bathing. Hopefully the new hotel development planned for this area will not spoil it.

Hampstead
Just along the coast from Batibou is Hampstead Bay. Look for a sign saying '**Number 1 Beach**'. The vehicle track is located on the apex of a sharp bend opposite the Windblow Road, so watch out for traffic. Also be careful of the deep drainage gutter and the road itself, which is narrow, steep and often muddy. If driving, I recommend parking safely on the main road and walking down. It takes about 20 minutes on foot. Hampstead Bay is broad and the black-sand beach very long. For *Pirates of the Caribbean* fans, this beach was where the cannibals were chasing Captain Jack Sparrow and friends back to the *Black Pearl*. Be careful of the surf, it can be a little rough with a strong undertow.

Hodges Bay
To the southeast of Calibishie and Pointe Baptiste is Hodges Bay. Infrequently visited, this is a very lovely place. The bay is quite sheltered, making it safe for bathing, and the beach is very long and clean. To find it, look for the signs to Sea Cliff Cottages and follow the road down towards Calibishie Cove. Before reaching it, you should see a track on the right-hand side of Villa Vista that goes down to the beach. It is short but quite steep. At the bottom you have to cross the small river mouth to get to the beach proper. The islet offshore is accessible to good swimmers and those with kayaks, and there is a track that runs along its spine and goes right to the end. If you have a mask and snorkel, there is a large bank of sea fans between the shore and the islet that is worth a look. Be careful of sea surge and currents when you get close to the islet.

Purple Turtle
Located north of Portsmouth in the area called Lagoon (sometimes Lagon) on the road to the Cabrits National Park and the 'top end'. A mixture of light and dark sand with shallow and calm bathing make this a popular beach hangout. It is especially good for children and you will always meet visiting yachties here. The Purple Turtle Beach Club has a mix of pretty good local and international food, cold drinks and a washroom. Shower facilities are located a little to the south of the bar. **Note:** because this beach attracts a lot of visitors it can also be a draw for petty theft. Try to keep valuables out of sight and reach of wandering hands.

Ripaton Beach
A remote and very pretty beach, few seem to know nor visit Ripaton. You'll find it to the south of Picard, on the straight stretch, just before Ti Bay Villas (residential villas). There may be a sign. Follow a small road to the north of the private land and veer right down a rough vehicle track until it comes to an end at the beach. It can be muddy and you may have to cross a stream to get out on to the beach.

Sandy Bay
An unofficial 'secret beach', Sandy Bay is a lovely spot. Find beach access near My Father's Place Guest House. There's a small sign. Follow the track and steps for about 10 minutes and you'll be on a nice beach, which is actually in two parts, separated by a rocky outcrop and cave. The inshore waters are protected by a reef system that is actually not bad for snorkelling, though you should stick to the inshore side. The beach is quite popular with local people at weekends.

Secret Beach
The only way to get to Secret Beach is by water. Rent a kayak from Wave Dancer Watersports on Coconut Beach (page 197) and head south to the end of the bay and then around the rocky coastal bluff (they will guide you there or even drop you off and pick you up later if you don't fancy kayaking yourself). The beach is worth

the trip; although it cannot claim to be a secret, it is one of the island's prettiest and the snorkelling around this area reveals shallow reefs, corals and plenty of aquatic life.

Toucari Bay Toucari is a picture postcard village and bay located along the northwest coast of the island. The bay has a black-sand beach and is usually very calm. Bring your snorkel and investigate the coral reef formations and volcanic activity along the northern end of the bay. You can also rent paddleboards here (see page 197).

Woodford Hill Woodford Hill has a long beach of white sand. There is usually no sign for it, but it is quite easy to find. Along the coastal road that passes through the village of Woodford Hill, look for a narrow paved road on a bend that goes down towards the sea. The verges are sometimes quite overgrown, disguising it a little, but you should see it. Go down to the bottom and, if you have come by car, park up under the trees. Be sure to leave your valuables locked away out of sight as there have been very occasional incidents of opportunist theft on this beach. Do not let this put you off though. This is as nice a beach as any in the Caribbean.

COLD SULPHUR SPRINGS At the base of the large 'drive-through' crater on Morne Aux Diables you should see a sign for the **Cold Sulphur Springs** (also called **Cold Soufriere**). A very easy 15-minute walk takes you along a track and a series of small steps down to the base of the crater. You reach a small wooden viewing platform over the cold springs. Though not especially photogenic, this area is fascinating, with a number of bubbling freshwater pools and streams that are effervescent with the release of sulphurous gas bubbles from beneath the ground. A volcanic Zen garden of large rocks, bright green mosses and clear pools, the springs are surrounded by *kaklen* (*Clusia mangle*), a very typical species of fumarole vegetation found at most volcanic sites on Dominica and very prevalent here. These particular sulphur springs are cold because the magma layer from where the hot gases are released is thought to be much lower down than those, say, in the Wotten Waven area. This means that by the time they reach the surface they have cooled down.

This area is the subject of scientific study as some of the more recent volcanic swarms recorded on Dominica have come from the Morne Aux Diables Volcano.

Farm feeder roads The feeder roads up to and around the banana farms along the ridges behind the village of Calibishie are very accessible and offer some excellent scenery. Good starting points are the Windblow Road to the west of Calibishie, and the Calibishie Ridge Road from the east of the village. The roads wind around the ridges and hook up with each other, eventually looping back down to the village itself.

If you are driving, you should have a 4x4 as the terrain is a little rough in places. It is also a nice place to hike or take an evening stroll. The views are good, the area interesting, and there is always a chance you will be able to meet and chat with farmers. Don't be surprised if some offer to sell you land; this has been a relatively popular area for overseas investors looking to build homes.

HORSERIDING Trail riding and lessons are offered by **Brandy Manor Riding Center** (*Brandy, Bornes*; ☏ *767 235 4871, 767 612 0978*; e *brandymanor@ymail. com; www.brandymanor.wix.com/ridingcenter;* ⨍). Whether you are a novice or a seasoned rider, enjoy the trails through semi-deciduous woodland and rainforest around Brandy Estate and Wai'tukubuli National Trail Segment 11; or ride around Sugarloaf Mountain and enjoy superb views of Prince Rupert Bay and the Morne

Diablotin National Park. It costs around US$20 per 30 minutes per horse for either trail riding or lessons and you can go out for around 3 hours at a time. Ask either for a picnic or a barbecue ride or enjoy refreshments at Brandy Manor when you return. Riders who would like to extend their stay for even longer should ask about Brandy Manor's riverside cottage accommodation. Alternatively, contact **Rainforest Riding** (*Portsmouth;* \ *767 445 3619, 767 265 7386;* e *rainforestriding@yahoo.com; www.rainforestriding.com;* f); Valerie Francis offers accompanied horseriding around the Cabrits National Park trails, on part of WNT Segment 14, and also along Purple Turtle Beach. She will also teach you how to ride and has a training ring at her farm near Douglas Bay. Accompanied tours are usually US$45–100 and lessons are US$40 per hour.

INDIAN RIVER BOAT TRIP (*Site pass required; prices pp US$20 for the trip plus US$5 for the site pass if you don't already have one*) Boat tours along the Indian River begin at the visitor centre near the Indian River bridge to the south of Portsmouth on Michael Douglas Boulevard. Small, colourful wooden fishing boats carry up to eight passengers each along a one-mile stretch of the Indian River. This stretch of the Indian River actually lies below sea level, making it quite deep and therefore one of the few rivers on Dominica that is accessible by boat – most are too shallow or full of boulders, rapids and cascades to go far. The river is lined with a type of mangrove that is known locally as the bloodwood tree because of its reddish sap. It has large buttress roots that weave their way across the banks like giant tendrils before disappearing beneath the water.

The river is a good place for birdwatching. Common water birds seen here include the green heron, the mangrove cuckoo, both the belted and ringed kingfisher, the common moorhen and the Caribbean coot (see pages 7–8 for more information on Dominica's birds and pages 68–9 for more on birdwatching).

The Indian River runs along the northern edge of the **Glanvillia Swamp**, one of two large areas of swampland in this region. For fans of the *Pirates of the Caribbean* feature films, the Indian River was the location of the hideaway of Tia Dalma (Calypso) in *Dead Man's Chest*. Ask your riverboat guide to take you there before calling in for refreshments at the rustic bar that marks journey's but not World's End. It is nice to take the river trip in the late afternoon when birds are on the move and the return journey is bathed in the soft yellow and purple light of dusk.

INDIGO ART GALLERY & COTTAGE ✳ (\ *767 445 3486; www.mariefrederickgallery. com; visit the gallery, relax & enjoy free Wi-Fi & bush tea; stay and hang out for US$5 pp/hr*) Located in the northern village of Bornes is the Indigo Art Gallery & Cottage. Marie Frederick's unique treehouse gallery is as much a masterpiece of natural design, originality, simplicity and beauty as her Fauvist-style artwork. It enjoys expansive views of the forest canopy and the lush tropical garden, and birds regularly fly in and out enjoying fruits and other treats laid out or hanging for them. Marie was born in Deauville, France but has been living on Dominica for many years after falling in love with the place. She finds her inspiration in the daily life of Dominica, its natural environment and simple wooden *ti-kai* houses. Marie works in pen and ink, watercolour, acrylic and oil pastel. She also creates colourful hand-painted T-shirts that make for very original 'nature island' souvenirs.

The treehouse cottage has to be seen to be believed; there really is nothing else quite like it and it is a fabulous place to stay for anyone looking to hang out with nature, seek some artistic inspiration, or even spend a few romantic nights. Check with Marie for availability and rates.

POINTE BAPTISTE ✳ Pointe Baptiste is located on the northeast coast, a short distance south of Calibishie. It is noted for its **Red Rocks**, a very unusual and extremely photogenic coastal formation of smooth red earth that has been compacted and shaped by both ocean and weather. It looks other-worldly and is often cited by travellers as one of their favourite places on the island. As well as admiring the beauty of the formations themselves, you can explore a small cave, short trails along the coast to further formations and a black-sand beach along the margins of the Pointe Baptiste Estate, and fabulous views back across the bay to Calibishie, Morne Aux Diables and the northern interior. This is an especially magical place at dusk when the sun begins setting behind the mountains.

The second area worth visiting at Pointe Baptiste is the white-sand beach at Pointe Baptiste Bay – it's a nice place for a bathe and a picnic and if you call in at **Pointe Baptiste Estate**, you could taste and buy some of the many variations of chocolate that are made there (box, page 188).

To get to Pointe Baptiste you have to follow the coastal road from Calibishie towards Woodford Hill. Very shortly after leaving Calibishie village, look for a small and often hidden sign to Pointe Baptiste on your left. A sharp turn up a small road brings you into the village. To get to the beach, take the first right turn down a rough feeder road. Follow it as it curves to the right and then left all the way down to the beach.

To get to Red Rocks, drive straight through Pointe Baptiste and keep going without turning off. The road ends – there may be a chain across it – and beyond it is a vehicle track that soon ends at a small parking area. Either park up before the chain or at the end of the track. Look for a trail in the bush by the wooden hut and keep going straight. Ignore all the spurs for now, you can explore them afterwards. The trail passes through coastal brush and then down a few steps to the formation. Have fun exploring, but don't get too close to the edges.

WATERSPORTS Prince Rupert Bay and Douglas Bay are great places to enjoy the water, both above and below. If you just want to swim, try Purple Turtle Beach, Ripaton Beach, Toucari Bay, or the two beaches at Douglas Bay.

JC Ocean Adventures Cabrits; ☎ 767 449 6957; e jorgama60@gmail.com; www. jcoceanadventures.com; f. Located within the Cabrits National Park near the main reception building, JC Ocean Adventures offers boat diving, snorkelling & PADI dive tuition.

Keepin' It Real Toucari Bay; ☎ 767 225 7657; f ToucariBay. Located along the main road through Toucari, Keepin' It Real rents paddleboards & snorkelling gear & also offers 'eco tours' of the bay. Chill with a coffee or cold drink & enjoy the peace & quiet of this very tranquil spot. Ask about their cottage rental.

Wave Dancer Watersports Coconut Beach, Portsmouth; ☎ 767 265 3654; e limbodancer@ hotmail.com; f. Coconut Beach isn't easy to find – it's between Ripaton Beach & Picard Beach – look for an old narrow road off the straight stretch to Picard. Wave Dancer rents kayaks, Hobie-Cats, sailboards & jet skis. You can also go on a banana-boat ride, try waterskiing or wake & knee boards. You can also learn to windsurf, sail & kite board. If you are interested in going to Secret Beach & don't fancy kayaking there yourself, you can pay for a boat drop-off & pick-up.

HIKES

BWA NEF WATERFALL (*Difficulty: T: 2; R: 1; E: 2; D: 1; Rating = 3.8; Guide not essential*) This is a fun little river hike to an interesting waterfall that is inside a tall, narrow canyon. It is tricky to get to the trailhead by bus as they travel very infrequently along this stretch of road. You really need a car or you could hitch a ride from Pennville or Vieille Case. For bus information from Portsmouth see page 50.

To find the trail, head south from Pennville and stop at the second hairpin bend on a river gulley. The road passes over the river and on the right-hand side of the road, a little to the right of the apex of the bend, you should see a sign and a narrow trail leading down to the river.

Follow the river upstream. From time to time you will see the trail appearing on each bank, but ultimately you are brought back to the river again. There is a very short section that passes through some private land and the owner may request a small 'contribution' (it should not be much as the section of private land is very short). Eventually you will come to a tall, narrow canyon where you will find the cascading waterfall.

LA CHAUDIERE   (*Difficulty: T: 2; R: 1; E: 2; D: 1; Rating = 3.0; Guide not essential*)   On the main road between Blenheim and Hampstead you will see a sign for the village of Bense and La Chaudiere Pool. Drive through the village until you come out the other side to a feeder road that heads out along Hampstead Ridge. This road is quite broken in places so a 4x4 will certainly help. If you are travelling by bus, you will have to walk here from the village. For bus information from Portsmouth see page 50. Continue along this road (it will be a lot further than you expect) until you reach a small sign for La Chaudiere pointing to a track on the left-hand side of a farmer's hut. It is quite a distance along the rough road, so stick with it and enjoy the views. If you are driving and don't really fancy it, just park up out of the way and walk. If you do drive to the sign, park up opposite the hut. There may well be farmers working here so be sure you are not blocking the road or obstructing them in any way.

You could choose to drive down this road – it leads to a water catchment for the village – but you really do need a 4x4 and a strong nerve for that. Alternatively, walk down the road for about 15 minutes until you see a sign on the left-hand side before you reach the bottom. The trail is fairly short (don't panic when you find yourself going uphill again – it does feel rather odd – but you will end up at the right place on the river if you stick with it). When you emerge from the trail you will see a river in front and a smaller one to the right. You have to cross over the one on your right (careful!) and then work your way down to the point below. Work your way around it until you are facing upstream on the second, larger river. You should see La Chaudiere in front of you. Make your way up the right-hand side until you are there. You can climb up the rocks on the right to get above the cascade, but be wary about jumping in (I'm not really much of a jumper myself but I know it was a popular pastime here). It used to be very deep but at the time of writing, following Tropical Storm Erika, it was very silted up and far too shallow for jumping in from above. It is, however, a very beautiful bathing and picnic spot.

LAPLUY (LAPLI) WATERFALL   (*Difficulty: T: 1; R: 1; E: 1; D:1; Rating = 2.5; Guide not essential*)   A little-known waterfall at the time of writing, Lapluy (Lapli) Waterfall can be found at the end of a short and easy track inland from the coastal hamlet of Tanetane. The waterfall is inside a canyon and is in two sections. There isn't much by way of a pool, and the river is more like a stream, but the rock formation of the canyon is interesting and Lapluy is certainly worth a short diversion if you can be bothered with the fee collection.

At the time of writing there's a sign at the trailhead telling you that the track runs across private land and that you have to pay an access fee. It doesn't tell you how much and asks you to call one of two telephone numbers. It's hard to think of a more effective way to put people off than this so hopefully it will change.

If you do make it past this point, then the trail itself is actually very easy to follow; indeed for some of the way it is even lined with stones and has a couple of wooden bridges. Essentially you are following the diminutive Salt River (look for the water snails, they are prolific) through a deep gulley. You will pass through coconut groves and alongside a liana-covered cliff before you eventually reach the canyon; it should take less than an hour to get here. Wade through the first pool into the canyon to see the waterfall proper. Occasionally someone has manufactured a way to get up to the top of the lower section (it was a rough wooden ladder when I went), but be careful if you do attempt this. At the top is a very small rock-filled pool within the conical formation that has been created by the water that is falling from above.

LAMOTHE RIVER FALLS (*Difficulty: T: 2; R: 2; E: 2; D:2; Rating = 5.0; Guide strongly recommended*) The Lamothe River begins life in the region of Cold Soufriere on Morne Aux Diables and meanders down the western slopes of the volcano between the small coastal hamlets of Cottage and Clifton. The trailhead is difficult to find and the trail itself is rather tricky to follow in places so, for this reason, taking along a local guide is a very good idea. You will also be climbing up and over river boulders and cascades – a helping hand and a bit of reassurance are worth having.

Heading north up the coastal road from Toucari, take the paved road inland at the junction in Cottage. At a fork, the route heads down an unpaved track to the left (you really need a 4x4 here if you are driving) and then you must look for a walking trail that heads steeply down to the river, also on your left.

Cross the river and then follow the trail as it meanders inland through abandoned estate lands – you will see coconut, cocoa and coffee trees – along the elevated northern bank of the river. There are a couple of open, rocky areas where the trail seems to disappear. Hug the right and you pick it up again. Eventually you will arrive at the river.

From here it is a river hike. You will come to a deep pool and cascade that has a ladder propped up against it (unless it has washed away by the time you read this). Make your way over this cascade and keep heading up river until you reach the tiered falls. If you can manage it, climb up the rocks on the left-hand side of the lower waterfall to the pool above.

DOUGLAS BAY BATTERY AND GARRISON RUINS (*Site pass required. Difficulty: T: 2; R: 0; E: 2; D:1; Rating = 3.1; Guide not essential*) A knowledgeable guide would make for a great companion on these trails, but it is not essential and there is plenty of information around to give you a good understanding and appreciation of the place. And you have this guidebook, of course.

Follow the signposted trail to the Douglas Bay battery from the wide clearing and stone footpath that leads up to the restored Fort Shirley garrison. After a short distance you will reach a sign pointing to the commandant's quarters up a spur trail to the right. Take this trail up to the ruins of the **commandant's quarters**. From here continue northwards along the main trail until you see the impressive ruins of the officers' quarters down to your left. Walk down to them and take a look around. Trees and vines embrace and weave themselves around the stone ruins. Three cannons lie abandoned beside the ruins of the defensive wall and a gateway leads to the remains of the battery. Take care when exploring the ruins as there are many sharp rocks and plenty of things that can trip you up. The woodland area to the south of these ruins was once a parade ground. Also in this area and at the foot of East Cabrit, there were stables, further troops' barracks and a cistern.

To the west of these impressive ruins, heading steeply uphill, are some steps. Climb up to the top where you meet a wide path. Head to the right for 15–20 minutes around the northern edge of West Cabrit, along the partially restored ruins of a wall, until you come to the end of the path. There are nice views across Douglas Bay and along the coast towards Capuchin. To the north you can usually also see The Saints and Guadeloupe.

Walk back along the wide track all the way to Fort Shirley.

EAST CABRIT TRAIL (*Site pass required. Difficulty: T: 2; R: 0; E: 2; D:1; Rating = 3.1; Guide not essential*) This is a nice trail with panoramic views from the summit of East Cabrit. In the wide clearing below the Fort Shirley garrison, follow the signposted trail to the Douglas Bay battery. When you reach the sign pointing up to the **commandant's quarters**, follow it. At the ruin, the wide trail running north leads to the officers' quarters and the Douglas Bay battery (above), but there is also a narrow spur trail on the north side of the ruin that heads upwards through the trees. This is the East Cabrit Trail. It is a pretty walk that gradually climbs up East Cabrit in a series of long but fairly gentle switchbacks. It takes around 30–45 minutes to reach the ruins of the East Cabrit guardhouse, ordnance store and powder magazine. Up the stone steps are the ruins of a battery position with views across to the east. Take time to explore and then continue along the East Cabrit Trail until you reach the end at the ruined northeast battery emplacement. From here there are views from Douglas Bay to Prince Rupert Bay. Immediately below is the patchwork swamp of the Cabrits with its distinctive clumps of fern and sedge. This trail is also a good place to encounter the *kouwès* grass snake, hermit crabs, and tree and ground lizards.

WEST CABRIT TRAIL (*Site pass required. Difficulty: T: 2; R: 0; E: 2; D:1; Rating = 3.1; Guide not essential*) From the top of the Fort Shirley garrison, behind the restored officers' quarters, a sign points to the start of the West Cabrit Trail. The track passes through dry coastal woodland and climbs gradually to the top of West Cabrit via a series of fairly gentle switchbacks. You will see some fine examples of the naked

THE BATTLE OF THE SAINTS

One of history's most famous naval battles was fought off the northwest coast of Dominica. In 1782 Admiral the Comte de Grasse set sail from Martinique with 35 warships and a plan to meet up with a Spanish fleet of 12 warships and together they would attack the British-held island of Jamaica. De Grasse was pursued by 36 ships of the British fleet that had set out from St Lucia under the command of Admiral James Rodney. On 12 April the fleets lined up for battle off Les Îles des Saintes, a small group of islands between Guadeloupe and Dominica.

It is said that a sudden shift of wind allowed Rodney's flagship, *Formidable*, and several others to break the French line in two places, firing upon and scattering them as they did so. The resulting confusion and disorder of the French fleet ended in defeat and de Grasse surrendered on his flagship, *Ville de Paris*. No-one can be certain whether the manoeuvre to break the French line was deliberate or just pure luck, but it became a tactic that was repeated in later battles. The French and Spanish failed to capture Jamaica and Rodney was made a peer.

Indian tree, known locally as *gòmyé wouj* (*Bursera simaruba*), and the savonnet (*Lauchocarpus latifolius*), which is the most common tree found growing on the Cabrits headland. It is also highly likely that you will encounter one of Dominica's grass snake species, the *kouwès*, along this trail, as well as hermit crabs, land crabs and tree and ground lizards. After around 30–45 minutes of steady climbing, you reach the cannon emplacement of the West Cabrit battery. There is a nice view westwards out over the Caribbean Sea.

In addition to the battery placement, West Cabrit was also the location for a hospital and surgery, surgeons' quarters, further troops' barracks, artillery quarters and the commandant's bungalow.

9

Heart of Dominica, Morne Diablotin National Park, and the West

In this chapter we explore the dense and largely untouched forest and parrot habitats of the Morne Diablotin National Park and Northern Forest Reserve. We travel along the rugged Caribbean coastline, and follow the Layou River inland to the 'Heart of Dominica', where we find the Central Forest Reserve, hidden waterfalls, and Maroon legends.

GETTING THERE AND AWAY

BY CAR It takes about an hour to travel the west-coast highway between Roseau and Portsmouth. Flooded rivers and landslides brought about by Tropical Storm Erika in August 2015 destroyed three west-coast bridges at Macoucherie Estate, Batali Bay and Point Ronde, and a section of road near the Layou River mouth. At the time of writing, short diversions and Bailey bridges were in place enabling the

GREAT DAYS OUT

Here are some suggestions for great days out in the west and Heart of Dominica. You will find details of all the places mentioned in this chapter.

JACKO STEPS AND BEACH OR RAINFOREST LUNCH Spend the morning hiking one of Dominica's greatest and most historic trails and follow it up with a late lunch either at Romance Café on Mero Beach or Riverstone Bar & Grill in Bells.

JACKO AND SOLTOUN FALLS, LUNCH AND EMERALD POOL From Pont Cassé head through the interior towards Bells, first stopping off at the Jacko Waterfall and then the twin Spanny Falls. Enjoy lunch at Riverstone Bar & Grill in Bells (there's sometimes live music on a Sunday) and then take a leisurely afternoon stroll to the Emerald Pool when all the cruise ship tourists have gone.

SYNDICATE FALLS, NATURE TRAIL AND LUNCH Walk the Syndicate Nature Trail on the lookout for parrots (even better in the company of Birdy) and then hike the short river trail to see the Syndicate Falls (you may well see parrots here too). Head down the coast to enjoy a late lunch at either Sunset Bay Club or Tamarind Tree (draught Kubuli!).

free flow of vehicular traffic along the west coast. Bells, Pont Cassé and the region often referred to as the Heart of Dominica, are located on the main road between Roseau and Marigot. This road also suffered some damage from Erika and forms the main traffic artery between the capital, the airport, and the northeast.

BY BUS Buses run frequently along the west-coast highway between Roseau ·and Portsmouth and through the Heart of Dominica between Roseau and Marigot. The Layou Valley road between Layou and Pont Cassé is currently in poor shape from both the Mathieu Dam burst and Tropical Storm Erika. Hardly any buses pass this way and to explore it you must have your own car or private taxi. Public buses do not travel up to Syndicate and the Morne Diablotin National Park. For more information see page 50.

WHERE TO STAY

HEART OF DOMINICA

⌂ **Harmony Villa** [map, page 217] (4 bedrooms) Pont Cassé; ☎767 612 4166; e info@harmonyvilla.com; www.harmonyvilla. com; ⨍. This is an exquisite open-plan villa in a secluded & peaceful forest location in the Heart of Dominica. Beautifully designed & constructed with wide verandas, living area, Wi-Fi, fully equipped kitchen, 4 bedrooms & bathrooms, Harmony suits couples, families & friends. Set in nearly 1ha of forest garden, with tall wooden ceilings & spiral staircase, & walls decorated with the original & colourful artwork of owner Carla Armour, this is a beautiful, stylish & luxurious getaway. Guests receive welcome drinks on the veranda, a complimentary first dinner & daily b/fast. Harmony is linked to Anchorage Hotel (page 97) & Picard Beach Cottages (page 175) so discounted rates are offered to travellers combining these accommodation options. Land & sea tours, car rental & other activities can be arranged via sister company Dominica Tours (page 35). **$$$$$**

⌂ **Ramelton Estate** [map, page 217] (3 bedrooms) Layou Valley; ☎+1 246 425 2788; e edp@caribsurf.com; www.rameltondominica. net. Plantation-style accommodation set in 9ha of beautiful garden & forest surroundings, Ramelton has 3 bedrooms, each with a large private bathroom with shower. There is a kitchen, a lounge with open fire, internet access, & a large veranda with lovely views. A long trail leads down to a river. A caretaker lives in the grounds & there is a daily maid service. This is a peaceful & private accommodation choice, ideal for couples or a group of friends. Weekly stays are preferred & there are discounts if you stay longer. **$$$$$**

⌂ **Crescent Moon Cabins** (4 cabins) Riviere La Croix; ☎767 449 3449; e jeanviv@cwdom.dm; www.crescentmooncabins.com. Crescent Moon Cabins is nestled on a forested hillside above a river & is surrounded by lovely gardens. Family owned & managed, it comprises 4 wooden cabins, tastefully furnished with dbl bed, en-suite bathroom & verandas, all overlooking the valley towards the sea. The cabins sleep couples & families of up to 4. The quaint dining terrace serves great food, much of which is grown organically on site, & there is a small communal lounge with library & internet. Crescent Moon has an organic farm, a large greenhouse, & colourful tropical gardens that guests are welcome to explore. A natural spring provides clean drinking water. Try the homemade goat's cheese, soap, essential oils & balms. Let Ron know your dietary needs before you arrive & he'll do his best to prepare appropriate meals for you. Crescent Moon is very hands-on, sensorial & natural accommodation with excellent personal service. It is also well located for exploring the natural sights of the Heart of Dominica & the Morne Trois Pitons National Park. **$$$**

⌂ **Liberty Jungle** [map, page 217] (3 cottages) Bells; ☎767 613 9425; e libertyjungle@ gmail.com; www.libertyjungle.com; ⨍. Secluded, peaceful & private wooden cottages are set within nearly 1ha of lush & colourful tropical gardens in the Heart of Dominica near the village of Bells. The One Love Studio is the smallest of the 3, with queen-size bed, private balcony, hammock & separate bathroom facilities. The Lovers Cabin also sleeps 2. It has a king-size bed, a unique shower with sky view, private veranda & hammocks. The largest cottage is Guardian Angel. Very popular with honeymooners, it has a king-size bed, a sunken bathtub, & an outside shower built into the large private veranda. Liberty Jungle has an on-site bar & restaurant serving high-end international fusion with a strong hint of France. Your host, Marielle, will also be happy to take you on bespoke island tours. Surrounded by forest & gardens, Liberty Jungle is both a romantic retreat & a centrally located base for exploring the island at a relaxed pace. At the time of writing, the short access road was extremely rough & required a 4x4 vehicle. English & French spoken. **$$$**

🏠 **Roots Jungle Retreat** [map, page 146] (4 cottages) Pagua Hills; ☏767 276 1473; e rootsjungleretreat@gmail.com; www. rootsjungleretreat.com; 📘. The name of this accommodation option speaks volumes – it's hard to think of many places in such a remote setting. A rough 3km feeder road from the western margins of Concord takes you into the lush forests of Pagua Hills where you eventually arrive at Roots (yes, you definitely need to rent a 4x4). Surrounded by thick forest, 4 cottages each comfortably sleep 2, but could take up to 6. 2 cottages are stand-alone, the other 2 form a duplex & have large private verandas. All cottages have private bathroom facilities, mosquito nets & Wi-Fi. Roots is off-grid & is powered by a hydro system from the bounding river. The hillside gardens have beds of flowers & vegetables & there is an off-ground covered platform where you could pitch a tent. There is a nearby river cascade & pool. There is a restaurant & bar for guests only. Managers live on site. **$$–$$$**

🏠 **Zen Gardens** [map, page 217] (3 cottages) D'Leau Gommier, Bells; ☏767 449 3737; m 767 612 5128; e zengardens37@gmail.com; www. zengardensdominica.com; 📘. Zen Gardens is located near the village of Bells. It is a remote & beautiful location in the lush Heart of Dominica, surrounded by rivers, forest & tropical gardens. There are 3 rustic & colourful wooden cottages, each with cooking facilities & running cold water from a local spring. Shower & toilet facilities are shared. There is a chef on call who can prepare meals for you with prior notice. Zen is a great escape for those looking for peace, natural solitude & simplicity & is about as laidback – & indeed Zen – as it gets. **$$**

🏠 **D-Smart Farm** [map, page 217] Corona; ☏767 295 2605 or 767 315 5128; e d-smartfarm@ hotmail.com; 📘. D-Smart Farm offers educational tours & classes on organic farming on Dominica. It is popular with local schools & travellers are also welcome (see page 215). If you wish to stay on the farm there is the basic but clean Bwa Bandé Cottage (with 1 bed, living area, bathroom, kitchenette) & a very natural forest campground where pitches are on wooden platforms; there are creative canvas & wood 'tents', a kitchen, shower & changing room, & composting toilets. Bring your own tent & camping gear or simply use those provided. Research students & visiting scientists could easily make D-Smart Farm their base, as electricity, Wi-Fi & covered classroom mean it could be used as a forest field station. **$**

WEST COAST

🏠 **Sunset Bay Club & Seaside Dive Resort** [map, page 209] (12 rooms, 1 suite) Batali Beach, Coulibistrie; ☏767 446 6522; e sunset@cwdom.dm; www.sunsetbayclub.com. Sunset Bay offers well-maintained & comfortable accommodation in coastal garden surroundings with easy access to the beach & sea. Each dbl room has ceiling fans, en-suite bathrooms, mosquito nets, Wi-Fi & safe. Family rooms have bunks to sleep 4. There is also a spacious honeymoon suite available. Services & facilities include laundry, a large swimming pool, poolside showers & sauna. The hotel has its own dive centre with instructors & 2 dive boats. The Four Seasons Restaurant (page 206) serves local & international cuisine daily. Sunset bay also offers an anchorage & provisioning service for visiting yachts. **$$$**

🏠 **Mango Island Lodges** [map, page 210] (4 rooms) St Joseph; ☏767 617 7963; e mangoislandlodges@yahoo.com; www. mangoislandlodges.com; 📘. Perched on the hillside between St Joseph & Mero, Mango Island Lodges offers stylish, laid-back & very comfortable accommodation. The rooms have en-suite bathroom, ceiling fans, mosquito net, TV & Wi-Fi. The garden terrace has an infinity pool & jacuzzi with uninterrupted Caribbean Sea views. Scuba diving, snorkelling, hiking & other island tours can be arranged for you (you can rent dive & snorkelling equipment here). Mango Island's restaurant (page 206) is open to guests & the public & is also a relaxing place to chill out with a coffee, juice & a good book. English & French spoken. **$$$**

🏠 **The Tamarind Tree Hotel & Restaurant** [map, page 210] (15 rooms, 2 cottages) Salisbury; ✆767 449 7395; e hotel@tamarindtreedominica.com; www. tamarindtreedominica.com. A popular & well-placed family-owned & -managed hotel located along the cliffs to the south of Salisbury, Tamarind has 15 dbl rooms with en-suite bathrooms, ceiling fans, Wi-Fi, & porch. Superior rooms on the upper floor also have AC. All the rooms have great Caribbean Sea views. The 2 SC cottages are located nearby & each has 2 bedrooms, fully equipped kitchen, living area & large deck. Tamarind's terrace restaurant & bar (see below) is at the foot of the gardens on top of the cliff & serves good local & international cuisine. It also has Kubuli beer on tap! Also within the gardens is a swimming pool & sun terrace. Your host Annette can take you on personal tours, or arrange them for you. German,

Swiss, Italian, Spanish & French as well as English are spoken here. Scuba diving packages are also available using the services of East Carib Dive (page 81). Very popular with European travellers, Tamarind Tree is in a great spot for exploring the east coast & hiking trails such as Syndicate, Diablotin, WNT Segment 10, Kachibona Lake & others. $$$

🏠 **The Beach House** Layou; e thebeachhouselayoudominica@gmail.com; www.thebeachhousedominica.com. Located in Layou village & right on the shoreline, The Beach House has 1 bedroom & a futon in the living room, 2 kitchens, 2 bathrooms, hammocks & open upstairs deck overlooking the Caribbean. Simple, functional, laid-back & great value accommodation on the mid-west coast. $

✖ WHERE TO EAT AND DRINK

HEART OF DOMINICA
Map, page 217

✖ **Liberty Jungle** Bells; ✆767 613 9425; f. The quaint bar & restaurant at Liberty Jungle is also open to the public by reservation. Surrounded by colourful rainforest gardens, it's a tranquil, romantic & scenic place to dine on high-quality international dishes. Call ahead. $$$

✖ **Riverstone Bar & Grill** Bells; ✆767 449 3713; f. Nestled on the banks of the Laurent River near the village of Bells, Riverstone is a great place to drop in for food & refreshments after exploring some of the sights of the Heart of Dominica. Serving good value Creole & international food, it is usually open Wed–Sun with occasional live music at the w/end (check FB page). Just turn up. $$

WEST COAST

✖ **Four Seasons Restaurant** [map, page 209] Sunset Bay Club, Coulibistrie; ✆767 446 6522. Also open to the public, Sunset Bay's lunch & dinner menu is varied & offers a wide selection of Creole & international dishes. Seafood is a speciality. Just turn up. $$–$$$

✖ **Mango Island Lodges** St Joseph; ✆767 617 7963; f Enjoying panoramic Caribbean Sea views from a hillside position between St Joseph & Mero, Mango Island's restaurant is open to hotel guests & the public. Serving a wide range of Creole & international dishes (including French, Mexican &

sushi), the food is fresh & high quality. Turn up for lunch & snacks; dinner by reservation. $$–$$$

✖ **East Carib Dive** [map, page 210] Salisbury; ✆767 449 6575. East Carib Dive has a rustic, laid-back beach bar & restaurant serving a mix of local & international dishes. Calling ahead is advisable. $$

✖ **Romance Café** [map, page 210] Mero; ✆767 449 7922; f. Located on the beach at Mero, Romance Café is a very popular bar & restaurant – for good reason. Frédérique serves great food – a blend of local with a hint of French cuisine. Her menu changes daily according to what is available. There's always a wide range on offer & it's always fresh, tasty & good value. Cool & convivial, Romance is a great place to chill by the sea. It has a small boutique selling local products & it hosts regular cultural activities & events inc the annual Reggae On The Beach. Just turn up for lunch & dinner. $$

✖ **The Tamarind Tree Hotel & Restaurant** [map, page 210] Salisbury; ✆767 449 7395. Tamarind Tree has an appetising daily lunch & dinner menu offering very good value local & international cuisine in a pleasant terrace restaurant on the cliffs. With Kubuli beer on draught, it's always a great option! Just turn up. $$

✖ **Connie's Mero Beach Bar** [map, page 217] Mero; ✆767 449 6513. Located towards the northern end of Mero Beach, Connie serves a range of local lunches as well as snacks, take-away & a variety of beverages. Just turn up. $

THE MORNE DIABLOTIN NATIONAL PARK When it was formed in 1977, the **Northern Forest Reserve** covered 8,900ha of mountains and rainforest. In January 2000, 3,335ha were taken from the reserve to form the **Morne Diablotin National Park**, which was created primarily as a sanctuary to protect the natural habitat of Dominica's two endemic parrots, in particular its national bird, the **sisserou** (*Amazona imperialis*). Morne Diablotin gets its name from the French name for the black-capped petrel (*Pterodroma hasitata*), a bird that used to inhabit the cliff faces of the mountain. The name translates to 'little devil' and was given because of its apparent demonic-sounding call. The petrel typically nests on high cliff faces, burrowing a hole or using natural clefts. Though rarely seen these days, experts believe the bird may be returning to the mountain.

The higher elevations of Morne Diablotin are cloaked in elfin woodland. Low-growing *kaklen* (*Clusia mangle*) dominates the terrain, growing in a dense, tangled blanket some 2–3m above the ground. The *palmiste moutan*, or mountain palm (*Prestoea montana*) pushes its way through the *kaklen*, together with other low-growing trees and ferns. The lower elevations give way to montane forest and then dense swathes of rainforest. Trees such as the *gommier* (*Dacryodes excelsa*) and several species of *chatanier* (*Sloanea dentata*, *Sloanea caribaea* and *Sloanea berteriana*) can be found here, its unmistakable buttress roots reaching out across the forest floor. Other trees known locally as the *mang blanc, mang wouj, bwa kanno* and *kwé kwé* can also be found in this habitat and have prop roots. The karapit (*Amanoa caribaea*) produces both buttress and prop roots and is one of the most abundant species of large tree growing in the rainforest.

Within the Morne Diablotin National Park is the Syndicate Nature Trail, one of Dominica's most popular birdwatching trails (see details on pages 216–18). There is also an extremely tough trail to the 1,447m summit of Morne Diablotin (pages 218–19).

The visitor centre was opened in October 2006 and has an interpretation room where visitors can learn about the rainforest habitat, including the trees, animals and birds that may be seen within it. The centre also has toilets and a small shop selling refreshments. Unfortunately it is often closed, catering more to cruise ship tour buses than independent travellers.

THE HEART OF DOMINICA Established in 1952, the 410ha **Central Forest Reserve** is Dominica's oldest forest reserve. As the name suggests, it is located centrally, between the Morne Trois Pitons National Park and the Northern Forest Reserve. It has a rich biodiversity and consists of dense tropical rainforest, rivers, streams and waterfalls. It also provides a habitat for free-roaming fauna such as the agouti, and birds such as the endemic jaco parrot (*Amazonia arausiaca*). The *gommier* trees that grow in abundance in this dense forest have traditionally been used by the Kalinago for canoe building.

Bisecting the Central Forest Reserve is the main artery for vehicle traffic passing between Douglas Charles Airport and the capital, Roseau. Located along this road is the sprawling village of **Bells**, a farming community to the south of the Central Forest Reserve and along the Layou River. There are a number of accessible natural attractions around this village as well as sites of historical interest. They include the Layou River itself, the Spanny Falls (pages 220–1), the Jacko Falls (page 216) and the interesting and historic Jacko Steps (pages 221–2).

The **Layou River** is Dominica's longest, originating in the heights of the Northern Forest Reserve in the area of Mosquito Mountain (you climb this summit on WNT

Segment 8 – see pages 240–2), and emptying into the Caribbean Sea just south of St Joseph. It is a beautiful river that runs through deep gorges and wide expanses of rainforest. It is alive with mountain mullet and crayfish, and many species of bird, including heron and kingfisher, can be seen along its banks or buzzing across its surface for insects. The river has stretches of rapids as well as both shallow and deep pools that are perfect for bathing and, until recently, river tubing.

In 1997, on a section of the river where it is joined by one of its tributaries, the Mathieu River, there was a series of dramatic landslides that changed the shape of the landscape forever. The two rivers meet in a gorge where the cliffs are easily 100m tall. Upstream from this junction, in the region of Carholm, the valley walls of the Mathieu River collapsed, sliding into the river and passing into the gorge where the two rivers join. A landslide dam was created, plugging both rivers. Water backed

JACKO AND THE MAROONS

'Maroons' is the name given to the runaway slaves of 18th- and 19th-century Dominica. Before the French arrived on the island, bringing with them their own slaves, it is thought that a number of runaways from other islands had already arrived on Dominica and had either befriended the indigenous Kalinago or were living in remote forest locations. It is quite amazing to think that 'free' Africans were living on this island for over 100 years before the Europeans came here. For all those years, Dominica was left alone, its landscape too rugged and inaccessible to be either safe or commercially viable. But land pressures on other, flatter islands meant that there was a need to expand sugarcane production here. Once the Europeans had established an economic foothold, the slaves that were brought to Dominica to work on estates soon outnumbered their colonial masters. Some of them escaped and lived in camps in the interior – presumably joining up with those already there. These Maroons, or *nègres marrons*, used the island's rugged terrain to their advantage, protected by tall peaks, deep ravines and dense rainforest. They cut trails across the island to other Maroon encampments and to estate settlements which they raided for ground provisions and livestock. Establishing a large and secret network of forest camps and trails, the Maroons were led by a number of prominent chiefs including Robin, Hill, Quashie, Battrebois, Pharcelle, Clemence, Nico, Congo Ray, Moko, Zombie, Jacko, Goree Greg, Balla, Sandy, Juba, Elephant, Cicero, Soleil, Nicholas, Diano, Lewis and Jupiter. Areas of the interior of Dominica where these chiefs had their camps still retain their names today.

By the late 18th century the number of camps and the network of trails stretched the entire length of the island's dense interior. In 1813 Major General George Robert Ainslie arrived to become Governor of Dominica. A violent, oppressive, perhaps even psychopathic man, his brutality against runaway slaves and those who helped them was manifested in the Maroon trials, torture and executions that became the hallmark of his reign. On 12 July 1814, Chief Jacko, who had spent upwards of 40 years as a runaway, was shot and killed in a bloody battle with the Loyal Dominica Rangers, a militia of 'trusty' slaves who were offered the reward of freedom in exchange for killing a Maroon chief. His death marked the end of the Maroon wars.

Many of Dominica's hiking trails, including Jacko Steps (see pages 221–2) and WNT segments 2, 3, 5 and 8 (see *Chapter 10*), follow former Maroon traces.

up behind the dam and three days later it was breached, sending wave upon wave of water and mud racing down the Layou River to the sea. A second landslide took place on the Mathieu River the following week, creating exactly the same effect at the same river junction. The Mathieu River was plugged more solidly this time but it was only three days before the backed-up volume of river water along the Layou breached the dam again. The Mathieu River was plugged a final time, it seemed, and a large lake formed in the river valley behind the landslide dam. That lake, known as Lake Mathieu (or Miracle Lake) was dramatic and beautiful and could easily have become a popular natural attraction had the dam not burst one final time in 2011, sending rocks and silt down the Layou in a raging torrent that wrecked agricultural stations and the Wacky Rollers zip-lining park. The piles of sand you see at the river mouth today hark back to this event and were supplemented by the devastation wreaked by Tropical Storm Erika in 2015.

WEST COAST VILLAGES Located along the shoreline between the communities of Picard and Dublanc, **Morne Espagnol** is a 365m conical volcanic peak. There is a communications mast on the summit and a rough and steep access track has been built to maintain it. A walk up to the top is a very steep climb but the views are excellent. You will also see lots of *bwa kwaib*, Dominica's national flower (page 6). If driving north to Picard and Portsmouth, the track can be found on the left-hand side once you are beside the mountain.

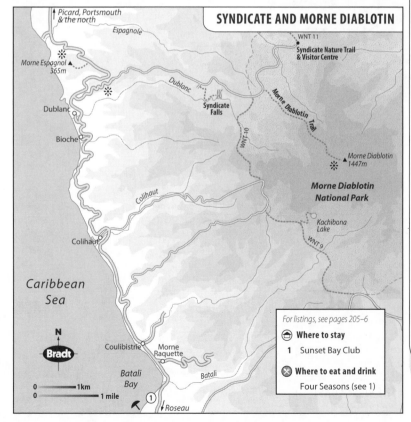

SYNDICATE AND MORNE DIABLOTIN

Picard, Portsmouth & the north

Espagnole

WNT 11

Syndicate Nature Trail & Visitor Centre

Morne Espagnol 365m

Dublanc

Morne Diablotin Trail

Syndicate Falls

Dublanc

WNT 10

Bioche

Morne Diablotin 1447m

Morne Diablotin National Park

Colihaut

Kachibona Lake

Colihaut

WNT 9

Caribbean Sea

N

Bradt

Coulibistrie

Morne Raquette

Batali Bay

Batali

0 ▬ 1km
0 ▬ 1 mile

1

Roseau

For listings, see pages 205–6

⊜ **Where to stay**
1 Sunset Bay Club

⊗ **Where to eat and drink**
Four Seasons (see 1)

Heart of Dominica, Morne Diablotin National Park, and the West WHAT TO SEE AND DO 9

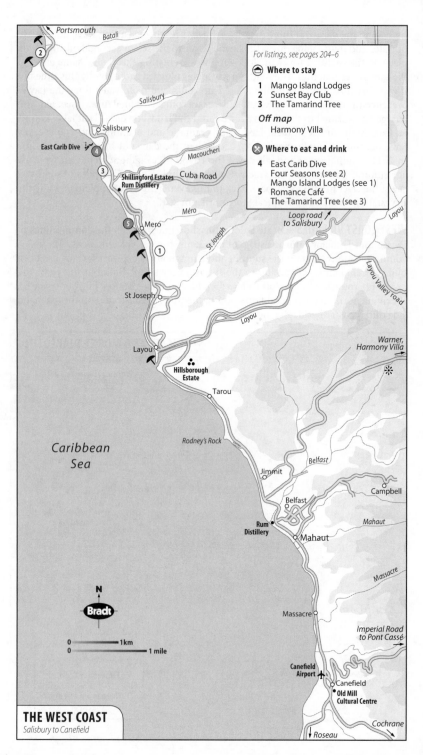

For listings, see pages 204–6

🏠 Where to stay

1 Mango Island Lodges
2 Sunset Bay Club
3 The Tamarind Tree

Off map
  Harmony Villa

⊗ Where to eat and drink

4 East Carib Dive
  Four Seasons (see 2)
  Mango Island Lodges (see 1)
5 Romance Café
  The Tamarind Tree (see 3)

Portsmouth
Batali
Salisbury
Salisbury
East Carib Dive
Macoucheri
Cuba Road
Shillingford Estates
Rum Distillery
Méro
Mero
Loop road to Salisbury
Layou
St Joseph
Layou
St Joseph
Layou
Layou Valley road
Layou
Hillsborough Estate
Warner, Harmony Villa
Tarou

Caribbean Sea

Rodney's Rock
Belfast
Jimmit
Campbell
Belfast
Mahaut
Rum Distillery
Mahaut
Massacre

N
Bradt
0   1km
0   1 mile

Massacre
Imperial Road to Pont Cassé
Canefield Airport ✈
Canefield
Old Mill Cultural Centre
Cochrane
Roseau

THE WEST COAST
Salisbury to Canefield

The French and Creole term for Carnival (*carne* = flesh, *vale* = farewell) is *masquerade*, and it is from this word that *mas* is derived, an abbreviated form which is used by Dominicans to describe the period of carnival (you may come across the term 'Mas Domnik' or 'Real Mas'). This two-day festival before Lent combines costume, music and dance with origins in West Africa and French Creole. Following emancipation in 1838, the festivities of *mas* moved to the streets of the capital, where bands from villages all around the island would come to celebrate. Each band had its own distinct style of music, dance and costume. One such costume is the *sensay*, which is a full dress of long strips of material with a headpiece that may include horns and a mask. The mask is of tribal origin and many demonic variations exist (unfortunately many seem to have been replaced with cheap plastic variations today). The costumes of these groups, called *ban mauvais*, were deliberately intimidating, threatening terror with whips, sticks and batons. Today one of Dominica's best-known *ban mauvais* groups hails from the village of Colihaut.

During the Carnival season there is always a *ban mauvais* parade accompanied by the drums of a *la peau cabwit* (goatskin drum) band through the streets of Roseau, and sometimes also in Colihaut itself. It is always atmospheric and stirring as the *sensay* dance their way through the streets accompanied by a cacophony of drums, horns and whistles. If you are visiting Dominica during Carnival, be sure to experience *ban mauvais* and *la peau cabwit* at the *j'ouvert* (opening) parade in Roseau, from around 04.00 on Carnival Monday.

The two villages of **Dublanc** and **Bioche** are situated between Colihaut and Picard to the south of Portsmouth. The road into Bioche follows the small river to the shoreline where fishermen land their catch. The road across the bridge is a dead end. The village of Dublanc is also located on a river, the source of which is high up in the area of Syndicate in the shadow of Morne Diablotin. It is along this river that the Syndicate (Milton) Falls are located (pages 219–20). Dublanc is a residential community with a small primary school and playing field located along its shoreline. A road loops through the village from the main coastal highway.

The French Roman Catholic priest, Father Raymond Breton, who visited Dominica between 1642 and 1650 in an attempt to convert the Kalinago to Christianity, built the first church on the island in a settlement at **Colihaut**. In 1795 Colihaut was the scene of a revolt when settlers who were sympathetic to the French attempted to aid an invasion from the north. Unfortunately for them, the invasion failed and the British military captured and deported a number of people from Dominica.

Colihaut is located at the foot of the Colihaut River valley. From the coastal highway heading north, the main part of the village is to the left, between the shore and the road, though residences have spread further up the valley to the right where you will also see a large quarry. A narrow street lined with mango trees takes you alongside the river and into the heart of the village, where the Roman Catholic church dominates the small houses, convenience stores and bars. Built in 1950, the Church of St Peter is constructed from stone with large wooden louvre windows and a tall bell tower. On the north side of the church is a small garden and in front of the entrance gate a message of love has been tiled into the pavement.

Painted on a nearby wall is a mural of the *ban mauvais* parading through the streets in their *sensay* costumes accompanied by a band playing their *la peau cabwit*

9

goatskin drums at carnival time. A little further down the road is a beautiful old wooden house belonging to the Shillingford family. The house has large verandas with intricately carved, decorative fretwork, jalousie windows and large wooden hurricane shutters. There are a number of bars and snackettes in this area as well as a traditional stone-oven bakery. Towards the sea you may see colourful boats pulled up and fishing traps scattered along the rocky shoreline.

Like many coastal villages, **Coulibistrie** sits either side of a river (the Coulibistrie) that runs from the interior down through a deep valley and to the sea. The river is fast-flowing with small rapids and bathing pools higher up. In August 2015, Tropical Storm Erika turned the river into a torrent that brought destruction to this village and, for a long time afterwards, roads and houses were full of mud. Coulibistrie has several small residential houses, snackettes and convenience stores located each side of the river. The Coulibistrie Roman Catholic Church is a pretty stone building with wooden framed windows that are half stained glass and half louvre. A makeshift bell tower hugs the building on one side.

The name of the village of **Morne Raquette** is derived from the French word for prickly pear cactus, which grows wild in the area. The Kalinago word for the cactus is *bata* and the original name for the settlement below Morne Raquette was Batali, a name still given to the area today. The beach at Batali is predominantly used by local fishermen to store their boats and fish traps. A little further to the south at Sunset Bay Club, the beach is much nicer and the sea excellent for bathing and even snorkelling.

The village of Morne Raquette is a small community located high up on the slopes of Morne Jalousie, above Batali Bay and Coulibistrie. Access to the village is via a small road that joins the main coastal highway on the southern edge of Coulibistrie. The road is well signposted and is a steep climb. The village itself is pretty with excellent views of the Caribbean Sea. The road climbs up through the village and into dry coastal woodland and scrub that is dominated by the yellow blossoms of *kampech* trees (*Haematoxylum campechianum*) until it reaches the summit of the mountain. The views along the coast to the south are superb and it is possible to see the unmistakable shape of Scotts Head when the weather is clear. If you are feeling adventurous, the drive along this road really requires a 4x4 vehicle because of its gradient and also because the surface deteriorates in places. From the summit, the road descends a little and runs high along the side of the river valley. As it heads inland, the views of Dominica's interior are breathtaking and, on a clear day, it is possible to see the peaks of several volcanoes as well as nearby Mosquito Mountain. The road continues on through banana plantations and becomes part of the island's network of farm feeder roads.

Salisbury is a village that until fairly recently was still commonly called Baroui, its original Kalinago name. The Kalinago village was located in the area of the present Salisbury cemetery. The name Salisbury of course reflects the British influence on the island. Following emancipation, a settlement was established on the slopes of the Salisbury (or Baroui) River valley and now extends to the heights of Grande Savanne and along the southern ridge of the Batali River valley. Bananas and citrus fruits such as oranges and grapefruit are grown above the village, all the way up to Petit Macoucheri beneath the peak of Mosquito Mountain. The feeder roads up to these heights that are used extensively by local farmers make for an excellent drive into the interior, with impressive views from up above the river valleys. They also provide access points for National Trail segments 8, 9 and 10. Such a trip also gives an interesting insight into the rural farming activities of the people in the area, and passing along rough vehicle tracks through orchards and banana plantations, seeing farmers hard at work cultivating and harvesting their crops, offers a truly vivid impression of rural Dominica life. Many of the people you see hard at work in the fields these days are actually migrant workers from Haiti.

The Roman Catholic Church of St Theresa at Salisbury was built in 1929 and has been recently renovated. It is a beautiful stone church situated above the main coastal highway to the south of the village. A rough vehicle track directly opposite, on the other side of the coastal highway, leads down to Salisbury beach, where the Salisbury fish landing site is located. There is a small concrete jetty and usually a scattering of fishing boats and fish traps along the beach.

The village of Salisbury is accessed via a signposted road that leaves the main highway and then turns sharply to the left. The road through the village heads straight up to the heights of the ridge above the river valley. On each side of the narrow road are houses, small convenience stores and several bars and snackettes. From the top of the village there are good views down towards the sea and along the coast.

Macoucheri is home to the Shillingford Estates distillery, which produces rum from sugarcane that it grows on its estate. The distillery produces several types of Macoucheri Rum, which is consumed domestically as well as exported. It is often considered to be the best base for the many variations of rum punch that are sold around the island. The distillery is located next to the Macoucheri River and what used to be the H D Shillingford Cricket Ground. Both the distillery and the cricket ground were severely impacted during Tropical Storm Erika. At the time of writing the distillery was back up and running, but the cricket ground was not.

When rum is in production, the distillery offers short tours demonstrating how the home-grown sugarcane is turned into bottled rum (☏ 767 449 6409).

Mero is a pretty little seaside community located between St Joseph and Salisbury. Look for a small one-way road off the west-coast highway that runs in a crescent through the village and back out again. Residential areas of Mero extend to the inland side of the coastal road up towards the heights of Cuba.

The beach at Mero is a long and very beautiful stretch of dark volcanic sand. The sea is usually very calm and clear and excellent for bathing. The people here are used to visitors, indeed it is a stopping-off point for a number of cruise ship shore excursions during the high season. But don't let that put you off; it is a nice place to relax and enjoy the sea. There are several beach bars and restaurants in and around Mero; Romance Café (page 206) is a particular favourite.

The village of **St Joseph** is located just north of the Layou River at the base and around the steep slopes of a river valley that runs down to the sea. There is not much for the traveller here; the village is largely residential.

Commanding the heart of St Joseph is the large Roman Catholic church, built in the late 19th century and dedicated to Saint Gerard. A walk along the river and through the village takes you past homes, small bars and grocery stores but little more.

Tarou is a tiny fishing and farming community located along a small river valley beneath the dry scrubland slopes of Desjardin and Warner. In the summer time the area becomes vulnerable to wildfires that scorch the dry bush along the slopes above the village, forcing locals to abandon their houses and stand helplessly along the shoreline in the hope that the quickly spreading fires can be subdued before they reach their homes. The name of the village is thought to be derived from the Kalinago name for a seabird that nests in the face of the nearby cliffs. In the late afternoon you may come across the fishermen of Tarou retrieving their seine nets. This involves a line of people pulling hard on a rope that extends right across the main road. The traffic halts and the catch is brought a little nearer to the dinner plate. From time to

9

time, to let the traffic pass and to take a well-earned breather, the fishermen tie off the seine rope on a pole by the side of the road before hauling once again.

A little to the south of Tarou is Tarou Point, more popularly known as **Rodney's Rock**. A reminder of the island's volcanic history, this prominent lava formation is an interesting natural feature as well as the source of rather dubious local legend. The story goes that when Admiral Rodney returned to Dominica following the British victory at the Battle of the Saints in 1782, the French who were occupying the island at the time used the rock to delay his continued pursuit of their retreating fleet. They placed lights on the rock and dressed it up to give the impression of a ship at anchor. In the darkness, Rodney is said to have been completely fooled and spent all night firing his cannon at this seemingly invincible foe. Historical records would seem to indicate that Rodney was elsewhere at the time however, but it is a nice story nevertheless.

Located further south along the west-coast highway is the busy village of **Mahaut**. In a similar fashion to the Lallay road of Grand Bay village, the main road through Mahaut is lined with small bars, rum shops, snackettes and convenience stores. Loud music often blasts out on to the street, people dance, argue, debate or just hang out, watching the world pass by before them. There is a small village market on Saturday mornings and fishermen sell their catch on the roadside throughout the week – listen out for the conch shells being blown, if you can hear them above the heavy bass and the traffic noise. To the north of Mahaut is the community of Belfast, a residential district and also home to what used to be **Dominica Coconut Products**, owned by Colgate Palmolive. Before Tropical Storm Erika it was an important employer in the area producing wonderful soaps made from coconut and branded as **Refresh.** It seems Erika was the final straw for Colgate Palmolive who closed down the factory shortly after the storm. At the time of writing there were some noises about a government rescue package.

The name 'Mahaut' is thought to be derived from the Kalinago word *maho*, which means a plant or tree bark that can be used to make rope. *Maho* was used extensively by Kalinago for any type of work, tool or fixing that required the use of cordage.

Massacre, a small village of fishermen and farmers, is located between Canefield Airport and Mahaut. Above the road and framed by a number of very beautiful flamboyant trees is the pretty Roman Catholic church of St Ann. Built of stone and brightly painted, the church was constructed in 1921.

The name of the village is said to have come from a French account of the massacre in 1764 by British soldiers of the Kalinago who were settled in the area. Chief Thomas 'Indian' Warner, son of Sir Thomas Warner and a Kalinago woman, rose to prominence as a popular leader of the Amerindian people of this region. For a number of years he led Kalinago fighters in conflict against the British occupying forces until his half-brother, Philip, offered a truce and invited the Kalinago to agree a treaty. During the celebrations of this new peace, Philip is said to have murdered his rebel half-brother as a signal to begin the massacre of the entire Kalinago settlement. There is a mural painted on a wall along the main coastal road in Massacre depicting this event.

ACTIVITIES AND SPECIAL INTERESTS

BIRDWATCHING *(Site pass required at Syndicate)* The Syndicate Nature Trail is located within the Morne Diablotin National Park. It is naturally beautiful and a very accessible introduction to the elevated rainforest environment of the island. The forest-covered hillsides of Morne Diablotin and Morne Turner have become one of the last remaining habitats for the endangered sisserou parrot (*Amazonia imperialis*), an Amazonian that is endemic to Dominica. This unspoilt and very scenic habitat has become a draw for birdwatchers visiting the island. In the high season you may meet cruise ship visitors here, also hoping to catch sight of the island's rare parrots.

Birds you may encounter at Syndicate, in addition to the jaco and the sisserou parrots, may include the four species of hummingbird that are found on Dominica; including the endemic blue-headed hummingbird (*Cyanophaia bicolor*). Other sightings may include the forest thrush (*Cichlerminia lherminieri*), the scaly-breasted thrasher (*Margarops fuscus*), the trembler (*Cinclocerthia rufcauda*), and the plumbeous warbler (*Dendroica plumbea*).

The Layou River and the Pagua River are also good places to watch water birds such as the ringed and belted kingfisher (*Ceryle torquata* and *Ceryle alcyon*), the green-backed heron (*Butorides striatus*) and the least sandpiper (*Calidris minutilla*). Along the riverbanks you may see the cattle egret (*Bubulcus ibis*) and the snowy egret (*Egretta thula*).

For bird enthusiasts who would like the company of an expert guide, see pages 68–9. For more about Dominica's birds, see pages 7–8.

ORGANIC FARM TOURS Discover what it is like to live a self-sufficient life, living simply off the land, growing what you eat and eating what you grow. **D-Smart Farm** (\ 767 295 2605 or 767 315 5128; e *d-smartfarm@hotmail.com; www.ecobalanceda. com;* 🛈) is located in Corona – between Sylvania and Pont Cassé – and is 1ha of managed farm and natural rainforest. Your host, Dawn Francis, and her team will give you a tour of the property, talking about and showing you the crops that are grown there, and about traditional bush medicines. You can even join in with planting and harvesting. This is a working farm and a sustainable lifestyle; chickens provide eggs and droppings, goats and rabbits also provide manure for the crops. Gommier tree sap is collected to make a fire, provisions and vegetables are cooked over a traditional coal pot, and there are demonstrations of arts and crafts from nature. If you wish to stay on the farm, see listing on page 205.

THE EMERALD POOL (*Site pass required*) The Emerald Pool is a very popular attraction, especially during the cruise ship season, at weekends and on public holidays. The small waterfall and pool is perhaps one of Dominica's most photographed natural sites and is certainly one of the most visited. Located on the northern edge of the national park, within sight of Morne Trois Pitons itself, the Emerald Pool is a very accessible and beautiful rainforest attraction. Its accessibility means that it is a shore excursion for every visiting cruise ship and heavy footfall has not been without cost. Please resist the temptation to scratch your name on the walls and rocks behind the waterfalls.

The Emerald Pool is easy to find, just off the road to Castle Bruce and the Kalinago Territory. See page 50 for information on buses from Roseau. If travelling by car from the Roseau area, once you reach the Pont Cassé roundabout in the interior, take the road towards Castle Bruce and La Plaine (the third exit). After around 15 minutes you will come to a signposted junction with the road to Castle Bruce and the Kalinago Territory to the left, which is where you should turn. After a very short distance the entrance to the Emerald Pool visitor centre is on the left. If you are not in possession of a site pass, you can buy one from the Emerald Pool visitor centre, where you will also find vendors selling souvenirs and refreshments. On cruise ship days do not be surprised to find the car park teeming with people and a queue all the way along the trail to the pool (see page 110 for information on cruise ship days).

Getting to and from the Emerald Pool requires a short, gentle walk in two easy sections; the first part is a 15-minute stroll through the rainforest along a well-maintained path. There is a nice viewpoint to the right and a wooden bridge across a cascading river. Some steps up, and then eventually down, lead to the waterfall and the pool. Just follow the signs.

On the return trip, take the path that leads upwards, rather than the path to the left across the bridge. This is an old Kalinago trail that loops back to the visitor centre. It is also now part of Wai'tukubuli National Trail Segment 5 (see pages 233–5). It is a pleasant and easy walk through the rainforest.

SOLTOUN FALLS Before someone erected a sign that you can probably see from outer space, Soltoun was actually rather a secret place known to few people. It was a tough scramble down a steep river valley to a completely unspoiled series of waterfalls. Things have changed, but it is still a very lovely spot and well worth a visit. In addition to the sign and car park, there is a rough concrete road down into the river valley and a short series of trails to the main waterfalls. If the weather is dry, the top waterfall can be rather disappointing but the one beneath is always very beautiful, with a deep pool. Both are very accessible and well worth the short walk. Expect a small entry fee.

JACKO FALLS Just before you get to the village of Bells from Pont Cassé, you'll come across what must be Dominica's most accessible waterfall. Look for colourful signage, and a wooden shelter selling fruit and souvenirs. The waterfall is located within a river gully which you can view from a platform at the top. If you wish, and are able, you can also go down to it. There are concrete steps leading to the river, the waterfall and the pool. Unless there are hordes of cruise ship tourists looking down on you, it is quite a nice place for a river bath. The surroundings are pretty; there is a cave, rainforest vegetation, moss-covered boulders, tropical flowers and birdlife. The waterfall is not particularly tall but, like the Emerald Pool, its draw is its accessibility for those who do not wish to do much walking or hiking. Expect a small entry fee.

SCUBA DIVING The central west coast of Dominica has some excellent dive sites which have beautiful, healthy coral reefs, steep vertical walls and an abundance of interesting marine life. They are less visited than those in the Soufriere Scotts Head Marine Reserve and are in excellent condition. At the time of writing, large grouper, rays, nurse sharks, frogfish and sea horses had all been commonly sighted on the reef formations here. See pages 80–1 for more details about the dive sites and dive operators in this area.

HIKES FROM THE WEST COAST

SYNDICATE NATURE TRAIL (*Site pass required. Difficulty: T: 1; R: 0; E: 0; D: 1; Rating = 1.3; Guide not essential but recommended if birdwatching – see pages 68–9*) The Syndicate Nature Trail is a loop through the rainforest habitat of the Morne Diablotin National Park. It is very popular with bird enthusiasts as this area is a protected parrot habitat. It also has a wide variety of other birdlife as well as some magnificent tree specimens. The trail is well marked and there are signs beside many of the most prominent trees along the route, giving you both the standard as well as the local name. If it is open, the visitor centre has an interpretation room, washroom facilities and a small snack bar. You can also buy your site pass here.

To get to Syndicate, look for a very clear sign along the west-coast highway, a little to the north of Dublanc. The narrow road climbs uphill and passes a number of small farmsteads, many of them growing citrus. The road is quite long and fairly

LAYOU AND THE HEART OF DOMINICA

For listings, see pages 204–6, unless otherwise stated

Where to stay

1. Liberty Jungle
2. Mango Island Lodges
3. Ramelton Estate
4. Villa Incognito p241

Off map

Harmony Villa
Zen Gardens

Where to eat and drink

5. Connie's Mero Beach Bar
   Liberty Jungle (see 1)
   Mango Island Lodges
   (see 2)
6. Riverstone Bar & Grill
7. Romance Café

Heart of Dominica, Morne Diablotin National Park, and the West   HIKES FROM THE WEST COAST

9

narrow. Use your horn on bends as you may well encounter farmers' vehicles. Pass the sign for the Syndicate Falls and also for the Morne Diablotin Trail. Keep going until you come to the visitor centre and car park. It is quite a way in, so do not become anxious that you may have gone the wrong way. The road is simply longer than you probably expected it to be.

Public buses do not go up this road. You could get off on the west-coast highway and walk; it will take 45–60 minutes to get here, or you could get lucky and hitch a ride with a farmer. However you manage it, the road is quiet and very scenic.

Pass through the visitor centre to reach the start of the trail and follow the signs. As it is a loop, you can choose which direction to go. At some point during your hike you will come to a viewpoint across a river valley to Morne Turner. This is a popular place for birdwatchers and there is always a good chance of seeing parrots in flight above the forest canopy. Sit and wait here for a while and you are sure to be rewarded. In all likelihood the parrots you see will be jacos. They are large and green, and have red wing-tips and a distinctive yellow tail-feather. They tend to fly in pairs and have the kind of call you would expect from parrots. The sisserou is larger and looks more ungainly in the air. It does not have the yellow tail-feather and has a much more high-pitched call.

If you walk the loop trail without stopping, it will take less than an hour. You should try to take longer, however, as this rainforest habitat, the tree species and the birdlife are all very special. The best times for parrots are early morning or late afternoon. For information on guided birdwatching, see pages 68–9.

MORNE DIABLOTIN (*Site pass required. Difficulty: T: 4H; R: 0; E: 4; D: 4; Rating = 7.5H; Guide strongly recommended*) The hike to the 1,447m summit of Morne Diablotin is a challenge. It involves a relentless uphill hike, a scramble up steep rocks and then a lengthy climb through tree branches and roots. For the most part the trail is very obvious, and, if you get a cloudless sky when you reach the summit (please note, this is rare), the views across the island and beyond are spectacular. Before you begin the hike, it is important to be prepared to get wet and very muddy. Also, as the summit is often windy and cloud-covered, it can be quite cold. Bring something to keep you warm, to protect you from wind and rain, and ensure you have a change of clothes and somewhere to keep them dry.

You will find the trailhead on the road to the Syndicate visitor centre (see above). It is on the right-hand side, about three-quarters of the way there, and there is a sign.

From the very beginning, the trail lets you know you are climbing a mountain. The first hour is a steep climb up steps made from wood or tree fern, through the dense rainforest of the mountain's lower elevations. The forest is raw and untouched, full of magnificent *chatanier* trees with their giant buttress roots, tall and incredibly straight *gommier* trees, *bwa mang* with their prop roots, giant tree ferns and an abundance of epiphytes. The first hour of the hike also has a background symphony of birdsong, including those of both species of endemic parrot, the sisserou and the jaco. If you take a break and stand still beneath their calls, you may be lucky enough to see them flying above the canopy. Look for seed fall; it often reveals where parrots are hanging out in the canopy above.

After the first hour of climbing, the trail becomes a combination of steps, roots and rocks. It also begins to get very muddy and, for the next 30 minutes or so, you will have to scramble up a number of boulders and steep slopes. As you do this, take a look around at the vegetation. You should notice that it is beginning to change from rainforest to montane forest, with the girth of the trunks smaller and the trees themselves shorter than at lower elevations.

After around 90 minutes or so you will encounter yet another change. You are now moving into elfin woodland, or cloudforest, and you begin climbing over and under the branches of *kaklen* (*Clusia mangle*), a tree that is prolific on Dominica at both these higher altitudes and around fumaroles. The *kaklen* has twisting branches and roots with broad, fattish green leaves. The climb through them is tricky, but easier than losing your boots in the swampy mud below. Take care with your footing and look out for sharp branches at eye and chest level, especially where they may have been cleared back with a machete. The chances are it will be very wet now – everywhere – and so the *kaklen* branches and roots will be greasy and moss-covered. Take your time. Use your hands and arms to support your legs, and test each branch before giving it your full weight.

For the remainder of this climb, you are required to use both upper and lower body strength to get you to the rocky bluff near the top of the trail, known as Imray's View after Dr John Imray, who made the first recorded ascent in 1862. The bluff is a little to the southeast of the actual summit of the mountain (not really worth another painful hour, especially if cloudy), and, for most, marks the end of this long and difficult hike. Hopefully your views are not obscured by thick clouds but if they are, it is sometimes worth waiting a while (unless it is too cold, of course) and you may be fortunate enough to catch a break and enjoy the panoramas from the top of Dominica's highest mountain.

SYNDICATE (MILTON) FALLS (*Difficulty: T: 2; R: 2; E: 1; D: 1; Rating = 3.8; Guide not essential*) The Syndicate Falls, also known as Milton Falls, are found in the Syndicate area. The waterfall is attractive and very accessible. The trailhead is at the end of a rough vehicle track that begins on the road to the Syndicate visitor centre, next to a large mango tree. You may see a small sign; you will almost certainly see a large, somewhat faded red-and-white one informing visitors that the waterfall is a water source for the settlements in the area. This means that introducing foreign substances or pollutants to the falls and river may have a detrimental effect on the people who rely on its water, particularly the villagers of Dublanc on the west coast. A fine and imprisonment await those found guilty of this offence, apparently. For this reason it is probably prudent and considerate simply to view the waterfall and resist bathing in the pool or river.

The track to Syndicate Falls passes through private land and the owner will request a nominal entry fee. He has a couple of rustic wooden cabins he rents (handy for National Trail through-hikers) and there are also washrooms.

To get there follow the road to Syndicate from the west-coast road (see above) and look for the sign on the right-hand side about two-thirds of the way to the Syndicate visitor centre. The rough vehicle track immediately forks. Go left and follow it through until you come to another junction with a rough vehicle track going quite steeply uphill to the left. You will need a 4x4 to get up there, but it's not really necessary. My advice is to park up out of the way and walk up this last section. If you do want to drive up, there is a small parking area at the top.

From the small parking area follow the wide track to a building. This is where you will be asked to deposit your entry fee in a box or hand it over if there is someone there. This building also houses the washroom. From here follow the wide track gradually downhill. You will see an open valley on your right that is fringed with banana plants, with grapefruit trees beyond. If you want to see parrots, just hang around here – there is a really good chance you will see jaco.

At the bottom of the hill, the wide track appears to end, but pick up the trail on the left and follow it down to the river. The water is fairly shallow and it is easy to cross. On the other side you should see a trail along the right-hand bank, through the trees, but

x

essentially all you have to do is follow this river upstream. Tropical Storm Erika changed the landscape here and quite a bit of the forest trail washed away. If you do find it, avoid any uphill spur to the right and simply hug the river until you have no other option than to hike along the bed and over the rocks. Do this for a short distance – perhaps 15 minutes – until you are within sight of the waterfall. Approach it up the left-hand side.

KACHIBONA LAKE (*Difficulty: T: 3; R: 1; E: 2; D: 2; Rating = 5.0; Guide suggested*) I have included this hike on the off-chance it gets a little better. At the time of writing I'd say it ought to be very low on your hiking priority list, especially if you have limited time on the island, but its history and significance to the people of Colihaut, plus the fact that you may well see road signs for it, means that it ought to get a mention here.

Maroon (runaway slave) chief Pharcelle is said to have had one of his camps in the area of Kachibona Lake. It is located on a high ridge beyond the Colihaut River and protected by cliffs and dense forests. The lake has suffered a series of landslides and would currently be better described as a rather murky and unattractive pond. But nature works wonders on Dominica and the people of Colihaut are proud of its legacy, so it may get better with time.

The hike itself is a pretty one, starting in the extremely scenic heights of Colihaut where farmlands seem to cling to vertiginous mountainsides and farmers work harder than many of us could ever imagine.

Access the trailhead from the west-coast highway. Either drive up the road that heads inland from the village of Colihaut (look for the Busy's Honey sign) or another road a little to the south of Colihaut (there may well be a sign here). Follow this very long, looping feeder road inland and up to the high hills above Colihaut and stop when you see the big National Trail sign and shelter.

The trail to Kachibona Lake follows Wai'tukubuli National Trail Segment 9 but in reverse. Follow the painted blazes through farmland and then into lush forest. Some sections are a little difficult to follow, especially where slides have occurred, so if you do get a little confused, retrace your steps, look for the last painted blaze you saw and then scan the forest for the next one. Don't just wander along without taking note of where you are and where you have come from. In the vicinity of a rather splendid wooden shelter, look for one of the island's largest *gommier* trees.

The trail will bring you steeply down to the Colihaut River which you must cross. Tropical Storm Erika turned this river into a raging torrent and caused considerable devastation to the village below. Climb down the steep and muddy bank and then make your way a short distance upstream and look for the continuation of the trail on the right. Once you make it up the opposite bank and around a large tree (this isn't especially obvious) it is a relatively short distance to a fork in the trail. WNT Segment 9 continues to the right and the Kachibona Lake trail to the left.

From this point on, the trail is very difficult to follow so please take your time and even consider leaving yourself memorable markers along the way. Also look out for the remnants of plastic banners that were tied to trees during a village race here some years ago. It is only around 20 minutes or so from the trail fork to the lake.

HIKES IN THE HEART OF DOMINICA

SPANNY FALLS (*Difficulty: T: 3; R: 0; E: 3; D: 1; Rating = 4.4; Guide not essential*) Two pretty waterfalls separated by a steep ridge make up Spanny Falls (sometimes called Penrice Falls, or Spanny Twin Falls). It is the climb up and down this ridge that gives this very short hike a moderate rating. If you do not fancy the climb, you can satisfy yourself with just visiting the first waterfall which is very easy to reach.

Spanny Falls takes its name from the owner of Spanny's Disco, a bar and snackette that is located on the western edge of the village of Bells in Dominica's interior. It is impossible to miss. To get there from Roseau, take the road to Marigot from Pont Cassé. The bar is on the left, about 15 minutes' drive from Pont Cassé and before you reach Bells. For information about buses passing along this route see page 50.

If you are driving, park up near the bar and pay a nominal entry fee for trail maintenance. The bar is also a good spot for a drink afterwards.

Just next to the bar is a rough vehicle track heading into the woods. This is the start of the trail.

Follow the track past a farm for around ten minutes until it ends with a spur straight ahead and another to the left. Take the trail to the left into the forest, over a couple of small wooden bridges, until you reach some steps with a hand rail. Follow them down. Be careful with your footing as this trail is often wet and the steps can be slippery. After another ten minutes you should reach the first waterfall. Surrounded by greenery, and in particular tree ferns, this pool is a lovely spot to cool off.

To get to the second waterfall, walk down to the pool and follow the small path to the right. Negotiate the boulders and then use the rope and tree roots to help you climb up to the top of the ridge. It is steep and a little tricky, but very short and good fun. At the top, head left along and down the narrow ridge to the second waterfall using the rope to help you. Watch your footing on tree roots and be careful on the last part down to the boulders near the pool as it is rather steep.

Spanny Falls welcomes cruise ship visitors in the high season. To avoid them, go later in the afternoon.

JACKO FLATS AND STEPS ✻ (*Difficulty: T: 3; R: 3H; E: 2; D: 2; Rating = 6.3H; Guide recommended*) Jacko was a Maroon chief who escaped captivity and fled to the forest shortly after arriving on Dominica. He established a camp on a high natural plateau above the Layou River until he was eventually killed in a bloody battle on 12 July 1814. For more on Jacko and the Maroons, see box, page 208.

Jack Flats is the name given to the area on top of the plateau where the camp was located and Jacko Steps refers to a steep staircase that was carved into the cliff by Maroons. The staircase joined the elevated camp to the Layou River and survives today.

This is truly a world-class hike that affords breathtaking scenery and challenging terrain. Its history also serves to make it both soulful and haunting.

There are several ways to hike it, but by far the best is to begin by the schoolhouse in the village of Bells. Follow the wide track at the side of the school down towards the river and look for a trail on your right when you are at the bottom. Cross the river here. The trail continues on the opposite side, slightly upstream. Climb up the steep bank and, when in sight of the house, turn sharply right up to the top of the ridge where you will come to a trail junction. Go left and follow the ridge. The river will be down below to your right. The trail passes a small wooden house (on your left) and then goes through a gate up to another rustic wooden home. This is where you may meet Eunice and Mal. They are lovely people who live very simply and in harmony with nature. It is they, and not the government, who maintain this historic trail and put up the signs. Please make a donation (around US$5 per person) to help them out. If you are thirsty, enjoy a fresh juice or a bush tea with them, and, if you feel you need a guide, you could ask them about that too.

The trail continues from the back of their home and climbs steeply up to the top of the plateau. Follow the fence on the left. At the top you should see the Jacko Flats sign. The area you now pass through was roughly the location of the Maroon camp. The forest is dense and beautiful. Take a moment to stop and think about how it must have been for the runaway slaves who lived up here and the terrible consequences they would face if caught. Think about the final battle with the militia when they finally found and attacked this place. Think of Jacko shooting two of them dead before taking a fatal bullet himself.

When you are ready to move off, follow the trail through the woods in a northwesterly direction until you find yourself walking along the spine of an extremely narrow ridge with steep drops on either side. It should take about 20–30 minutes to walk from Jacko Flats to the top of Jacko Steps.

Take care descending the steps; they are steep and often leaf-strewn, making them slippery. The iron loops you may see now and again were put here by a landowner in the 1980s. A cable ran through them to make ascent and descent of the steps easier. Personally I am happy it is no longer here, for the steps should be difficult to negotiate; they were made that way.

The foot of the steps is especially slippery and eroded so take it easy. Once down, you will find yourself in a tributary of the Layou River. Head left until you meet the Layou and then begin your journey upriver (left), looking ahead and picking your route across sand banks, rocks, rapids and pools.

There is one particularly tricky section where the river curves to the right around a cliff. Here the river runs fast and is deep. My recommendation is to hug the cliff on the right, all the way around. But look to your left at this point and see if you can find the waterfall hidden within a small conical cavern.

Further upstream, ignore the rivers and rapids on the right. The basic rule of thumb is always to stick to the left and follow the main river. The last section is testament to Tropical Storm Erika. The river has been forced way over to the right and the left is now a vast landscape of rocks, boulders and river sand. Walk up the dry left side until you come to a large junction. The schoolhouse should be visible ahead of you. Cross over to the far side and climb the bank to the flat ground behind the school. Head left to the road you came down at the beginning of the hike.

10

The Wai'tukubuli National Trail

The Wai'tukubuli National Trail runs from the south of the island at Cachacrou to the northwest where it reaches an end at the Cabrits National Park. It is about 200km in length and is split into 14 connected segments. Each segment has its own unique set of challenges as well as areas of historic, cultural and natural interest.

Although the trail has been in existence for several years now, it has not really developed to its full potential. Accommodation, dining and provisioning options *en route* are still quite scant, and there is little or nothing offered by the authorities when it comes to updates on trail status, recording hikers in and out, and emergency support. Some of the segments were affected by Tropical Storm Erika in August 2015, others have fallen into neglect. There is a Wai'tukubuli National Trail management and maintenance team, but you get the impression that they lack the funding and resources to raise the level of the trail and its peripheral and support offerings to what they really ought to be. For this reason you should prepare carefully your approach to tackling the trail, especially if your plan is to through-hike. As there is no official way of recording hikers on trail segments, be sure to share your hike plan with someone.

Camping, in theory, is not allowed, but the authorities acknowledge that it would be impossible to through-hike the trail without pitching a tent or a hammock on some of the segments. The subject has therefore become a grey area that, at the time of writing, no-one seems particularly eager to deal with. So if you have to overnight, keep your impact on the environment to a minimum and stick to the trail. You may find it very difficult to find flat and even ground. I use a Hennessy Hammock (*www.hennessyhammock.com*) which is very flexible, lightweight and has minimal environmental impact. If you are through-hiking please be aware that this is a very tough trail with some steep and muddy ups and downs, some narrow ledges, and river crossings. A heavy pack makes it even harder. I like the National Trail very much and am happy we have it, but I do feel that in many places it is more like an assault course than a hiking trail. Please bear in mind when planning that many of the segments are very challenging indeed.

Trail signage takes the form of signposts, information boards and yellow-and-blue painted blazes. In some areas signage is quite poor or sparse so don't walk for too long with your head down. Always be sure you can see a blaze or you at least remember where the last one was.

The following trail descriptions were updated in March 2016. There is currently no way to find updated trail information online; the official website hasn't changed since it was launched in 2011 – perhaps something will materialise. The hiking guides and operators I have listed on pages 76–7 are likely to know the latest trail status should there continue to be a lack of official updates.

Please note, though I tried, I could not hike segments 8 and 9 before the deadline for this manuscript. Both the trails and access to them were in bad shape following

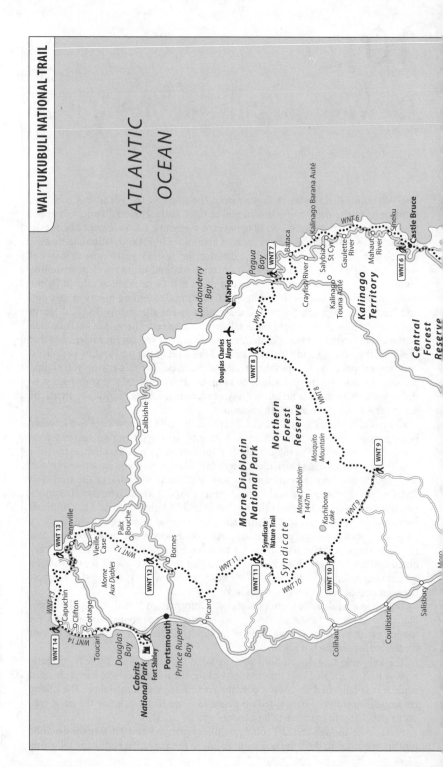

ATLANTIC
OCEAN

Londonderry
Bay

Pagua
Bay

Marigot

WNT 7

Bataca

Kalinago Barana Auté

WNT 6

Crayfish River

Salybia

St Cyr

Sineku

Kalinago
Touna Auté

Gaulette
River

Castle Bruce

Mahaut
River

WNT 6

Douglas Charles
Airport

WNT 7

Kalinago
Territory

WNT 8

Central
Forest
Reserve

Calibishie

Northern
Forest
Reserve

WNT 8

Mosquito
Mountain

Morne Diablotin
National Park

Morne Diablotin
1447m

WNT 9

Pennville

Kachibona
Lake

WNT 9

WNT 13

Paix
Bouche

Vieille
Case

WNT 12

Syndicate
Nature Trail

Bornes

Syndicate

WNT 11

Clifton

Morne
Aux Diables

WNT 12

WNT 11

WNT 10

Capuchin

WNT 13

WNT 10

Cottage

Picard

WNT 14

Toucari

Coulibistrie

Colihaut

Meso

WNT 14

Douglas
Bay

Portsmouth

Fort Shirley

Cabrits
National Park

Prince Rupert
Bay

Salisbury

Coulibistrie

224

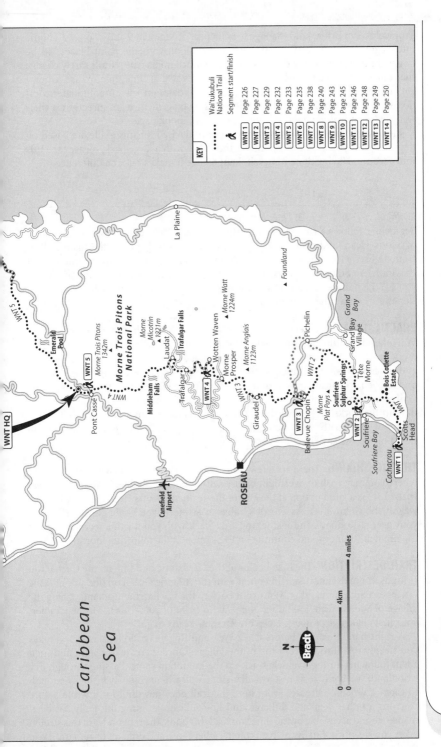

Caribbean
Sea

Morne Trois Pitons
National Park

La Plaine

Emerald
Pool

WNT 5

Pont Cassé

WNT HQ

WNT 5

Morne Trois Pitons
1342m

Morne
Micotrin
▲1221m

Laudat

Trafalgar Falls

**Middleham
Falls**

Trafalgar

Morne
Prosper

Wotten Waven

▲ *Morne Watt*
1224m

▲ *Morne Anglais*
1123m

▲ *Foundland*

WNT 4

WNT 4

WNT 3

Giraudel

Canefield
Airport

ROSEAU

Bellevue Chopin

WNT 3

Morne
Plat Pays ▲

**Soufriere
Sulphur Springs**

WNT 2

Pichelin

Grand
Bay

Grand Bay
Village

Tête
Morne

WNT 2

Soufriere

Soufriere Bay

**Bois Cotlette
Estate**

Cachacrou

WNT 1

Scotts
Head

WNT 1

N

Bradt

0   4km

0   4 miles

KEY

•••••• Waï'tukubuli
National Trail

⋏ Segment start/finish

WNT 1 Page 226
WNT 2 Page 227
WNT 3 Page 229
WNT 4 Page 232
WNT 5 Page 233
WNT 6 Page 235
WNT 7 Page 238
WNT 8 Page 240
WNT 9 Page 243
WNT 10 Page 245
WNT 11 Page 246
WNT 12 Page 248
WNT 13 Page 249
WNT 14 Page 250

The Waï'tukubuli National Trail

10

225

Tropical Storm Erika. I did manage to walk part of Segment 9 and also get 2½hours into Segment 8 before the trail disappeared along with the paint blazes. To be honest I think the existing description pretty much holds true – trails rarely change that much – but they clearly needed sorting out at that time. In any case, when I get another chance, I will hike them and post updates on www.bradtupdates.com/dominica. You could also contact the WNT management team directly via their website (*www.waitukubulitrail.com*) or their Facebook page.

Please also note that the trail ratings I have devised for this guide are based on day-hiking. If you are through-hiking the WNT with a large pack, please take this into account. Having done it myself, I appreciate it makes rather a difference.

SEGMENT 1: SCOTTS HEAD TO SOUFRIERE

(*Difficulty: T: 3; R: 0; E: 3; D: 2; Rating = 5.0*)
Segment 1 follows a route from the isthmus of Cachacrou, up through the village of Scotts Head, and over the peak of Morne Crabier. It passes the historic Bois Cotlette Estate (pages 141–2) and several farm holdings before finally emerging at the Soufriere Sulphur Springs (page 141). Crabier will seem a fitting name when you see the number of land crabs scuttling around on the mountain's dry southern slopes at certain times of the year.

PRACTICALITIES Segment 1 is a short but challenging beginning to the Wai'tukubuli National Trail, especially following a massive landslide that tore away much of the original trail above the village of Scotts Head. The steep ascent and descent of Morne Crabier is tiring and in places the terrain is loose, slippery and uneven. The farmlands and dry forest countryside between the foot of Morne Crabier and the Sulphur Springs are very scenic and remind me a little of my earlier days in the Yorkshire Dales (the Dales with coconut palms – imagine that). Take plenty of water with you because this is a very dry part of the island and you will not come across any rivers or places to top up.

THROUGH-HIKING There are a few small guesthouses in the village of Scotts Head where you may wish to overnight before setting out and **Rodney's Wellness Retreat** (page 131) is a good option at the end of the segment. Scotts Head has very little by way of shops, however. As Morne Crabier is so steep, you could consider leaving your gear at Rodney's and just taking a daypack with you for this segment. Spend the night at Rodney's and continue on to Segment 2 the following morning.

TRAIL DESCRIPTION The hike begins at the Caribantic building on the Cachacrou isthmus. It is a dramatic starting point with the Atlantic Ocean on one side and the Caribbean Sea on the other. With your back to the Cachacrou headland, facing the village of Scotts Head, look up at the peak in front of you. This is Morne Crabier; your first challenge of many. Deep breath then, ready to go?

A right-hand turn just before Chez Wen and Rogers (good local eateries) takes you steeply uphill to the very top of the village. Once there, take a right and then a left, following a rough vehicle track up the mountain slope. Passing through dry woodland, you come to a crest by a dry-stone wall where you may be lucky enough to catch a welcome breeze. From here the trail goes downhill for a while before reaching a rather deep and difficult landslide gulley. Assuming this gully has been made safe and accessible by the time you read this book, the remainder of this stretch takes you steeply uphill over what is often rather loose and difficult terrain until you reach Crabier Plateau; an area of lush pasture land, planted rather incongruously on the side of the mountain, and looking rather more like the English countryside than the eastern Caribbean. It is a lovely place to rest and catch your breath while enjoying the fabulous view down to the Cachacrou isthmus where your hike began. When ready, head up to the left-hand corner of this valley and make your way around some ruined buildings. A short but steep section takes you up to a small tree-covered plateau at the top of the mountain.

Walk straight across the top, past the shelter, and begin a very steep descent. Though there are steps made from rocks and tree roots, the ground can be slippery here and it is not always possible to get a firm footing. Take your time, resist the urge to go quickly, be careful and use the trees on either side to support you. If you have them, walking poles really help here.

When you arrive at the bottom you will be in a small glade with a wide, grass-covered track that becomes a stony feeder road. Follow it all the way to the main paved road between Soufriere and Galion. Turn right on to this road and walk uphill for about 1km. The hiking trail resumes on the right-hand side. It is signposted. Follow the track along a pretty valley of farmland, dry forest and volcanic rocks. It veers to the left at a small farmstead and piggery and, after a short distance, the views open up a little more and you can see the impressive Morne Plat Pays volcano. Stick with this trail as it runs downhill and then emerges at another rough vehicle track. To the right is the Bois Cotlette Estate (page 141) and to the left is the continuation of the National Trail. A further 20 minutes or so brings you to a main road. To the left is the village of Soufriere and Rodney's Wellness Retreat, to the right is the Soufriere Sulphur Springs (page 141) where Segment 1 ends and Segment 2 begins.

SEGMENT 2: SOUFRIERE TO BELLEVUE CHOPIN ✳

(Difficulty: T: 2; R: 0; E: 3; D: 3; Rating = 5.0)
Segment 2 is a long but steady hike from Soufriere Sulphur Springs to the heights of Tete Morne and then across the mountainside to the elevated village of Bellevue Chopin. A section of the trail from the heights of Morpo to Bellevue Chopin was actually cut by slaves who were forced to create a route from the inland estates to the southern coastline where produce could be loaded aboard ships. You will also see active sulphur deposits, simple farmsteads and lots of aromatic bay trees. Just as you may have met charcoal burners and villagers using the trails on Segment 1, here you may well meet people on the way to or returning from their 'gardens'; small allotments or pieces of land where they grow vegetables and *ground provisions*, perhaps rear pigs, goats, graze cows and so on. It is a trail that is functional for many people and allows you, the visitor, to look through a window into everyday Dominica.

PRACTICALITIES Segment 2 is quite challenging because it has some steep climbs and it is also quite long. You need to give yourself plenty of time and it is imperative that you carry sufficient water; aside from a stand pipe in Tete Morne you will not find any water until you reach Bellevue Chopin. You will also be presented with a choice of routes when you reach Morpo Junction. The route via Pichelin and New Florida is no longer maintained. The route to the top of Morpo and via the 'old slave trail' is now the 'official' route.

THROUGH-HIKING At the beginning of this segment, Soufriere has a few accommodation options (see above) including **Rodney's Wellness Retreat** where you can also camp. There is also a minimart in the village, but don't count on it having an especially wide selection of produce. Through-hikers reaching the end of Segment 2 have simple accommodation and camping options at Bellevue Chopin. Behind the organic composting facility, just 15 minutes into Segment 3, is **Broad Meadow Farm** (behind the organic composting facility – see page 135) where you can give Gordon Royer a shout and spend a comfortable night in a hammock.

TRAIL DESCRIPTION This segment begins at Soufriere Sulphur Springs. You can either start inside the springs and walk up to the top and then right, or you can follow the wide track at the end of the road, next to the car park. Both meet at the same point. Follow the track up the mountain. On your left you can see the large volcanically active area; a vast scar of steam and sulphur above the springs.

The trail climbs to the top of the ridge in a series of switchbacks through dry forest and thickets of bamboo. From time to time you are rewarded with great views down to Soufriere. If conditions are good, you can actually see reef formations in the bay.

When you reach the top of the ridge, pass over it and walk down into the village of Tete Morne. Up to your right is the Palmiste Estate and Morne Vert (see pages 143–4 for hike directions). Walk down the village road past the stone cross and look for the trail sign on the left. Follow this side road a short distance to a rather pretty avenue of bay trees and look for the trail sign, once again on the left, towards the bottom of the lane. If you have never come across bay before, take a leaf, crunch it up in the palm of your hand and then smell it.

Follow the trail downhill and cross over a dry river gully. The trail undulates a little and comes to a small glade. Stick to the left and enjoy views of the interior and the southeast. Skirt around the perimeter of a second glade and then descend very steeply down a narrow ridge. If you suffer from vertigo it may be a good idea not to look down to your left at this point. The track down this ridge is a little tricky and it is important to take your time and be sure of your footing. At the bottom you will arrive in another dry river gully. Cross it and walk alongside a small farmstead and piggery before coming to a paved road. Go left and then look for a continuation of the trail on your right, running along the left-hand side of a large house.

Follow the track to a junction and stick to the wide path until it reaches a paved road. Walk down it for a short distance to a junction and then take the trail to the left along a dirt track. To your right you should see fields of yams or dasheens and have good views of Grand Bay beyond. Continue along this well-used farm trail, skirting plots of vegetables and *ground provisions*. Look out for sorrel, low-growing bushes with deep red flowers that are used to make a seasonal drink at Christmas time. To your right you should be able to see the Atlantic Ocean and ahead of you the verdant mountains of Dominica's interior.

At a sharp turn, follow the trail down a steep hill and alongside more fields of dasheen until you come to a paved feeder road. Go right and follow it downhill to another paved road where you must turn left. Walk uphill to Morpo Junction. Take a left and begin a long and tedious trudge up a paved farm feeder road to the top of the Morpo peak. It will take you at least 45 minutes to reach the top where you'll find a sign pointing to a forest trail. The views from the top are great. Take a well-earned rest and look down on the Grand Bay coastline. If it is a clear day you can also see the French island of Martinique to the south.

Starting quite wide and then narrowing to a trail, the journey through lush woodland is an interesting and occasionally challenging one. It climbs steeply and narrowly further up the mountain and then winds its way northwards around trees and cliffs. Occasionally it gets very narrow and there are steep drops so take it steady, especially if you are carrying a large pack. Eventually you will come to the apex of a bend where the route passes through a cleft and then heads back along a pretty woodland trail and down some rather steep steps. This section is said to have been cut by slaves in order for produce to be shifted from inland plantations to the south coast. Views of the mountainous interior finally open up ahead of you. The very pointed peak is Morne Anglais, which is the southernmost volcano of the Morne Trois Pitons National Park (pages 142–3). To the right of it are Morne John, Morne Watt and Foundland, which is in the southeast.

The small clearing at the bottom of a steep scramble, with what looks like a wall, is the remains of an old quarry, known locally as a 'tarrish pit'. For some reason there are rather a lot of picnic tables around here. I can think of nicer places to sit with a sandwich, but there you go. The trail widens and runs downhill for a rather tedious 15 minutes or so before it reaches the outskirts of Bellevue Chopin where it becomes a paved road all the way to the main junction and bus stop, which marks the end of this hike (you can catch a bus to Roseau from here). Grab a well-deserved bite to eat and something good to drink at the snackette by the bus stop. To the side of this snackette is a great view down to Roseau.

SEGMENT 3: BELLEVUE CHOPIN TO WOTTEN WAVEN

(Difficulty: T: 3; R: 1; E: 3; D: 3; Rating = 6.3)
In terms of distance, this is one of the longest segments of the National Trail. It begins in the elevated community of Bellevue Chopin and introduces you to some of the organic farming for which this area has become known. Following a former Maroon trail, you walk from Bellevue Chopin across the foothills of Morne Anglais to the flower village of Giraudel. From there you drop down into the River Claire Valley and then climb steeply up to the farmlands of Morne Prosper. The final stretch is a descent to the volcanically active spa village of Wotten Waven and then on to Trafalgar if you so wish. Along the route you can enjoy great views of Roseau, the Roseau Valley, the west coast and the volcanic peaks of the Morne Trois Pitons National Park. You will also meet villagers and farmers, giving you a little insight into the lives of people who live and work here.

PRACTICALITIES Duration and the steep River Claire Valley combine to give this hike its high rating. The climb up out of the valley to Morne Prosper is particularly steep and vertigo sufferers may have a little difficulty with it. The segment is long so you should set off as early as possible and take plenty of water. The bridge over the River Claire was destroyed by Tropical Storm Erika so you will have to wade across. It is narrow and not especially deep, though the climb up the far bank can be a challenge.

THROUGH-HIKING If you have spent the night in Bellevue Chopin then provisioning for this segment will be difficult. Some fruit and plenty of water should see you through to Giraudel where there is a small village shop and a couple of snackettes and bars. After that you won't get much respite until Wotten Waven and Trafalgar where there are several places to stay and eat (see pages 111–12). You should try to make time for a hot volcanic spa (pages 116–18). The River Claire is fine for a water top-up as there are no farms or villages upstream from your crossing.

TRAIL DESCRIPTION The trailhead for Segment 3 is located on the main road through Bellevue Chopin by the bus stops and snackettes. Follow the wide vehicle

10

track from the sign. It is an easy and pleasant introduction to the walk. Notice the start of rainforest vegetation: tree ferns, bromeliads, ginger lilies and heliconia.

Soon you will come to an organic composting facility. This is an integral component of the Bellevue Chopin organic farming community (see page 135). The production of organic pesticides and fertilisers is small and only serves the local farmers at present. Behind the facility is Broad Meadow Farm (see page 135).

Eventually the track comes to a signposted T-junction. Take the trail to the right. You now move from wide feeder road to forest trail and an environment of semi-deciduous forest mixed with rainforest vegetation.

The trail begins a long uphill climb through the forest to the brow of a hill where you can rest for a while before heading down again. Take another break where the trail evens out for a stretch and enjoy the serenity of the forest.

The terrain gets a little muddy in places and you have to negotiate a few loose stones and tree roots. Be careful not to stumble. It is always best to step between tree roots rather than on them as they can be surprisingly slippery. Follow the steep slope down to a dry creek. The banks of this creek were damaged by Erika and it may not be obvious where the trail continues. It's almost directly ahead of you; slightly to the left. The climb up the steep bank is tricky. Be careful on the rocks too as they can be slippery. Soon you will come to a pretty moss-covered bridge over another dry river bed.

As you close in on Giraudel another climb begins. It is quite long and steep and the terrain is a little troublesome in places. You will see anthuriums and crotons growing to your left as you follow the contours of the mountainside and negotiate very narrow ledges where previous landslides have worn away the trail. Take care here; in some places the track is barely one-person wide! Views begin to open up on your left; you can see the pointed volcanic peak of Morne Canot and the larger Morne Plat Pays further to the southeast as you look back towards Bellevue Chopin.

A final short but steep climb brings you to the outskirts of Giraudel. At the road, head uphill to the right and follow it to a T-junction. Go left and, when you reach the two-way sign, head left through the village. The shop and snackettes are on the main road. Follow this road right out of the village and continue along it for about 1km until you see a sign pointing to a rough feeder road on the right opposite a wooden church. From this road there are good views of Roseau and the west coast. Pass the next church and keep going, following the rather broken feeder road all the way as it curves around to the left and continues to wind its way uphill. Very soon it levels out again and you can take a breather while enjoying more great views; this time of Morne Trois Pitons, Morne Micotrin and the west coast. If you look carefully you should be able to make out a village on a high narrow ridge between you and the mountains beyond. This is Morne Prosper, where you are heading next.

Stick to the main track and head downhill until you reach a fork. Take the signposted track to the left and follow it downhill. Be careful, the surface can be slippery. After about 20 minutes or so you should come to a sign pointing to the right. It will be just before a steel gate indicating private property. Climb the bank and pick up the forest trail.

You are now making a rather long and steep descent to the River Claire. A series of switchbacks and a rather severe slope finally brings you to the bottom of this valley. Be careful: it is very steep and extremely tricky if you are carrying a large backpack. Notice, if you can, how the vegetation shifts from rather dry semi-deciduous woodland and bamboo thickets at the top to much wetter rainforest vegetation towards the bottom.

You will reach a trail junction. To the left is a wide track that used to run to the community of Elmshall in the Roseau Valley (about 45 minutes away), but was ripped to bits by the river during Tropical Storm Erika. The National Trail continues to the right. Very soon you will arrive at the river crossing. So long as the day is not closing in on you, this is a nice place to stop for a rest. Despite the wrecked bridge (if it is still there), the River Claire is a pretty spot that is rarely visited, and the series of cascades and pools are a real joy. Refresh yourself before moving on. You have a very steep climb ahead, but try to comfort yourself with the fact that it is the last major climb on this segment.

Over the other side, pick up the trail and climb the ridge up to Morne Prosper via a series of switchbacks and rather steep steps. The ascent is hard and very narrow in places. Deep breaths, take your time, and be especially cautious if you are carrying a heavy pack. This is actually an old path down to the river from Morne Prosper and was here long before anyone ever dreamed up the National Trail. It was where villagers would come to bathe and wash clothes, so as you are hauling yourself up, imagine carrying a basket of laundry on your head... You will know when you are close to the top of the ridge when you begin to smell the lemon grass that grows there.

Catch your breath on the benches at the top and enjoy the view of Morne Anglais. The houses you see along the western slopes of the mountain are actually Giraudel, where you have just come from.

If you are sitting on the bench looking at the view, you must now follow the trail to your left. Where it forks, go left again and you will come to a paved road and some houses. Follow the road to the junction. This is the main road through Morne Prosper. Turn right and follow the main road uphill to a four-way junction. Go straight on up the rough feeder road. Stick to this track as it runs alongside farmlands and then around a bend to the left, where you come to another junction at a sign for the Morne Hill Farm access road. To the right is the optional trail to Morne Nicholls and the Boiling Lake (page 125). Don't even think about it. A cold beer and a hot sulphur bath probably sound far more appealing than an endless muddy trudge to Morne Nicholls right now so take the road straight ahead and down the hill. You should have great views of farmland, Morne Micotrin and the village of Laudat across the Roseau Valley.

The feeder road soon ends and turns into a rough track. A short, steep climb up the hill brings you to more farmland. Head along the edge of the fields, following the signs until you reach a wide woodland path. It is quite steep in places and there are a few steps to negotiate. The woodlands are beautiful, however. Can you smell the sulphur yet? You will soon, and this is a good sign; it means you are near the end of the journey.

This area is very picturesque. Look at the vegetation to your left. You should see a whole forest of tree ferns and colourful ginger lilies. The village of Wotten Waven also comes into view now. As you approach, you begin to get a sense of how volcanically active it is around here; the smells, the colour of the soil.

A short downhill stretch brings you to a stream. Cross over and climb the short but steep hill on the far side. You will now arrive at the rear of some houses. Follow the fence and the signs to the main road. The end of the trail and the main village junction (and bus stop) are to your left. You will find accommodation and hot volcanic spas in the village. If your goal is Trafalgar, take a right at the three-way junction, passing Screws Sulphur Spa and then downhill to the bridge across the volcanically active River Blanc. A steep climb up the hill is followed by a 20-minute stretch of road across the valley and the Roseau River to another T-junction. To your right is Papillote Wilderness Retreat and the Trafalgar Falls, to your left the village of Trafalgar and the continuation of the trail.

(Difficulty: T: 2; R: 1; E: 3; D: 3; Rating = 5.6)

Segment 4 runs from the spa village of Wotten Waven at the head of the Roseau Valley all the way to Pont Cassé in the interior. It connects you with some of Dominica's most notable hiking trails and natural attractions. Optional additions to this segment therefore include Trafalgar Falls (pages 115–16), Ti Tou Gorge (page 115), the Boiling Lake Trail (pages 118–20), the Freshwater Lake (pages 122–3), the Boeri Lake (pages 120–1), Morne Micotrin (pages 124–6) and Middleham Falls (pages 123–4).

From Wotten Waven the trail leads you to Trafalgar and then it climbs steeply up to Dominica's highest village, Laudat. Primary gateway to the Morne Trois Pitons National Park, Laudat is a village where most hikers end up sooner or later. From here the trail passes through the Middleham Estate and skirts the Morne Trois Pitons National Park, winding its way through a truly beautiful area of unspoilt rainforest until it emerges at Pont Cassé in the shadow of Morne Trois Pitons itself.

PRACTICALITIES There are a couple of very steep ups and downs on this hike but many stretches are in fact quite flat or gently undulating. River crossings are few and do not present much of a hazard, though at the time of writing the steep riverbanks created during Tropical Storm Erika were quite a challenge for a shorty like me. A nice optional diversion on this segment is the Middleham Falls, which is just a 15–20-minute hike from the main trail.

THROUGH-HIKING Both Wotten Waven and Trafalgar have good and affordable accommodation and dining options (see pages 111–12) but Pont Cassé has very little to offer hikers other than the Wai'tukubuli National Trail HQ building which marks the beginning of Segment 5. **D-Smart Farm** (page 205) is an option and just a short bus ride away.

TRAIL DESCRIPTION From Wotten Waven, follow the paved road across the Roseau Valley to Trafalgar, passing Screw's Sulphur Spa and Da-Scape (pages 117–18). When you reach the road junction, left is Trafalgar and the continuation of the trail, right is Trafalgar Falls and Papillote Gardens, both just 15 minutes or so away. Follow the road left into Trafalgar and look for signs on the right leading you up through the narrow backstreets of the village. The paved road climbs and then ends, turning into a trail and then ascending very steeply via a series of worn and muddy switchbacks. This is actually an old track and is still used by villagers as a short-cut between Trafalgar and Laudat. When you reach the top of the ridge there are good views down to your right (you are up above Papillote Wilderness Retreat). The trail evens out and then descends for a stretch before making a final short climb to the farmlands of Laudat. Follow the signs to a paved feeder road which heads into the village. You will come to a junction by a bar. To the right is Ti Tou Gorge and the Boiling Lake trailhead. The National Trail continues to the left. At the next junction go right and follow the road uphill until you reach another road junction. To the right are the Freshwater Lake, Boeri Lake, Chemin L'Etang and Morne Micotrin (see references above). The National Trail continues along the main road to the left. Follow it until you see the signs on your right for both the National Trail and the Middleham Falls.

Follow the long feeder road all the way to the Middleham Falls trailhead. Once on the trail proper you will come to a shallow river crossing. Take the trail uphill via a series of steps and switchbacks until you come to the flat. Continue all the way to the signposted trail junction. To the left is the trail down to Middleham Falls, straight on goes to Cochrane, and to the right is the continuation of the National Trail.

The next section is very beautiful. Though there are no views, the rainforest is quite magical. Listen out for jaco parrots and the distinctive call of the mountain whistler. The forest contains a wide variety of tree species and a lack of dense undergrowth means that you can see quite far into it. Stop and rest; listen to the sounds of nature. Look for movement; perhaps you will see an agouti foraging for fallen fruit or woodland birds such as the trembler or the forest thrush. Seeds dropping beneath *gommier* trees is a sign parrots are feeding in the canopy above; they are usually in pairs and the sudden sound of squawking means they are likely to take flight.

The trail climbs very gently up a ridge in the heart of the Middleham Estate before descending again. You will come to a junction where there is a shelter and rest area. Straight on is Sylvania and the main road between Roseau and Pont Cassé; it takes about 20 minutes to get there. To the right is the continuation of the National Trail. The route follows the national parks boundary for a distance before leaving it near a very large *gommier* tree (see how people have been bleeding it for its sap) and then heading quite steeply uphill. As you climb you will pass the large buttress roots of magnificent *chatanier* trees. Pay attention to the route; it is easy to stray off track if your head is down. Take a breather on the benches and complete the ascent by squeezing through tall trees and huge boulders and finally using ropes to help you get to the top. Here you will find another covered rest area. Now follow the trail sharply down the other side of the ridge (the ropes are both a help and a hindrance) until you come to a bridge spanning a deep gorge. Once over the other side, there is another river gully and rather pretty cascade to negotiate. The descent is tricky, the egress a climb. After this the trail is very easy-going all the way to a final river crossing and then Pont Cassé where it emerges at the traffic island. Segment 5 continues on the road to Bells via the Wai'tukubuli National Trail HQ building, which is clearly signposted 100 yards or so on the right.

SEGMENT 5: PONT CASSÉ TO CASTLE BRUCE

(*Difficulty: T: 2; R: 2; E: 1; D: 3; Rating = 5.0*)
Segment 5 follows a historic route that was originally used by the indigenous Kalinago, then by bands of escaped slaves (Maroons, or *nègres marrons*), and more recently by people travelling from the east-coast village of Castle Bruce to Roseau where they would meet the newly constructed Imperial Road at Pont Cassé. One of the many benefits of the Wai'tukubuli National Trail is that it keeps historic routes like this one alive and allows both residents and visitors to experience and enjoy the journey taken by many before them. When hiking this segment, in particular the stretch between Pont Cassé and the Emerald Pool, you will be walking on fragments of the stone road that was here before its more modern counterpart just a couple of hundred metres away.

PRACTICALITIES This is a fairly easy trail, gently undulating with few steep inclines. The main challenges on this journey are the often muddy terrain, a few narrow ledges, and occasional river and stream crossings. There are also a few lengthy road sections that are not much fun, though walking through the village of Castle Bruce at the end of the day or early morning can be lively and interesting.

10

THROUGH-HIKING At Pont Cassé there is very little for through-hikers. Replenish water from fast-running streams and, if you get really desperate and cannot wait until Castle Bruce, the Emerald Pool visitor centre has a snackette. *En route* are Beyond Vitality and Eden Heights (pages 150–1). The Sea Breeze Inn (page 152) is a great place to overnight towards the end of this segment. It is located on the beach at Castle Bruce, it serves good food and it has Wi-Fi. There is also a minimart along the road from the Sea Breeze Inn where you can stock up on foodstuffs, liquids, even sandwiches.

TRAIL DESCRIPTION From the WNT HQ building near Pont Cassé, head into a dense, lush and often very wet rainforest environment. Even when it isn't raining, the terrain is usually fairly soggy here; catch it on a wet day and it can be like wading through mud soup. You will frequently come across the rocks that made up the old road though quite often you'll simply be concentrating on not losing your boots to the mud. Be warned: this section can be a trudge.

You do get a brief respite from this rather claustrophobic environment when the trail emerges briefly from the forest and offers views across the interior to the north where you will see the conical peak of Morne Nègres Marrons (also known as Morne Laurent), so named because it was once the location of a Maroon camp. The trail continues through the forest, interrupted briefly as it passes down a rough feeder road and then through the remains of a pig farm. After around 3 hours, you will be relieved to meet up with the Emerald Pool trail where you have the option of taking a very short diversion to enjoy this frequently visited natural attraction (see page 215). If you feel like bailing out, this is the place to do it. Also, if your supplies are running low, there is a small snackette at the visitor centre. Follow the National Trail signs from the Emerald Pool through the forest for just under an hour until you emerge at the main highway to the east in an area called Fond Melle. Follow the road for about 1.5km before heading back into the forest. (Look for a sign on the right-hand side of the road).

The trail descends rather sharply down to the L'Or River after leaving the road. Look to the left and you will see where this pretty waterway joins the Fond Figues River to create the Belle Fille. This convergence of several rivers and streams is quite lovely and, if you are feeling a little hot and bothered, is a great place to cool off. Cross the bridge (careful – the wooden boards are often very slippery) and pick up a narrow trail that snakes around rock face and old landslide in a rather hair-raising manner. Take care here; the ledge is narrow and high. Once past this rather precarious section, follow the undulating track as it continues along the course of the river. It will even out and cross a paved road by a bridge. Keep going straight, sticking to the river. Look out for all the tree ferns and heliconia. It is a lovely forest and river environment.

You will come to a river crossing with some gorgeous cascades and pools. Make a short diversion to the left to take a look at the river gorge. Over the other side, the trail climbs quite high above the river before descending again, crossing a couple of small streams along the way. You will come to a croton-lined path that runs alongside a small farmstead. Pass by the small wooden house (don't worry about the dogs) and greet the owners if they are around. Crossing some rather rough ground, head back into the bush and then return to the river where you must make a crossing. You may see the remains of the rope bridge here; another victim of Tropical Storm Erika – or perhaps by the time you use this guide a new one has been built. If you do have to wade across the river, you will find it to be fairly shallow and the current not especially strong. But take care nonetheless. On the other side you will arrive at a farmstead. Pass through the gardens and to the right of the house. You will come out on to the main highway once again.

Head right towards Castle Bruce and follow the road for about 2km. Once on the straight section, look for a small bridge. Around 100m beyond it, on the right, the trail leaves the road and heads into banana plantations. Follow the wide feeder road in a straight line all the way through these farmlands. It is completely flat and very easy-going. Soon you may hear the sound of the ocean. Cross a couple of small streams and come to a paved road. The Atlantic Ocean is in front of you, the road to Saint Sauveur is to your right, and Castle Bruce is to your left. Head left and at the junction go right. Follow the road past St David's Bay and into the village. Alternatively, crash at the very friendly and perfectly located Sea Breeze Inn (page 152). Just after the old Roman Catholic church, take the road downhill on the right and follow it for about 3km as it meanders through and around the lower part of the village. Eventually it joins the main highway again. To the right is the beginning of Segment 6.

SEGMENT 6: CASTLE BRUCE TO HATTON GARDEN

(*Difficulty: T: 2; R: 1; E: 2; D: 3; Rating = 5.0*)
This segment passes through the Kalinago Territory (pages 147–72). It brings you either through or very close to most of the Territory's villages and it also incorporates the Kalinago Barana Auté (pages 154–6) and L'Escalier Tete Chien (page 158). The route follows woodland, village and farm tracks that offer great views of the east coast, and it also follows fairly substantial sections of the main highway through the Territory. This is no bad thing. You will meet Kalinago people at work or at rest, you will have an opportunity to see and perhaps purchase craft products such as tree-fern carvings, calabash bowls and *larouma* basketware, and you will get a taste of what life is like for Dominica's indigenous people.

PRACTICALITIES This is not an especially difficult hike, it is just rather long. There are a few small river and stream crossings, there are some short but steep ups and downs – especially on Horseback Ridge near the end of the segment – and in a few places the terrain is quite slippery. Start early. This is key, especially if you wish to take your time and enjoy the views, the crafts, and meeting people as well as visit the Kalinago Barana Auté and L'Escalier Tete Chien.

THROUGH-HIKING As already mentioned, the Sea Breeze Inn is a good place to spend the night before hiking Segment 6. Other options include Domcan's, Sunrise Farm Cottages or, if you fancy a bit of luxury, Beau Rive (page 150). *En route*, a great accommodation option is Aywasi Kalinago Retreat, where you can either stay in a cottage, camp or hang up a hammock. There is a fairly well-stocked minimart in Castle Bruce village near Sea Breeze Inn and another in Bataca. As you will be on the main highway for a good portion of this hike, use roadside standpipes to fill up with water. Towards the end of the segment, near Bataca, is the Carib Territory Guesthouse and, if you have very deep pockets, you could opt for Pagua Bay. You should note that this is the last segment where you will have any accommodation or provisioning options for a while.

TRAIL DESCRIPTION The trailhead is at the Richmond Estate to the north of Castle Bruce, just before you enter the Kalinago Territory. Look for a sign on the right and a wide section of old paved track that was actually the original coastal road. Pass

10

alongside plantains, coconut palms and breadfruit trees until you come to some gates and a house. Pass to the left of the gates and follow the track downhill through woodland. It gets quite steep, muddy and slippery in some places so watch it. At the bottom of this slope you come to a river. Cross over it carefully and climb up the short hill before heading downhill again. Soon you will hear the sound of the ocean and then you will see it on your right-hand side.

The trail levels out for a stretch. Ignore spurs and stick to the main track as it meanders downhill through coastal woodland and coconut palms towards the sea. Continue downhill, again it is quite steep and slippery, until you come close to the shoreline. The National Trail continues to the left but you will also see a track on your right that goes down to the sea at Raymond Bay. Walk alongside the pretty Madjini River and cross the bridge. Chill out for a while and catch your breath before continuing up the clear trail. Notice how all the trees and shrubs have been shaped by the trade winds. This is very typical of the littoral woodland all along the exposed east coast. Climb a short, rocky and rather muddy path that can be quite slick in the wet until it becomes paved and meets up with the main highway through the Kalinago Territory.

At the road, go right and head to Sineku. A short walk brings you to the trailhead for L'Escalier Tete Chien, which is also your turning point. By the way, if you are asked by the drinkers at the bar if you need a guide, you don't. And if you feel uncomfortable – this spot is notorious for harassment – ignore this spur and simply continue along the main road until you pick up the National Trail further down near Mahaut River. Follow the wide track down to the L'Escalier Tete Chien reception buildings. Walk past them and look for a trail sign on your left. If you know your trees, it is near a large mango. The track straight ahead continues to L'Escalier Tete Chien (10 minutes away – page 158).

The National Trail continues through coastal woodland with occasional views on your right. Again some of the downhill stretches can be a little steep and slippery. You will come to a junction. The National Trail goes to the left and there is a track down to the sea on your right. You will be able to see the volcanic formations that are very typical along this coast.

Stick to the left and follow the signs. The trail now follows the coast, up and down a series of river gullies. It is a bit of a trudge, often wet and overgrown, and not very interesting, but you are rewarded with nice coastal scenery from time to time. You will also cross a couple of small streams. Eventually the trail widens and you find yourself walking away from the sea through fields of bananas, coconut palms, paw-paws and mangoes. And then you arrive at the main road again, this time near the village of Mahaut River.

Turn right and follow the road downhill. You will pass the craft shop and home of Israel and Victoria Joseph. Israel carves tree ferns (known locally as *fougère*, or *fwigè*) into masks, plant holders and reliefs. His work is excellent. Victoria makes traditional *larouma* basketware.

At the bottom of the hill, just around the bend, pick up the trail again on the right-hand side. Follow the wide track downhill to the Mahaut River. Cross the bridge and then follow the trail uphill until you come to the rear of the Sineku Primary School. Up above the school you will see the roof of the Mahaut River Church. On the right-hand side of the school you should see a sign. Pass between two large thickets of bamboo and follow the trail to a small river. Cross and head uphill again. Ignore spurs and continue straight until you come to some houses. Follow the paved road. Enjoy the heliconias, crotons, ginger lilies, and banana plants that fill the verges with colour. Once again, you will arrive at the main road.

THE 'CARIB WAR'

On 19 September 1930 a rather heavy-handed attempt by armed policemen to search for and confiscate contraband, namely smuggled rum and tobacco, turned into a pitched battle with local people. The police retaliated by firing their weapons, killing two Kalinago and injuring two others. Incensed, the Kalinago beat the policemen, who somehow managed to escape. The Crown Colony Administrator perpetuated the heavy-handedness of the affair when he decided to call on a British naval vessel, *HMS Delhi*, which was in the area, to lend assistance. The *Delhi* arrived firing flares across the coastline to frighten the Kalinago and landing marines to round up those who were suspected of being the troublemakers. The incident became known as the 'Carib Uprising' or the 'Carib War'.

Turn right and follow the highway. Look out for further craft stalls as well as fresh fruit and vegetables for sale. Try a jelly coconut; the water is refreshing and it may give you the burst of energy you probably need by now. Continue along the highway to the community of Gaulette River and look for a trail sign on the right-hand side near a bus stop. Follow the paved vehicle track downhill. The track curves to the left around a playing field and becomes a trail that runs downhill for quite a distance towards the sea. Enjoy nice coastal views of Pointe Belair and Gros L'Illet before arriving at the very pretty Gaulette River. Cross and then follow the trail uphill. At the top of the ravine stick to the left and keep going uphill. The landscape opens up to farmland and you will come to some dwelling houses. Take the route uphill to the left and rejoin the main highway in the settlement of St Cyr.

Go right and, just after the Salybia Primary School, look for a trail sign on the right. A wide vehicle track runs quite steeply downhill. At a junction, go straight and continue downhill towards the sea. Take a break and enjoy the views.

Continue downhill and pass a memorial to the 'Carib War' of 1930. Follow this coastal bush and woodland stretch, ignoring spurs and sticking to the main track.

Be careful on the rocks as you approach the pretty Salybia River. Cross the bridge. Notice the small shrine cut in the rockface and follow the track to a junction. The road to the right comes to a dead end at the river mouth. It is worth a short trip down to see the views of the coast. Follow the road uphill. You will soon catch sight of a cemetery. On your left you may also see the ruins of the original Salybia Roman Catholic Church that was built in the latter half of the 19th century. Despite its condition, it has some interesting architectural features as well as a pretty mural that is still largely intact on an internal wall (see box, page 156 for more information about this area and its proposed regeneration).

Follow the track uphill and look for a trail sign to the right of the church, opposite the mural. Follow it uphill and go right at a junction. The trail passes to the left of a wooden house and then up the bank on the far side. You will come to more houses. Bear left along the wide track. This settlement is Crayfish River.

The road becomes paved as it climbs uphill and then joins up with the main road leading down to the Kalinago Barana Auté. Turn right at this junction and follow this rather steep road all the way down to the reception building. Before you get there, you will pass the entrance to Aywasi Kalinago Retreat (page 150), which is a good accommodation option if your energy is beginning to wane. You now have a choice of touring the Kalinago Barana Auté (pages 154–6) or continuing on your

The Wai'tukubuli National Trail SEGMENT 6: CASTLE BRUCE TO HATTON GARDEN

10

237

journey. (Not that I would ever deliberately lead you astray on these hikes but I feel it is only right to inform you that the KBA has a bar.)

The National Trail continues up the road to the left of the reception building, across the Crayfish River and up past the *karbet*, *ajoupa* and cassava press structures to the very end of the paved road. Look for a trail on the left through a field which can sometimes be quite overgrown. Notice all the colourful wild flowers, a variety of heliconia, as you pass through. Stick to the main track as it curves away from the sea and heads inland and reaches a brook. Cross over and follow the uphill path until you come to the Buluku River where there are some pretty cascades. Cross over and follow the trail to a small clearing by a house. There is a junction here. Ignore the trail immediately to the left and take the one on the right of it, on the outside. At another clearing the track becomes paved and continues to the left. Follow it all the way uphill until it comes to the main highway at Bataca.

Take a left (yes, left) and follow the main road for about 1km. Look for a painted sign on the right and follow the road uphill. Keep going straight up the very steep Horseback Ridge Road towards the Bataca water tank where you will see a trail heading into woodland. Follow it steeply downhill. Look for a spur on the left and keep going down. Now look for another spur, this time on the right. Some parts of this descent can be very steep and just as slippery so take care. The views across to the north are great. (Look for some communications masts in the distance. You will come to them on Segment 7.) Follow the stream down to the bottom of the hill where the trail eventually widens and crosses some rather rough open terrain. At a junction take the wide track to the right and follow it alongside the Pagua River, which should be on your left. The track climbs for a short stretch but then flattens out. It can be swampy around here. After passing through a banana plantation you come to a main road. To your right is the road to Antrizle, Atkinson and the Kalinago Territory. To your left is Hatton Garden, the end of this segment and the start of Segment 7. Take a left, cross the bridge, then take a right at the junction. The start of Segment 7 is on your left. This road heads towards Marigot.

SEGMENT 7: HATTON GARDEN TO FIRST CAMP ✳

(*Difficulty: T: 2; R: 1; E: 3; D: 3; Rating = 5.6*)
This segment of the National Trail runs between the Hatton Garden Estate and the farmlands of Hanover in the forested hillsides to the southwest of Marigot. It is a very nice trail that passes through farmland, wet and dry forest habitats, and over rivers. Regions in this area such as First Camp, Captain Bruce, La Guerre, Gregg and Newcastle reflect a history of exploration, battles, Maroon leaders and lands that were named after places back home during colonial times. The trail itself is a combination of old hunting tracks, farm feeder roads, and historic traces. You can expect to see and hear jaco parrots as well as meet farmers and learn a little about what they are growing. There are also some great views of the northeastern coastline as well as westwards across the volcanoes of the interior.

PRACTICALITIES The most difficult parts of this trail are the rather steep ups and downs where it crosses ridges and river gullies in the latter stages of the segment. Another challenge if you are day-hiking is that the trail ends in a rather remote location – following the farm feeder roads east down towards the Douglas Charles Airport will take up to a couple of hours. For this reason, when crossing the Coffee River near the end, it may be a good idea to make sure you have a good supply of water.

THROUGH-HIKING The issue of water at the end of Segment 7 continues into Segment 8, where there is no access to water until you reach Gravel Gutter which is about 90 minutes or more into the trail. At the beginning of Segment 7, nearby accommodation options include Hibiscus Valley Inn (page 151), but there is nothing much by way of provisioning options. Prior to this point, the last shop would have been a minimart in Bataca (page 154). Essentially, once you begin Segment 7 you are on a long trek into Dominica's wilderness that will continue through segments 8, 9, 10 and 11.

TRAIL DESCRIPTION This segment begins in Hatton Garden, close to the shoreline of Pagua Bay. Look for the trailhead sign between the river bridge and the sea. Follow the vehicle track to its end, ignoring any spurs, and cross over the Marechal River, which has been running towards the ocean on your right-hand side. The forest trail climbs gradually and emerges into an open valley of abandoned farmland. Round a corner and cross a small brook. Pass between some cocoa trees and then carefully cross another small stream before climbing up a steep hill. It can get a little overgrown here, but the track is usually easy to follow. Stick to the tree-line on the left. The trail heads back into the forest and climbs through deciduous woodland and rainforest via a couple of switchbacks. Turn a corner and descend with care into a second, rather pretty river valley and cross over a small river. Enjoy views of Pagua Bay and the east coast.

After passing through more overgrown and abandoned farmland, head back into the forest and begin climbing up a ridge. The views start to open up a little more. Pass through a small banana plantation and come to a feeder road. Go right and follow it for about 500m, keeping an eye out for a sign on your left. Take the steep trail uphill towards a line of coconut palms along the ridge line. You come to another vehicle track at the top. Go left and then left again after just a few yards. It is a short but steep climb. There are good views of the northeastern coastline on your right.

You will come to a communications mast. Walk around the perimeter and follow the feeder road. At the junction go left and walk towards a second and then a third mast. There are good views all around. As you face the mast: Morne Diablotin is at 3 o'clock; Morne Aux Diables is at 4 o'clock; Pagua Bay is at 9 o'clock; and at 12 o'clock, behind the mast, is Horseback Ridge in the Kalinago Territory (if you hiked Segment 6, this is where you came from). Follow the road. On your right is an abandoned banana plantation. The track becomes paved and there are cocoa trees on your left. At the main feeder road junction, go left and then almost immediately right.

The trail now passes through a farm belonging to Mr Walter Williams and family. It is a large citrus and banana farm that also has lots of cocoa and breadfruit trees as well as less common fruits such as golden apple, known locally as *pom sitè*, which makes a very refreshing drink. Creeping along the ground between fruit trees and banana plants you may also see pumpkins. A major attraction to hikers, yet a pest to the farm itself, is the number of jaco parrots in this area. You are guaranteed to see and hear them flying around so have your camera or binoculars at the ready. Whilst they are an attraction to visitors, you may wish to spare a thought for citrus farms like this one. They can lose fairly substantial portions of their crops to marauding jaco parrots.

As you exit the farm and descend through what can often be a rather overgrown stretch into a river gully you will notice a dramatic transition from farmland to a wet forest habitat. This area has some very large heliconia species growing alongside the trail. Cross over the very pretty Manitipo River bridge and begin a steep ascent to the top of a ridge where you will notice the habitat changes once again. Here the forest is a drier woodland habitat that reflects its proximity to the coast. A short descent brings you to a viewpoint where you can see the Atlantic Ocean, Douglas Charles Airport and the very flat French island of Marie-Galante. Descending further you will reach a junction where the National Trail heads inland once again. The vehicle track to the right is a feeder road that will bring you to the coastal village of Marigot.

Back in the forest the trail makes a gradual ascent. Look out for torch ginger on your right-hand side. As the trail becomes a little steeper, the views behind you open up and you can see the island's northeastern coastline. At a junction with some farmland, the National Trail heads to the right. To the left you can see the depths of the interior and the ridgeline running up to Mang Peak. Curving back around into the forest, the trail climbs steeply to the top of a ridge. Notice the *gommier* trees (they are tall and straight with rounded trunks and occasionally seeping white sap), *balata* (the bullet tree, known for its strength), *bwa bandé* (Dominica's now notorious 'natural Viagra'), and the *savonette* whose roots used to be used by the Kalinago to stun river fish before catching them.

Begin a long descent into a river valley. The terrain is steep and challenging in places. Pass through an environment of wet forest, tree ferns and tall *gommier* and enjoy views to the north. The trail continues descending until it finally reaches a junction. The National Trail continues to the left. After a flat stretch, the trail meanders downhill to a river. Across the river it is a short but steep climb up the ridge, followed by a downhill trail through the forest until you reach open farmland. The trail now turns into a feeder road that passes between farms. Please do not stray from the path and on to these farmlands; the farmers are quite sensitive about this.

The vehicle track runs downhill until it fords the Coffee River. This is the last river you will meet for at least a couple of hours so fill up if you need to. I like to stay here for a while and have a soak to cool down before continuing. On the other side of the river, the trail climbs all the way up to a junction with another feeder road. To the left is First Camp and the start of Segment 8. To the right, the feeder road passes through farmland estates before rounding the back of the Douglas Charles Airport runway and emerging at the Atlantic coast. If you do wish to exit, turn right and look for trail blazes on rocks at a second junction where you should take the right-hand fork. It will take you a couple of hours to walk to the main coastal road from here.

SEGMENT 8: FIRST CAMP TO PETITE MACOUCHERIE ✳

(*Difficulty: T: 4H; R: 2; E: 4; D: 4; Rating = 8.8H*)
Running right across Dominica through the Northern Forest Reserve, this segment is as remote and unspoilt as it gets. It begins in the farmland of Hanover and First Camp on the east coast and ends in the elevated farmland of Petite Macoucherie, high above Mero, on the west coast. The rainforest *en route* is beautiful with magnificent specimens of *gommier, chatanier, karapit* and other trees, and the canopy sometimes seems alive with parrots, mostly jaco, though sisserou can also be heard here. The trail reaches its highest point at the summit of Mosquito Mountain where rainforest is replaced by montane thicket and a wet covering of mosses and lichens.

This is a trail that really began as a hunter's trace. You may come across pits that were dug to trap wild pigs and you may even see signs of the animals themselves. Look for evidence of digging in wet soil around tree roots where they have been looking for worms. You may also see trees where moss or lichen has been worn off the bark from pigs rubbing themselves against it for a good scratch. Notice how high the marks are; big pigs. You are unlikely to meet them, however, as they are elusive and very easily spooked. Hunters still operate in this area but apparently they no longer use pit traps.

PRACTICALITIES The ratings indicate this to be Dominica's toughest hike and I think this is right. It is very long; between 7 and 9 hours, meaning you must set off at first light in order to reach the end before darkness falls. The first 4 hours are relatively easy-going; the trail undulates without too much severity and there is a cluster of river crossings around a third of the way. The ascent and descent of Mosquito Mountain is severe and very draining after 4 to 5 hours of remote rainforest hiking, but there is a simple cabin before it, offering you a chance to hole up for the night if you so wish. It is a very steep ascent up Mosquito Mountain (I wonder why the trail doesn't simply go around it?) and you must use both upper and lower body strength, together with a very focused mind, to make it. It really feels like an assault course. From the summit, a very narrow ridge line with tricky terrain maintains your altitude and concentration for a further hour before dropping you back down into the rainforest. From there, thankfully, the trail is easier again.

This segment needs proper planning; do not take it lightly. I recommend a guide for all but the most experienced and well-equipped hikers.

The starting and ending points of this segment are also remote. There are no public buses and even farm vehicles are rare. You must therefore arrange for a drop-off, pick-up or carry camping gear.

Please note: I was unable to re-hike the entirety of this segment prior to the submission of the new edition of this guide. The trail was in pretty poor shape and many of the blazes had faded away to nothing. Entry and egress from rivers was also challenging because of the torrents created by Tropical Storm Erika. I did manage to hike about 2½ hours of the segment before calling it quits when the trail disappeared along with all the blazes and I didn't much fancy getting myself lost in the Northern Forest Reserve. So please check for updates before you go (you should do this anyway, of course) by contacting the WNT management team via their website (*www.waitukubulitrail.com*). I will also post trail updates from time to time on www.bradtupdates.com/dominica.

THROUGH-HIKING There is a rudimentary wooden shelter at the eastern foot of Mosquito Mountain, between 3 and 4 hours into the trail depending on your pace. There are no accommodation or provisioning options near the end of Segment 7 or at the beginning of Segment 8, and the last place for a water refill before you reach Gravel Gutter (see description below) is the Coffee River on Segment 7 (pages 238–40). If you make it to the end of Segment 8, you may see a sign for **Villa Incognito** (✆ 767 614 7646, *see map, page 217*), which is about a mile down the road towards Mero and where you can spend a night or two and get well fed by Chita Goedkoop who maintains an organic farm in the area.

TRAIL DESCRIPTION In Hanover follow the farm feeder road and trail signs uphill until you reach the large sign indicating the beginning of Segment 8. Follow the trail along a ridge and into the forest. There are good views of the interior to your left. The trail undulates and meanders through the semi-deciduous and rainforest habitat of First Camp, so named because in 1964 it was used as a camp by the First Battalion of the Worcestershire Regiment, who came to Dominica for jungle training. The rainforest crowds around you as you enter the Northern Forest Reserve, with large concentrations of *gommier* attracting riots of feeding jacos at canopy level. The trail is wide and easy to follow for a long stretch, though eventually the terrain becomes a little trickier and there are a couple of short but steep ascents and descents. Use tree roots to help you. The trail evens out again and eventually arrives at Gravel Gutter, a shallow and pretty mountain stream that is full of watercress. It runs right across the trail so look for the sign on the other side. Wade across and refill your flask. Walk through a lovely rainforest environment to a deep river gully. Climb down the bank and up the other side carefully and continue your rainforest walk.

Negotiate a second small river and, at a very clear trail junction, go right. The forest continues to be dominated by large *chatanier*, *gommier* and *karapit*. Notice the different layers of forest growth; primary, secondary and tertiary – all competing for space and light. The trail undulates through this lush and unspoilt forest reserve and you will eventually find yourself on a high ridge. Down to your left you may hear a river. The trail now descends steeply to meet it. This is the Melville Hall River (the one that eventually runs alongside the Douglas Charles Airport). Cross carefully; it is fairly deep in places as well as fast-flowing. Over the other side you pass over a small tributary and then meet the same river again. Cross carefully and head back into the forest. Soon you come to another tributary. Though quite wide, it is fairly shallow so wading across is easy. The trail climbs though it gives you a respite with flat stretches. Look out for signs of wild pigs in this area. Cross a small stream. This will be the last chance to fill up on water for the next 3 hours or more. You will come to a rudimentary wooden shelter that is a handy place to bunk down if it is raining or you wish to postpone any mountain climbing.

Continue your uphill journey until you come to a very steep section. This is the beginning of the climb to the top of Mosquito Mountain. It is at least 3 hours to the end of the segment from this point. The climb to the top of the mountain takes about an hour. It is a steep and difficult climb. You must use tree roots and ropes to pull you up. Pack away your hiking poles and take your time, always be sure of your footing before moving on, and test each root or branch before giving it your full weight. The environment transitions from rainforest to montane thicket; the trees become shorter and branches tend to be covered in dripping wet mosses and lichens. Follow a narrow ridge to the top. Once there you should enjoy views if the surrounding thicket is not too high though this is not a place to dwell; it can get cold, wet and windy. Take a rest and move on.

The descent to Petite Macoucherie takes around 2 hours, the first of which is a rather tricky hike along the southern ridge of the mountain. There is a series of short but steep descents and ascents though you do not lose much by way of elevation. From time to time the vegetation opens up to give you views. The terrain is difficult, steep and often slippery and eroded, and your legs are tired. Be careful not to trip, slide or stumble on all the tree roots. Eventually you come to a long, steep descent which drops you into a rainforest environment once more. Again, take your time going down.

At the bottom you will come to a small stream. The water is good for drinking if you need a top-up. Follow a much easier trail out of the forest to some abandoned farmland. The grassy trail may be a little overgrown. Cross a small brook and come to a rough feeder road. Keep going until you come to a junction with a paved road. This is Petite Macoucherie and the end of the segment. To your left is a very long walk down to Mero (at the junction further down, go left), and to your right is Segment 9.

SEGMENT 9: PETITE MACOUCHERIE TO COLIHAUT HEIGHTS

(*Difficulty: T: 3; R: 3; E: 3; D: 4; Rating = 8.1*)

The remoteness of Segment 8 continues into Segment 9. You leave behind the farmlands and beautiful scenery of Petite Macoucherie and enter an unspoilt environment of primary rainforest and semi-deciduous woodland, emerging several hours later at the farmlands of Colihaut Heights. Along the way you should encounter parrots, you will see lots of magnificent species of *gommier*, *karapit* and *chatanier* trees, and you will come across a hidden waterfall.

PRACTICALITIES This trail ought to be dubbed the 'segment of ridges'. Though it starts and ends on farm feeder roads, the middle section of the trail is replete with steep ridge climbing and river crossings. Both technically and physically challenging, this hike needs planning and lots of time. Give yourself at least 7 to 8 hours.

Please note that I was unable to re-hike this segment prior to my manuscript deadline. I did manage some of it from the other end on a hike to Kachibona Lake, but my efforts to walk the whole trail were scuppered because of access problems following Tropical Storm Erika. I doubt very much that the trail has changed its route, so much of the following description should still be good. One thing you should definitely expect is a little difficulty getting in and out of rivers; the banks may be steeper (they were ripped apart by raging torrents) and trail markers over the far side may be difficult to spot. Most will continue dead opposite, but take your time looking and you should find them all right.

THROUGH-HIKING If you are through-hiking from Segment 8, first of all, well done for making it this far. Other than camping out on the trail, at the time of writing **Villa Incognito** (✆ *767 614 7646*) was the only other layover option in the area (a mile down the Mero road from the end of Segment 8). Other than chancing upon a farmer with fruit to sell, there is no hope of provisioning here, though if you have stayed at Villa Incognito you should at least be able to begin your day on a full stomach. There is also nothing but farmlands at the end of this segment. You will cross plenty of streams at the bottom of each of the ridges you climb, all of which are good for water refills as there are no farmlands or villages above.

TRAIL DESCRIPTION Follow the paved feeder road from the junction where Segment 8 ends (see page 240) for about an hour. You will pass alongside both working and abandoned farms of banana, plantain, dasheen, christophene, passionfruit and citrus crops. The road crosses a pretty little river and begins to climb. Hopefully you are here on a nice day because the scenery is absolutely gorgeous. Stick with the road – it is very broken up and a little overgrown in places – as it climbs a little more steeply and reaches a junction. Take the rough feeder track to the right (the paved feeder road to the left goes all the way to Salisbury – about 20 minutes by car). Stick with this feeder road as it climbs alongside banana fields and then ends rather abruptly at a shed. Before continuing, enjoy the view; without doubt one of the most beautiful on the island. You are looking south across farmland and countless valleys. The large mountain is Morne Trois Pitons. The pointed peak to the right is Morne Anglais; the mountain to the left is Foundland.

The trail passes to the right of the shed. It may well be a little overgrown so take your time picking out the route which heads downhill and circles back beneath the structure. The terrain is a little tricky so be careful. The trail soon widens and

10

heads rather steeply downhill. You are following the western boundary line of the Northern Forest Reserve. At the bottom of the hill you will arrive at your first river crossing. Negotiate it carefully and then begin a steep uphill climb. Use tree roots and ropes to help you whenever you can but be sure to test everything first. It can be very muddy and slippery so please take your time, especially if you are carrying a heavy pack. At the top of the ridge, take a breather and then head very steeply down the other side. Once again, cross over the river at the bottom. If you need a refill, the water is good.

The next ascent is yet another steep one. At the top of the ridge you will see a trail junction. Go straight ahead and down the next ridge to a dry river gully. Climb up and out – a little shorter distance this time – and you will hear a river down to your left. You may also hear jaco parrots. Head steeply down to a lovely river and take a well-deserved breather.

The next ascent is interrupted for a short distance by a flattish area before heading very sharply uphill. Cross over the peak and negotiate the severe drop down the other side. You are passing through some of Dominica's oldest forest; remote and untouched for centuries. Again the trail is quite even for a while as it passes through a beautiful forest environment. Head down to the next river where you may see a small cascading waterfall.

Ready for the next climb? It is another steep one up to the top and then down the other side of the next sharp ridge where you come to a lovely river. Cross over carefully and almost immediately negotiate two further rivers before climbing again. Be careful on these rivers; the stones are slippery, the entry and exit points steep and crumbling. At the top of the next ridge you come to a more open area with abandoned farmlands. Stick to the right, following the boundary of the forest reserve for a short distance before coming to a junction. Take a sharp left and head uphill. The trail widens; this whole area was once full of thriving banana farms. It is hard to believe. Now abandoned to the forest, this area is yet another reminder of the decline of small island agriculture.

The trail narrows again as you head downhill. It undulates for a distance before dropping steeply to a river. Cross it and after a very short distance on the other side, turn around to your left. You ought to be able to see a tall, cascading waterfall. Take a seat and enjoy being where you are (which is high above the west coast village of Coulibistrie).

The trail heads upwards again; it is a steep hike this time rather than a climb. From the top head down again and cross over a small river. At the top of the next steep ridge you will come to a junction where you must go right. The trail is a little easier, meandering through the forest and passing through thickets of tall bamboo. Again, listen out for parrots.

Use the ropes (if they are still there) to help you down the next steep descent, cross the river at the bottom and follow the trail until it joins up with another one. This is the trail to Kachibona Lake (page 220). Stick to the left (right goes to the lake) and follow the very clear and wide trail downhill to your final river crossing. Over the other side head uphill and use the ropes to help you up alongside the log. The steps are rather eroded and slippery. Eventually you will come to a wooden shelter. Take a rest; you have about 20 minutes to go.

Continue the climb through much drier forest until you come to a farm. Follow the trail along its margins until you arrive at a roughly paved feeder road. Go right and walk a short distance downhill. At the next junction go right. Walk for about ten minutes to reach the end of Segment 9 and the beginning of Segment 10. The feeder road continues down to the village of Colihaut (about 20 minutes by car).

(Difficulty: T: 2; R: 1; E: 1; D: 2; Rating = 3.8)

Like many trails, this one began as a route that people used to access hillside lots where they grew *ground provisions*, bananas and so on. Many of these trails were developed into feeder roads so that farmers could use vehicles more easily to access their land and bring produce to market. In more recent times agriculture has been in a state of decline as it has become more and more difficult for small island farmers to compete. Many family farms have been abandoned and young people tend to find the business unappealing due to the imbalance of effort to reward. To a certain extent this trail tells a little of that story. The route follows one of the very first feeder roads that was constructed on the island and it passes both abandoned and active farmsteads. You may meet farmers who seem to be working land in the middle of nowhere, growing yams or dasheen on steep hillsides, or bananas on the slopes of river valleys. In Syndicate, a traditional farming area, you will see a number of larger farms where citrus fruit and coffee is grown in abundance, yet you will also see signs advertising land for sale.

This is an interesting walk with nice views of the west coast and the forest-covered peaks of the Morne Diablotin National Park. It ends at Syndicate, a very beautiful area and notable habitat of Dominica's endemic Amazonian parrots.

PRACTICALITIES This is an easy walk and should take no longer than 3 to 4 hours to complete. For the most part the trail is downhill. The terrain is also easy-going. The practical challenges are how to get to the start and end points of the trail. If you are not through-hiking you will either need to arrange for a drop-off and pick-up, drive to one end and walk there and back, or go with a guide. Another option is to lengthen this hike by tagging on the first section of Segment 11; effectively walking from Colihaut to Picard. You would need a drop-off but you could walk out to Picard. This would take around 6 hours.

This segment did suffer damage caused by Tropical Storm Erika. Several landslides blocked the trail, but well-marked and well-trodden tracks over them offer no serious challenges to hikers.

THROUGH-HIKING There is nothing to support through-hikers at the beginning of this segment though you could spend the night in a wooden cabin or tent on the Syndicate Falls trail (pages 219–20) when you reach the end. If you are really lucky the Syndicate visitor centre may be open, catering for cruise ship visitors, but don't count on it. If it is open, you may be able to get a simple bite to eat and a drink. If you want to walk out, the main west-coast highway is a 45-minute walk from the end of the segment.

TRAIL DESCRIPTION The start of Segment 10 is on a feeder road in the hillside high above the village of Colihaut.

Follow it around the heights of the Colihaut River Valley as it winds its way around and down the hillside. It is very easy-going. You will see heliconias, ginger lilies, bamboo thickets and tree ferns. The track crosses a couple of streams before reaching a small farm of bananas and citrus fruit. Note the crotons and colourful hibiscus. There are also nice views of the Caribbean Sea.

Continue around the slopes of the river valley, sticking to the main track. You will come to another viewpoint before beginning a gentle climb. Tree ferns and bamboo continue to line the trail as you ascend. Once over a crest, you begin a gentle descent. Notice the small and rather cloudy pond down to your left; rather fittingly this area is called L'Etang (pond or lake). The track continues its gentle ascent meandering upwards around the margins of a wide valley and then in a series of switchbacks until it evens out again. Stick to the main track as you round the apex of a bend and begin a gradual descent.

Soon you come to a wonderful view of volcanic peaks and Caribbean Sea. If conditions are good, you may also see the Saints (see box on page 200) and Guadeloupe on the horizon. Around the next corner the views continue. This time you can see Morne Diablotin, Dominica's highest mountain.

If you haven't heard them already, listen out for parrots as you get ever closer to Syndicate and the Morne Diablotin National Park. Look on the ground for the remains of grapefruit; munched at by parrots and finished off by ants and other insects. The track is a little steep in places and the terrain uneven and often muddy, but it is fairly easy-going. Towards the bottom of the slope the track crosses a river and arrives at some of the larger farmsteads of Syndicate. You will see bananas and citrus trees on the left, yams and dasheen beyond the tree ferns on your right. At a junction go right and stick to the main feeder road which continues downhill and soon becomes paved. A farm on your left is full of citrus trees and its road boundary is lined with bananas and coffee trees.

Eventually you come to the main Syndicate road. To the left is the west coast highway and to the right is the Syndicate visitor centre. It takes about 20 minutes to walk to the visitor centre and the beginning of Segment 11, about 45 minutes to reach the west-coast highway where you can catch a bus.

SEGMENT 11: SYNDICATE TO BORNES

(*Difficulty: T: 2; R: 2; E: 3; D: 4; Rating = 6.9*)
This hike takes you from the visitor centre at the start of the Syndicate Nature Trail to the village of Bornes which is located on the main road between Portsmouth and Calibishie. The first section of the hike follows an abandoned logging road and then continues through semi-deciduous, rainforest and coastal woodland habitats. You will also enjoy some great views of Prince Rupert Bay and the Cabrits National Park.

PRACTICALITIES Though it starts very gently, this segment is extremely long (perhaps too long, to be honest) and it has some very steep ups and downs which, at the time of writing, had suffered some erosion, turning them into mud slides in wet conditions. There are some river crossings, the largest of which has a rather slippery swing bridge and is not for the faint-hearted.

At Bornes, if you are not through-hiking, you can catch a bus to either Portsmouth or Calibishie.

THROUGH-HIKING While you have simple accommodation options near the end of this segment (Lily's Guesthouse and Brandy Manor – page 178), your only real option at the beginning is at the Syndicate Falls trail (pages 219–20), where you could overnight in one of the simple wooden 'cottages' or camp. There are no provisioning options at either end other than the 'Survival' shop along the main road in the village of Bornes, where you can get the basics. Most river water is fine for refills, though once you near Bornes you should either refrain or use a filter or purifier.

Some of the steep ups and downs on this segment are very tricky with a large pack and there are some sections that are rope-assisted. Again, they feel rather more like an assault course than a hiking trail, so take care.

TRAIL DESCRIPTION The start of Segment 11 is at the Syndicate visitor centre. As you face the centre and car park you will see that the paved road continues to the left and becomes a rough track that passes through citrus orchards. There is a large sign. At a junction, take the wide trail to the right and follow it to the rusting skeleton of a Timberjack logging vehicle. Rather like an artificial reef in the ocean, it is slowly being enveloped by nature and, rather ironically, becoming part of the environment it was once brought here to destroy.

The woodland trail is wide and often overgrown and muddy for a long stretch – around an hour or so – until it finally arrives at a turn-off to the right on the apex of a bend. Saying farewell to the old logging road also marks the end of the easier part of this hike. From now on it becomes rather more challenging.

The trail meanders through a very pretty section of forest along a ridge before heading rather steeply downhill, winding its way through the trees until the gradient eventually becomes a little shallower. This is a pretty area of semi-deciduous woodland and rainforest. The descent is steep again as you make your way down the side of a ridge. Use trees, rope and roots to help you negotiate the route safely. At the bottom of a gully pass over a small stream and then, after a short climb, enjoy your first real views. You can see Prince Rupert Bay, the twin peaks of the Cabrits National Park, the northern edge of Picard, Glanvillea and Portsmouth.

The trail heads downhill again, through a banana plantation and then to a junction with a dirt road where there are also more great views. Follow the road until you reach the sign by a building and then follow the fenced track downhill to the Picard River bridge. Take care crossing; the surface of the bridge is often extremely slippery.

Climb up out of the river gully and follow the trail through the forest. You are now faced with a very steep climb up a high ridge where you are eventually rewarded with another great view of Prince Rupert Bay and Portsmouth. A short but steep descent brings you into a gully of large boulders which is followed by a long and tiring climb to the top of another ridge. Once you are there, the trail widens and levels out for a while, with just a few gentle undulations through what is now a rather dry coastal forest habitat. Watch out for razor grass.

Descend steeply again into a river gully and follow it to the left. After about 25m, pick up the trail on your right and climb out. Look for the sign. Upstream to your left, if you fancy a diversion at this point, there is a small cascading waterfall. Follow the trail down into a second gully but go straight across this one and climb up the other side. It is another long and arduous climb to the top of a ridge where the view opens up and you are rewarded with your final panorama of Prince Rupert Bay, Portsmouth and Morne Aux Diables ahead of you; even the Saints and Guadeloupe across the sea may be visible in the distance.

Follow the trail along an undulating ridge. Descend steeply into a dry river gully and then climb up and out to the left before descending steeply again into a wet valley. Follow the trail up out of the valley and then along a gradual gradient downwards until the surroundings begin to open up around you and the trail reaches a wide feeder road. You should see Brandy Manor in front of you.

If you are not spending the night here, walk left along the feeder road past Brandy Manor to a junction. Segment 11 continues along the left-hand spur. If you have decided this is really enough after all, you can bail out by following the paved road to the right, over the river and up to the main road in just a few minutes. At the main road, left goes to Portsmouth, right to Calibishie. Buses and vehicles pass frequently so you should be able to get a ride without having to wait too long.

For the die-hards who want to make it to the very end of this long segment, follow the spur through a rather swampy habitat which is typical for this area (you

10

are not that far from the Indian River and the Glanvillea Swamp). The trail actually follows the route of Dominica's first and last railway line that once ran from the Brandy Estate to the Indian River. It was part of a short-lived logging endeavour and was used to transport timber from the forest to the Indian River and then the coast. The project was abandoned after just two years and rail sections were plundered and used in building construction in Portsmouth. Brandy Manor has some remnants of the rolling stock for those who are interested.

The trail follows the river and then crosses it. There are some interesting examples of mangrove vegetation here, notably the *Rhizophora*, known as red mangrove or bloodwood, with its unique, contorted roots. The trail eventually meets the main highway. Follow the signs and pick it up again on the other side. The pretty woodland trail runs east towards Bornes, crossing a couple of small rivers *en route*. It eventually reaches a feeder road which emerges near the Indigo Art Gallery (page 196) and a junction which leads either to the main Portsmouth to Calibishie road (to the right) or to the continuation of the National Trail (to the left).

SEGMENT 12: BORNES TO PENNVILLE ✹

(*Difficulty: T: 3; R: 1; E: 3; D: 4; Rating = 6.9*)
On a clear day, this is one of the most scenic segments of the National Trail. It runs from Bornes up to Morne Destinée, through the farmlands of the Moore Park Estate, and up and across the lower elevations of the Morne Aux Diables volcano. It emerges in the pretty village of Vieille Case and continues along a very beautiful stretch of coastline to Pennville, before heading up again to the remote and idyllic farmlands of Delaford. The views on this trail can be spectacular so try to pick a day with good weather.

PRACTICALITIES This segment has some steep ups and downs and occasionally fairly challenging terrain, especially above Moore Park and then down to Vieille Case. Towards the end, on the section from Pennville to Delaford (where Segment 12 ends and Segment 13 begins), you have to walk on the main highway for around 3–4km, which is not ideal, though the views along the way are lovely.

At Delaford you may be able to catch a ride or an occasional bus across Morne Aux Diables to Portsmouth or back down to Vieille Case.

THROUGH-HIKING Accommodation options near the end of Segment 11 include Brandy Manor and Lily's Guesthouse (page 178). Provisioning options in Bornes are limited to a small village shop or two. Don't expect much. There are no accommodation options at the end of Segment 12 (though you can always ask around in the village of Vieille Case). With permission, you can camp out on private land near Delaford. Alternatively, continue into Segment 13 and find a spot on the trail to hang a hammock or pitch a tent. The top end is a fairly dry area and river fills are seldom. Use standpipes or ask for a fill-up from a kindly soul in Vieille Case.

TRAIL DESCRIPTION Starting near the Indigo Art Gallery in Bornes (see page 196), follow the trail up a paved feeder road. It is a steep climb up towards Morne Destinee past farmlands of bananas, mangoes, avocados, and coconuts, but the views are great. If the weather is clear, you should be able to see Morne Diablotin and the volcanoes of the south behind you.

At the top of the hill the paved road comes to an end. A grassy track becomes a narrow trail and heads steeply downhill and then along the sides of a wide valley full of coconut palms. There are views to your right of the Atlantic coastline all the way down to the Red Rocks at Pointe Baptiste (page 197). The village you see is Paix Bouche. The undulating trail continues through semi-deciduous woodland and runs down into the Grand Riviere Valley and across a bridge at the bottom.

Up and out the other side, the trail widens and joins with a paved feeder road. To the right is the village of Paix Bouche. This area is the Moore Park Estate. Head left and follow the feeder road to its conclusion. Continue along the trail through farmlands and, if the weather is fine, enjoy the mountain views all around. Pass around a beautiful river valley, alongside fields of yams and bananas, and over a pretty brook until you reach the narrow spine of a steep ridge (if you are refilling, use a filter or purifier here). It is a tough climb up to the top, but you can pause for breath and enjoy fabulous views behind you. The trail up this ridge is grassy so do not be surprised if it is a little overgrown. Follow it up and then take a right when you near the top. Look for the sign.

Now follow the trail steeply downhill. Soon you will see the village of Vieille Case below you. The views are fabulous. Continue all the way down to a paved feeder road (often slippery) which runs to the village. Walk through it until you reach the main highway at the bottom where you must turn left. Follow the highway for about 1km until you see a sign and gazebo on the right-hand side.

This section of the trail takes you down into a river valley and then back up and out the other side in a series of switchbacks. It is a lovely area, perhaps because of its simplicity and remoteness, but also because Amerindians once occupied it and, when you reach the large volcanic boulders along the river, you can almost imagine them still here. Notice also the littoral woodland; the way the coastal trees have been shaped by the weather on this windward coast. And look out across the Atlantic. The flat island you may see on the horizon is Marie-Galante. It is a French island that now belongs to Guadeloupe but was also once home to Amerindians. A bridge carries you over a second river crossing and then the trail leads you uphill. You will reach a lovely viewpoint where you should sit and rest for a while. The rugged coves, bays, inlets and beaches of Autou, Wombati Bay, Ans Soldat, Batibou Bay and Hampstead run all the way around the northeast coast to the unmistakable Red Rocks formation at Pointe Baptiste.

From the viewpoint you come to the village of Lower Pennville. Follow the steep paved road all the way up through the village to the main highway. To the left is Vieille Case. Take a right and follow the highway for about 3–4km, all the way to the Delaford Estate where this segment ends and the next one begins. *En route* you will pass the Demitrie River cascade, which is a nice spot to freshen up.

SEGMENT 13: PENNVILLE TO CAPUCHIN

(*Difficulty: T: 1; R:1; E: 2; D:2; Rating = 3.8*)
This segment takes you along the very north coast of Dominica. It begins at the remote Delaford Estate and ends at Canna, near the village of Capuchin. Before the road across Morne Aux Diables was constructed, this route was used to get across the island as well as to access small farm holdings. It is still commonly used by farmers today.

PRACTICALITIES This is an easy hike that follows steady uphill and then downhill gradients. It crosses one very small river that barely registers in terms of difficulty, and it is also a short hike that you should be able to complete within 3 hours.

THROUGH-HIKING You should plan on hiking segments 13 and 14 together; it can easily be done in 5 or 6 hours. Water is a bit of a problem until you get to Capuchin where you can either ask for a fill or use a standpipe. If you do feel the need to break and spend the night at the end of this section I am told you can pitch a tent in the Canna Heritage Park.

TRAIL DESCRIPTION The start of the trail is by a very small building in Delaford, just off the main road to Pennville. It passes a few simple buildings and farmland, curving around the Delaford River Valley and then beginning a gradual climb. A very easy route to follow, the track hugs the hillside along a series of broad coastal valleys. In some areas the trail is a little narrow and the terrain loose and rocky scree, but it is not especially challenging. The incline grows a little steeper but reaches its highest point about an hour or so into the hike. The best views of the coastline are also up to this point.

Now follow the clear route downhill through dry coastal woodland, coffee trees and coconut palms in a series of switchbacks, through the ruins of an abandoned coffee estate, until you meet the Taffia River which, once it meets the northern cliffs, tumbles as a waterfall into the sea. An easy river crossing brings you back out towards the coast where the trail becomes wide track. Stick with it all the way to Dominica's most northwesterly point, where this segment comes to an end at Canna. This area, settled by Amerindians and later by Capuchin monks, has a small cannon battery at its most westerly point from where there are great views of the Saints and Guadeloupe on a clear day. This is also where Segment 14 begins.

SEGMENT 14: CAPUCHIN TO CABRITS

(*Difficulty: T: 2; R: 0; E: 2; D: 2; Rating = 3.8*)
The final leg of the Wai'tukubuli National Trail is mostly a road walk, though not without interest or nice scenery. From Canna on the northwestern tip of the island, the trail takes you down to the rocky shoreline which you follow to the Capuchin fishery building and join the road. If you don't fancy the rough terrain of the rocky shoreline, you can simply follow the road. From there a rather long walk along the highway brings you through the villages of Clifton, Cocoyer and Cottage, the pretty seaside community of Toucari, past the equally beautiful Douglas Bay, and through the Cabrits Swamp to the end of your journey. Canna, where the hike begins, was the site of an Amerindian settlement and then a gun battery emplacement. Capuchin monks are also thought to have lived in this region, giving the area its name. A cannon is still *in situ*, pointing out across the sea towards the Saints, where the famous battle of 1782 took place (see page 200).

PRACTICALITIES Hiking along a main road isn't ideal but, other than trying to negotiate the rocky shoreline, it is the only way to get you from Capuchin to the Cabrits. The short section from Canna to the Capuchin fishery building is really for the die-hards; my advice is to go with the road and enjoy a bit of colourful Dominican village life *en route*.

TRAIL DESCRIPTION From the sign at Canna, either follow the trail down to the coast or simply follow the road. The coastal trail heads downhill through dry coastal woodland. Look out for ruins on your left. Towards the bottom it gets quite steep and you must negotiate the rocky mouth of a ravine before emerging on the shoreline.

With cliffs to your left and the sea to your right, take it easy along the pebble beach. You may find yourself constantly looking down so remember to stop, take a rest and a look around. After negotiating your first set of boulders you will come to a jetty, a boatshed and a sea wall. This is the Capuchin fishery building where you should rejoin the main road.

Follow the main road through the tiny villages of Clifton and Cocoyer. Before you reach the village of Cottage, there is an optional route off the road that bypasses the heart of the village via the Lamothe playing field. Personally, I don't think this short diversion is worth it; but it's your choice. If you continue along the road you will come to Cottage where there are a couple of local bars and a fairly well-stocked minimart. From Cottage the road heads downhill to the pretty village of Toucari, where it is worth pausing to enjoy the scenery and perhaps grab a snack or a drink at a roadside bar. You then have a very steep road climb out the other side to the residential communities of Morne A Louis and Savanne Paille. From here it is downhill all the way. Pass through Tantane and along the shoreline of the very pretty Douglas Bay. At the end of the bay, the gazebos and picnic benches are the sign to head into the Cabrits Swamp for the final leg. There is a great stretch of beach here too. Follow the trail through the swamp (it really is quite swampy and desolate) along the margin of the Cabrits National Park. Keep going until you reach the road and Prince Rupert Bay. To the right is the Cabrits National Park and Fort Shirley (pages 173–90); to the left, Lagoon and Portsmouth (pages 183–4). A good place to rest up is Purple Turtle Beach, to the left, where there is a bar and restaurant (page 194).

Congratulations! You have completed the Wai'tukubuli National Trail. It is quite an achievement.

SEND US YOUR SNAPS!

We'd love to follow your adventures using our *Dominica* guide – why not send us your photos and stories via Twitter (@BradtGuides) and Instagram (@bradtguides) using the hashtag #dominica. Alternatively, you can upload your photos directly to the gallery on the Dominica destination page via our website (*www.bradtguides.com*).

10

Appendix 1

Accommodation name	Location	Type	Price Code	Page
3 Rivers Eco Lodge	Rosalie	SC	$	151
767 Ecologic	Soufriere	SC	$–$$	131
Anchorage Hotel	Castle Comfort, Roseau	H	$$$	97
Arial Sea Villa	Calibishie	SC	$$$$–$$$$$	176
Atlantique View	Anse de Mai	H	$$$$$	175
Aywasi Kalinago Retreat	Crayfish River	H	$$$	150
Banana Lama Eco Villa	Rosalie	SC	$$$$$	149
Bay View Lodges	Calibishie	SC	$$	177
Beau Rive	Castle Bruce	H	$$$$	150
Beyond Vitality	Belle Fille	SC	$–$$	150
Calibishie Cove	Hodges Bay, Calibishie	SC	$$$$	176
Calibishie Gardens	Calibishie	SC	$$	177
Calibishie Lodges	Calibishie	H	$$$	177
Carib Territory Guesthouse	Bataca	H	$	151
Castle Comfort Dive Lodge	Castle Comfort, Roseau	H	$$–$$$	98
Chez Ophelia Cottage Apartments	Copthall	H	$$	111
Citrus Creek Plantation	La Plaine	SC	$$$	150
Classique International Guest House	Marigot	H	$$–$$$	177
Cocoa Cottages	Shawford	H	$$$–$$$$	111
Coffee River Cottages	Melville Hall	SC	$$$	177
Comfort Cottages	Blenheim	SC	$$$$	177
Crescent Moon Cabins	Riviere La Croix	H	$$$	204
D'Auchamps Cottages	Shawford	SC	$–$$	112
D-Smart Farm	Corona	SC	$	205
Domcan's Guesthouse	Castle Bruce	H/SC	$	151
Dominica's Sea View Apartments	Calibishie	SC	$$	177
Eden Heights	Castle Bruce	SC	$	151
Evergreen Hotel	Castle Comfort, Roseau	H	$$$	97
Exotica Cottages	Gommier, Giraudel	H	$$–$$$	131
Fort Young Hotel	Roseau	H	$$$–$$$$	97
Garraway Hotel	Roseau	H	$$$	97
Gingerlily Cottage	Riviere Cyrique	SC	$	152
Harmony Villa	Pont Cassé	SC	$$$$$	204
Hibiscus Valley Inn	Concord	H	$–$$	151
Hide-Out Cottage	Geneva, Grand Bay	SC	$	131
Hotel The Champs	Picard	H	$$$	175

Hummingbird Inn	Castaways, Roseau	H	$$–$$$	98
Itassi Cottages	Morne Bruce, Roseau	H	$$	98
Jacoway Inn	Calibishie	H/SC	$$	178
La Bou Country Cottage	Soufriere	SC	$$$$$	130
La Flamboyant Hotel	Roseau	H	$$	98
Le Petit Paradis	Wotten Waven	H/SC	$	112
Liberty Jungle	Bells	H	$$$	204
Lilly's Guesthouse	Brandy	H	$	175
Ma Bass Central Guesthouse	Roseau	H	$	98
Mango Island Lodges	St Joseph	H	$$$	205
Manicou River	Tanetane, Portsmouth	SC	$$$$	175
Mermaid's Secret	Rosalie	SC	$–$$	151
My Father's Place	Marigot	SC	$$$	177
Ocean View Apartments	Scotts Head	SC	$	131
Pagua Bay House	Marigot	H	$$$$$	175
Papillote Wilderness Retreat	Trafalgar	H/SC	$$$$$–$$$	111
Picard Beach Cottages	Picard	H	$$$$	175
Pointe Baptiste Estate	Pointe Baptiste, Calibishie	SC	$$$$$–$$$	176
Ramelton Estate	Layou	SC	$$$$$	204
Rodney's Wellness Retreat	Soufriere	SC	$$$–$	131
Roots Jungle Retreat	Pagua Hills	H	$$–$$$	205
Rosalie Bay Resort	Rosalie	H	$$$$$	149
Roxy's Mountain Lodge	Laudat	H	$$	111
Sea Breeze Inn	Castle Bruce	H	$	152
Sea Cliff Cottages	Calibishie	SC	$$	178
Sea World Guesthouse	Citronnier	H	$	99
Secret Bay	Petite Baie, Portsmouth	SC	$$$$$	174
Secret Garden	Wotten Waven	SC	$	112
Sisserou Lodge	Reigate, Roseau	SC	$$$	98
Sisters Beach Bar & Lodge	Picard	SC	$$	175
St James Guesthouse	Goodwill, Roseau	H	$	98
Stowe Ocean Vista	Stowe	SC	$	131
Sunrise Farm Cottages	Castle Bruce	SC	$$	150
Sunset Bay Club	Batali, Coulibistrie	H	$$$	205
Sunshine Cottage	Shawford	H	$$	112
Sutton Place Hotel	Roseau	H	$$–$$$	98
Symes Zee Guesthouse	Roseau	H	$	99
Tamarind Tree Hotel	Macoucherie	H/SC	$$$	205
The Beach House	Layou	SC	$	206
Tia's Bamboo Cottages	Wotten Waven	H	$$	112
Vanil Vaness	Citrus Creek	SC	$$	150
Veranda View Guesthouse	Calibishie	H	$$	178
Villa Christina	Soufriere	SC	$	132
Villa Vista	Calibishie	SC	$$$$$	176
Villa Passiflora	Calibishie	SC	$$$$$	176
Windblow Estate	Calibishie	SC	$$	178
Zandoli Inn	Stowe	H	$$$	131
Zen Gardens	Gleau Gommier, Bells	SC	$$	205
Zion Valley	Delices	SC	$	152

Appendix 2

HIKES AT A GLANCE

TRED RATING

Terrain	Unchallenging	Easy	Moderate	Challenging	Severe	Hazard!
Score	0	1	2	3	4	H
River X	No crossings	Easy	Moderate	Challenging	Severe	Hazard!
Score	0	1	2	3	4	H
Elevation	Flat	Easy	Moderate	Challenging	Severe	Hazard!
Score	0	1	2	3	4	H
Duration	< 1 hour	1–2 hours	2–4 hours	4–6 hours	> 6 hours	
Score	0	1	2	3	4	

For more information about this rating system see page 73.

HIKES

Hike	T	R	E	D	Rating	Page
Boeri Lake	2	1	2	1	3.8	120
Boiling Lake from Ti Tou Gorge	3	2	3	4	7.5	118
Bwa Nef Waterfall	2	1	2	1	3.8	197
Charles Warner 'Secret Pool'	2	2	1	2	4.4	167
Chemin L'Etang	2	0	2	2	3.8	121
Dernier Falls	2	0	3	1	3.8	168
Douglas Bay Battery & Garrison Ruins	2	0	2	1	3.1	199
East Cabrit Trail	2	0	2	1	3.1	200
Freshwater Lake Trail	2	0	3	1	3.8	122
Galion & Morne Crabier	2	0	3	2	4.4	144
Glassy Trail	2	0	1	1	2.5	169
Jacko Steps	3	3H	2	2	6.3H	221
Kachibona Lake	3	1	2	2	5.0	220
La Chaudiere	2	1	2	1	3.0	198
Lamothe River Falls	2	2	2	2	5.0	199
Lapluy Waterfall	1	1	1	1	2.5	198
Madjini Ridge Trail	4	0	4	2	6.3	168
Middleham Falls from Cochrane	2	1	2	1	3.8	124
Middleham Falls from Laudat	2	1	2	1	3.8	123
Morne Anglais	3	0	4	3	6.3	142
Morne Diablotin	4H	0	4	4	7.5H	218
Morne Micotrin	3H	0	4	3	6.3H	124
Morne Trois Pitons	4H	0	4	3	6.9H	126
Palmiste Ridge	2	0	3	1	3.8	143
Perdu Temps	3	3	2	3	6.9	144

Sari Sari Falls	3	3	2	2	6.3	170
Spanny Falls	3	0	3	1	4.4	220
Syndicate (Milton) Falls	2	2	1	1	3.8	219
Syndicate Nature Trail	1	0	0	1	1.3	216
Victoria Falls	3	3	0	2	5.0	170
Wavine Cyrique	4H	0	4	1	5.6H	171
West Cabrit Trail	2	0	2	1	3.1	200
WNT Seg 1: Scotts Head to Soufriere	3	0	3	2	5.0	226
WNT Seg 2: Soufriere to Bellevue Chopin	2	0	3	3	5.0	227
WNT Seg 3: Bellevue Chopin to Wotten Waven	3	1	3	3	6.3	229
WNT Seg 4: Wotten Waven to Pont Cassé	2	1	3	3	5.6	232
WNT Seg 5: Pont Cassé to Castle Bruce	2	2	1	3	5.0	233
WNT Seg 6: Castle Bruce to Hatton Garden	2	1	2	3	5.0	235
WNT Seg 7: Hatton Garden to First Camp	2	1	3	3	5.6	238
WNT Seg 8: First Camp to Petite Macoucherie	4	2	4	4	8.8	240
WNT Seg 9: Petite Macoucherie to Colihaut Heights	3	3	3	4	8.1	243
WNT Seg 10: Colihaut Heights to Syndicate	2	0	1	2	3.1	245
WNT Seg 11: Syndicate to Bornes	2	2	3	4	6.9	246
WNT Seg 12: Bornes to Pennville	3	1	3	4	6.9	248
WNT Seg 13: Pennville to Capuchin	1	1	2	2	3.8	249
WNT Seg 14: Capuchin to Cabrits	3	1	2	3	5.6	250

Appendix 3

If you have enjoyed Dominica and wish to pursue your interest, here is a selection of further reading options. The listings below are by no means comprehensive; they are just meant as a starting point for further research.

Dominica has a number of talented writers and poets, many of whom self-publish their work locally and in very small quantities. A good way of seeking them out is to attend the annual Nature Island Literary Festival & Book Fair (see page 61) and also to visit the Roseau Public Library (page 95).

NON-FICTION
History and culture
Andre, Irving & Christian, Gabriel *Death By Fire* Pont Cassé Press, 2007; ISBN 978 0973734768

Bell, Stewart *Bayou of Pigs* Wiley, 2008; ISBN 978 0470153826

Boyd, Stanley A W *A Brief History of the Cathedral of Roseau* Roseau Public Library archives

Burton, Eileen *National Dress of Dominica* Paramount, 2003. Available from Dominica book stores.

D'jamala Fontaine, Marcel *Dominica's Diksyonne, English Creole Dictionary* ISBN 1 85465074 2

Honychurch, Lennox *The Dominica Story* Macmillan, 1975; ISBN 0 333 62776 8

Honychurch, Lennox *Negre Mawon, The Fighting Maroons of Dominica* Island Heritage Initiatives, 2014

Jacob, Jeno J *Dominica's Folk Beliefs* 2008. Available from Dominica book stores.

Pattullo, Polly *Your Time is Done Now: Slavery, Resistance and Defeat: the Maroon Trials of Dominica (1813–1814)*; Papillote Press, 2015; ISBN 978 0957118775

Natural history
Adams, C Dennis *Caribbean Flora* Nelson Caribbean, 1976; ISBN 0 17 566186 3

Bannochie, Iris & Light, Marilyn *Gardening in the Caribbean* Macmillan, 1993; ISBN 0 333 56573 8

Evans, Peter G H & James, Arlington *A Guide to Geology, Climate and Habitats*. Available from Dominica book stores and Forestry, Wildlife & Parks Division.

Evans, Peter *Birds of the Eastern Caribbean* Macmillan Caribbean, 2009; ISBN 978 0333521557

Evans, G H & James, Arlington *Wildlife Checklists*. Available from Dominica book stores and Forestry, Wildlife & Parks Division.

James, Arlington; Durand, Stephen; & Baptiste, Bertrand Jno *Dominica's Birds*. Available from Dominica book stores and Forestry, Wildlife & Parks Division.

James, Arlington *Plants of Dominica's Southeast*. Available from Dominica book stores and Forestry, Wildlife & Parks Division.

James, Arlington *Flora and Fauna of Cabrits National Park*. Available from Dominica book stores and Forestry, Wildlife & Parks Division.

Lennox, G W & Seddon, S A *Flowers of the Caribbean* Macmillan, 1978; ISBN 0 333 26968 3

Lennox, G W & Seddon, S A *Trees of the Caribbean* Macmillan Caribbean, 1980; ISBN 978 0333287934

Malhotra, Anita & Thorpe, Roger S *Reptiles and Amphibians of the Eastern Caribbean* Macmillan Caribbean, 2007; ISBN 978 0333691410

Guides and travelogues

Bird, Jonathan *Dominica, Land of Water* Jonathan Bird Photography, 2004; ISBN 978 0972863414

Bond, James *Birds of the West Indies* Houghton Mifflin Harcourt, 1993; ISBN 978 0618002108

Bourne, M J; Seddon, S A; & Lennox, G W *Fruits and Vegetables of the Caribbean* Macmillan, 1988; ISBN 978 0333453117

Evans, P C H & Honychurch, Lennox *Dominica, Nature Island of the Caribbean* Hansib Publishing, 2009; ISBN 978 1906190255

Evans, Peter G H & James, Arlington *A Guide to Nature Sites*. Available from Dominica bookstores and Forestry, Wildlife & Parks Division.

Fermor, Patrick Leigh *The Traveller's Tree, A Journey Through the Caribbean Islands* John Murray Publishers Ltd, 2005; ISBN 978 0719566844

James, Arlington *An Illustrated Guide to Dominica's Botanic Gardens*. Available from Dominica bookstores and Forestry, Wildlife & Parks Division.

Kamyab, A *Dominica, A Tropical Paradise* AuthorHouse, 2009; ISBN 978 1438915678

Lawrence, Michael *Diving & Snorkelling Dominica* Lonely Planet, 1999; ISBN 0 86442764 6

Pattullo, Polly & Baptiste, Anne Jno *The Gardens of Dominica* Papillote Press, 1998; ISBN 0953222403

Pattullo, Polly *Roseau Valley Guide* Papillote Press, 2007. Available directly from the publisher, Papillotte Wilderness Retreat gift shop and Dominica bookstores.

Sullivan, Lynne M *Adventure Guide, Dominica & St Lucia* Hunter, 2005; ISBN 978 1588433930

Biographical

Higbie, Janet *Eugenia, the Caribbean's Iron Lady* Macmillan Caribbean, 1993; ISBN 978 0333572351

Kalinago People of Dominica *Yet We Survive* Papillote Press, 2007; ISBN 978 09532224 21

Napier, Elma *Black And White Sands, a bohemian life in the colonial Caribbean* Papillote Press, 2009; ISBN 978 09532224 45

Paravisini-Gebert, Lizabeth *Phyillis Shand Allfrey, a Caribbean Life* Rutgers University Press, 1996; ISBN 0 813 52265

Pattullo, Polly & Sorhaindo, Celia, compiled by *Home Again, Stories of migration and return* Papillote Press, 2009; ISBN 978 09532224 52

Pizzichini, Lilian *The Blue Hour, a life of Jean Rhys* W W Norton & Company, 2009; ISBN 978 0393058031

FICTION
Novels and short stories

Aaron, Philbert *Decorated Broomsticks, a novel of political independence* Paramount, 2007; ISBN 978 97682121 84

Allfrey, Phyllis Shand *It Falls Into Place* Papillote Press, 2004; ISBN 978 0 9532224 14. Short stories.

Allfrey, Phyllis Shand *The Orchid House* Rutgers University Press, 1996; ISBN 978 0813523323

Brand, Pete *Harken's Caribbean Sea* Authorhouse, 2006; ISBN 978 1425947514

Children of Atkinson School, Dominica *The Snake King of the Kalinago* Papillotte Press, 2010; ISBN 978 0 9532224 69

Christian, Gabriel *Rain on a Tin Roof* Pont Cassé Press, 1999; ISBN 978 0966845419

John, Marie-Elena *Unburnable* Harper Paperbacks, 2007; ISBN 978 0060837587

Kincaid, Jamaica *The Autobiography of My Mother* Plume, 1997; ISBN 978 0452274662

Lazare, Alick *Kalinago Blood* Abbott Press, 2013; ISBN 978 1458212641

Lazare, Alick *Pharcel, runaway slave* iUniverse, 2006; ISBN 978 0595395781

Rhys, Jean *Wide Sargasso Sea* W W Norton & Company, 1998; ISBN 978 0393960129

Shillingford, Christborne *Most Wanted, street stories from the Caribbean* Papillote Press, 2007; ISBN 978 0 9532224 38

Poetry and storytelling

Brumant, Lawrence *Ki Mannyè Donmnik Touvé Non'y (How Dominica Got its name and Four Other Konts)*. Available from Dominica book stores.

Cooke, Trish (illustrations by Caroline Binch) *Look Back!* Papillote Press, 2013; ISBN 978 095711872

Dominican Writers Guild *Words, Sound and Power, a collection of Dominican poetry.* Available from Dominica bookstores.

Grell, Jane Ulysses *Praise Songs* Papillote Press, 2013; ISBN 978 0957118744

John, Giftus *The Island Man Sings His Song* Writer's Showcase, 2001; ISBN 0595180906

John, Giftus *Mesyé Kwik! Kwak!* Virtualbookworm.com Publishing, 2005; ISBN 1589397649

Shand Allfrey, Phyllis *Love For An Island, collected poems* Papillote Press, 2014; ISBN 978 0957118751

Sorhaindo, Paula *Pulse Rock* Parnassus Publishing, 1993; ISBN 978 1871800401

MAGAZINES

Dominica Traveller (*www.dominicatraveller.com; see ad page 30*)
Domnitjen (*www.domnitjen.com*)
Experience Dominica (*www.dhta.org*)

WEBSITES

www.dhta.org Dominica Hotel & Tourism Association
www.dominica.dm Website of the Discover Dominica Authority
www.dominica.gov.dm Government of Dominica
www.dominicawatersports.com Dominica Watersports Association

Index

Page numbers in **bold** indicate major entries; those in *italics* indicate maps

INDEX TO ADVERTISERS